MW00564014

BAY AREA RIDGE TRAIL

The Official Guide for Hikers, Mountain Bikers, and Equestrians

4th Edition

BAY AREA RIDGE TRAIL

The Official Guide for Hikers, Mountain Bikers, and Equestrians

4th Edition

Elizabeth Byers
and
Jean Rusmore

WILDERNESS PRESS ... *on the trail since 1967*

Bay Area Ridge Trail: The Official Guide for Hikers, Mountain Bikers, and Equestrians

Fourth edition, second printing 2020

Copyright © 2019 by Elizabeth Byers
Copyright © 1995, 2002, 2008 by Jean Rusmore

Editor: Scott Alexander Jones
Project editor: Ritchey Halphen
Photos: Elizabeth Byers, except where noted
Maps: Ben Pease / Pease Press
Cover design: Scott McGrew
Text design: Annie Long
Indexer: Sylvia Coates

Library of Congress Cataloging-in-Publication Data for this book is available at catalog.loc.gov.
ISBN 9780899979052 (pbk.); ISBN 9780899979069 (ebook); LCCN 2018049388

Manufactured in China
Distributed by Publishers Group West

 Bay Area Ridge Trail Council
1007 General Kennedy Ave., #3
San Francisco, CA 94129
415-561-2595, ridgetrail.org

 **WILDERNESS PRESS**
An imprint of AdventureKEEN
2204 First Ave. S., Ste. 102
Birmingham, AL 35233
800-443-7227, fax 205-326-1012

Visit wildernesspress.com for a complete listing of our books and for ordering information. Contact us at info@wildernesspress.com, facebook.com/wildernesspress1967, or twitter.com /wilderness1967 with questions or comments. To find out more about who we are and what we're doing, visit blog.wildernesspress.com.

Cover photos: Top, San Francisco Peninsula Watershed (see page 279); bottom left, summit of Loma Alta (see page 66); bottom right, Dias Ridge Trail (see page 50); back cover, Mission Peak Regional Preserve (see page 200)

Frontispiece: The view of San Pablo Bay and Mount Tamalpais from Skyline Wilderness Park (see page 114)

All rights reserved. No part of this book may be reproduced in any form, or by any means electronic, mechanical, recording, or otherwise, without written permission from the publisher, except for brief quotations used in reviews.

SAFETY NOTICE Although Wilderness Press and the author have made every attempt to ensure that the information in this book is accurate at press time, they are not responsible for any loss, damage, injury, or inconvenience that may occur to anyone while using this book. You are responsible for your own safety and health while in the wilderness. The fact that a trail is described in this book does not mean that it will be safe for you. Be aware that trail conditions can change from day to day. Always check local conditions and know your own limitations.

To my sister, Lindsay Terzian,
who always wanted to hike on the Ridge Trail with me,
and to my children,
Jane and Will Cavagnero, who love trails as much as I do

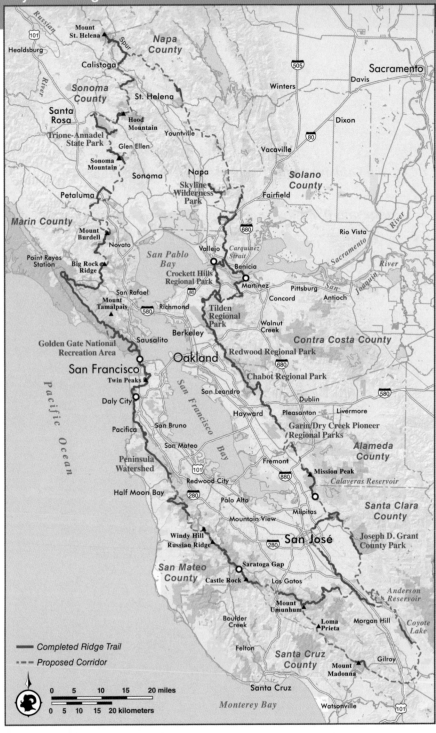

Contents

East Bay   141

South Bay   207

Foreword

MY FAMILY HAS LIVED IN CALIFORNIA for six generations, and I grew up exploring its beautiful regional parks and protected open spaces. These public lands, preserved for all people and all time, captured my imagination early on and ignited a passion for nature, history, and the outdoors, which enriched my life beyond measure.

After graduating from college, I lived, worked, and traveled far afield, but when I moved back to the Bay Area in 1983, I fell head over heels in love all over again with my home state's parks and open spaces. That romance has deepened over the years, and so has my appreciation for how rare and innovative our conservation legacy truly is.

Thirty years ago, I was inspired by the audacious notion of creating a trail that could ring the ridgelines around the bay and connect all nine Bay Area counties. Two of the principals who promoted this seemingly impossible dream were people I liked and admired immensely: Bill Mott and Brian O'Neill. Bill had been general manager of the East Bay Regional Park District and director of both California State Parks and the National Park Service. Brian was the longtime general superintendent of the Golden Gate National Recreation Area. They were always brimming with big ideas and contagious enthusiasm. They knew how to fire up the rest of us and build teams to get things done. If Bill and Brian believed the Bay Area Ridge Trail could eventually become a reality, who was I to argue? They signed me and countless others up for the long run, and now the Ridge Trail is nearing 400 miles, with exciting new stretches being added every year as we close in on its eventual completion at 550 miles.

Over the years I've had the pleasure, both personally and professionally, to explore many sections of the Ridge Trail. I've seen stunning vistas in all directions and have enjoyed many long, quiet, and healing hours in the company of nature so close to our busy and noisy urban landscape. And maybe most importantly, I've met thousands of fellow travelers of all ages and ethnicities soaking up the scenery with warm and welcoming smiles on their faces.

I hope you enjoy this new Ridge Trail guidebook and saunter in the hills as often as you can. I look forward to seeing you out there, maybe with my young granddaughters in tow, as I try to pass the gift of nature on to them the way my family did for me. And when we meet, let's make a date to join the big party when the last golden spike is nailed to the final trailhead and the Ridge Trail loop is complete. It will be the most epic urban trail through nature the world has ever known, another global treasure in our own backyard.

—*Doug McConnell*
Emmy Award–winning environmental journalist and host
of the television program OpenRoad with Doug McConnell

An Inspired Vision to Connect People, Parks, and Open Space

AS TRAIL ENTHUSIASTS, we stand on the shoulders of the visionary leaders who came before us. These visionaries dreamed big and worked tirelessly to preserve the Bay Area's treasured natural heritage. William Penn Mott Jr., park leader extraordinaire, sparked and captured the imagination for a regional trail network, and others charmed, cajoled, and fought to conserve the peaks, ridgelines, and wild spaces in between, creating a necklace of parks and open-space jewels all around the region.

The Bay Area Ridge Trail Council is led by a small but mighty group of dedicated board, staff, and volunteers. It derives much of its success from deep-rooted collaborations and a broad coalition of public and private partners, including elected and community leaders, park agencies, land trusts and other managers, the California State Coastal Conservancy, individual donors, businesses, and nonprofits.

With more than 375 miles of the trail now dedicated, we're proud of the progress to date and the beautiful trails boasting panoramic vistas. But there is much more work to do: Many new sections are in design and under construction. Each new trail opening is a cause for celebration. The excitement and big smiles are like an adrenaline rush pushing us to press ahead, even when the path forward is rocky, steep, or obscured.

As with any long-distance trail, the Ridge Trail truly is more than the sum of all the individual sections. It's all about connection—connecting communities, parks, people, and open space. People who experience nature want to protect it. Connected corridors, as well as recreational trails, support habitat and wildlife. And as longer and longer stretches are knit together, new opportunities for epic multiday treks come into being. Today, it's possible to hike 87 continuous miles from northern Marin to CA 92 on the Peninsula, or 46 continuous miles in the East Bay. Creating a network of overnight accommodations to support multiday trekking and circumnavigation is just one of the exciting initiatives we're working on.

A Bay Area Ridge Trail was never preordained. Instead, every inch of trail exists because someone spoke out, stepped up, and acted to protect, build, or restore it and make it open to the public to enjoy forever. And now the legacy is ours to cherish and carry forward.

This book is designed to be your guide as you explore the wonder of these trails. I hope your travels inspire you to join our quest. Visit ridgetrail.org for news about trail progress, events and outings, exploration tools, trail stewardship days, and other ways to engage. Join us today!

—*Janet McBride*
Executive Director, Bay Area Ridge Trail Council

Acknowledgments

I WAS INTRODUCED TO THE BAY AREA RIDGE TRAIL project in 1988, when I was working at the Trust for Public Land. I then joined the Ridge Trail steering committee, helped move the group toward becoming a nonprofit, and served on the board of directors for a number of years. In 2000, I started working with the organization again, this time as its newsletter editor, and I served in that capacity for 16 years. Because I love being out on the trails, and have lived in the San Francisco Bay Area for most of my life, I have always found the Bay Area Ridge Trail to be a very compelling vision.

I want to thank Tim Jackson at AdventureKEEN for hiring me to update the guidebook; it gave me a good excuse to spend a lot of time hiking and biking the entire trail. Also at AdventureKEEN, Ritchey Halphen worked tirelessly as the managing editor, pulling the book together with his team in a short amount of time.

I am extremely grateful to Jean Rusmore, who researched and wrote the first three editions of this guidebook. Without her very hard work over the decades, this guidebook would have been much more challenging to assemble. Her trail descriptions show how much detail she noticed while hiking on the trails, and how much time she spent researching relevant information.

Over the years, so many people have contributed their time and enthusiasm into creating 375 miles of the trail, and I am grateful to every one of them. In particular, the Bay Area Ridge Trail Council's staff and board of directors have been instrumental in moving the trail project forward. Jean Rusmore worked with many staff members over the years, and I also want to thank the council staff who helped me with this book: Louisa Morris and Liz Westbrook, who reviewed the text, and Janet McBride and Eileen Morris, who helped with other aspects of the project. Ben Pease, the cartographer, was an invaluable resource. He spent countless hours patiently reviewing the maps with me and making updates.

I am grateful to my family and friends who hiked or biked the trail with me and helped me with car shuttles: my sister, Lindsay Terzian; Will Headapohl; my children, Jane and Will Cavagnero; and Claire Kingsley and Isa Giannini. Thanks to Bay Area Ridge Trail board member Bob Siegel, who led the group hike through the San Francisco Peninsula Watershed. Finally, I want to thank Will Headapohl for all of his support while I worked on this project.

I hope to see you on the trail, and I look forward to many more hikes as the Ridge Trail gets closer to 550 miles.

—*Elizabeth Byers*

The San Francisco Bay Area

THE SAN FRANCISCO BAY AREA, with its remarkable juxtaposition of bay, mountains, and sea, is one of the world's premier natural settings. The jewel of this region is San Francisco Bay, one of the largest bays in the United States and a unifying feature for the nine counties that ring its shores. Two arms of the Coast Range cradle the bay as they run northwest–southeast along the length of the region. The hills and valleys of the North and South Bay counties loosely connect the Inner and Outer Coast Ranges.

A wealth of natural beauty resides in the Bay Area's coastal mountains and their rolling foothills: redwood forests, lush streamsides, grasslands, oak woodland, rocky peaks, and sunny chaparral slopes. The tradition of land conservation began more than a century ago in the Bay Area, and extensive public open space now occupies the land between the Coast Ranges. Today, public agencies and private land trusts have set aside tracts of land in the mountains, foothills, valleys, and cities that are parks, open-space preserves, and watersheds. In several Bay Area counties, this land now forms a continuous open-space corridor—a Bay Area greenbelt.

These public open spaces are peaceful backdrops to a bustling urban area—places for adventure, discovery, recreation, and relaxation. They are habitat for diverse plant and animal species, and areas for forests to thrive and cleanse our air. Within this greenbelt is the route of the multiuse Bay Area Ridge Trail. When complete, 550 miles of trail will link public parks and open spaces on the ridgeline surrounding San Francisco Bay.

The route of the Bay Area Ridge Trail lies close to the homes of more than 7 million residents, most of whom live in the valleys of the Coast Range and on the sloping plains that border the bay. From almost any place in the Bay Area, the ridgelands, accented by taller peaks, are visible to Bay Area residents. For them, the sun rises and sets over these mountains, literally and figuratively. Bay Area natives, especially, are fiercely proud and protective of their mountains.

The Bay Area's Heritage of Outdoor Enjoyment

The physical grandeur of this setting and its moderate climate, influenced by the bay and the Pacific Ocean, make the Bay Area ideal for outdoor recreation. You can hike, run, bike, or ride horseback somewhere in the area on almost any day of the year. The area's earliest inhabitants—the Ohlone, Yurock, Pomo, and other American Indian tribes—considered this a gentle land. The first explorers marveled at its beauty, its great redwood forests, and its Mediterranean climate. After the gold rush, a wave of settlers

1

arrived to farm and work in its salubrious weather. The first California Geological Survey team report, written in the early 1860s, delighted in the variety of terrain and glowingly praised the marvelous scenery.

As the Spanish built missions and settlements in California, the Spanish government awarded large land grants to some colonists for their service. On vast domains known as ranchos, these colonists, or rancheros, kept thousands of cattle, which they managed with well-trained horses. Anglo cattle ranchers blazed trails as they herded their stock and allowed friends—and a relatively small public interested in walking and riding—to cross their lands on these trails, some of which are still in public use.

European immigrants who grew up in the mountains of Germany, Austria, and Switzerland recognized the natural beauty of the Bay Area and took pleasure in walking with friends on weekends. They could wander freely through orchards, along farm roads, through friendly neighbors' meadows, and along hillside animal paths. Mount Tamalpais became a favorite destination after passenger-ferry service from San Francisco reached Marin County in the 1920s.

Eventually many hiking and horseback riding groups sprang up to offer trips in the Bay Area countryside on trails made by the rancheros, cattlemen, early settlers, and weekend explorers. Today, trail enthusiasts can find outings geared for a great variety of skills and interest levels.

A Land-Conservation Ethic

The nine Bay Area counties that border San Francisco Bay recognize the need for cooperation and collaboration to ensure the preservation of the area's natural resources. The Association of Bay Area Governments, the Metropolitan Transportation Commission, the Bay Area Air Quality Management District, the Bay Conservation and Development Commission, and the California State Coastal Conservancy seek unity by organizing and managing regional affairs. The Coastal Conservancy has funded the planning and design of many miles of Ridge Trail.

Nonprofit grassroots organizations address current needs or glaring deficiencies in government long-range regional planning and land-use problems. Recognizing that the Bay Area needed a defining greenbelt of open space for its cities, far-sighted citizens and committed activists in the 1960s joined Dorothy Erskine to form a group dedicated to achieving this ideal. Known first as People for Open Space, then Greenbelt Congress, and now Greenbelt Alliance, this organization mobilized a regional effort to establish a ring of parks, preserves, open spaces, farms, and ranches around the Bay Area and continues its mission to this day. As the crusaders grew in numbers, so too did the greenbelt around the bay.

Development of Parks and Open Spaces

As the Bay Area population grew, especially in the years following World War II, outdoors lovers began to appreciate the importance of preserving recreation lands for all to enjoy. More and more people gravitated to the outlying hills and valleys to walk or ride horseback freely.

Even before World War II, East Bay citizens began to realize the need for parks adjacent to their growing cities. Inspired and dedicated citizens of Alameda and Contra Costa Counties, aided by civic leaders, launched the East Bay Regional Park District (EBRPD) in 1934 by an overwhelming vote. The EBRPD's first acquisition, Tilden Regional Park, marked the beginning of its present-day greenbelt of parks, historic units, and recreation complexes of nearly 121,400 acres.

Other cities and counties eventually followed suit, setting aside small and large areas for parks and open space. Many of these parklands lie on the ridges, mountainsides, and foothills of the Coast Ranges. However, with the recognition that San Francisco Bay was diminishing in size and purity due to landfills and wastewater and garbage dumping, agencies around the bay began establishing shoreline parks to increase stewardship and appreciation of the bay. A notable example is the 30,000-acre Don Edwards San Francisco Bay National Wildlife Refuge, a unit of the U.S. Fish & Wildlife Service.

As the appreciation of the Bay Area's need for breathing space and stretching room grew, other new agencies also took up the cause. Successful examples include the Marin County Open Space District and the Midpeninsula Regional Open Space District in Santa Clara and San Mateo Counties. In 1990, Sonoma County organized an Agricultural Preservation and Open Space District; Santa Clara County established an Open Space Authority in 1993; and in 2006 Napa County residents approved a measure to establish the Napa County Regional Park and Open Space District. Several cities and

The Julian Trail overlooks Rodeo Valley in the Marin Headlands (see page 43).

The Bay Area Ridge Trail Council's Mission

The Bay Area Ridge Trail Council plans, promotes, and sustains a connected hiking, cycling, and equestrian trail on the ridgelines around San Francisco Bay—linking people, parks, and open space for current and future generations.

---

counties passed bond measures and initiatives to promote good land use, limit urban sprawl, provide recreational opportunities, and preserve agriculture at city edges.

Today, as a result of these many efforts, hundreds of thousands of protected acres in the foothills and mountainsides surround the urbanized bayside, and more acreage lines the bay's shores. In coastal counties—particularly Marin, San Francisco, and San Mateo—the National Park Service permanently protects thousands of acres. There is at least one unit of the California State Parks system in each Bay Area county, and most Bay Area counties have a county park system and/or a regional park agency.

Many Bay Area parks were established on closed military bases. The military designated Forts Baker, Barry, Cronkhite, and Funston as surplus bases during post–World War II downsizing, along with Milagra Ridge and Sweeney Ridge Military Reservations. In 1994, the San Francisco Presidio became a national park under the jurisdiction of the Golden Gate National Recreation Area and Presidio Trust. A provision of federal law that required these military lands to be offered to public entities before the commercial market led to the creation of many of the parks that grace our ridgetops and baylands.

Watersheds, too, preserve open space in Bay Area counties. In order to ensure a steady water supply for San Francisco's growing population, a group of individuals formed the Spring Valley Water Company in the mid-1880s; the City of San Francisco purchased the company in 1930 and began to pipe water from the Sierra Nevada to service the needs of its customers—now more than 2.7 million people—in San Francisco, in the East Bay, and on the Peninsula. The San Francisco Public Utilities Commission now manages 59,000 acres of watershed lands on the Peninsula and in Alameda and Santa Clara Counties.

Other jurisdictions began to develop stable water supplies and to store water in reservoirs. Most of these storage areas are in the foothills surrounding the bay plain. For many years these reservoirs were off-limits to the public. However, with the development of modern purification techniques, some agencies began to open their gates to quiet, passive recreation, such as nature walks and hiking. Today, most water agencies allow some public access.

Private nonprofit Bay Area organizations, such as the Peninsula Open Space Trust, Sonoma Land Trust, Solano Land Trust, and John Muir Land Trust, have worked for many years to preserve and protect open-space lands for eventual public use. Through gifts, purchases, and easements, these organizations can make choice lands available to the public.

The
Bay Area Ridge Trail

A COMBINATION OF UNIQUE CHARACTERISTICS primed the Bay Area for the establishment of the Bay Area Ridge Trail: a glorious physical setting; a long history of outdoor recreation; a growing greenbelt; a conservation ethic; and a population of avid outdoor enthusiasts, conservationists, and willing volunteers. Designed as a multiuse ridgeline route for hikers, bicyclists, and equestrians (and some sections for wheelchair users), this planned 550-mile trail, nearly 70 percent complete, connects public parklands and watersheds of the Bay Area greenbelt that circles San Francisco Bay.

The Bay Area Ridge Trail traverses ridgelines and crosses valleys, providing iconic 360-degree views, glimpses of the area's cultural heritage, and firsthand experience of the Bay Area's diverse ecosystems. It offers places to sit, contemplate, relax, test endurance, build stamina, and restore the spirit. The scenic trail links communities along the ridgeline and connects to bayside population centers via feeder trails through existing city, county, regional, and federal parks.

For those who want to experience all that the Bay Area Ridge Trail has to offer, they can circumnavigate the entire 375 (and growing) miles, either in one intensive effort, or over time. The list of circumnavigators grows every year. Walking or riding every mile gives one the opportunity to explore new parts of the Bay Area; for the curious and adventurous, this is an extremely satisfying experience.

The Beginnings

When William Penn Mott Jr. was general manager of the East Bay Regional Park District in the 1960s, he proposed that a trail be established around the entire ridge of the Bay Area. His vision also included a trail around the bay, close to the water, and connector trails to the Sierra Nevada. Mott went on to serve as director of California State Parks and later of the National Park Service. In the late 1980s, he lent his strong support and encouragement to achieving his vision of a ridgeline trail around the bay.

In 1986, People for Open Space (POS), the predecessor of Greenbelt Alliance, began an effort to acquaint the City of San Francisco with the public-access policies of the region's water departments. POS brought together the managers of water departments; county, regional, state, and federal parks departments; trail activists; and leaders of environmental organizations at a meeting in 1987, intending to demonstrate to San Francisco that less restrictive public-access policies used in other Bay Area watersheds did not harm water quality. As an important outgrowth of that meeting, these groups recognized that watershed lands, parks, and preserves that surround the bay could be linked with a regional trail.

A coalition of activists, spurred by the energy and commitment of William Penn Mott Jr., established the Bay Area Ridge Trail Council in late 1987. Brian O'Neill, superintendent of the Golden Gate National Recreation Area (GGNRA), was the first chairman, and the National Park Service was a major financial supporter of the project during the first seven years. The outpouring of support for the Bay Area Ridge Trail led the informal council to incorporate in 1992 as a nonprofit organization. Today, the council has seven staff members and a dedicated corps of grassroots volunteers.

Accomplishments

As of late 2018, 375 miles of the Ridge Trail have been completed and are dedicated, signed, and in use. Many additional miles of trail are being planned or are under construction for dedication in the near future. Nearly three quarters of the dedicated miles are open to all users (hikers, equestrians, and mountain bicyclists). The total Ridge Trail mileage is primarily calculated along the main route on a single alignment and does not include alternative, spur, or access trails to the main route. Most of the developed trail traverses public parklands around the Bay Area, but about 7 percent of the trail miles cross private lands, many held by nonprofits.

The Bay Area Ridge Trail vision has always included the idea that ultimately one could travel continuously around—or circumnavigate—the entire route. As increasingly longer stretches are joined, multiday, overnight trips become possible. As of 2018, hikers can explore 87 miles of continuous Ridge Trail from CA 92 in San Mateo County to northern Marin County (with only a 0.9-mile-long navigable gap), and 46 contiguous miles in the East Bay.

The far northern section of the Ridge Trail route has changed significantly over time, with two major northward extensions in 1990 and 2012. After the publication of this guidebook's third edition, the alignment was shifted north across the upper Napa Valley to include Bothe–Napa Valley State Park, the city of Calistoga, and the valley's eastern ridgeline. The route includes a spur through Robert Louis Stevenson State Park to the summit of 4,386-foot Mount St. Helena, the highest point on the Ridge Trail.

In the southern part of the Bay Area, the alignment splits to include one route across Santa Clara Valley, below San José, and a southern extension route that extends as far south as Gilroy. A new Ridge Trail segment, opened in 2017, reaches the summit of 3,486-foot Mount Umunhum, the second-highest point on the Ridge Trail.

This fourth edition features entirely new segments in parks and watersheds that the Ridge Trail had not yet traversed, including Vargas Plateau Regional Park, North Sonoma Mountain Regional Park and Open Space Preserve, Fernandez Ranch, and the Pinole Valley Watershed. A new trail section crosses another major bridge, the Benicia–Martinez Bridge, and new segments run along urban creek trails in San José and Petaluma.

The Next Step: Closing the Gaps

Since the first trail dedication in 1989, the Bay Area Ridge Trail Council has been particularly successful in completing Ridge Trail segments on public lands. Going forward, nearly 60 percent of the planned route will be on public land, 36 percent on privately held lands, and 5 percent on lands held by land trusts and other nongovernmental organizations. In addition, the Bay Area Ridge Trail Council works to address multiuse gaps, so that both equestrians and mountain bikers can travel on either a shared route with hikers or on a parallel route when necessary.

The Bay Area Ridge Trail Council reaches out to private landowners, works to build sound public policies that support the Ridge Trail, and assists community partners in fundraising and trail maintenance efforts, which are critical to completing the remaining Ridge Trail miles.

Closing these gaps in the Bay Area Ridge Trail presents an immediate and immense challenge that will take years to fulfill. Success in this effort relies on the council's leadership and the ongoing involvement and commitment of its members, volunteers, and public agency partners. Volunteers play a key role in the programs and projects of the council. From an active corps that serves on the board of directors, to those who build trails and plan and carry out Ridge Trail events, and others who raise needed funds, the volunteers are the heart of the Bay Area Ridge Trail Council.

Routes Shared with Other Bay Area Regional Trails

After World War II, Californians' enthusiasm for an around-the-state, border-to-border loop trail surged, and easements were secured and rights of way developed for the California Riding and Hiking Trail. However, due to rapid building activity along the route and lack of legal rights to the trails, most trail segments fell into disrepair and were subsequently closed. Today, the Bay Area Ridge Trail follows some segments of this early trail in Marin, Contra Costa, and San Mateo Counties.

The Anza Trail, a 1,200-mile National Historic Trail, follows Captain Juan Bautista de Anza's 18th-century attempt to find a land route from Mexico to San Francisco. In the Bay Area, the Anza Trail runs through Santa Clara, San Mateo, San Francisco, Alameda, and Contra Costa Counties and shares the Ridge Trail route in several sections in most of these counties.

Two other Bay Area trails with national trail status that follow the Ridge Trail route are the 31-mile Skyline National Recreation Trail in the East Bay Hills and the Penitencia Creek Trail, a national recreation trail in San José.

The statewide Coastal Trail hugs the shoreline through San Mateo, San Francisco, Marin, and Sonoma Counties. In Marin, San Francisco, and San Mateo Counties, the Ridge Trail and Coastal Trail share an alignment in certain sections.

The San Francisco Bay Trail, the Ridge Trail's sister trail, will ultimately circle the shoreline of the entire bay, following a plan originally developed and funded by legislation introduced by Senator Bill Lockyer. The Association of Bay Area Governments, the Metropolitan Transportation Commission, and the nonprofit San Francisco Bay Trail Project oversee the planned 500-mile Bay Trail, and as of 2018, more than 354 miles are dedicated. The San Francisco Bay Trail and the Bay Area Ridge Trail share alignments across several bay and strait bridges and along the waterfronts of Benicia and Martinez. These entities are also collaborating on the Carquinez Strait Scenic Loop Trail, which has many miles in place and includes a 32-mile outer loop, a 26-mile inner loop, and a 27-mile southern loop.

Bigleaf maples on Sonoma Mountain's east slope show their brilliant colors in November.

The Bay Area Ridge Trail Council seeks to connect neighboring communities by linking the Ridge Trail to other regional trails and to local trail networks. The connecting trails offer many local residents the opportunity to reach the long regional trails without ever starting a car.

Other Long Trails

Long-distance trails connecting several sites, cities, and/or regions are a challenge to distance hikers and a source of volunteer action and pride in the areas they traverse. The oldest of these trails in the United States is the Appalachian Trail, which stretches from Springer Mountain in Georgia to Mount Katahdin in Maine. Other well-known trails include the Long Trail in New England, the John Muir Trail in California's Sierra Nevada, the California Coastal Trail, the aforementioned Anza Trail, and the Continental Divide National Scenic and Pacific Crest Trails from Mexico to Canada. Around Lake Tahoe, the Tahoe Rim Trail traverses ridgetop lands. Other communities and regions are taking up the long-trail idea as well.

How to Use This Book

THE TRAIL DESCRIPTIONS HERE are arranged clockwise around San Francisco Bay, beginning in San Francisco on the Golden Gate Bridge, followed by Marin County, Sonoma County, Napa County, and so on around the bay. Hence, the Marin County descriptions start at the south end and finish at the north end of each segment. As the route heads across the interior valleys of the North Bay, trail descriptions begin at the west end and finish at the east end. The East Bay descriptions start in the north and end in the south, and across the Santa Clara Valley the trips go from east to west. Heading up the Peninsula and into San Francisco proper, the route is described from south to north.

Summary of Trail Features

Starting on the next page, this helpful table lists at-a-glance information for all of the trips in this book, including whether dogs, bikers, or horses are allowed on the trail; whether restrooms, picnic facilities, or camping is available; and any applicable parking fees.

Ridge Trail Tracker

Starting on page 16, this handy tool enables Ridge Trail users to plan and record their trips and measure their progress toward completing the entire trail.

Trip Descriptions

Summary Information

The summary information for each trip lists the mileage of that particular Ridge Trail segment, the elevation gain and loss, the different types of users who may access it, the managing agencies, the most important regulations that visitors must observe, any nearby facilities, and the location of the trailheads. For more information about public-transit access to trailheads, see Appendix 2 (page 312) or visit 511.org.

The agency and regulations sections list the name of each public agency or private entity responsible for the area, its hours of operation for the park or preserve, dog and bike rules, and fees. Rules regarding dogs range from their prohibition on trails altogether to simply requiring them to be under voice control (see the Summary of Trail Features table, page 10, for details). In general, where allowed on trails, dogs must be on a 6-foot leash. Some trails pass through the jurisdictions of more than one agency, each with different dog regulations, all of which are noted.

(continued on page 21)

Summary of Trail Features

Region/Trail Name	Dogs Allowed	Restroom(s)	Parking Fee	
The North Bay				
The Golden Gate Bridge	Only service dogs	Both sides of bridge	South side of bridge	
Marin Headlands from the Golden Gate Bridge to Tennessee Valley	Only Coastal Trail, portion of SCA Trail, and Julian Trail, on leash	Top of Julian Trail, Gerbode Valley Trailhead, and Tennessee Valley Trailhead	No	
Marin Headlands from Tennessee Valley to Shoreline Highway	Only on Miwok Trail, on leash	Tennessee Valley Trailhead	No	
Mount Tamalpais State Park and Dias Ridge Trail	No	Pantoll	Pantoll	
Mount Tamalpais State Park and Bolinas Ridge	Prohibited in state park, on leash in GGNRA	Pantoll	Pantoll	
Bolinas Ridge and Samuel P. Taylor State Park	On leash	Samuel P. Taylor State Park	Samuel P. Taylor State Park	
Samuel P. Taylor State Park to White Hill Open Space Preserve	On leash in state park, under voice control on preserve fire road and watershed	Samuel P. Taylor State Park	Samuel P. Taylor State Park	
Loma Alta Open Space Preserve and Loma Alta Fire Road	On leash on Lucasfilm land, under voice control on preserve fire roads	No	No	
Lucas Valley Open Space Preserve	On leash on Lucasfilm land, under voice control on preserve fire roads	No	No	
Indian Tree Open Space Preserve	On leash on trail, under voice control on preserve fire road	No	No	
Stafford Lake Watershed to O'Hair Park	On leash on trail, under voice control on preserve fire road	No	No	
Mount Burdell Open Space Preserve	On leash on trail, under voice control on preserve fire roads	No	No	
Helen Putnam Regional Park	On leash	Yes	Yes	
City of Petaluma	On leash	Several parks along route with restrooms	No	
Jack London State Historic Park and East Slope Sonoma Mountain Trail	No	Trailhead	Yes	
Jack London State Historic Park and North Sonoma Mountain Regional Park and Open Space Preserve	No	Both trailheads	Both trailheads	
Spring Lake Regional Park and Trione-Annadel State Park	On leash in county park, prohibited in state park	Spring Lake Regional Park	Spring Lake Regional Park	
Hood Mountain Regional Park and Open Space Preserve	On leash	Upper Trailhead	Yes	
Bothe–Napa Valley State Park	Prohibited on trail	Yes	Yes	
Robert Louis Stevenson Park: Lower Oat Hill Mine Trail and Table Rock/Palisades Trails Spur	Only Lower Oat Hill Mine Trail	No	No	
Robert Louis Stevenson State Park: Mount St. Helena Spur	No	No	No	

Picnic Tables	Camping	Bikes Allowed	Horses Allowed	Wheelchair Access
No	Kirby Cove	Yes	No	Yes
Gerbode Valley Trailhead, Tennessee Valley Trailhead	Kirby Cove, Hawk Camp, Haypress	Alternative route	Part of route	No
Tennessee Valley	Haypress	Yes	Yes	No
Pantoll	Frank Valley Horse Camp, Pantoll, Bootjack	Alternative route for section of trail	Yes	No
Pantoll	Pantoll, Bootjack	Alternative route	Alternative route for section of trail	No
On route, Samuel P. Taylor State Park	Samuel P. Taylor State Park	Yes	Yes	Cross Marin Trail
Samuel P. Taylor State Park	Samuel P. Taylor State Park	Yes	Yes	Cross Marin Trail
No	No	Yes	Yes	No
No	No	Yes	Yes	No
No	No	Alternative route	Yes	No
No	No	Doe Hill fire road only	Yes	No
No	No	Except for Dwarf Oaks Trail	Yes	No
Yes	No	Yes	Yes	No
Several parks along route have picnic tables	No	Yes	No	Some sections accessible, sidewalks
Near trailhead	No	Yes	Yes	No
Both trailheads	No	Except 0.7-mile section	Yes	No
Spring Lake Regional Park and along trail	Spring Lake Regional Park	Yes	Yes	No
Along trail	Backpacking campsites	Yes	Yes	No
In state park	In state park	Except last 1.2 miles	Yes	No
No	No	Only Lower Oat Hill Mine Trail	Only Lower Oat Hill Mine Trail	No
Stevenson Memorial Trailhead	No	Yes	Yes	No

Summary of Trail Features *(continued)*

Region/Trail Name	Dogs Allowed	Restroom(s)	Parking Fee	
The North Bay *(continued)*				
Moore Creek Park	No	Trailhead	No	
Skyline Wilderness Park and Napa Solano Ridge Trail	Prohibited on trail	Trailhead	Yes	
Rockville Hills Regional Park and Vintage Valley Trail	On leash	Yes	Park entrance fee	
Lynch Canyon Open Space and McGary Road	No	Lynch Canyon Trailhead	Yes	
Hiddenbrooke Open Space	No	No	No	
Blue Rock Springs Park to Vallejo–Benicia Buffer	On leash, prohibited in Blue Rock Springs Park	Blue Rock Springs Park	Blue Rock Springs Park	
Vallejo–Benicia Waterfront	On leash	State park, 9th Street Park	State park	
Benicia–Martinez Bridge	On leash	No	No	
The East Bay				
Carquinez Bridge and Crockett	On leash	Carquinez Park	No	
Crockett Hills Regional Park	Under voice control on trails and fire roads	Trailhead	No	
Fernandez Ranch	Under voice control on trails	Trailhead	No	
Martinez City Streets	On leash	Martinez Regional Shoreline	No	
Carquinez Strait Regional Shoreline to John Muir National Historic Site	Under voice control on EBRPD trails and fire roads, on leash in national historic site	EBRPD Trailhead	No	
Contra Costa County Feeder Trail #1	Under voice control on trails and fire roads	No	No	
Pinole Valley Watershed	No	No	No	
Pinole Valley Watershed West and Sobrante Ridge Regional Preserve	Prohibited in watershed, under voice control on preserve trails and fire road	No	No	
Kennedy Grove Regional Recreation Area to Tilden Regional Park	Under voice control on trails, prohibited on Eagle's Nest Trail, on leash on Nimitz Way	Kennedy Grove, Inspiration Point	Kennedy Grove	
Tilden Regional Park to Redwood Regional Park	Under voice control on EBRPD trails and fire roads, on leash in Sibley, prohibited in EBMUD section	Steam trains, Sibley, Redwood's Skyline Gate	No	
Redwood and Anthony Chabot Regional Parks	Under voice control on trails and fire roads	Skyline Gate, Wayside, Bort Meadow	No	
Anthony Chabot Regional Park	Under voice control on trails and fire roads	Bort Meadow, Chabot and Proctor Staging Areas	No	

	Picnic Tables	Camping	Bikes Allowed	Horses Allowed	Wheelchair Access
	No	No	Yes	Yes	No
	Yes	Yes	Yes	Yes	No
	Yes	No	Yes	Only on Vintage Valley Trail	Vintage Valley Trail
	Yes	No	Yes	Yes	No
	No	No	Yes	Yes	No
	Blue Rock Springs Park	No	Except hiking trail in Blue Rock Springs Park	Only on Buffer Trail	Columbus Parkway paved path and sidewalks
	State park, 9th Street Park, Glen Cove Waterfront Park	No	Except Carquinez Overlook Trail	Only from Glen Cove Waterfront Park to K Street	State Park Waterfront Trail, Benicia Marina, sidewalks
	No	No	Yes	No	Yes
	Carquinez Park	No	Yes	Prohibited on bridge	Yes
	Trailhead	No	Yes	Yes	No
	Trailhead and along trail	No	Yes	Yes	Other trail in park
	Martinez Regional Shoreline	No	Yes	Yes, not advised	Sidewalks
	EBRPD Trailhead and Mt. Wanda Trail	No	Yes	Yes	No
	No	No	Yes	Yes	No
	Along bike route	No	Alternative route	Yes	No
	Along trail in preserve	No	Prohibited in watershed, allowed in preserve, except for 0.7-mile section	Yes	No
	Kennedy Grove	Wildcat View, New Woodland, ES Anderson, Gillespie	Yes	Yes	Nimitz Way
	No	Sibley Backpack Camp	Allowed between Inspiration Point and Lomas Cantadas Dr., between Old Tunnel Road and Sibley Staging Areas	Yes	No
	Redwood Bowl, Bort Meadow	Fern's Dell Girls' Camp, Trail's End, Fern Dell, Bort Meadow	Yes	Yes	No
	Bort Meadow	Bort Meadow, several other campgrounds in park	Yes	Yes	No

Summary of Trail Features *(continued)*

Region/Trail Name	Dogs Allowed	Restroom(s)	Parking Fee	
The East Bay *(continued)*				
East Bay Municipal Utility District Lands and Cull Canyon Regional Recreation Area	Prohibited in watershed, under voice control on EBRPD trails and fire roads	Both trailheads	No	
Cull Canyon Regional Recreation Area to Five Canyons Parkway	On leash	Cull Canyon and Don Castro Regional Recreation Areas	No	
Five Canyons Parkway to Garin/ Dry Creek Pioneer Regional Parks	Under voice control on EBRPD trails and fire roads, on leash in Stonebrae	Garin Regional Park Southern Trailhead	No	
Vargas Plateau Regional Park	Under voice control on EBRPD trails and fire roads	Trailhead	No	
Mission Peak Regional Preserve and Ed R. Levin County Park	Under voice control on EBRPD trails and fire roads, on leash in county park	Peak Trail/Hidden Valley Trail junc- tion, Eagle Spring Backpack Camp, Ed R. Levin County Park	Both trailheads	
The South Bay				
Penitencia Creek	On leash	Penitencia Creek Gardens and Peniten- cia Creek Park	No	
Alum Rock Park and Sierra Vista Open Space Preserve	No	West Trailhead, Quail Hollow	Yes	
Sierra Vista Open Space Preserve	No	No	No	
Joseph D. Grant County Park	On leash	Main entrance (not along trail)	Main entrance (not at trailhead)	
Coyote Creek Parkway North	On leash	Hellyer County Park, Metcalf Park	Hellyer County Park	
Coyote Creek Parkway South	On leash	Metcalf Park, model airplane site, Ander- son County Park	No	
Coyote Lake–Harvey Bear Ranch Trail	On leash	North Trailhead	No	
Mount Madonna County Park	On leash	Sprig Recreation Area Trailhead	Main entrance, not on route	
Santa Teresa County Park and Calero/ Los Alamitos Creeks Trails	On leash	Pueblo Group Picnic Area	Yes	
Almaden Quicksilver County Park	On leash	Both trailheads	No	
Sierra Azul Open Space Preserve and Lexington Reservoir County Park	Except Woods Trail	Sierra Azul Trailhead and Lexington Reser- voir County Park	No	
Sierra Azul Open Space Preserve: Mount Umunhum	No	All trailheads	No	
Sanborn County Park: John Nicholas Trail	On leash	Sunnyvale Mountain Trailhead	No	
Sanborn County Park and Castle Rock State Park	On leash in county park, prohibited in state park	Sunnyvale Mountain Trailhead	No	

	Picnic Tables	Camping	Bikes Allowed	Horses Allowed	Wheelchair Access
	Cull Canyon Trailhead	No	No	Yes	No
	Cull Canyon and Don Castro Regional Recreation Areas	No	Only south section	Only north and south sections	Sidewalks
	Garin Regional Park Southern Trailhead	Arroyo Flats	Yes	Yes	No
	Trailhead	No	Yes	Yes	No
	Ed R. Levin County Park	Eagle Spring Backpack Camp	Yes	Yes	No
	Penitencia Creek Gardens and Penitencia Creek Park	No	Yes	Yes	Yes
	Yes	No	Yes	Yes	No
	On route	No	Yes	No	No
	On route	Woodland Youth Camp	Yes	Yes	No
	Stonegate Park, Hellyer County Park, Metcalf Park	No	Yes	Yes	Yes
	Metcalf Park, model airplane site, Anderson County Park	No	Yes	Yes	Yes
	In park, not on trail	Yes	Yes	Yes	No
	Main entrance	Yes	No	Yes	No
	Pueblo Group Picnic Area	No	Yes	Yes	Calero/Los Alamitos Creeks Trails
	Mockingbird Hill Trailhead and along trail	No	Yes	Yes	No
	Lexington County Park	No	Yes	Yes	No
	Near summit	No	Yes	Yes	No
	Sunnyvale Mountain Trailhead, Lake Ranch Reservoir	Sanborn County Park	Yes	Yes	No
	Sunnyvale Mountain Trailhead	Castle Rock State Park	Yes	Yes	No

Summary of Trail Features *(continued)*

Region/Trail Name	Dogs Allowed	Restroom(s)	Parking Fee	
The Peninsula				
Saratoga Gap Open Space Preserve to Skyline Ridge Open Space Preserve	Allowed on leash only in one section of preserve, on leash in county park	North Trailhead	No	
Skyline Ridge Open Space Preserve and Russian Ridge Open Space Preserve	No	South Trailhead, Alpine Pond, Alpine Road	No	
Windy Hill Open Space Preserve	Allowed on leash only in certain sections	Skyline Blvd. Picnic Area	No	
Wunderlich County Park to Huddart County Park	No	El Corte de Madera Creek parking, North Trailhead	Huddart Park main entrance	
Purisima Creek Redwoods Open Space Preserve	No	Both Skyline Blvd. trailheads, Purisima Creek Road Trailhead	No	
Skylawn Memorial Park	On leash	No	No	
San Francisco Peninsula Watershed	No	South Trailhead, every 2 miles in watershed, Sweeney Ridge	No	
Sweeney Ridge	On leash, prohibited on Notch Trail	Sweeney Ridge and Sneath Lane junction	No	
Skyline College, Milagra Ridge, and Pacifica	On leash	Milagra Ridge	No	
Mussel Rock to Lake Merced	On leash	Lake Merced	No	
San Francisco				
Lake Merced to Stern Grove	On leash	Lake Merced, Pine Grove Park, Stern Grove	No	
Stern Grove to the Presidio	On leash	Larsen Park, Panhandle	No	
San Francisco Presidio	On leash	Presidio Clubhouse, Rob Hill Campground, Golden Gate Bridge	Golden Gate Bridge	

Ridge Trail Tracker

Region/Trail Name	Hiker Miles	Equestrian Miles	Biker Miles	Miles Hiked or Ridden	Date	Notes
The North Bay						
The Golden Gate Bridge	1.9	n/a	1.9			
Marin Headlands from the Golden Gate Bridge to Tennessee Valley	5.2	4.7	7.7			
Marin Headlands from Tennessee Valley to Shoreline Highway	3.1	3.3	3.3			
Mount Tamalpais SP and Dias Ridge Trail	5.5	5.5	6.2			Mountain bikers must ride an additional 2.1 miles on a road that is not dedicated Ridge Trail.

Picnic Tables	Camping	Bikes Allowed	Horses Allowed	Wheelchair Access
Horseshoe Lake	Portola Redwoods State Park	Yes	Yes	Horseshoe Lake
Horseshoe Lake, Alpine Pond	No	Yes	Yes	Horseshoe Lake, Alpine Lake
Skyline Blvd. picnic area	No	Only on Fenceline Trail	Yes	No
Huddart Park main entrance, Purisima Creek Redwoods Trailhead	Huddart County Park	No	Yes	No
South Trailhead	No	Yes	Yes	0.2-mile segment
No	No	Yes	Yes	Yes
Along route	No	Yes	Yes	Contact sfwater.org
No	No	Prohibited on Notch Trail	Prohibited on Notch Trail	No
No	No	Yes	Yes	Sidewalks
No	No	Yes	Prohibited in San Francisco	Sidewalks
Lake Merced, Pine Grove Park, Stern Grove	No	Yes	No	Sidewalks
No	No	Yes	No	Sidewalks
Rob Hill Campground	Rob Hill Campground	Yes	No	Some sidewalks

Region/Trail Name	Hiker Miles	Equestrian Miles	Biker Miles	Miles Hiked or Ridden	Date	Notes
Mount Tamalpais SP and Bolinas Ridge	6.4	5.6	n/a			Bicyclists can ride 5.2 miles on roads that are not dedicated Ridge Trail.
Bolinas Ridge and Samuel P. Taylor SP	12.5	12.5	12.5			
Samuel P. Taylor SP to White Hill OSP	10.8	10.8	10.8			
Loma Alta OSP and Loma Alta Fire Road	4	4	4			
Lucas Valley OSP	3.2	3.2	3.2			
GAP						
Indian Tree OSP	3.1	3.1	2.4			

Ridge Trail Tracker *(continued)*

Region/Trail Name	Hiker Miles	Equestrian Miles	Biker Miles	Miles Hiked or Ridden	Date	Notes
GAP						
Stafford Lake Watershed to O'Hair Park	3.2	3.2	0.7			
Mount Burdell OSP from Novato Blvd.	4.2	4.2	n/a			
Mount Burdell OSP from San Andreas Dr.	n/a	n/a	2.9			Hikers and equestrians may also use
GAP						
Helen Putnam Regional Park	1.1	1.1	1.1			
GAP						
City of Petaluma	6.6	n/a	6.6			Plus 0.4-mile return on spur
GAP						
Jack London State Historic Park and East Slope Sonoma Mountain Trail	5.5	5.5	5.5			Includes 2.1-mile connector trail
Jack London State Historic Park and North Sonoma Mountain Regional Park and OSP	7.4	7.4	6.7			Includes 2.1-mile connector trail
GAP						
Spring Lake Regional Park and Trione-Annadel SP	10.8	10.8	10.8			
GAP						
Hood Mountain Regional Park and OSP	5.5	5.5	5.5			Includes 0.3-mile summit spur (not Ridge Trail)
GAP						
Bothe–Napa Valley SP	3.4	3.4	2.2			
GAP						
Robert Louis Stevenson State Park: Lower Oat Hill Mine Trail	4.5	4.5	4.5			
Robert Louis Stevenson State Park: Table Rock and Palisades Trails Spur	6	n/a	n/a			Spur trail—not main Ridge Trail route
Robert Louis Stevenson SP: Mount St. Helena Spur	5	5.5	5.5			Spur trail—not main Ridge Trail route
GAP						
Moore Creek Park	4.9	4.9	4.9			
GAP						
Skyline Wilderness Park and Napa Solano Ridge Trail	4.8	4.9	4.9			
GAP						
Rockville Hills Regional Park and Vintage Valley Trail	4.2	0.8	4.2			Includes 0.5-mile connector trail and 0.1-mile Ridge Trail gap
GAP						
Lynch Canyon Open Space	4.3	4.3	4.3			
McGary Road	3.5	3.5	3.5			
Hiddenbrooke Open Space	2.5	2.5	2.5			

Region/Trail Name	Hiker Miles	Equestrian Miles	Biker Miles	Miles Hiked or Ridden	Date	Notes
GAP						
Blue Rock Springs Park to Vallejo–Benicia Buffer	5.5	3.1	5.1			Plus 0.4 mile return on Blue Rock Springs Park hiker trail. Includes 0.1-mile gap.
Vallejo–Benicia Waterfront West	5.2	3.2	4.5			
Vallejo–Benicia Waterfront East	4.6	0.8	4.6			
GAP						
Benicia–Martinez Bridge	2.5	n/a	2.5			
GAP						
The East Bay						
Carquinez Bridge and Crockett	2.8	n/a	2.8			
GAP						
Crockett Hills Regional Park	5.4	5.4	5.4			
GAP						
Fernandez Ranch	1.4	1.4	1.4			
Martinez City Streets	2.2	n/a	2.2			
Carquinez Strait Regional Shoreline to John Muir National Historic Site	4.2	4.2	4.2			Plus 1.1-mile return on Mount Wanda Trail
GAP						
Contra Costa County Feeder Trail #1	3.3	3.3	3.3			Includes 0.9-mile connector trail
GAP						
Pinole Valley Watershed	6.5	6.5	6.9			
Pinole Valley Watershed West and Sobrante Ridge Regional Preserve	2.7	2.7	1.3			Mountain bike miles includes 0.3-mile connector
GAP						
Kennedy Grove Regional Recreation Area to Tilden Regional Park	5.2	5.2	5.2			Plus 0.5-mile return on Laurel Loop and Kennedy Creek Trails
Tilden Regional Park to Redwood Regional Park	9.3	9.3	4.3			Noncontiguous miles for bikers
Redwood and Anthony Chabot Regional Parks	7.5	7.5	7.7			
Anthony Chabot Regional Park	6.6	6.6	6.7			
East Bay Municipal Utility District Lands and Cull Canyon Regional Recreation Area	6.6	6.6	n/a			
Cull Canyon Regional Recreation Area to Five Canyons Parkway	2.6	1.3	1.4			Equestrian miles are non-contiguous
Five Canyons Parkway to Garin/Dry Creek Pioneer Regional Parks	10.6	10.6	10.6			Includes 0.2-mile and 2.9-mile connector trails. Add 0.6 miles if ending at Dry Creek Park instead of Garin Park.

Ridge Trail Tracker *(continued)*

Region/Trail Name	Hiker Miles	Equestrian Miles	Biker Miles	Miles Hiked or Ridden	Date	Notes
GAP						
Vargas Plateau Regional Park	2	2	2			
GAP						
Mission Peak Regional Preserve and Ed R. Levin County Park	9.9	9.9	9.9			
GAP						
The South Bay						
Penitencia Creek	3.9	3.9	3.9			Includes 0.2 mile from BART
GAP						
Alum Rock Park and Sierra Vista OSP	3.9	3.9	3.9			
Sierra Vista OSP	4.9	n/a	4.9			
GAP						
Joseph D. Grant County Park	5.9	5.9	5.9			
GAP						
Coyote Creek Parkway North	9.3	9.3	9.3			
Coyote Creek Parkway South	9.2	9.2	9.2			
GAP						
Coyote Lake– Harvey Bear Ranch Trail	5.6	5.6	5.6			Includes 0.9-mile connector trail
GAP						
Mount Madonna County Park	3.5	3.5	n/a			
GAP						
Santa Teresa County Park and Calero/Los Alamitos Creeks Trails	6.3	6.3	6.3			Plus 1.1-mile return trip from Coyote Peak
GAP						
Almaden Quicksilver County Park	4.6	4.6	4.6			
Sierra Azul OSP and Lexington Reservoir County Park	11.7	11.7	11.7			
Sierra Azul OSP: Mount Umunhum (from Jacques Ridge)	8.1	8.1	8.1			Includes 2.8 miles on Woods Road from previous segment
Sierra Azul OSP: Mount Umunhum (from Bald Mountain)	3.8	3.8	3.8			Includes 3.4 miles from previous segment
GAP						
Sanborn County Park: John Nicholas Trail	3.5	3.5	3.5			
Sanborn County Park and Castle Rock SP	6	6	6			

Region/Trail Name	Hiker Miles	Equestrian Miles	Biker Miles	Miles Hiked or Ridden	Date	Notes
The Peninsula						
Saratoga Gap OSP	8.1	7.8	7.8			
Skyline Ridge OSP and Russian Ridge OSP	5.1	5.3	5.3			Includes 0.1 mile on Rapley Road
GAP						
Windy Hill OSP	3.3	3.1	0.5			
GAP						
Wunderlich County Park to Huddart County Park	5.9	5.9	n/a			
Purisima Creek Redwoods OSP	5.8	7.5	7.5			
GAP						
Skylawn Memorial Park	1.1	1.1	1.1			
GAP						
San Francisco Peninsula Watershed	12.8	12.8	12.8			Includes 2.9-mile Sneath Lane connector
Sweeney Ridge	3.2	2.2	2.2			Does not include connector-trail mileage for equestrians and mountain bikers
Skyline College, Milagra Ridge, and Pacifica	3.4	3.4	3.4			
GAP						
Mussel Rock to Lake Merced	4.5	4.5	4.5			
San Francisco						
Lake Merced to Stern Grove	4.1	n/a	4.1			
Stern Grove to the Presidio	6.6	n/a	6.6			
Mount Sutro Trail and Phil Arnold Trail	2.1	n/a	2.1			
San Francisco Presidio	2.7	n/a	2.7			

(continued from page 9)

Many parks charge an entrance fee, although some require it only on weekends. A fee is generally charged for amenities such as camping, horseback riding, and swimming. Because fees are subject to change, we've elected not to list exact prices in this book. *Call the park or check its website for the very latest information.*

Biking rules vary depending on the managing agency. Some allow mountain bikers on fire or service roads; a few allow them on narrow trails. Biking access is included in the introductory material for each trip; bikers will find Ridge Trail routes on the maps in this guide, as well as on agency maps and on trailhead signs. See Appendix 1 (page 310) for a complete list of agency addresses, phone numbers, and websites.

Getting Started

This section lists trailhead locations, along with GPS coordinates for reaching them.

On the Trail

This section describes the route, gives directions for trail junctions, tells you what you may see along the way, mentions animal and plant life, and sketches some geological, historical, and cultural features that add to the interest of the trip.

Maps

A general overview map for the entire Ridge Trail is opposite the Table of Contents, on page vi. Each regional chapter begins with an overview map of the Ridge Trail route through that particular region, with the Ridge Trail segments shown as bold red lines.

Map Legend

Trails & Uses

Bay Area Ridge Trail	Connector Trails	Other Trails
▬ ▬ ▬ ▬	▬ ▬ ▬	▬ ▬
Multi-Use		
▬·▬·▬·▬	·▬·▬·▬	·▬·▬·
Hiking/Bikes		
▬▬▬▬▬▬	▬ ▬ ▬ ▬	▬ ▬ ▬
Horse/Hiking		
••••••••	••••••	·············
Hiking only		

▬ *Hikers on Sidewalk; Bikes on Street*

O━ ━O   *Start and End of Segment*

o 1.0 o   *Mileage Between Points*

Regional Trails

🔵 **Bay Area Ridge Trail**

◾ *San Francisco Bay Trail*

◎ *California Coastal Trail*

🔵 *Juan Bautista de Anza National Historic Trail*

🍃 *East Bay Parks Regional Trails*

Roads & Transit

═══	*Freeway*
═══	*Highway*
═══	*Road*
───	*Local Road*
═ ═ ═	*Unpaved Road*
(280)	*Interstate Highway*
(101)	*U.S. Highway*
(1)	*State Highway*
┼━◻━┼	*Rail Transit and Station*
┼·┼·┼·┼	*Freight Railroad*

Regional Maps

▬▬▬ *Completed Ridge Trail Segments*

▬ ▬ ▬ *Proposed Ridge Trail Corridor*

Symbols

P	*Trailhead Parking*
EP	*Equestrian Parking*
LP	*Limited Parking*
🪑	*Picnic Table*
⛺	*Campground*
⛺	*Group Campground*
🏠	*Ranger Station*
❓	*Visitor Center or Museum*
🚻	*Restroom*
♿	*Handicap Accessible*
⏜	*Bridge*
▪	*Point of Interest*
904'▲	*Peak (Elevation in Feet)*
⊷	*Gate*
🌲	*Redwood Tree or Grove*
〰	*Stream*
⬭	*Body of Water*
〰	*Marsh or Wetland*
🗺	*Elevation Contours (200-Foot Intervals)*
▭	*Area Shown on Inset Map*

Land Management

▨	*Parks and Open Space Preserves*
▨	*Other Public Lands*
▭	*Watersheds*
▨	*Campus*
▨	*Private Property*
— ·· —	*County Line*

A separate map for each trip marks the Ridge Trail segment, as well as other trails, park trailheads, and major landmarks. Different thicknesses and dash patterns indicate the trails and their user groups at a glance. The combination of user-group symbols on the map, the accessibility information at the beginning of each trip, and the material in the text clarify the Ridge Trail route and appropriate users within each park or preserve. Other trails are shown with thin red lines, with similar dash patterns indicating users.

Additional information on the maps includes trailhead parking areas, major roads, and nearby landmarks, which, combined with the text, will direct you to the park. A legend explaining the symbols on these maps is on the opposite page.

The maps are generally based on the 7.5-minute series of U.S. Geological Survey (USGS) topographic maps, which are available from some sporting goods and outdoor stores and from the USGS online at store.usgs.gov.

For complete information, look online for a park map from the managing agency. Maps are available at some trailheads, but they may not be in stock when you visit.

Sharing the Trails

Hikers, mountain bikers, and equestrians share many segments of the Bay Area Ridge Trail. Wherever possible, the Ridge Trail tries to accommodate all users on a single route. If this is not possible, Bay Area Ridge Trail policy states that "due to policy or regulation restrictions, environmental concerns, safety or physical terrain, the Bay Area Ridge Trail Council works cooperatively to secure an additional route that offers an equivalent trail experience."

Variations in speed, height, and power of each type of user require some trail etiquette rules. Some general rules include the following:

- Observe trail-use signs.
- Be responsible, safe, and considerate.
- Stay on the trail.
- Respect private property.
- Minimize your impact.
- Protect plants and wildlife.
- Hikers and mountain bikers yield to equestrians—stop and remain quiet while an equestrian is passing.
- Mountain bikers yield to hikers—dismount and allow a hiker to pass.

A number of agencies have adopted additional rules for bikers. Maximum speed is 15 miles per hour, but slow down to 5 miles per hour when passing or when sight distance is limited. Helmets are a standard requirement of most agencies. Some agencies use radar systems to increase awareness of park speed limits and to help bikers know their speed.

Hazards for Trail Users

Poison oak is ubiquitous in the Bay Area. It takes different forms, most often as a trailside shrub but mature plants climb trees and occasionally become small trees themselves.

The plant *(right)* has three-lobed leaves that are shiny green in spring and turn shades of red and orange in the fall. Most people have allergic reactions; just to touch its leaves, berries, or leafless twigs can cause an itchy, blistery rash that takes several weeks to heal. Learn to recognize it and carefully avoid it.

Rattlesnakes are indigenous to the Bay Area but are far less widespread than poison oak. As shown below, they have triangular-shaped heads and diamond markings on their backs, and they rattle using the segmented sections on their tails. They generally try to avoid contact with humans. However, as you hike on warm spring days, it's advisable to look down for rattlesnakes that may be sunning themselves on the trail. Also, be sure to look where you put your hands when climbing on rocks.

Lyme disease is a potentially serious disease caused by the bite of the **western black-legged tick.** In their active months, between December and June, these tiny ticks can brush off trailside grasses and bushes and cling onto your clothes. Wear light-colored clothing so you can see the ticks, keep your arms and legs covered, and tuck your pant legs into your socks.

Mountain lions also inhabit wild lands in the Bay Area. Sightings of these shy creatures have become more frequent in recent years due to increased human use of their habitat. Trail users should stand facing any mountain lion they encounter and make loud noises while waving their arms; do not run away because that may cause a mountain lion to see you as prey.

Feral pigs have spread over many acres of wild lands since they were introduced as hunting animals in the 19th century. While generally not dangerous to humans, they can be fierce when cornered, so don't approach them.

What to Wear and Take Along

Some basic rules for all trail users are to carry plenty of water, food, and snacks; bring the appropriate equipment for your mode of travel; take an extra sweater or fleece and a windbreaker; wear a hat; and carry (and use) sunscreen. A basic first aid kit is good to have as well. All of these items can easily fit in a light day pack. Finally, don't forget your phone in case of an emergency.

Specialized equipment for trail users is readily available but not required. Many hikers prefer to wear boots; others find that sturdy shoes with good tread and adequate support are appropriate for most Bay Area trails. Some bikers prefer clip-in biking shoes, and many equestrians prefer to wear a protective helmet.

Camping and Multiday Trekking

For those who want to have a true outdoor experience on Ridge Trail outings, there are numerous opportunities for camping near the trail. This is an appealing option for areas with contiguous Ridge Trail segments, which could take days to complete. The Summary of Trail Features table (page 10) states whether the park offers camping; the websites for these parks provide detailed information about the camping, including hike-in camps. Also, the Ridge Trail Council has maps online showing campgrounds in the general vicinity of the Ridge Trail. Hostels, huts, yurts, and adjacent inns offer additional opportunities to extend your time on the trail.

Bikers pedal the Dias Ridge Trail.

Trail Sampler:
Trips for Many Reasons

Consult this quick-reference list to find the right trip for your particular interest.

For Peak Baggers

THE NORTH BAY

- Marin Headlands from the Golden Gate Bridge to Tennessee Valley (p. 45): Slacker Hill, 928'
- Mount Tamalpais State Park (pgs. 50 and 55): East Peak, 2,571'
- Samuel P. Taylor Park to White Hill Open Space Preserve (p. 64): White Hill, 1,430'
- Loma Alta Open Space Preserve and Loma Alta Fire Road (p. 66): Loma Alta, 1,592'
- Lucas Valley Open Space Preserve (p. 70): Big Rock Ridge, 1,895'
- Mount Burdell Open Space Preserve (p. 77): Mount Burdell, 1,558'
- Jack London State Historic Park (p. 90): Sonoma Mountain, 2,463' (trail ends near summit)
- Hood Mountain Regional Park and Open Space Preserve (p. 98): Hood Mountain, 2,730'
- Robert Louis Stevenson State Park (p. 109): Mount St. Helena, 4,343'
- Skyline Wilderness Park (p. 114): Sugarloaf Mountain, 1,638'
- Hiddenbrooke Open Space (p. 126): Sulphur Springs Mountain, 1,112'

THE EAST BAY

- John Muir National Historic Site (p. 153): Mount Wanda, 643'
- Tilden Regional Park to Redwood Regional Park (p. 171): Wildcat Peak, 1,250'; Vollmer Peak, 1,905'; and Round Top Mountain, 1,763'
- Redwood and Anthony Chabot Regional Parks (p. 177): Redwood Peak, 1,619'
- East Bay Municipal Utility District Lands and Cull Canyon Regional Recreation Area (p. 185): Dinosaur Ridge, 1,000'
- Mission Peak Regional Preserve and Ed R. Levin County Park (p. 200): Mission Peak, 2,517', and Monument Peak, 2,594'

THE SOUTH BAY

- Alum Rock Park (p. 211): Eagle Rock, 796'
- Sierra Vista Open Space Preserve (p. 211): Unnamed hill on side trip from Boccardo Loop Trail, 1,896'
- Mount Madonna County Park (p. 230): Mount Madonna, 1,897'
- Santa Teresa County Park and Calero Creek/Los Alamitos Creek Trails (p. 233): Coyote Peak, 1,155'
- Sierra Azul Open Space Preserve (pgs. 241 and 245): Mount El Sombroso, 2,999', and Mount Umunhum, 3,486'

THE PENINSULA
- Skyline Ridge and Russian Ridge Open Space Preserves (p. 262): Borel Hill, 2,572'
- Windy Hill Open Space Preserve (p. 266): Windy Hill, 1,905'

SAN FRANCISCO
- Stern Grove to the Presidio (p. 297): Twin Peaks, 904'/922', and Mount Sutro, 909'

Ocean Views

THE NORTH BAY
- The Golden Gate Bridge (p. 40)
- Marin Headlands from the Golden Gate Bridge to Tennessee Valley (p. 45)
- Marin Headlands from Tennessee Valley to Shoreline Highway (p. 48)
- Mount Tamalpais State Park and Dias Ridge Trail (p. 50)
- Mount Tamalpais State Park and Bolinas Ridge (p. 55)
- Bolinas Ridge and Samuel P. Taylor State Park (p. 59)

THE EAST BAY
- Kennedy Grove Regional Recreation Area to Tilden Regional Park (p. 167)
- Tilden Regional Park to Redwood Regional Park (p. 171)

THE SOUTH BAY
- Sierra Azul Open Space Preserve: Mount Umunhum (p. 245)

THE PENINSULA
- Saratoga Gap Open Space Preserve to Skyline Ridge Open Space Preserve (p. 258): from Long Ridge Open Space Preserve
- Skyline Ridge and Russian Ridge Open Space Preserves (p. 262): from Borel Hill
- Windy Hill Open Space Preserve (p. 266): from Windy Hill
- Purisima Creek Redwoods Open Space Preserve (p. 273): from Harkins Ridge Trail
- Skylawn Memorial Park (p. 277)
- San Francisco Peninsula Watershed (p. 279)
- Sweeney Ridge (p. 282)
- Skyline College, Milagra Ridge, and Pacifica (p. 285)
- Mussel Rock to Merced Lake (p. 288)

SAN FRANCISCO
- Stern Grove to the Presidio (p. 297)
- San Francisco Presidio (p. 305)

Inland Vistas

THE NORTH BAY
- The Golden Gate Bridge (p. 40)
- Marin Headlands from the Golden Gate Bridge to Tennessee Valley (p. 43)
- Marin Headlands from Tennessee Valley to Shoreline Highway (p. 48)
- Mount Tamalpais State Park and Dias Ridge Trail (p. 50)
- Mount Tamalpais State Park and Bolinas Ridge (p. 55)

Inland Vistas *(continued)*

Good for Families

Good for Families *(continued)*

THE SOUTH BAY

- Penitencia Creek (p. 208): Picnic areas in Penitencia Creek Gardens and Penitencia Creek Park
- Alum Rock Park (p. 211): Play area in middle of park and picnic tables throughout park
- Joseph D. Grant County Park (p. 217): Picnic tables at main entrance
- Coyote Creek Parkway North (p. 220): Walk or ride bikes on the trail; picnic at several parks along the trail.
- Coyote Creek Parkway South (p. 224): Walk or ride bikes or horses; picnic along the trail
- Coyote Lake–Harvey Bear Ranch County Park (p. 227): Picnic areas along Coyote Lake
- Mount Madonna County Park (p. 230): Picnic tables near main entrance
- Santa Teresa County Park (p. 233): Picnic tables at Pueblo Day Use area
- Sierra Azul Open Space Preserve: Mount Umunhum (p. 245): Picnic tables near parking area at summit

THE PENINSULA

- Skyline Ridge Open Space Preserve (pgs. 258 and 262): Picnic at Horseshoe Lake or Alpine Pond
- Windy Hill Open Space Preserve (p. 266): Picnic area adjacent to Skyline Boulevard
- Purisima Creek Redwoods Open Space Preserve (p. 273): Picnic area at Redwood Trail near Skyline Boulevard
- Mussel Rock to Lake Merced (p. 288): Neighborhood parks (Northridge Park and Palisades Park) just off the trail in Daly City

SAN FRANCISCO

- Lake Merced to Stern Grove (p. 294): Parks along the Ridge Trail route with picnic facilities (Harding Park, Pine Lake Park, Stern Grove)
- Stern Grove to the Presidio (p. 297): Parks along the Ridge Trail route (Larsen Park, Buena Vista Park, Golden Gate Park)
- San Francisco Presidio (p. 305): Picnic at Rob Hill Campground

Segments That Are
Almost Level and Mostly Paved

THE NORTH BAY

- The Golden Gate Bridge (p. 40)
- Samuel P. Taylor State Park (pgs. 59 and 64): Cross Marin Trail
- Helen Putnam Regional Park and City of Petaluma (p. 81)
- Spring Lake Regional Park (p. 94): Spring Creek Trail
- Vintage Valley Trail (p. 119)
- Vallejo–Benicia Waterfront (p. 132)
- Benicia–Martinez Bridge (p. 137)

THE EAST BAY

- Carquinez Bridge and Crockett (p. 142)
- Martinez City Streets (p. 150)
- Tilden Regional Park (pgs. 167 and 171): Nimitz Way

THE SOUTH BAY

- Penitencia Creek (p. 208)
- Coyote Creek Parkway North (p. 220)
- Coyote Creek Parkway South (p. 224)
- Calero Creek/Los Alamitos Creek Trails (p. 233)

THE PENINSULA

- Skyline Ridge Open Space Preserve (pgs. 258 and 262): Alpine Pond and Horseshoe Lake trails
- Skylawn Memorial Park (p. 277)
- Mussel Rock to Lake Merced (p. 288): section from Mayfair Drive to Lake Merced

SAN FRANCISCO

- Lake Merced to Stern Grove (p. 294)
- Stern Grove to the Presidio (p. 297): section from the Panhandle to the Presidio

Segments with More Than 1,000 Feet of Elevation Gain

THE NORTH BAY

- Marin Headlands from the Golden Gate Bridge to Tennessee Valley (p. 43): 1,170' for mountain bikers
- Mount Tamalpais State Park and Dias Ridge Trail (p. 50): 1,505' for hikers and equestrians, 1,745' for mountain bikers
- Samuel P. Taylor State Park to White Hill Open Space Preserve (p. 64): 1,540'
- Loma Alta Open Space Preserve and Loma Alta Fire Road (p. 66): 1,040'
- Lucas Valley Open Space Preserve (p. 70): 1,115'
- Indian Tree Open Space Preserve (p. 71): 1,200'
- Mount Burdell Open Space Preserve (p. 77): 1,400' (from Novato Blvd.) or 1,200' (from San Andreas Dr.)
- Jack London State Historic Park and East Slope Sonoma Mountain Ridge Trail (p. 86): 1,495'
- Jack London State Historic Park and North Sonoma Mountain Regional Park and Open Space Preserve (p. 90): 1,695'
- Spring Lake Regional Park and Trione-Annadel State Park (p. 94): 1,120'
- Hood Mountain Regional Park and Open Space Preserve (p. 98): 1,950'
- Bothe–Napa Valley State Park (p. 101): 1,120'
- Robert Louis Stevenson State Park: Lower Oat Hill Mine Trail (p. 104): 1,860'
- Robert Louis Stevenson State Park: Table Rock and Palisades Trails Spur (p. 107): 1,280' north–south
- Robert Louis Stevenson State Park: Mount St. Helena Spur (p. 109): 1,790' for hikers, 1,990' on multiuse route
- Skyline Wilderness Park and Napa Solano Ridge Trail (p. 114): 1,400'

THE EAST BAY

- Crockett Hills Regional Park (p. 144): 1,250'
- Carquinez Strait Regional Shoreline and John Muir National Historic Site (p. 153): 1,025'
- Pinole Valley Watershed (p. 160): 1,195' for hikers and equestrians
- Kennedy Grove Regional Recreation Area to Tilden Regional Park (p. 167): 1,045'
- Tilden Regional Park to Redwood Regional Park (p. 171): 1,785'

Segments with More Than 1,000 Feet of Elevation Gain *(continued)*

THE EAST BAY *(continued)*

- East Bay Municipal Utility District Lands and Cull Canyon Regional Recreation Area (p. 185): 1,050'
- Five Canyons Parkway to Dry Creek/Garin Regional Parks (p. 192): 1,470'
- Mission Peak Regional Preserve and Ed R. Levin County Park (p. 200): 2,190'

THE SOUTH BAY

- Alum Rock Park and Sierra Vista Open Space Preserve (p. 211): 1,775'
- Sierra Vista Open Space Preserve (p. 214): 1,290'
- Mount Madonna County Park (p. 230): 1,150'
- Almaden Quicksilver County Park (p. 238): 1,160'
- Sierra Azul Open Space Preserve and Lexington Reservoir County Park (p. 241): 1,830'
- Sierra Azul Open Space Preserve: Mount Umunhum (p. 245): 2,435' from Jacques Ridge Parking Area; 1,150' from Bald Mountain Parking Area
- Sanborn County Park: John Nicholas Trail (p. 248): 1,160'

THE PENINSULA

- Purisima Creek Redwoods Open Space Preserve (p. 273): 1,215' for hikers, 1,710' for equestrians and mountain bikers
- San Francisco Peninsula Watershed (p. 279): 1,725'

Trips Less Than 5 Miles Round-Trip

THE NORTH BAY

- The Golden Gate Bridge (p. 40)
- Helen Putnam Regional Park (p. 81)
- Hiddenbrooke Open Space (p. 126)
- Benicia–Martinez Bridge (p. 137)

THE EAST BAY

- Fernandez Ranch (p. 147)
- Martinez City Streets (p. 150)
- Cull Canyon Regional Recreation Area to Five Canyons Parkway (p. 189)
- Vargas Plateau Regional Park (p. 197)

THE PENINSULA

- Skylawn Memorial Park (p. 277)

Trips Less Than 5 Miles One-Way with a Shuttle

THE NORTH BAY

- Marin Headlands from Tennessee Valley to Shoreline Highway (p. 48)
- Loma Alta Open Space Preserve and Loma Alta Fire Road (p. 66)
- Stafford Lake Watershed to O'Hair Park (p. 74)
- Rockville Hills Regional Park and Vintage Valley Trail (p. 119)
- Vallejo–Benicia Waterfront (p. 132): from state park entrance to Military East

THE EAST BAY

- Carquinez Bridge and Crockett (p. 142)
- Contra Costa Feeder Trail #1 (p. 157)
- Pinole Valley Watershed West and Sobrante Ridge Regional Preserve (p. 164)

THE SOUTH BAY

- Penitencia Creek (p. 208)
- Alum Rock and Sierra Vista Open Space Preserve (p. 214)
- Mount Madonna County Park (p. 230)
- Almaden Quicksilver County Park (p. 238)
- Sierra Azul Open Space Preserve: Mount Umunhum (p. 245): from Bald Mountain Parking Area
- Sanborn County Park: John Nicholas Trail (p. 248): between Sanborn Road and Sunnyvale Staging Area

THE PENINSULA

- Windy Hill Open Space Preserve (p. 266)
- Skylawn College, Milagra Ridge, and Pacifica (p. 285)
- Mussel Rock to Lake Merced (p. 288)

SAN FRANCISCO

- Lake Merced to Stern Grove (p. 294)
- San Francisco Presidio (p. 305)

Trips 5–10 Miles Round-Trip

THE NORTH BAY

- Lucas Valley Open Space Preserve (p. 70)
- Mount Burdell Open Space Preserve (p. 77)
- Bothe–Napa Valley State Park (p. 101)
- Robert Louis Stevenson State Park: Lower Oat Hill Mine Trail (p. 104)
- Robert Louis Stevenson State Park: Mount St. Helena Spur (p. 109): hiker route
- Moore Creek Park (p. 112)
- Skyline Wilderness Park and Napa Solano Ridge Trail (p. 114)
- Lynch Canyon Open Space (p. 123)

THE SOUTH BAY

- Sierra Vista Open Space Preserve (p. 214)
- Joseph D. Grant County Park (p. 217)

THE PENINSULA

- Sweeney Ridge (p. 282)

Trips 5–10 Miles One-Way with a Shuttle

THE NORTH BAY

- Marin Headlands from the Golden Gate Bridge to Tennessee Valley (p. 43)
- Mount Tamalpais State Park and Dias Ridge Trail (p. 50)

Trips 5–10 Miles One-Way with a Shuttle *(continued)*

THE NORTH BAY *(continued)*
- Mount Tamalpais State Park and Bolinas Ridge (p. 55)
- City of Petaluma (p. 83)
- Jack London State Historic Park and North Sonoma Mountain Regional Park and Open Space Preserve (p. 90)
- Blue Rock Springs Park to Vallejo–Benicia Buffer (p. 128)

THE EAST BAY
- Carquinez Strait Regional Shoreline and John Muir National Historic Site (p. 153)
- Pinole Valley Watershed (p. 160)
- Kennedy Grove Regional Recreation Area to Tilden Regional Park (p. 167)
- Tilden Regional Park to Redwood Regional Park (p. 171)
- Redwood and Anthony Chabot Regional Parks (p. 177)
- Anthony Chabot Regional Park (p. 181)
- East Bay Municipal Utility District Lands and Cull Canyon Regional Recreation Area (p. 185)
- Mission Peak Regional Preserve and Ed R. Levin County Park (p. 200)

THE SOUTH BAY
- Coyote Creek Parkway North (p. 220)
- Coyote Creek Parkway South (p. 224)
- Coyote Lake–Harvey Bear Ranch County Park (p. 227)
- Santa Teresa County Park and Calero Creek/Los Alamitos Creek Trails (p. 233)
- Sierra Azul Open Space Preserve: Mount Umunhum (p. 245): from Jacques Ridge Parking Area
- Sanborn County Park and Castle Rock State Park (p. 251)

THE PENINSULA
- Saratoga Gap Open Space Preserve to Skyline Ridge Open Space Preserve (p. 258)
- Skyline Ridge and Russian Ridge Open Space Preserves (p. 262)
- Wunderlich County Park to Huddart County Park (p. 269)
- Purisima Creek Redwoods Open Space Preserve (p. 273)
- Sweeney Ridge (p. 282)

SAN FRANCISCO
- Stern Grove to the Presidio (p. 297)

Trips More Than 10 Miles
(ONE-WAY OR ROUND-TRIP)

THE NORTH BAY
- Bolinas Ridge and Samuel P. Taylor State Park (p. 59): One-way
- Samuel P. Taylor State Park to White Hill Open Space Preserve (p. 64): One-way
- Jack London State Historic Park and East Slope Sonoma Mountain Ridge Trail (p. 86): Round-trip
- Spring Lake Regional Park and Trione-Annadel State Park (p. 94): One-way
- Hood Mountain Regional Park and Open Space Preserve (p. 98): Round-trip

- Robert Louis Stevenson State Park: Mount St. Helena Spur (p. 109): Round-trip (multiuse route)

THE EAST BAY

- Crockett Hills Regional Park (p. 144): Round-trip
- Five Canyons Parkway to Garin/Dry Creek Pioneer Regional Parks (p. 192): One-way

THE SOUTH BAY

- Sierra Azul Open Space Preserve and Lexington County Park (p. 241): One-way

THE PENINSULA

- San Francisco Peninsula Watershed (p. 279): One-way

Contiguous Trail Segments of 15-Plus Miles

THE NORTH BAY

- **53 MILES** *(hiker route)*: South entrance of the Golden Gate Bridge through the Marin Headlands, Mount Tamalpais State Park, Bolinas Ridge, Samuel P. Taylor State Park, Gary Giacomini Open Space Preserve, White Hill Open Space Preserve, Loma Alta Open Space Preserve, and Lucas Valley Open Space Preserve
- **16 MILES:** Robert Louis Stevenson State Park (Lower Oat Hill Mine Trail, Palisades Trail, Table Rock Trail, and Mount St. Helena Trail)

THE EAST BAY

- **46 MILES:** Kennedy Grove Regional Recreation Area, EBMUD Lands, Wildcat Canyon Regional Park, Tilden Regional Park, Sibley Volcanic Regional Preserve, Huckleberry Botanic Regional Preserve, Redwood Regional Park, Anthony Chabot Regional Park, Cull Canyon Regional Recreation Area, Castro Valley streets, Don Castro Regional Recreation Area, Five Canyons Open Space, Garin Regional Park, and Stonebrae subdivision

THE SOUTH BAY

- **19 MILES:** Coyote Creek Parkway North and South
- **22 MILES:** Almaden Quicksilver County Park, Sierra Azul Open Space Preserve, and Mount Umunhum

THE PENINSULA AND SAN FRANCISCO

- **23 MILES:** Sanborn County Park, Castle Rock State Park, Saratoga Gap Open Space Preserve, Long Ridge Open Space Preserve, Upper Stevens Creek County Park, Skyline Ridge Open Space Preserve, and Russian Ridge Open Space Preserve
- **17 MILES:** San Francisco Watershed, Sweeney Ridge, Skyline College, Milagra Ridge, and Pacifica streets
- **18 MILES:** Mussel Rock, Daly City, to the Presidio, San Francisco (connects to 52 miles in North Bay, creating a 70-mile stretch)

Linger by a Lake or Pond

THE NORTH BAY

- Mount Burdell Open Space Preserve (p. 77): Hidden Lake
- Helen Putnam Regional Park (p. 81): fishing pond
- Jack London State Historic Park (pgs. 86 and 90)

Miner's lettuce is abundant along the trail in San Mateo County's Bear Gulch Watershed.

Linger by a Lake or Pond *(continued)*

THE NORTH BAY *(continued)*

- Spring Lake Regional Park (p. 94)
- Trione-Annadel State Park (p. 94): Lake Ilsanjo
- Hood Mountain Regional Park and Open Space Preserve (p. 98): Merganser and Blue Heron Ponds
- Skyline Wilderness Park (p. 114): Lake Marie
- Rockville Hills Regional Park (p. 119): Grey Goose Lake
- Lynch Canyon Open Space (p. 123): Lynch Reservoir
- Blue Rock Springs to Vallejo–Benicia Buffer (p. 128): Blue Rock Springs Park

THE EAST BAY

- Kennedy Grove Regional Recreation Area to Tilden Regional Park (p. 167): San Pablo Reservoir
- Anthony Chabot Regional Park (p. 181): Lake Chabot
- Cull Canyon Regional Recreation Area (pgs. 185 and 189): swimming lagoon
- Cull Canyon Regional Recreation Area to Five Canyons Parkway (p. 189): swimming lagoon and fishing lake at Don Castro Regional Recreation Area
- Garin Regional Park (p. 192): Jordan Pond
- Ed R. Levin County Park (p. 200): Sandy Wool Lake

THE SOUTH BAY

- Penitencia Creek Park (p. 208): Penitencia Creek Gardens
- Joseph D. Grant County Park (p. 217): Grant Lake
- Coyote Creek Parkway North (p. 220): Hellyer County Park and Metcalf Park
- Coyote Creek Parkway South (p. 224): Quarry ponds and Anderson Lake
- Coyote Lake–Harvey Bear Ranch County Park (p. 227): Coyote Lake
- Sanborn County Park: John Nicholas Trail (p. 248): Lake Ranch Reservoir

THE PENINSULA

- Saratoga Gap Open Space Preserve to Skyline Ridge Open Space Preserve (p. 258): Jikoji Pond and Horseshoe Lake
- Skyline Ridge and Russian Ridge Open Space Preserves (p. 262): Horseshoe Lake and Alpine Pond
- Mussel Rock to Lake Merced (p. 288): Lake Merced

SAN FRANCISCO

- Lake Merced to Stern Grove (p. 294): Lake Merced and Pine Lake

Shady Hikes

THE NORTH BAY

- Samuel P. Taylor State Park (pgs. 59 and 64): Cross Marin Trail
- Indian Tree Open Space Preserve (p. 71)
- Jack London State Historic Park and East Slope Sonoma Mountain Ridge Trail (p. 86): some open sections
- Jack London State Historic Park and North Sonoma Mountain Regional Park and Open Space Preserve (p. 90): some open sections
- Hood Mountain Regional Park and Open Space Preserve (p. 98), except summit, which is exposed
- Bothe–Napa Valley State Park (p. 101)

THE EAST BAY

- Redwood and Anthony Chabot Regional Parks (p. 177): some open sections

THE SOUTH BAY

- Sierra Azul Open Space Preserve: Mount Umunhum (p. 245), except summit, which is exposed
- Sanborn County Park: John Nicholas Trail (p. 248)
- Sanborn County Park and Castle Rock State Park (p. 251)

THE PENINSULA

- Wunderlich County Park to Huddart County Park (p. 269)
- Purisima Creek Redwoods Open Space Preserve (p. 273): some open sections

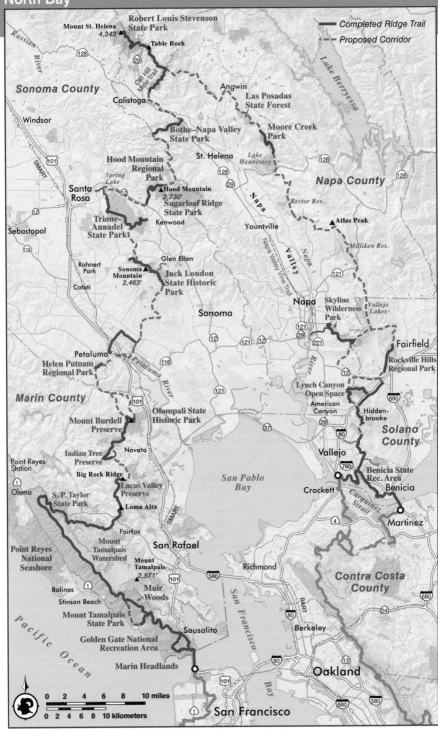

Completed Ridge Trail
Proposed Corridor

Mount St. Helena
4,343'

Robert Louis Stevenson
State Park

Table Rock

Russian River

Sonoma County

Windsor

Calistoga

Angwin

Las Posadas
State Forest

Bothe–Napa Valley
State Park

Moore Creek
Park

Hood Mountain
Regional
Park

St. Helena

Lake
Hennessey

Napa County

Spring
Lake

Santa
Rosa

Hood Mountain
2,730'

Sugarloaf Ridge
State Park

Kenwood

Rector Res.

Sebastopol

Trione-
Annadel
State Park

Napa

Yountville

Atlas Peak

Milliken Res.

Rohnert
Park

Glen Ellen

Sonoma
Mountain
2,463'

Jack London
State Historic
Park

Cotati

Napa Valley Vine Trail

Sonoma

Napa

Skyline
Wilderness
Park

Vallejo
Lakes

Fairfield

Petaluma

Helen Putnam
Regional Park

Petaluma River

Rockville Hills
Regional Park

Marin County

Olompali State
Historic Park

Lynch Canyon
Open Space

American
Canyon

Hidden-
brooke

Solano
County

Mount Burdell
Preserve

Novato

Vallejo

Point Reyes
Station

Indian Tree
Preserve

Big Rock Ridge

Benicia State
Rec. Area

Benicia

Olema

Lucas Valley
Preserve

S. P. Taylor
State Park

Loma Alta

Crockett

Carquinez
Strait

San Pablo
Bay

Martinez

Fairfax

Point Reyes
National
Seashore

Mount
Tamalpais
Watershed

Mount
Tamalpais
2,571'

San Rafael

Contra Costa
County

Richmond

Bolinas

Stinson Beach

Muir
Woods

Mount Tamalpais
State Park

Sausalito

San Francisco Bay

Berkeley

BART

Golden Gate National
Recreation Area

Pacific Ocean

Marin Headlands

Oakland

0 2 4 6 8   10 miles
0 2 4 6 8 10 kilometers

San Francisco

38

NORTH BAY

The Golden Gate Bridge

LENGTH 1.9 miles one-way; car shuttle possible

ELEVATION GAIN/LOSS 190'/120' one-way

ACCESSIBILITY Hikers and bicyclists; access for wheelchair users ends at Vista Point in Sausalito

AGENCIES Golden Gate Bridge Highway and Transportation District and National Park Service

PARKS Presidio and Golden Gate National Recreation Area

REGULATIONS Hikers and wheelchair users permitted on the bridge's east sidewalk from 5 a.m. until either 6:30 p.m. Pacific Standard Time (November–March) or 9 p.m. Pacific Daylight Time (March–November). Bicyclists may use sidewalks anytime (side is determined on a daily basis); after daylight hours, bike use is subject to a remotely controlled security check at gates on both ends of east sidewalk. Electric bikes must be manually pedaled. Only service dogs allowed.

FACILITIES Viewing deck, Welcome Center (open 9 a.m.–6 p.m.), and cafés (open 9 a.m.–6 p.m.) at San Francisco end of bridge; water and restrooms at both ends of bridge

THIS FAMOUS BRIDGE SPAN, dedicated in 1937, is one of the world's most spectacular and visited sites. A trip by foot, bike, or wheelchair offers visitors an excellent opportunity to understand Bay Area geography and the route of the Bay Area Ridge Trail. The bridge can be windy and/or foggy, so wear layers.

Getting Started

SOUTH TRAILHEAD Golden Gate Bridge Welcome Center, south of bridge, San Francisco. Parking lots (some with fee) next to the Welcome Center; farther east, on the north side of Lincoln Boulevard; and on the west side of US 101/CA 1. (**GPS: N37° 48.454', W122° 28.500'**)

NORTH TRAILHEAD North Tower Golden Gate Bridge parking lot, Sausalito. From US 101/CA 1 heading north or south in Marin County, take the Alexander Avenue exit and turn left at stop sign; then go right on Conzelman Road and immediately left downhill into the parking lot. (**GPS: N37° 49.933', W122° 28.936'**)

On the Trail

On March 28, 1937, President Franklin Delano Roosevelt pressed a telegraph key in the White House that signaled the opening of the Golden Gate Bridge. Since that ceremonial event, this iconic San Francisco structure has been in continual daily use. More than 112,000 vehicles cross it every day, and 1 million people cross it by foot or bike every month.

Start your trip outside the Welcome Center at the bridge's south end. To get to the bridge, **bicyclists** can head up the ramp to the right of the Round House Café (and connect with the appropriate bike path) or venture north into the plaza to see the statue of Joseph Strauss, the chief engineer of the Golden Gate Bridge, and the man who insisted upon strict safety guidelines—helmets for all workers and supervisors and the installation of safety nets for the bridge workers. To read more about the so-called Halfway to Hell workers, see the Carquinez Bridge trip on page 142.

The Golden Gate Bridge

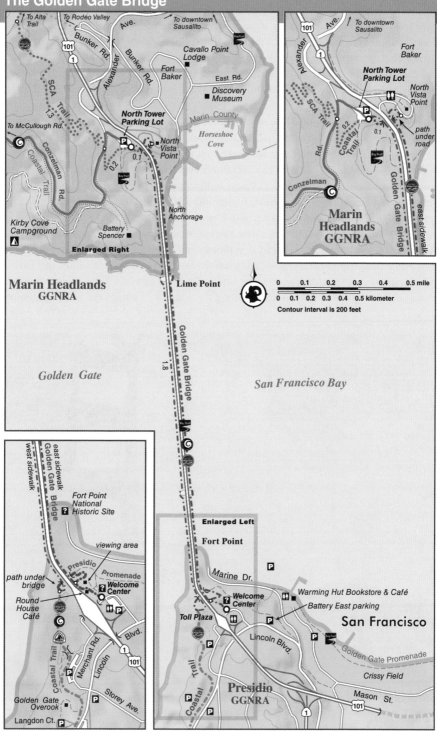

41

Hikers can continue past the statue to view information panels that tell the story of how the bridge was built before walking up a ramp for more exhibits. From here, stairs take you up to the viewing area. The expansive panorama includes fine views of the bridge, Marin Headlands, Tiburon Peninsula, Alcatraz and Angel Islands, and downtown San Francisco. As you look out to sea, think of the first explorers happening onto this slot in the coastline. Imagine those stalwart, adventurous men who risked foul weather, wild storms, lack of food and water, and uncharted ocean to sail north along this coast.

From the viewing deck, head straight out to the bridge's east sidewalk. Depending on the day and time, **bicyclists** use the east or west sidewalk. If you walk or ride across the bridge on a clear day, you can see northwest to the light station at Point Bonita and southwest to Mile Rock and Lands End, sentinels over the bay's entrance. At 0.3 mile, look directly down inside of historic Fort Point, built between 1853 and 1861 to defend San Francisco Bay. Surfers may be catching waves adjacent to the fort. The farther out you get on the bridge, the more you can see of San Francisco, especially the Presidio.

At midspan you're 220 feet above the mean high-water mark, and the top of the towers is 500 feet above you. From the walkway you can see an international parade of ships originating from exotic places: sleek naval vessels, elegant ocean liners, bay harbor cruise boats, sturdy tugs, container ships, and sailboats of all sizes. You can get a sense of the volume and speed of the tide by watching the water as it passes the bridge columns.

Pedestrians crossing the east side of the Golden Gate Bridge experience fantastic views of the bay and Marin Headlands.

As you approach the north end on the east side, look down to see what remains of the old Lime Point Lighthouse, built in 1883. Just beyond in a beautiful cove you can see Fort Baker, which has been renovated for many uses, including a resort and a children's museum.

When you see the parking lot above to your right, take the stairs up (**wheelchair users** can take the path just ahead and end this segment at the viewing area). Linger in the viewing area, where you have spectacular San Francisco views from a different perspective; then find the chain-link fence gate to descend stairs that take you under the bridge to the parking lot on the west side of the freeway.

◆ ◆ ◆

The next segment begins on the west end of this parking lot at the COASTAL TRAIL sign.

Marin Headlands from the Golden Gate Bridge to Tennessee Valley

see map on next page

LENGTH 5.2 miles one-way for hikers, 4.7 miles one-way for equestrians (from Gerbode Valley Trailhead), 7.7 miles one-way for mountain bikers; car shuttle possible

ELEVATION GAIN/LOSS 740'/805' one-way for hikers, 830'/680' one-way for equestrians, 1,170'/1,190' one-way for mountain bikers

ACCESSIBILITY Hikers, equestrians, and mountain bikers

AGENCY National Park Service

PARK Golden Gate National Recreation Area

REGULATIONS Leashed dogs allowed only on Coastal Trail between parking lot and Conzelman Road, SCA Trail south of Slacker Trail, and Julian Trail

FACILITIES Restrooms at Julian Trail parking, Gerbode Valley Trailhead, and Tennessee Valley; backcountry camping at Hawk Camp or Haypress Campground

THIS DRAMATIC TRIP takes you from the landmark Golden Gate Bridge into the hills of the Marin Headlands. Hikers climb through coastal chaparral and open grassland to the ridges above Sausalito and descend into the wide Tennessee Valley. Bicyclists ascend Conzelman Road with its breathtaking views and ride down into and out of scenic Rodeo Valley before dropping into Tennessee Valley, and equestrians begin in Rodeo Valley. You'll have spectacular views of San Francisco Bay, the Marin Headlands, and the Pacific Ocean. Come prepared for wind and fog.

Getting Started

SOUTH TRAILHEAD Hikers and mountain bikers use the North Tower Golden Gate Bridge parking lot, Sausalito. From US 101/CA 1 heading north or south in Marin County, take the Alexander Avenue exit and turn left at stop sign; then go right on Conzelman Road and immediately left downhill into the parking lot. (**GPS: N37° 49.933', W122° 28.936'**)

PARKING ALONG ROUTE Limited parking is available at the junction of Conzelman and McCullough Roads, Sausalito, which accesses the Julian Trail. (**GPS: N37° 50.033', W122° 29.670'**) A large parking lot for all trail users is available at the Gerbode Valley Trailhead (which accesses

Marin Headlands from the Golden Gate Bridge to Tennessee Valley

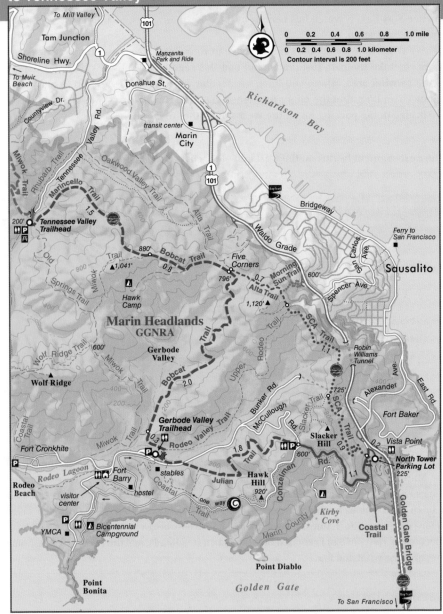

the Bobcat Trail), Bunker Road, 0.1 mile west of Simmons Road, Sausalito. (**GPS: N37° 49.960', W122° 30.993'**)

NORTH TRAILHEAD Tennessee Valley Trailhead, terminus of Tennessee Valley Road, 1.7 miles south of Shoreline Highway (CA 1), Mill Valley. Large parking lot for all trail users. (**GPS: N37° 51.663', W122° 32.142'**)

On the Trail

Hikers take a different trail for 2.9 miles to reach the multiuse Bay Area Ridge Trail route. From the northwest corner of the Golden Gate Bridge parking lot, take the Coastal Trail, which starts in a Monterey cypress forest, opens to views of the bridge and the bay, and climbs 0.2 mile to Conzelman Road. Cross Conzelman Road at the crosswalk to rail-road-tie steps and begin a 600-foot climb up the open hillside on the SCA Trail, named for and built by the Student Conservation Association. Zigzag along this narrow trail through coastal scrub, habitat for the endangered Mission blue butterfly.

The trail climbs steeply northwest above US 101; traffic sounds fade and the view northeast widens to include Richardson Bay and the Tiburon Peninsula. A small footbridge crosses seeping springs where moisture-loving yellow seep monkeyflower thrive. Turn around here to enjoy magnificent views of San Francisco's skyline, Alcatraz and Angel Islands, and the East Bay Hills beyond. Below you to the northeast, you can see the red-tiled roofs of Fort Baker's historic buildings in Horseshoe Cove.

At about 1 mile you begin climbing steps and then get to the ridge and a trail junction; to stay on the Ridge Trail route, go right on the SCA Trail. The Slacker Trail goes left to the Slacker Vista Point. If weather is clear, you'll have your first views west to the Pacific Ocean and northwest over the Marin Headlands.

Head steeply up the SCA Trail. This stretch is one of the highlights of the Ridge Trail, with dramatic views of the bay on one side and the ocean on the other. At 1.5 miles, the Ridge Trail heads west and follows the contour of the hillside below a row of houses. Look 600 feet down into Rodeo Valley and see the west entrance of the tunnel beneath the ridge you have just walked along.

The hiker route from the Golden Gate Bridge to Tennessee Valley yields vistas of San Francisco and the bridge from the Marin Headlands.

You pass through a small eucalyptus grove and begin to see more houses on the ridge. The chaparral slopes are covered in echium, which have dramatic purple-spiked flowers in the spring. At 2.2 miles, at the ridgetop high above Sausalito, you come to an intersection with three trails. The Upper Rodeo Valley Trail heads west down into the valley; Wolfback Ridge Road, the paved access road for the residences, is to your right; and the Alta Trail goes straight. Follow the signs for the Alta Trail. You soon round the east side of a hill in a eucalyptus grove, where you pass the Morning Sun Trail, a connector trail from the US 101 Spencer Avenue exit in Sausalito. Expansive views open to Sausalito, Tiburon, Mount Tamalpais, and north to San Rafael.

At 2.9 miles, you reach the convergence of five trails, known to Marin Headlands regulars as Five Corners, although no sign identifies it as such. Watch carefully for this junction; on foggy days it may be hard to see. Jog left about 30 feet to meet the Bobcat Trail and then turn right. This is where **mountain bikers and equestrians** coming up from Gerbode Valley meet **hikers.**

Mountain bikers also begin at the North Tower Golden Gate Bridge parking lot but exit on the road up to Conzelman Road. Take a left and begin the 1.2-mile ascent in the bike lane. This steep road winding up through the Headlands has plenty of traffic, as it offers phenomenal views out over the Golden Gate and San Francisco; you pass three parking areas at overlooks. When you reach the roundabout where McCullough Road turns off to your right, look for the parking lot just past this road turnoff.

From Rancho Sausalito to Golden Gate National Recreation Area

The open hills before you—from the Marin Headlands to Stinson Beach—were once part of the vast Rancho Sausalito. In 1841, the Mexican governor of California granted Englishman William Richardson the 20,000-acre Rancho Sausalito. Failing ventures forced Richardson into debt, and he had to sell his land to Samuel Throckmorton in 1860. The land was subdivided, and Portuguese immigrants from the Azores bought many ranches for use as dairies. Hay, needed to feed the dairy cows, did not thrive along this foggy coast, so by the mid-1890s the Portuguese had abandoned their dairies.

The U.S. Army also occupied land in the headlands. The Army bought the tract that now serves the north end of the Golden Gate Bridge in 1855, and in 1873, it began installing fortifications there, the last of which was a Nike missile site, dismantled in 1974.

Today, most of the original Rancho Sausalito is part of the Golden Gate National Recreation Area. The grizzlies and elk that vaqueros and early settlers hunted are long gone, but bobcats, deer, foxes, and an occasional mountain lion still range over these hills.

At the end of the lot, head down the Julian Trail, a dirt fire road. You are in an open chaparral landscape, with abundant fennel and mustard. In 0.2 mile, when the road takes a bend, you see sweeping views of the Pacific Ocean and the entire valley before you. After gently descending along the contours, at 2.4 miles you reach the historic rifle range on the valley floor, a huge open field. Cross Bunker Road at 2.8 miles, take a left, and in 0.1 mile head toward the Gerbode Valley Trailhead. At the SMITH TRAIL sign, turn right: this is where the route merges with the equestrian route (equestrians begin at the Gerbode Valley Trailhead, 0.1 mile to the west).

From the SMITH TRAIL sign, cross the wooden bridge over a riparian corridor lined with willows and turn left on the level Rodeo Valley Trail. You'll see fennel and Harding grass in the valley, as well as Hill 88, a prominent mountain in full view ahead. In 0.3 mile, turn right at the Bobcat Trail junction to begin your 2-mile trip up Gerbode Valley. Ahead is the site of the former Sam Silva dairy, one of the many Portuguese dairies located along this coast in the mid-1800s. All that remains today are the groves of eucalyptus and Monterey cypress and a few persistent fruit trees and rose bushes.

Past the dairy, the trail begins its climb up a hillside, and you look out over the floor of the valley. In the 1960s, developers planned the city of Marincello in this valley. Martha Gerbode and other staunch conservationists succeeded in preventing the development plans when The Nature Conservancy purchased the land and transferred it to the National Park Service in 1975.

The Bobcat Trail ascends to Five Corners, where **all trail users** follow the Bobcat Trail due west up a slight incline to a spectacular view of Mount Tamalpais to the northwest, Richardson Bay to the east, and the Pacific Ocean to the west. It's an open coastal scrub landscape, but in springtime you see buttercups, poppies, brodiaea, and scarlet Indian paintbrush, as well as native grasses waving in the breeze.

After a small dip and rise, you pass the trail that goes downhill to primitive Hawk Camp. Pause here to look back for a last glimpse of San Francisco's skyline and the tip of the Golden Gate Bridge tower. Hawks soar above, watching for field mice and voles in open grasslands and for wary rabbits hurrying across the road to the cover of chaparral. Go right to continue past the camp on the rocky road.

In 0.8 mile from Five Corners, veer right on the wide, 1.5-mile Marincello Trail. This is the road laid out in the 1960s to the proposed Marincello development. Modest stands of Monterey pines, cypresses, and eucalyptus planted by the would-be developers of this city now crown the steep road banks. Clumps of willows and tall woodwardia ferns watered by seeping springs dot the roadside, along with a profusion of Scotch broom.

The hillside falls off steeply to the east into Oakwood Valley, beyond which lie Mount Tamalpais, Richardson Bay, Belvedere, and San Pablo Bay in the distance. The trail makes a wide curve west as you near the trailhead in Tennessee Valley, and views open of Mill Valley and the headlands to the west. Soon you see the Miwok stables and corrals, part of an old dairy ranch. At the Tennessee Valley Trailhead, you will find picnic tables under a grove of pines.

◆ ◆ ◆

The next Ridge Trail segment starts on the northwest end of the parking lot.

Marin Headlands from Tennessee Valley to Shoreline Highway

LENGTH 3.1 miles one-way for hikers, 3.3 miles one-way for multiuse route; car shuttle possible

ELEVATION GAIN/LOSS 750'/280' one-way

ACCESSIBILITY Hikers, equestrians, and mountain bikers

AGENCY National Park Service

PARK Golden Gate National Recreation Area

REGULATIONS Leashed dogs permitted on Miwok Trail

FACILITIES Restrooms and picnic tables at Tennessee Valley Trailhead

THE TRAILHEAD IN TENNESSEE VALLEY lies at a low divide between Coyote and Wolf Ridges, from which creeks flow east to Richardson Bay and west to the ocean. The Bay Area Ridge Trail route climbs northwest along the Miwok Trail, which ascends steeply toward Coyote Ridge. From here you reach CA 1 on a gentle descent along a fire road. You'll have sweeping views of San Francisco Bay and Mount Tamalpais, see bountiful spring wildflowers, and catch cool ocean breezes. Fog and wind will often accompany you over these coastal hillsides.

Getting Started

SOUTH TRAILHEAD Tennessee Valley Trailhead, terminus of Tennessee Valley Road, 1.7 miles south of Shoreline Highway (CA 1), Mill Valley. Large parking lot for all trail users. (**GPS: N37° 51.663', W122° 32.142'**)

The Miwok Trail to Shoreline Highway affords sweeping views of Mount Tamalpais.

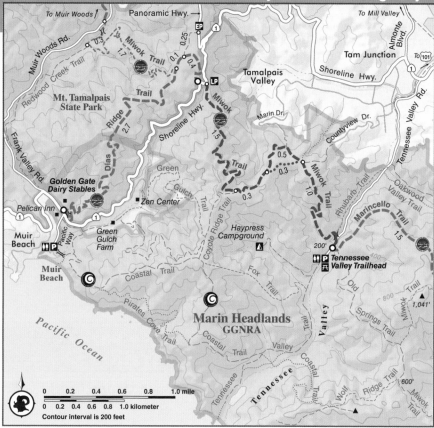

NORTH TRAILHEAD Shoreline Highway (CA 1), 0.4 mile west of Panoramic Highway, Mill Valley. Limited parking on either side of highway; *do not block the fire road gate.* (**GPS: N37° 52.776', W122° 33.285'**)

On the Trail

To begin this trip to Shoreline Highway, **hikers, equestrians, and mountain bikers** find the singletrack Bay Area Ridge Trail/Miwok Trail on the northeast side of the parking area. Cross a bridge over a small creek and follow its course upstream through a grove of native scrub oaks and nonnative eucalyptus.

After 0.4 mile, the trail takes a sharp turn and begins to climb steeply out of the canyon into a chaparral landscape. In spring, open grasslands are bright with flowers— pink mallow, blue brodiaea, golden poppy, and Douglas iris. You also see silver-leafed lupine, an important host plant for the endangered Mission blue butterfly.

At about 0.8 mile, look southwest to see the Pacific Ocean through a notch in the hills at the end of Tennessee Valley. Soon you see east across Richardson Bay to Belvedere and Angel Islands and beyond to the East Bay. Before you reach the Countyview Trail intersection in 1 mile, you begin to see neighborhoods in Mill Valley below to your right.

49

Turn left at the intersection to stay on the Miwok Trail, now a fire road. Above you to the north is a grove of tall eucalyptus crowning the hill. Hikers can take an unsigned singletrack trail shortcut to the left, which rejoins the main trail in 0.3 mile. The multiuse Miwok Trail circles north of the hill and descends and rises though eucalyptus before meeting the hiking route farther west. When the hiking and multiuse trails merge, you see the Miwok Trail extending north from Coyote Ridge and unobstructed views of Mount Tamalpais as you gradually ascend the fire road.

In 0.3 mile, you intersect the Coyote Ridge Trail; turn right on the Miwok Trail fire road. The route winds in and out of deep canyons and crosses chaparral-covered hills, offering fantastic views to the east of the bay, Angel Island, and Mount Diablo in the distance. About a mile from the trail junction, the trail begins to descend into Tamalpais Valley, with views of houses nestled in the hills. As you near the highway, you pass through eucalyptus groves on your right, where ferns line the trail and toyon and elderberry flourish.

When you reach the highway, you can see the Pacific Ocean to the west; turn left and walk along a short stretch of the road to where you have enough sight distance to safely cross Shoreline Highway.

The next section of the Ridge Trail continues at the trailhead here on CA 1.

Mount Tamalpais State Park and Dias Ridge Trail

From Shoreline Highway to Pantoll Ranger Station in Mill Valley

LENGTH 5.5 miles one-way for hikers and equestrians, 8.3 miles one-way for mountain bikers; car shuttle possible.

ELEVATION GAIN/LOSS 1,505'/660' one-way for hikers and equestrians, 1,745'/865' one-way for mountain bikers

ACCESSIBILITY Hikers, equestrians, and mountain bikers; cyclists must ride on 2.1 miles of undedicated roadway

AGENCIES California State Parks and National Park Service

PARKS Mount Tamalpais State Park, Golden Gate National Recreation Area (GGNRA), and Muir Woods National Monument

REGULATIONS State park and Dias Ridge Trail open 7 a.m.–sunset; Muir Woods National Monument open 8 a.m.–sunset; dogs prohibited

FACILITIES Water, restrooms, and walk-in campsites at Pantoll Ranger Station; Frank Valley Horse Camp on Muir Woods Road

WATCH RAPTORS SOAR ABOVE OPEN CHAPARRAL SLOPES, take in spectacular views of the Pacific Ocean, follow a moist creekbed, and cross shaded oak woodlands and redwood–fir forests; this trek through Mount Tamalpais State Park (as well as GGNRA lands on the Dias Ridge Trail) crosses the northwest corner of Muir Woods. Hikers and equestrians descend into Frank Valley on the Miwok Trail and mountain bikers descend the Dias Ridge Trail; all users then make a steady climb to the Pantoll Ranger Station.

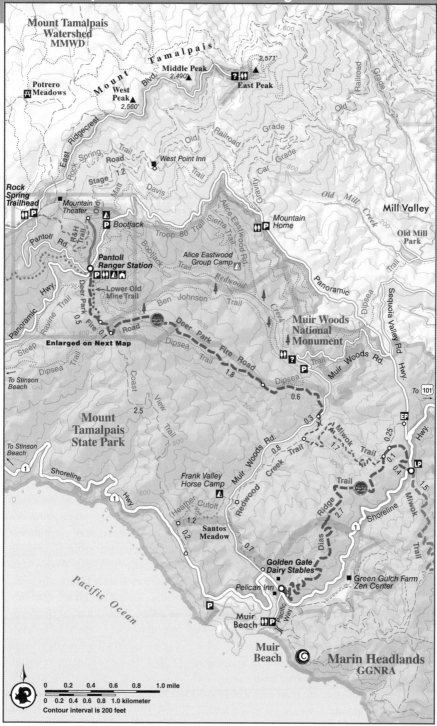

Getting Started

SOUTH TRAILHEAD Shoreline Highway (CA 1), 0.4 mile west of Panoramic Highway, Mill Valley. Limited parking on either side of highway; *do not block the fire road gate.* (**GPS: N37° 52.776', W122° 33.285'**)

NORTH TRAILHEAD Pantoll Ranger Station, Panoramic Highway and Pantoll Road intersection, Mill Valley. The parking area at the ranger station charges a parking fee. If it's full, additional parking is available across the road or at the Bootjack Picnic Area, 0.2 mile east of Pantoll, which also charges a fee. (**GPS: N37° 54.229', W122° 36.258'**)

EQUESTRIAN TRAILHEAD Horse trailer parking on the road shoulder along Panoramic Highway provides access to the Dias Ridge Trail. (**GPS: N37° W53.095', W122° 33.288'**)

On the Trail

This Bay Area Ridge Trail trip begins at the southeast corner of 6,300-acre Mount Tamalpais State Park. From Shoreline Highway the Miwok Trail ascends a gentle grade. In spring, Douglas iris and lavender bush lupine enliven the coyote brush–covered hillside. At 0.2 mile the view of Mount Tamalpais starts opening up, and when you come around the corner, it's breathtaking—the ocean sparkles in the distance and the entire ridge of Mount Tamalpais descends into Frank Valley. You also have far-reaching views to San Francisco and Richardson Bay, Belvedere, Angel Island, and across to the East Bay. Turn left when you reach the Dias Ridge Trail at 0.4 mile.

Hikers and equestrians turn right on the Miwok Trail after 0.1 mile on the Dias Ridge Trail and descend into Frank Valley. The narrow trail loses more than 600 feet on a comfortable grade; switchbacks pass through clearings and oak–bay groves, with views of the ocean, into the valley, and of the ridge you will follow on Deer Park Fire Road. Almost a mile down the trail a bench offers a good place to pause before entering the woods. Follow a tributary to Redwood Creek and arrive at a junction with the Redwood Creek Trail 1.7 miles from the previous junction. The Miwok Trail ends here; turn right to go upstream on the Redwood Creek Trail (this section was closed in 2018 due to storm damage).

Redwood Creek begins high in the canyons above Muir Woods and flows into the ocean at Muir Beach. In fall and winter, you may see fish swimming in the creek (fishing is prohibited). The trail follows the creek as it bends around a jumble of rocks where giant bay laurels spread a wide canopy. A pool reflects the sky and overhanging branches of alders, making this an inviting place to stop for a snack before the long climb to Pantoll. Continuing upstream, you cross a footbridge before reaching Muir Woods Road in 0.3 mile. Cross the road to the Deer Park Fire Road, where **mountain bikers** join you.

From the Dias Ridge Trail/Miwok Trail intersection, mountain bikers continue 2.7 miles down the Dias Ridge Trail to CA 1. The Dias Ridge Trail is part of the long-term Ridge Trail route, but currently the Ridge Trail terminates when the trail reaches CA 1. In 2010 the Dias Ridge Trail reopened after being rerouted off a heavily eroded ranch road that had deposited sediment into Redwood Creek, home to endangered coho salmon and threatened steelhead trout.

The Dias Ridge route traverses a chaparral landscape of coyote brush and California sage with fabulous views. Shortly after the Miwok Trail intersection you pass a short trail to a huge rock outcropping that hovers over the Miwok Trail below. In 0.2

mile, round a bend to the south; views of the ocean and Coyote Ridge open to the south. You can see the Green Gulch trails on Coyote Ridge and the Dias Ridge Trail out ahead through the coastal scrub. As you continue, you get more expansive views of the ocean and see CA 1 snaking down the mountain to your left. When the trail turns north, you have a full-on view of the spine of Mount Tamalpais. At 1.2 miles from the Shoreline Highway Trailhead, you pass through the few trees on the trail—bay and coast live oak. Shortly you start seeing views down the coast as far south as Pacifica. Turn around for views of the ridge along Panoramic Drive.

At 1.6 miles you enter GGNRA and the trail starts descending, with intermittent water bars and switchbacks. As you descend you begin to see the community of Muir Beach below as well as Green Gulch Farm, a Zen Center in the valley below. By 2.5 miles there is an unobstructed view of this valley, the wetlands of Redwood Creek, Muir Beach, and the slopes of heather (red in winter) to the north. As you get closer to the bottom you see more and more rock outcroppings. Just before the end of the trail, cross a bridge before coming to the Golden Gate Dairy barn and the line of iconic mailboxes on CA 1. The Pelican Inn is across the street. It is another 0.2 mile on the Muir Beach entrance road to the beach trailhead. Mountain bikers turn right and ride up Frank Valley Road for 2.1 miles; this section is not an official Ridge Trail route.

At the Deer Park Fire Road **bikers** join **hikers and equestrians** to ascend the broad, unpaved fire road, through scanty chaparral into oak–bay woodland. For 3 miles you climb steadily up the ridge to the Pantoll Ranger Station, a gain of almost 1,400 feet.

Just south of Pantoll on the Deer Park Fire Road, hikers can rest and soak in unsurpassed views of the coastal mountains and Pacific Ocean.

The Sleeping Lady

The 2,571-foot East Peak of Mount Tamalpais, upthrust by fault movement spanning millions of years, towers over the Bay Area. More than 7,000 years ago, Coast Miwoks revered the mountain and settled by its streams and along the nearby coast and bay waters. According to legend, the long flank of the mountain when viewed from the south is a beautiful maiden sleeping with her head to the east and her feet facing the sea. New arrivals to this area were drawn to its peaks and slopes, and by the late 1800s, thousands of hikers thronged its trails on weekends. In 1896, the Mount Tamalpais Railroad was extended to the summit but closed in 1929. The Tamalpais Conservation Club, formed in the early 1900s, and other hiking clubs helped construct and maintain trails. In 1928, Mount Tamalpais State Park was created. In 2014, the five agencies and nonprofits that manage land on the mountain—California State Parks, Marin County Parks, the Marin Municipal Water District, the National Park Service, and the Golden Gate National Parks Conservancy—formed Tamalpais Lands Collaborative, "One Tam," to administer Mount Tamalpais.

In about 0.5 mile, after entering a Douglas-fir forest, the fire trail crosses the Dipsea Trail, the route of the 7-mile foot race from Mill Valley to Stinson Beach, held every June since 1905. The Dipsea Trail offers an alternative route for hikers; it more or less parallels the fire road, crossing it several times as it climbs to the ridge. Shortly, the trail comes out into the open, where you look down into Frank Valley and Muir Beach, across to Dias Ridge, and up to Mount Tamalpais. In another 0.5 mile, after being in the trees, the fire trail emerges again into a stretch of meadow from which you can see the domes of a military installation on Mount Tamalpais's west peak. A little ways farther, you have views to San Francisco and down the Pacific Coast.

In spring, these grassy hillsides are bright with flowers. Red-tailed hawks and turkey vultures with wingspans of nearly 6 feet often circle above the meadows. Tracks along the trail reveal the presence of mule deer nearby.

Just short of 2 miles, tall redwoods remind you that you are on the edge of Muir Woods National Monument, which you enter farther up the trail. Soon, you get to the Ben Johnson Trail intersection; going right will take you to Muir Woods. Stay straight and the trail steepens, emerging into broad grasslands below Pantoll, 2.4 miles up from Muir Woods Road. The views are phenomenal: to the west is the expansive Pacific Ocean and to the south and east are San Francisco's skyline and the bay. The Deer Park Fire Road heads due north, passing the Dipsea Trail as it veers west on its way to Stinson Beach. Look for the bench up to your left and sit down to appreciate the unparalleled view.

For the last 0.6 mile, **hikers and equestrians** can follow the Old Mine Trail to Pantoll through a Douglas-fir forest; the trail begins just beyond the Lone Tree Trail junction and runs adjacent to the Deer Park Fire Road. Mountain bikers stay on the fire road to the Pantoll parking lot.

◆ ◆ ◆

The next Ridge Trail segment begins across the Panoramic Highway on the Matt Davis Trail.

Mount Tamalpais State Park and Bolinas Ridge

From Pantoll Ranger Station in Mill Valley to Bolinas–Fairfax Road in Bolinas

LENGTH 6.4 miles one-way for hikers, 5.6 miles one-way for equestrians, 5.2 miles one-way for mountain bikers on unofficial route; car shuttle possible

ELEVATION GAIN/LOSS 770'/730' one-way for hikers, 735'/740' one-way for equestrians, 540'/550' one-way for bicyclists

ACCESSIBILITY Hikers have access to full Ridge Trail route. Equestrians must use unofficial route for 2.7 miles. Mountain bikers must use an unofficial route.

AGENCIES California State Parks and National Park Service

PARKS Mount Tamalpais State Park and Golden Gate National Recreation Area (GGNRA)

REGULATIONS Mount Tamalpais State Park and West Ridgecrest Boulevard open 7 a.m.–sunset; dogs prohibited on unpaved trails. West Ridgecrest Boulevard may be closed at times of high fire danger or hazardous road conditions. Leashed dogs allowed on Bolinas Ridge Trail in GGNRA.

FACILITIES Water and restrooms at Pantoll Ranger Station; water and restrooms at Rock Spring Parking Area

HIGH ON THE SLOPES OF MOUNT TAMALPAIS and along Bolinas Ridge, this route takes full advantage of the mountain's breathtaking views, forested glades, and grassy slopes. The views to the ocean out over the steep open slopes are unsurpassed. Coastal fog often obscures vistas in the morning and late afternoon. Choose a clear winter or spring day to appreciate views up and down the coast and the wildflowers that bloom along the trail.

Getting Started

SOUTH TRAILHEAD Pantoll Ranger Station, Panoramic Highway and Pantoll Road intersection, Mill Valley. The parking area at the ranger station charges a fee. If the lot is full, additional parking is available across the street on Pantoll Road or at the Bootjack Picnic Area, 0.2 mile east of Pantoll, which also charges a fee. (**GPS: N37° 54.229', W122° 36.258'**)

NORTH TRAILHEAD Bolinas–Fairfax Road and West Ridgecrest Boulevard intersection, Bolinas. Pullouts allow for several cars to park here. (**GPS: N37° 56.368', W122° 39.512'**)

On the Trail

Hikers, equestrians, and mountain bikers start this trip at Pantoll and take different routes. Each route is described separately below.

Hikers begin on the Matt Davis Trail, at the stone steps across the Panoramic Highway from the Pantoll parking lot. This old but well-kept singletrack trail crosses the mountain and descends to Stinson Beach. A favorite of many hikers, it is named for the so-called dean of Mount Tamalpais trail builders and has been built and rebuilt over the years.

The trail crosses a clearing with serpentine rock outcroppings above the Panoramic Highway, and for the next 0.5 mile it contours through a forest of bays and firs. Soon it enters a small ravine where a stream splashes over moss-covered rocks, and giant ferns stand 6 feet tall. Around the next bend, a grassy spot above the trail is blue with hound's tongue blossoms in March. Douglas irises bloom by the trail in April. At about one mile you pass beautiful sculptural multi-trunked canyon live oaks. Then, as the trail rounds a south-facing slope, it emerges from the woods to cross a steep grassy hillside and climb over a saddle. From this vantage point, you see Bolinas Lagoon ahead in the distance and, looking back, the San Francisco skyline. The trail winds in and out of a tree-filled gully—again on grassy slopes—and at 1.6 miles reaches the junction with the Bolinas Ridge Trail. Veer right, and the Matt Davis Trail continues down to Stinson Beach.

The Bolinas Ridge Trail turns upward to round a steep slope. From these heights you look down on the town of Stinson Beach, and on a still day you can hear the roar of the surf. After passing through a forested ravine, you see the long curve of Stinson Beach, the Bolinas Lagoon, and the white line of waves breaking on Duxbury Reef beyond.

The trail continues across steep hillsides punctuated by great serpentine outcrops. Spreading bay trees, their roots buttressed by these rocks, cling to the hillside in gullies. In the sky, vultures with wingspans of 6 feet circle on strong updrafts that rise from the steep slopes. Bright-winged hang gliders often share the skies, born aloft by the same updrafts. From launch sites near West Ridgecrest Boulevard, they slowly wheel their way down to land on Stinson Beach. By March, buttercups and California poppies begin to appear in the grass, soon followed by a colorful array of spring wildflowers.

The trail continues in and out of folds across the ever-steeper hillside, climbing toward a spur of Bolinas Ridge. At 3.2 miles, you meet the Willow Camp Fire Road, which descends to Stinson Beach from West Ridgecrest Boulevard. You have expansive views down to Bolinas Lagoon and of the long Point Reyes Peninsula ridgeline. Continue on the Bolinas Ridge Trail across a small saddle and enter a ravine. On the other side of the ravine, a stone bench beside the trail overlooks the sea. It honors Bob Cook, the Eagle Scout who conceived this trail and worked with volunteers toward its completion.

Around another open slope, the trail enters bay-tree woods, where a lively creek rushes down Stinson Gulch. Across a bridge, ferns, mossy rocks, and a grove of moisture-seeking maples grow in damp contrast to the vegetation on the exposed hillsides. Then the trail traverses the hillside at a lower elevation before climbing back up the hillside to West Ridgecrest Boulevard. At 4.3 miles you walk on the road's edge around a bend for about 100 yards to the McKennan Gulch Trail gate. You have your first views of the Marin hills and mountain peaks to the northeast, and on clear days you can see Mount St. Helena in the distance.

The Bolinas Ridge Trail resumes beyond the McKennan Gulch Trail gate and then drops down below the road. Soon you leave Mount Tamalpais State Park and enter the Golden Gate National Recreation Area. The trail follows close to West Ridgecrest Boulevard. Below you, an old apple orchard in a green, spring-fed meadow marks the site of a mountain cabin. Here the unsigned equestrian trail from the east side of West Ridgecrest Boulevard joins the Bay Area Ridge Trail route.

The Ridge Trail (below left) traverses the grassy slopes of Bolinas Ridge.

Equestrians leave Pantoll Ranger Station, cross Panoramic Highway, and take the paved Old Stage Road in the forest past three left-branching hiking trails. Continue to the junction of the historic California Riding and Hiking Trail at 0.5 mile, turn left, and follow this trail up steep slopes through bay woodland and Douglas-fir forest. From the open grasslands at 0.8 mile, you have spectacular panoramic views of San Francisco, the ocean, and the peaks of Mount Tamalpais. Shortly after, you take a right on the Old Mine Trail and then climb to more fabulous views out over the grassy slopes. Many of the knolls offer ideal picnic spots. A left junction at 1.5 miles leads in 200 feet to Forbes Bench, a huge semicircular stone bench under a bay tree. From this intersection, West Ridgecrest Boulevard and the Rock Spring parking lot are 0.1 mile down the hill.

There is no signed equestrian trail for the next 2.7 miles, from Rock Spring to the "Apple Orchard." Therefore, from the Rock Spring parking lot, riders head northwest on the California Riding and Hiking Trail, which follows the east shoulder of West Ridgecrest Boulevard. Continue 0.5 mile beyond the McKennan Gulch Trail gate to join hikers on the Bolinas Ridge Trail.

Hikers and equestrians continue for 0.7 mile on the grassy hills and then bear west under the trees. The trail soon crosses a broad chaparral-covered hillside of oak, manzanita, toyon, and monkeyflower before descending into a dense moss-covered bay woodland. At 6 miles you begin to see redwoods and then climb to parallel West Ridgecrest Boulevard, winding through the redwood forest.

Trees in this forest, as large as 50 feet in circumference, were heavily logged in the 1850s to build San Francisco during the gold rush. Today, a grove of stately second-growth redwoods shades the summit of Bolinas–Fairfax Road at the end of West Ridgecrest Boulevard, where this segment of the Ridge Trail ends.

Bicyclists use Pantoll Road north from Pantoll Ranger Station to Rock Spring and then bear left on West Ridgecrest Boulevard for a ride on one of the most scenic roads on the West Coast. Stay on the road until reaching the next trail section at Bolinas–Fairfax Road.

The next leg of the Ridge Trail begins on the north side of Bolinas–Fairfax Road.

Bolinas Ridge and Samuel P. Taylor State Park

From Bolinas–Fairfax Road in Bolinas to State Park Entrance in Lagunitas

LENGTH 12.5 miles one-way to Samuel P. Taylor State Park; 12.2 miles one-way to parking at Platform Bridge, Tocaloma; 11.1 miles one-way to alternative trailhead at Olema Hill on Sir Francis Drake Boulevard; car shuttle possible

ELEVATION GAIN/LOSS 490'/1,800' one-way

ACCESSIBILITY Hikers, equestrians, and mountain bikers. Wheelchair users can access the 3-mile Cross Marin Trail.

AGENCIES Marin Municipal Water District (MMWD), National Park Service, and California State Parks

PARKS MMWD Watershed, Golden Gate National Recreation Area, and Samuel P. Taylor State Park

REGULATIONS Bolinas Ridge Trail and Cross Marin Trail open sunrise–sunset but subject to closure in times of high fire danger; state park hours 8 a.m.–sunset; leashed dogs permitted on Bolinas Ridge Trail and Cross Marin Trail. West Ridgecrest Boulevard open 7 a.m.–sunset but may be closed in times of high fire danger or hazardous road conditions.

FACILITIES Water and restrooms at Samuel P. Taylor State Park

AN UNPAVED ROAD, mostly downhill, runs along the crest of Bolinas Ridge, and from its heights you have magnificent views of the sparkling ocean, Tomales Bay, Point Reyes Peninsula, tree-covered ridges, deep canyons, oak-dotted hills, and distant peaks. On Bolinas Ridge, you travel through damp forests on soft and springy leaf duff; wind through tall chaparral on bare, rocky sandstone; and cross open, cattle-grazed grasslands. After descending to Lagunitas Creek, the shaded Cross Marin Trail is paved from Platform Bridge southeast through Samuel P. Taylor State Park. Weather and temperature vary: On Bolinas Ridge, long, exposed stretches of trail can be windy, hot, or foggy. For bikers, the Bolinas Ridge Trail can be bumpy and rutted.

Getting Started

SOUTH TRAILHEAD Bolinas–Fairfax Road and West Ridgecrest Boulevard intersection, Bolinas. Pullouts allow for several cars to park here. (**GPS: N37° 56.368', W122° 39.512'**)

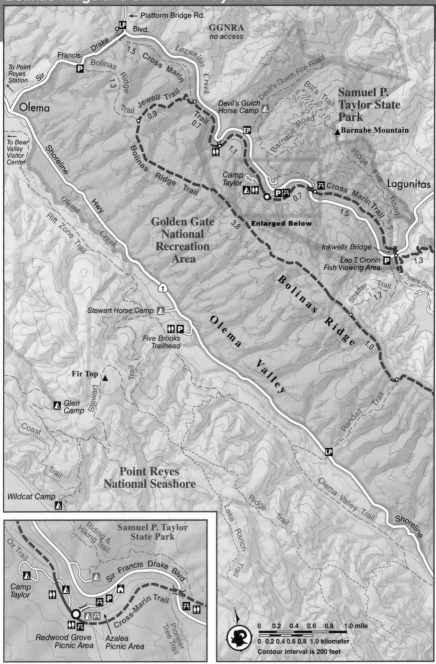

Enlarged Below

NORTH TRAILHEAD Cross Marin Trail at Samuel P. Taylor Park main entrance, 3.4 miles southeast of Platform Bridge Road, Olema. The park charges a day-use fee. (**GPS: N38° 01.104', W122° 44.013'**)

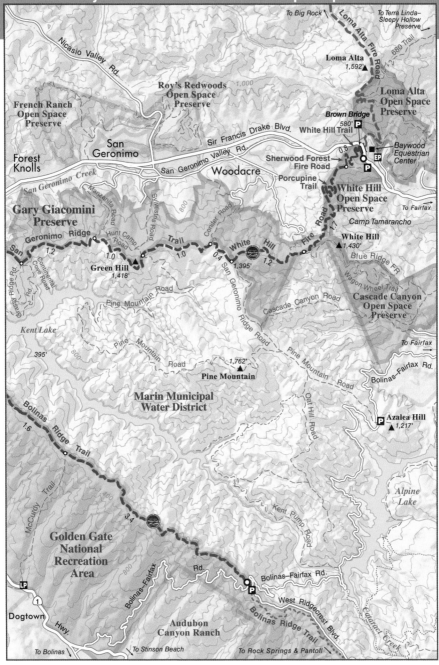

ALTERNATIVE NORTH TRAILHEAD North terminus of Bolinas Ridge Trail at Olema Hill on Sir Francis Drake Boulevard, 1.1 miles east of CA 1, Olema. Parking available on the south side of road for a 1.3-mile connector to the Ridge Trail. (**GPS: N38° 02.767', W122° 46.248'**) Alternatively, limited additional parking is available at the junction of Sir Francis Drake Boulevard and Platform Bridge Road, 3.4 miles northwest of the main state park entrance. Park along Platform Bridge Road and go southeast 1.5 miles on the Cross Marin Trail to the Jewell Trail junction. (**GPS: N38° 03.019', W122° 45.562'**)

EQUESTRIAN TRAILHEAD Park on roadside at Devil's Gulch Trailhead along Sir Francis Drake Boulevard, Olema. (**GPS: N38° 01.784', W122° 44.208'**)

On the Trail

To start your trip at the Bolinas–Fairfax Road summit, **hikers, equestrians, and mountain bikers** walk or ride into the cool dark Douglas-fir and redwood forest. Along the way you pass trails named for early landholders and tread the paths of Mexican ranchers, Anglo settlers, rugged loggers, and prosperous dairymen. At 0.6 mile, after you ascend a hill, the forest thins out and the ocean is far below on your left; farther down the trail you have views of Bolinas Lagoon. You then pass into chaparral of coyote brush and manzanita, where the dense vegetation makes a low, prickly border on both sides of the trail. Look south behind you to see Mount Tamalpais, Marin County's most prominent landmark.

Just before 1 mile, the view begins to open to the east, and at the top of the ridge you can see the bay and Mount Diablo. Coast live oak, madrone, monkeyflower, and chaparral pea also line the trail. When you reach the transmission lines, look back at the route you've traveled on Bolinas Ridge, and you feel like you are in a remote place. By 1.8 miles, you are back in the redwoods, with soft duff underfoot.

After 3.4 miles, you pass the McCurdy Trail, which descends to CA 1 at Woodville (also known as Dogtown), where a number of lumber mills once flourished. Stay on the Ridge Trail and continue through a luxuriant second-growth forest. At 5 miles, you reach the Randall Trail, which also descends to CA 1 in Olema Valley. The widowed

Those who make the long trek on the Bolinas Ridge Trail are rewarded with fabulous views across the open grassland to Tomales Bay and Inverness Ridge.

Redwood Logging on Bolinas Ridge

Like much of this area, this part of the ridge and surrounding slopes were once clothed in a majestic redwood forest. The demand for lumber during the gold rush obliterated the forest within a few years. Oxen dragged cut logs down to Bolinas Bay, which was deep enough for ships at that time, before erosion-born silt filled it. The devastation of the redwoods was so great that even some loggers expressed dismay. Today, some second-growth trees have attained splendid heights, and salal, Oregon grape, and huckleberry form a shiny understory.

Sarah Seaver Randall, a pioneer in the valley, operated a successful dairy and raised a large family, and her historic home is visible off CA 1.

Along the ridge beyond the Randall Trail, the forest thins and pastures edge the trail. Turkey vultures wheel through the skies, and bird song comes from the trees. At 6 miles you pass the Shafter Trail, named for the Shafter brothers, astute lawyers from Vermont who became rich landowners in Marin County. James McMillan Shafter's house, known as "the Oaks," still stands on private property near the Bear Valley Trail in Point Reyes National Seashore; it now functions as a retreat center for the Vedanta Society.

Beyond the Shafter Trail junction, the Bolinas Ridge Trail is completely out in the open; it drops into little ravines and then climbs rounded knolls to take in views toward wooded Inverness Ridge and Tomales Bay. On clear days, the blue waters of Tomales Bay shimmer in the sunshine, carrying your eye to the bay's outlet into the Pacific. The San Andreas Fault continues north through this long finger of water into the ocean. Just past a gate at about 6.4 miles, a picnic table next to a large rock outcropping makes a perfect resting point with exceptional views.

Continue through this beautiful pastoral scene: open grasslands extend up to the forested ridgeline and down to the barns nestled in Olema Valley. You pass through another gate at 7.8 miles and have a second chance to rest at a picnic table at 8.6 miles. Shortly before coming to the Jewell Trail junction at 9.8 miles, you reach the top of a ridge with excellent views of Black Mountain and Point Reyes Station. At the junction, take a right on the Jewell Trail; the Bolinas Ridge Trail continues 1.3 miles north to Sir Francis Drake Boulevard.

You descend the 0.9-mile Jewell Trail on a fire road that follows the ridge through steep grasslands punctuated by white, lichen-covered outcrops. Clumps of wind-sculpted oaks frame dramatic views of Barnabe Mountain in the east and Pine Mountain farther south. In spring, many-hued wildflowers brighten this spare landscape. Rounding a curve at the former Omar Jewell ranch homesite, you pass another line of eucalyptus and a few fruit trees.

Now you descend rapidly to a gate at the Cross Marin Trail on the edge of Lagunitas Creek. Samuel P. Taylor's mill on this stream, formerly called Papermill Creek, once produced paper bags and newsprint for San Francisco. The Bay Area Ridge Trail route turns right on the wooded Cross Marin Trail; in 0.2 mile it enters the 2,700-acre Samuel P. Taylor State Park, and in another 0.5 mile turns into pavement as it passes through campgrounds in the redwoods. If you parked at Platform Bridge, however, go left at the bottom of the Jewell Trail and travel 1.5 miles on the Cross Marin Trail.

The Cross Marin Trail follows Lagunitas Creek on the historic North Pacific Coast Railroad (later the North Shore and then the Northwestern Pacific Railroad) right-of-way. The railroad, bankrolled by the Shafter brothers and other financiers in the 1870s, extended from Sausalito to Samuel P. Taylor's mill and continued on to logging camps in Cazadero. Interpretive signs along the trail show the historic location of the mill and other buildings in the once-bustling place.

◆ ◆ ◆

To reach the end of this trail segment, continue 1.6 miles from the boundary of the park to where the road intersects the state park entrance road. This is the starting point for the next Ridge Trail segment.

Samuel P. Taylor State Park to White Hill Open Space Preserve

see map on p. 60

From Samuel P. Taylor Main Entrance in Olema to Brown Bridge in Fairfax

LENGTH 10.8 miles one-way; car shuttle possible

ELEVATION GAIN/LOSS 1,540'/1,265' one-way

ACCESSIBILITY Hikers, equestrians, and mountain bikers

AGENCIES California State Parks, Marin County Open Space District (MCOSD), and Marin Municipal Water District (MMWD)

PARKS Samuel P. Taylor Park, Gary Giacomini Open Space Preserve, White Hill Open Space Preserve, and MMWD Watershed

REGULATIONS State park hours 8 a.m.–sunset. Leashed dogs allowed on Cross Marin Trail; on MCOSD and MMWD trails, dogs can be off-leash on fire roads, but owner must carry leash at all times.

FACILITIES Water, restrooms, and picnic tables at Samuel P. Taylor State Park

THIS SEGMENT STARTS IN THE VALLEY on the old railroad trail, then climbs to San Geronimo Ridge. The ridge fire road is long and undulating, with rewarding 360-degree views of the North Bay, and deep canyons and wooded ridges crowned by Mount Tamalpais. The route feels remote and has a dramatic view down to scenic Kent Lake. After reaching its highest elevations in a unique Sargent cypress forest, the trail descends through White Hill Open Space Preserve, offering more beautiful views.

Getting Started

WEST TRAILHEAD Cross Marin Trail at Samuel P. Taylor Park main entrance, 3.4 miles southeast of Platform Bridge Road, Olema. (**GPS: N38° 01.104', W122° 44.013'**) The park charges a day-use fee. Alternative trailhead (for a shorter trip) is at the Shafter Bridge parking lot, 1.8 miles southeast of state park main entrance. (**GPS: N38° 00.269', W122° 42.537'**)

EAST TRAILHEAD Brown Bridge, Sir Francis Drake Boulevard, 0.6 mile north of Baywood Canyon Road, Fairfax. Look for roadside pullout parking on either side of the road before or after Brown Bridge. The main trail entrance is on the west side of road, on the south side of the bridge. (**GPS: N38° 00.585', W122° 37.055'**)

EQUESTRIAN TRAILHEAD Limited horse trailer parking is available at Baywood Equestrian Center, Fairfax. Call ahead (415-460-1480) to ensure that there's space. A spur trail leads up to the Ridge Trail. (**GPS: N38° 00.518', W122° 36.873'**)

On the Trail

Hikers, bikers, and equestrians start on the Cross Marin Trail where it intersects the Samuel P. Taylor State Park entrance road and head east. You pass through the group campground area and onto an unpaved path at a gate in 0.1 mile. Mostly in shade, the fire road follows the course of Lagunitas Creek and parallels Sir Francis Drake Boulevard. In another 0.5 mile it crosses a bridge over Sir Francis Drake and then reaches the Inkwells Bridge at 2 miles, where you can look down on the creek flowing through natural swimming holes that look like deep dark pools. During early winter, after the first rains, you may glimpse coho salmon moving upstream to spawn.

Carefully cross Sir Francis Drake Boulevard and continue up the fire road on the left (east) side of the creek into watershed lands. (A parking area is on the west side of the creek, where Shafter Grade connects to the Bolinas Ridge Trail.) Lush ferns grow on the embankment to your left under tall bays. In 0.2 mile, turn uphill onto the San Geronimo Ridge Trail, a wide, often rutted, and almost always rocky fire road. The road becomes a series of uphill segments followed by brief, somewhat level sections in a forest of Douglas-firs, madrones, and bigleaf maples. To the left, you get occasional filtered views out to distant hills.

The Ridge Trail in White Hill Open Space Preserve passes through open grassland.

At 3.4 miles you come to an intersection on the ridge, where the view opens. Take a left and stay on the San Geronimo Ridge Trail—you will pass a number of trails going off this main route. You soon head back into the fir, coast live oak, and tanoak forest. Stretches of the trail have fine views—of Pine Mountain to the south and San Geronimo Valley to the north. After 4 miles you see more manzanita and the trail starts ascending steeply into an open chaparral landscape, with coyote brush, chaparral pea, toyon, and chamise. Into the woods again, the trail undulates, and at about 5.3 miles you have spectacular views south down into scenic Kent Lake and of the rugged mountains in the Mount Tamalpais watershed.

Shortly, at the junction of Pine Mountain Road, you begin to see greenish serpentine rock outcroppings in an exposed landscape. By 5.9 miles you will begin passing through an extensive forest of pygmy Sargent cypress; the trees have limited heights due to high concentrations of serpentine rock in the soil. You are at the highest elevations on the route, and the road is very rocky.

By 6.6 miles you traverse scenic high grasslands and pass rounded hills. In less than 0.5 mile, you come to the White Hill Fire Road intersection, where you take a left and head down the open rocky road before reentering the trees. The trail goes up and down and in and out of the woods, with some of the open stretches providing rewarding views of Loma Alta, Mount Tamalpais, White Hill, and the San Geronimo Valley. Just after 9 miles, you pass a trail to Camp Tamarancho, where users of the challenging mountain biking trails must purchase a pass. The Boy Scouts own this property and granted an easement for a segment of the Ridge Trail.

The last section follows a zigzag course downhill. After views off to Woodacre, you descend through a fir and redwood forest, with a short trek on a singletrack trail when you turn right on the Porcupine Trail. After coming out on a grassy ridge with views of Loma Alta and Mount Tamalpais, take a left at the Sherwood Forest Fire Road at 9.9 miles; it will turn into a singletrack trail that passes through bays and madrones and descends to Sir Francis Drake Boulevard, ending at Brown Bridge.

The next leg of the Ridge Trail begins here at the trail sign.

Loma Alta Open Space Preserve and Loma Alta Fire Road

From Sir Francis Drake Boulevard in Fairfax to Lucas Valley Road in Nicasio

LENGTH 4 miles one-way; car shuttle possible

ELEVATION GAIN/LOSS 1,040'/800' one-way

ACCESSIBILITY Hikers, equestrians, and mountain bikers

AGENCY/LANDOWNER Marin County Open Space District and Lucasfilm Ltd.

PARK Loma Alta Open Space Preserve

REGULATIONS Leashed dogs permitted on Lucasfilm lands. Dogs must be under voice control on preserve fire road.

FACILITIES None

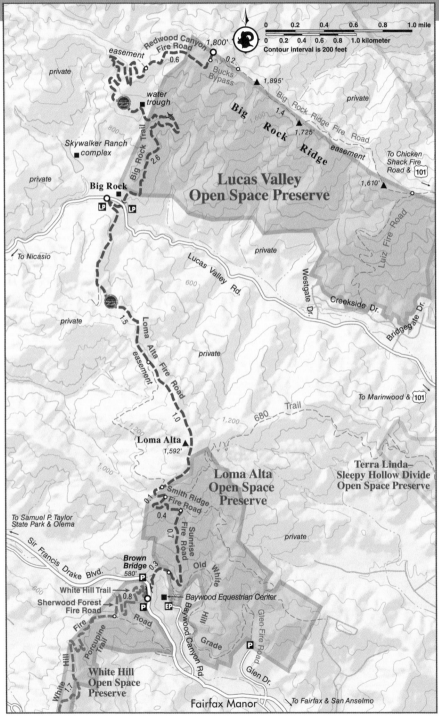

LOMA ALTA IS A MARIN COUNTY LANDMARK and one of the county's highest peaks. It divides the county's four major watersheds: Miller, Corte Madera, Lagunitas, and Nicasio Creeks. This Ridge Trail section climbs and descends open grasslands with spectacular 360-degree views at the summit. It's a steep, rocky, and exposed old ranch road, best traveled on cool mornings in summer or bright sunny days in winter.

Getting Started

SOUTH TRAILHEAD Brown Bridge, Sir Francis Drake Boulevard, 0.6 mile north of Baywood Canyon Road, Fairfax. Look for roadside pullout parking on either side of the road before and after Brown Bridge. The main trail entrance is on the west side of road, on the south side of the bridge. (**GPS: N38° 00.585', W122° 37.055'**)

NORTH TRAILHEAD Big Rock, Lucas Valley Road, 5.3 miles west of US 101, Nicasio. Roadside parking on south side of road. (**GPS: N38° 02.879', W122° 37.347'**)

On the Trail

Hikers, equestrians, and mountain bikers begin at the trailhead on the southwest side of Brown Bridge. Head under the bridge, where you get an excellent view of the bridge's colorful graffiti. The short singletrack trail passes through coast live oaks and buckeyes before meeting the Old White Hill Grade Fire Road, which was once the narrow-gauge North Pacific Coast Railroad. Take a right and, in 0.3 mile, turn left to head uphill on Sunrise Fire Road.

Equestrians ride with the summit of Mount Tamalpais in the distance.

To the south, Mount Tamalpais presides over the entire North Bay, while San Pedro Mountain and its long lower line of hills stretches east to the edge of the bay. When the trail turns sharply north at 0.4 mile, Loma Alta rises before you; as you turn around, your views expand to include the Richmond–San Rafael Bridge and all of San Francisco and San Pablo Bays.

At about 0.7 mile, you enter a shaded corridor where a cluster of oak trees flourishes; a creek runs through the narrow ravine below the trail. Beyond the tree canopy, the vegetation on this south-facing ridge reverts to sun-loving plants—coyote brush, sage, sticky monkeyflower, and ubiquitous poison oak. The trail continues unwaveringly straight up the fire road. At 1 mile the road intersects the Smith Ridge Fire Road; pause at this junction to take in splendid views south to Angel Island, the Bay Bridge, and the San Francisco skyline.

Turn left and the trail levels as it begins switchbacking up the hill. When the sun warms the air, you may detect the turpentine scent of yellow tarweed; Indians ground the seeds of this sticky-leafed plant into edible dry cakes. The blue-gray rocks underfoot contain serpentine, the California state rock, and rock outcroppings are scattered throughout these hills.

At 1.4 miles you reach the 680 Trail on your right and a rescue box for mountain bikers. Stay left on the fire road and at 1.5 miles you reach the top of the ridge. Fine views of sometimes fog-shrouded Bolinas Ridge and Pine Mountain open before you, and on clear days, you see all the high peaks of West Marin, from Mount Tamalpais to the south to Black Mountain to the north.

Go through the cattle gate, leaving the open-space preserve, and enter onto a trail easement on Lucasfilm Ltd. property, a working cattle ranch. Turn right after passing through the gate and ascend beside the fenced property line. The wide steep Ridge Trail route soon passes a junction, where you veer left toward the summit of Loma Alta. You reach the broad, rounded summit (1,592') at about 2 miles, where the trail levels and you can look down the other side of the mountain. Savor the expansive views in both directions: To the south, view Fairfax and the Ross Valley, the Tiburon Peninsula, San Francisco, the East Bay Hills, and the bay. To the west and north are grassy ridges indented by tree-filled canyons, valleys cut by rushing streams, and distant mountains traversed by other Ridge Trail routes. To the north lies Big Rock Ridge, a long line of mountain above Lucas Valley with two communication towers on its 1,895-foot summit.

The rocky road meanders down the east- and north-facing grassy hills of the Lucasfilm ranches; your descent is gentle and undulating at first, but it steepens farther along. Huge rocks are scattered among the grasslands; some shelter emerging oaks from sun and wind damage. The trail makes a wide swing west at about 2.4 miles and winds down the north side of an open hillside. Your view now takes in grassy Shroyer Mountain straight ahead, topped by a patchy forest of redwoods that extends into its south side.

By 2.8 miles you begin to get views east down Lucas Valley to the bay and Mount Diablo. Further on, you look down into canyons dense with bay and oak trees. In another mile you can see Big Rock and the next leg of the Ridge Trail route climbing up the ridge, as well as the extensive Skywalker Ranch complex. Shortly, you reach Lucas Valley Road, the end of this 4-mile Ridge Trail segment.

The next trail segment begins here.

Lucas Valley Open Space Preserve

see map on p. 67

From Lucas Valley Road to H Ranch in Nicasio

LENGTH 3.2 miles one-way (plus 3.2-mile return to trailhead)

ELEVATION GAIN 1,115' one-way

ACCESSIBILITY Hikers, equestrians, and mountain bikers

AGENCY/LANDOWNER Marin County Open Space District and Lucasfilm Ltd.

REGULATIONS Dogs allowed under voice control on fire roads and must be leashed on singletrack trails

FACILITIES None

CLIMB THROUGH GRASSLAND and some woodland to 1,800-foot Big Rock Ridge, the second-highest peak in Marin County. From here you can take in stellar views of Marin's mountains and valleys. The route is situated mostly on a well-graded singletrack trail, except for the fire road at the top, which has some steep sections. This is an exposed south-facing slope and all uphill, best traveled on cool mornings in summer or bright sunny days in winter.

Getting Started

TRAILHEAD Big Rock, Lucas Valley Road, 5.3 miles west of US 101, Nicasio. Park along south side of road. (**GPS: N38° 02.879', W122° 37.347'**)

Mountain bikers ascend the well-graded trail to Big Rock Ridge.

On the Trail

After parking on the south side of Lucas Valley Road, go through the underpass to get to the trail at the foot of Big Rock. The wide singletrack trail contours around a big hill and then heads directly toward the ridge. Below you on the right, one branch of Miller Creek flows through a beautiful wooded canyon of coast live oak, bigleaf maple, and buckeye.

At 0.6 mile you enter the shade, and for the next 0.5 mile pass in and out of the trees. You reach a hairpin turn at about 1 mile in a manzanita–chaparral landscape. Pause here to look out over the trail you've just ascended and the Ridge Trail route on the other side of the valley that climbs Loma Alta. Then the trail heads due west and at 1.2 miles comes to a gate, crossing into Lucasfilm Ltd. property. Trail users must stay on the trail.

Once through the gate on the ridge, you have views toward the hills you'll be crossing. The trail climbs steadily through grasslands accented by splendid live oaks clinging to the steep hillside and offering welcome shade on hot summer days. Tarweed is prolific. At one of the larger creeks, over which a bridge crosses, a trailside garden supports beautiful spring wildflowers—lupines, poppies, trillium, and farewell-to-spring—set against a backdrop of immense stony outcrops. **Equestrians** find a water trough on the trail installed by the Marin Horse Council.

At 1.7 miles the trail starts zigzagging uphill in wide sweeps through grasslands, where you can see its path above you. As you reach the ridge the trail comes out onto a relatively flat area where you have expansive views of the valley, West Marin, and Mount Tamalpais. At 2.6 miles you reach the Redwood Canyon Fire Road and climb steeply. Then in 0.5 mile, a gate leads into the upper reaches of the Lucas Valley Open Space Preserve, where the views are phenomenal. Continue about 0.2 mile on the road, passing Bucks Bypass Road, until you reach the gate at H Ranch, the end of the Ridge Trail segment until the next leg is completed.

The next leg of the Bay Area Ridge Trail begins in Indian Tree Open Space Preserve, 6 or 7 miles as the crow flies but 18 miles via roads to the trailhead on Vineyard Road in Novato.

Indian Tree Open Space Preserve

see map on next page

From Vineyard Road to end of Indian Tree Fire Road in Novato

LENGTH 3.1 miles one-way for hikers and equestrians (plus 3.1-mile return to trailhead); 2.4 miles one-way for mountain bikers (plus 2.4-mile return to trailhead)

ELEVATION GAIN 1,200' one-way

ACCESSIBILITY Hikers, equestrians, and mountain bikers. Cyclists take an alternative route.

AGENCIES North Marin Water District and Marin County Open Space District

PARKS Stafford Lake Watershed and Indian Tree Open Space Preserve

REGULATIONS Dogs allowed under voice control on fire roads and must be leashed on trails. Bikes allowed only on Indian Tree Fire Road.

FACILITIES None

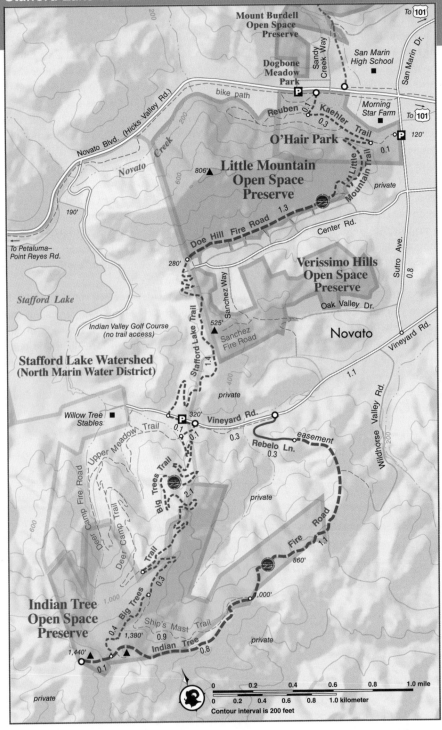

Mount Burdell
Open Space
Preserve

San Marin
High School

Dogbone
Meadow
Park

Sandy Creek Way

San Marin Dr.

To 101

bike path

Reuben

Kaehler Trail

Morning
Star Farm

To 101

0.1

0.3

Novato Blvd. (Hicks Valley Rd.)

Novato Creek

O'Hair Park

120'

0.1

806'

**Little Mountain
Open Space
Preserve**

Little Mountain Trail

private

190'

Doe Hill Fire Road

1.3

Center Rd.

Sutro Ave.

To Petaluma–
Point Reyes Rd.

280'

Sanchez Way

**Verissimo Hills
Open Space
Preserve**

0.8

Stafford Lake

Indian Valley Golf Course
(no trail access)

Stafford Lake Trail

525'

Sanchez
Fire Road

Oak Valley Dr.

Novato

Stafford Lake Watershed
(North Marin Water District)

1.4

Vineyard Rd.

1.1

Vineyard Rd.

Willow Tree
Stables

Upper Meadow Trail

P

320'

0.1

0.1

Vineyard Rd.

0.3

Rebelo Ln.

easement

Wildhorse Valley Rd.

0.3

Deer Camp Fire Road

Big Trees Trail

2.1

private

Deer Camp Trail

Fire Road

1.1

600'

860'

1,000'

1,000'

**Indian Tree
Open Space
Preserve**

Big Trees Trail

0.3

0.4

1,380'

Ship's Mast Trail

0.9

Indian Tree

0.8

private

1,440'

0.1

private

0   0.2   0.4   0.6   0.8   1.0 mile

0   0.2   0.4   0.6   0.8   1.0 kilometer

Contour interval is 200 feet

THERE IS NOT YET A TRAILHEAD at the south end of Indian Tree Open Space Preserve, so this segment of the Ridge Trail is an out-and-back trip, going from north to south. Hikers and equestrians explore Indian Tree's redwood and Douglas-fir forests on a shady and well-graded trip. A number of viewpoints on the trail look out to different parts of Marin. The mountain biker route has some steep ascents and is in a more open landscape, with especially nice views of Novato.

Getting Started

HIKER AND EQUESTRIAN TRAILHEAD Vineyard Road, 460 feet northwest of Woodside Court, Novato. Trailhead on south side of road when it becomes unpaved. Park on south side of street. (**GPS: N38° 06.171', W122° 38.025'**)

MOUNTAIN BIKER TRAILHEAD Rebelo Lane and Vineyard Road intersection, Novato. Access Indian Tree Fire Road 0.3 mile up Rebelo Lane. (**GPS: N38° 06.103', W122° 37.724'**)

On the Trail

Beginning in water district lands, **hikers and equestrians** descend gently from the trailhead on Vineyard Road along a fenced trail into a small meadow, lusciously green in springtime and sprinkled with shiny yellow buttercups. In 0.1 mile take a left at the junction and ascend on the Big Trees Trail through an oak and bay riparian woodland. The open understory allows a riot of springtime wildflowers to flourish—magenta shooting stars, white and light pink milkmaids, deep red Indian warriors, and later, blue hound's tongue.

Before long you reach a few viewpoints looking north. As you climb, you also pass under madrones, Douglas-fir, black oak, and buckeye. By 0.5 mile you've reached the first of many redwood groves. Before the trail turns sharply west, a clearing offers splendid views east to the bay and north to the 1,440-foot peak of Mount Burdell.

Trail users get unobstructed views of Mount Burdell from Indian Tree Fire Road.

Continue uphill and pass a trail that goes right. The forest is dense, especially on north- and east-facing slopes, where moss grows on older oak tree trunks and shade-loving plants thrive: maidenhair and printer's ferns, chocolate-colored mission bells, creamy-white globe lilies, and white coral bells. Fine-leafed huckleberry bushes fill the understory; deer and birds favor their small, blue-black berries.

At 2.2 miles you pass the Deer Camp Trail intersection and turn left to continue on the Big Trees Trail. Then shortly you emerge from the forest into chaparral on the edge of a deep canyon. A pause here will reward you with views east of the Novato Creek Baylands, the former Hamilton Air Base, and Mount Diablo in the distance. The Indian Tree Fire Road, the bike route to the Indian Tree Preserve summit, snakes up the opposite ridge. On a chilly day this southwest-facing stretch feels good; on a hot day, you will hurry by.

Back in the cool forest, you soon arrive at a junction with the Ship's Mast Trail; continue directly ahead on the Big Trees Trail and climb steadily through a Douglas-fir forest. At 2.9 miles the trail levels and then emerges into a wide meadow, joining the Indian Tree Fire Road in a gentle swale. Turn right up the fire road for about 0.1 mile until you reach a gate marking the end of this Ridge Trail segment.

Coming back down to the Big Trees Trail intersection, look for a narrow trail going uphill off to the right. It leads to a lush meadow bursting with spring wildflowers of every hue: cream-colored iris, purple lupine, and yellow buttercups. Ahead are the big trees—a solitary clump of immense redwoods. From the footpath between them, take a few steps left (be careful!) to stand at the edge of an abrupt drop-off above the deep canyon you saw from the trail. Now the whole North Bay spreads before you.

You can take your return trip down the Big Trees Trail or on the Indian Tree Fire Road, the bike route. If taking the fire road, a 0.3- mile connector trail running parallel to and south of Vineyard Road takes you back to the Big Trees Trailhead.

Mountain bikers are prohibited on the Big Trees Trail, so begin the out-and-back Indian Tree segment by following Rebelo Lane 0.3 mile to pick up the 2-mile Indian Tree Fire Road to the top of the preserve. The road is mostly uphill and quite steep in some places. It has more open grassland than the hiking trail, offering views to the north, east, and south, and passing entrances to a private ranch.

The next Ridge Trail segment starts at the hiker trailhead on Vineyard Road.

Stafford Lake Watershed to O'Hair Park

see map on p. 72

Vineyard Road to Novato Boulevard in Novato

LENGTH 3.2 miles one-way; car shuttle possible

ELEVATION GAIN/LOSS 200'/400' one-way

ACCESSIBILITY Hikers and equestrians; mountain bikers allowed only on Doe Hill Fire Road

AGENCIES North Marin Water District, Marin County Open Space District (MCOSD), and City of Novato

PARKS Stafford Lake Watershed, Little Mountain Open Space Preserve, O'Hair Park

REGULATIONS Dogs allowed under voice control on fire roads and must be leashed on singletrack trails. Mountain bikers allowed only on Doe Hill Fire Road.

FACILITIES Drinking water along trail in watershed

THIS SECTION OF TRAIL is at the rural western edge of Novato. Hikers and equestrians head north through woodland, over grassy hillsides with scenic views of Stafford Lake, around Little Mountain, and through forest and alongside Novato Creek in O'Hair Park. Mountain bikers are allowed on a 0.7-mile fire-trail section in Little Mountain Open Space Preserve that edges a residential neighborhood.

Getting Started

SOUTH TRAILHEAD Vineyard Road, 460 feet northwest of Woodside Court, Novato. Trailhead on south side of road after pavement ends. Then walk/ride west on Vineyard Road for less than 0.1 mile to the Stafford Lake Trail entrance, on the north side of the road. (**GPS: N38° 06.237', W122° 38.132'**)

NORTH TRAILHEAD Novato Boulevard, 300 feet west of Sandy Creek Way, Novato. Trailhead on south side of street. Parking at Dogbone Meadow Park, Novato Boulevard, 300 feet west of trailhead. (**GPS: N38° 07.203', W122° 36.961'**)

On the Trail

Start up a singletrack trail in a tight canyon, surrounded by teasel, coyote brush, willows, coast live oaks, and bay laurel. Making a switchback to the right, you begin an

The Kaehler Trail in Novato's O'Hair Park passes through a tree-lined meadow.

ascent up the east side of the canyon. At an overlook in 0.4 mile, you can see the densely forested hillside the Ridge Trail climbs in Indian Tree Preserve and the unobstructed view west down Vineyard Road.

The trail then heads north under intermittent shade of coast live oaks and bays. After reaching the top of the first hill, the trail follows the contour of the shady north-facing hillside and merges with a ranch road at 0.7 mile. There is a cattle gate here in the open grassland; stay on the Stafford Lake Trail, the singletrack trail that veers left. You now have views of the Indian Valley Golf Course below and the hills to the northwest. The narrow trail undulates up and down small hills, just below the eastern ridgeline boundary of the Stafford Lake Watershed. This part of the trail feels remote and peaceful. You pass a large water tank on your right with a drinking fountain provided by the North Marin Water District.

As hawks and turkey vultures quietly ride the wind currents above, you start seeing views of Stafford Lake, with its little island and the dairy farms surrounding it. You also get views into Novato, cross a paved road coming up from the golf course, and at 1.6 miles leave the hilltop and descend a north-facing hillside through a deciduous oak forest. When the young, yellow-green leaves unfurl in spring against the dark brown limbs, these trees are uniquely beautiful. After a cold snap in fall, their leaves turn a rich, tawny golden-brown. Rounding several switchbacks, you cross a road in a meadow; pass through the cattle gate on the other side and walk to the entrance of the Little Mountain Open Space Preserve at 1.5 miles.

You are now on Doe Hill Fire Road, which skirts the base of Little Mountain; the south-facing exposure can be hot in summer. A housing development is just below you. Tree-filled canyons indent the grassy hillside, collecting rain and spring water. **Mountain bikers** are allowed on the wide 0.7-mile Doe Hill Fire Road, accessible from Center Road, but must turn off when the wide trail ends. (GPS: start, N38° 06.765', W122° 37.786'; end: N38° 06.792', W122° 36.977')

Hikers and equestrians veer left onto the narrower Little Mountain Trail at the base of a steep creek canyon, looking out over residential neighborhoods. At 2.5 miles you get to the top of the hill where you have an excellent view of Mount Burdell and Novato. In May, early-blooming blue brodiaea wave above drying grasses, and clusters of orange poppies cover the sloping hillside. Then you enter a cool woods of bay trees and, after a couple of zigzags, descend gradually along the east side of Little Mountain.

After a long traverse, the trail turns right and descends quickly to a junction. Make a sharp left turn in O'Hair Park on the wide, level Reuben Kaehler Memorial Trail, which follows Novato Creek. At 3 miles you cross a row of eucalyptus trees before entering a large, tree-lined meadow. At the far end of the meadow, take a right at the junction and continue across the bridge to busy Novato Boulevard, where this trail segment ends.

◆ ◆ ◆

If you parked at Dogbone Meadow Park, take a left at Novato Boulevard to reach the parking lot in 140 feet. If you are going on to the next section of Ridge Trail in Mount Burdell Open Space Preserve, **hikers and equestrians** cross Novato Boulevard very carefully and go 0.1 mile past Sandy Creek Way to the trailhead just before San Marin High School. This section on Novato Boulevard, however, is not dedicated Ridge Trail.

Mount Burdell Open Space Preserve

see map on next page

From Novato Boulevard or San Andreas Drive to Mount Burdell Summit in Novato

LENGTH 4.2 miles one-way for hikers and equestrians (plus 4.2-mile return to Novato Boulevard) or 2.9 miles one-way for mountain bikers (plus 2.9-mile return to San Andreas Drive; alternative return route possible)

ELEVATION GAIN 1,400' one-way (from Novato Boulevard); 1,200' one-way (from San Andreas Drive)

ACCESSIBILITY Hikers, equestrians, and mountain bikers

AGENCY Marin County Open Space District

REGULATIONS Dogs allowed under voice control on fire roads and must be leashed on singletrack trails. Mountain bikers are prohibited on Dwarf Oaks Trail.

FACILITIES None

CLIMB THROUGH GRASSLANDS dotted with ancient oaks to spectacular vistas of North Bay ridges from the slopes of 1,558-foot Mount Burdell. The largest of Marin County Open Space District's holdings, these 1,627 acres of oak savanna and grasslands are interspersed with dense woodlands. Hikers and equestrians can begin from Novato Boulevard and cross a sensitive wildlife area on the Dwarf Oaks Trail. Mountain bikers join them at San Andreas Fire Road, and all users follow wide fire roads to the peak; the trails are mostly steep and rocky, with little shade. Summers are hot here, so be sure to get an early start.

Getting Started

NOVATO BOULEVARD TRAILHEAD Novato Boulevard, 300 feet west of San Marin Drive, Novato. Trailhead on north side of street. Parking at Dogbone Meadow Park, 0.2 mile west of trailhead on Novato Boulevard. (**GPS: N38° 07.164', W122° 36.833'**)

SAN ANDREAS FIRE ROAD TRAILHEAD San Andreas Drive, 0.6 mile north of San Marin Drive, Novato. Park along San Andreas Drive. (**GPS: N38° 07.806', W122° 36.257'**)

On the Trail

From Novato Boulevard to San Andreas Fire Road

Hikers and equestrians can begin this trip on Novato Boulevard across from O'Hair Park. From the trailhead, a shady 0.3-mile trail links to Mount Burdell Open Space Preserve. With the high school on the right and houses on the left, the trail runs up a narrow riparian corridor. When you come to a junction at 0.1 mile, stay right along the chain-link fence. You take a bridge over a creek and cross a road; after the last house on your left the trail comes out into the open and crosses a bridge to the preserve's information board.

This section of the park, until you get to the San Andreas Fire Road, is a sensitive wildlife area, home to many bird species that are scarce in Marin County. You're in a large meadow, and in spring it glows with bright orange California poppies and yellow suncups; by summer, golden oat grass covers the sloping fields. Red-tailed hawks soar overhead, and rusty-breasted bluebirds dart after insects.

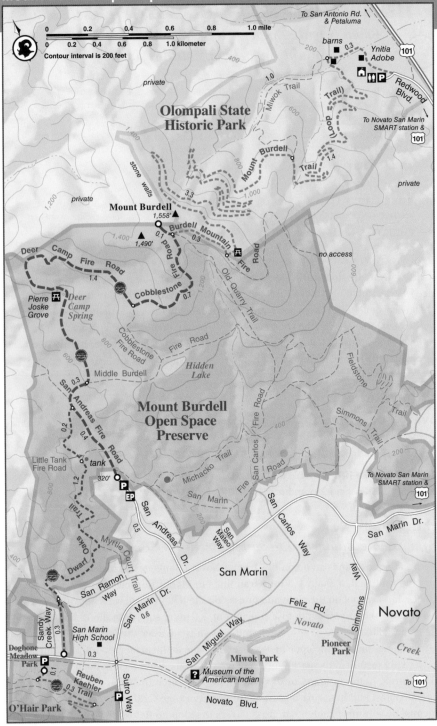

Head northwest and climb grassy slopes on the Dwarf Oaks Trail above a neighboring subdivision. At 0.5 mile, you begin getting distant eastern views of Novato, the bay, and Mount Diablo. Then, in 0.8 mile, you pass through beautiful deciduous oak woodland. The Myrtle Oak Trail goes down to a neighborhood on your right, and you continue to go in and out of coast live oak and bay woodland, with some black oak. Little streams tumble over rocks in shady canyons; white milkmaids and blue hound's tongue brighten the trailside. At 1.4 miles, the trail enters a clearing and Mount Burdell rises impressively before you. After passing a large water tank and reentering the woods again, the trail emerges from the trees and comes to a cattle gate. In the huge open expanse of grassland, head toward the San Andreas Fire Road just ahead; at 1.7 miles you reach the intersection with the multiuse Ridge Trail.

From San Andreas Drive to Mount Burdell Summit

The multiuse Ridge Trail route begins on the San Andreas Fire Road, a wide dirt road that heads north from the gate at San Andreas Drive. The trail ascends gradually through a canyon with bay–oak woodland to reach the preserve's open central valley. To the northeast, Mount Burdell rises 1,558 feet. At 0.4 mile the Dwarf Oaks Trail, the Ridge Trail route for hikers and equestrians, merges with the fire road. **All trail users** then veer east on the Middle Burdell Fire Road through sloping grasslands to a grove of ancient, deciduous valley oaks. One old giant's diameter measures close to 5 feet. In winter the gnarled, widespread limbs of these trees have striking, gaunt silhouettes against the greening fields.

Just across from this majestic grove, at 0.8 mile, the Ridge Trail route goes left on the Deer Camp Fire Road. Head due north through the grasslands, and then climb to a broad, wooded plateau; here, you can pause for a snack or lunch where you find hitch rails and a circle of log benches situated under some fine black oaks, large live oaks, and many bay trees.

Resuming your way uphill, at 1.4 miles from the San Andreas Trailhead, follow a long, steep curve around an isolated clump of buckeye trees on your right. Shortly after the trail levels off, you reach the Cobblestone Trail junction at 2.1 miles, where you turn left to head for the summit. This trail takes its name from the basalt rock that

Mount Burdell's Early Residents

The Coast Miwoks lived in this area from the 14th to mid-19th centuries, subsisting on shellfish from the marshes and acorns and wild game from the oak-studded hills to the west. The Miwoks' last chief, Camilo Ynita, received a Spanish land grant in 1834 and named the village and surrounding lands Rancho Olompali. Ynita later sold part of the rancho to James Black, who passed some of the land to his daughter as a wedding present. Mary Black married Galen Burdell, the first San Francisco dentist and the man for whom the mountain was named. The Burdells built a fine house on the east side of the mountain and developed orchards and gardens on the site of the large Miwok village, Olompali. Today, this is the site of Olompali State Historic Park.

The Dwarf Oaks Trail traverses beautiful oak woodland and provides views of Novato.

was quarried here to pave San Francisco streets in the 1860s and 1870s. Basalt, a dark igneous stone, can be readily split, chipped, and made into cobbles. From pits on the west side of Mount Burdell, Chinese laborers dug out and chipped rectangular stone blocks (about 6 inches wide, 15 inches long, and 4 inches thick). The workers loaded the cobbles onto wooden sleds and slid them down the steep mountainside. Scars of the sleds' descent are still visible from this trail.

Continue uphill on the rocky trail, past coast live oaks and lush clumps of California bay trees growing among boulders on east-facing slopes. As you approach the summit of Mount Burdell, at 2.8 miles you come to a private road on your left that leads to a relay tower, a telephone-company repeater station. On the right, the Old Quarry Trail, for **hikers and equestrians only,** drops 800 feet in elevation into the steep canyon. Cross the Burdell Mountain Fire Trail to take the singletrack trail up toward the summit. In 0.1 mile you'll come to the edge of the preserve at a rock wall with views north toward the Petaluma River. This is the end of the Ridge Trail segment, but heavy vegetation obscures the views from the top to the south.

Heading back from the summit, you have the option to turn left down the Burdell Mountain Fire Road leading to the rock quarries. The main quarry is on your left, well worth a short walk to see the exposed, layered rock walls of the pits where cobbles were removed. An overlook on the other side of the road offers a hawk's-eye view of the preserve and the distant, high ridges that almost encircle northern Marin County. On a clear day, you can make out Hicks Mountain to the northwest, Mount Tamalpais to the south, and the shoulder of Mount Burdell curving around to the west; when fog lies in the valleys, the ridgetops seem like islands floating in a misty sea.

Hikers and equestrians may consider a car shuttle and take the 5-mile Mount Burdell Trail to Olompali State Historic Park, which descends through oak and madrone woodlands to the site of the largest Miwok village in Marin County and the former

Burdell home and gardens. If returning to the San Andreas Fire Road, there are alternative routes down the mountain.

The next segment of the Bay Area Ridge Trail begins in Petaluma's Helen Putnam Regional Park, a 16-mile drive.

Petaluma

From Chileno Valley Road to
Casa Grande Road in Petaluma

IN PETALUMA, the 7.7-mile Ridge Trail ventures through a rural regional park and many neighborhoods and parks, including downtown; it also follows both the Petaluma River and Lynch Creek for a stretch. Northeast of US 101, you have an opportunity to explore newer neighborhoods of Petaluma. There is a 1-mile gap between Helen Putnam and the city route. The city section is an excellent bike ride; in May 2017, however, the route lacked RIDGE TRAIL signage. This is a temporary route until the planned route along the Petaluma River, Shollenberger Park, and Adobe Creek Trail is finished.

Helen Putnam Regional Park

From Chileno Valley Road to Oxford Court in Petaluma

LENGTH 1.1 miles one-way; car shuttle possible

ELEVATION GAIN/LOSS 170'/210' one-way

ACCESSIBILITY Hikers, equestrians, and mountain bikers

AGENCY Sonoma County Regional Parks

REGULATIONS Helen Putnam Regional Park open 8 a.m.–sunset. The southern entrance has a parking fee. Dogs must be leashed.

FACILITIES Water and restrooms

Getting Started

SOUTH TRAILHEAD 411 Chileno Valley Road, 1 mile south of Western Avenue, Petaluma. Parking lot. (**GPS: N38° 12.776', W122° 39.817'**)

NORTH TRAILHEAD Oxford Court, 420 feet southwest of Windsor Drive, Petaluma. Street parking. (**GPS: N38° 13.182', W122° 39.194'**)

On the Trail

Rural Helen Putnam Regional Park offers 6 miles of trails and panoramic views in a predominantly coast live oak and grassland landscape. The Bay Area Ridge Trail begins at the southwest corner of the park near the playground and picnic area. It veers to the right near the restrooms and offers two alternative routes for the first 0.3 mile: to the left on a singletrack trail over a grassy hill or to the right on a paved road. Both have excellent views of pastoral Chileno Valley to the right.

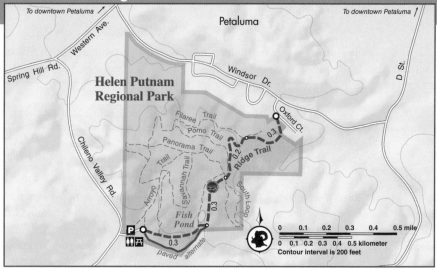

If taking the dirt trail, go left on the Cattail Trail and when you reach a wooden water tank at the cattail-lined fish pond, go right to meet the main paved trail traversing the east side of the pond. You pass coast live oaks, coyote brush, and California buckwheat. At 0.6 mile you reach a high point on the trail and an intersection with other trails that ascend the ridge. Stay straight and, as you head downhill ,you begin to see views of Petaluma to the east and by 0.8 mile you can see the residential neighborhood below you and the mountains to the east of the Petaluma Valley. The trail ends at the bottom of the hill at Oxford Court.

◆ ◆ ◆

There is a 1-mile gap between the end of this Ridge Trail section and the next section.

The Ridge Trail in Helen Putnam Regional Park begins by crossing grassland that overlooks Chileno Valley.

City of Petaluma

From Sunnyslope Avenue to Casa Grande Road in Petaluma

LENGTH 6.2 miles one-way (plus 0.8 round-trip through Steamer Landing Park); car shuttle possible

ELEVATION GAIN/LOSS 70'/50' one-way

ACCESSIBILITY Hikers and bicyclists

AGENCY City of Petaluma

PARKS McNear Park, Walnut Park, Lucchesi Park, Fox Hollow Park, Prince Park, Wiseman Airport Park

REGULATIONS Parks open during daylight hours. Dogs must be leashed in parks.

FACILITIES Water and restrooms in city parks (no restrooms at Fox Hollow and Wiseman Airport Parks)

Getting Started

SOUTH TRAILHEAD Sunnyslope Avenue and G Street intersection, Petaluma. Street parking. (**GPS: N38° 13.359', W122° 38.287'**)

NORTH TRAILHEAD Hidden Valley Drive and Casa Grande Road intersection, Petaluma. Parking at Wiseman Park. (**GPS: N38° 14.895', W122° 35.511'**)

On the Trail

Begin your tour through Petaluma on Sunnyslope Avenue and G Street, a residential neighborhood with wide streets and sidewalks. In a block, at 11th Street, McNear Park will be on your left. The park has tennis courts, a playground, a softball/baseball diamond, a dog run, picnic areas, and restrooms. Take a left on Sixth Street, where you pass under grand sycamore trees and view attractive old Victorian homes for three blocks. Take a right on D Street and in two blocks the neighborhood shifts from residential to commercial. On your right is Walnut Park, a one-square-block park with picnic areas, a playground, and restrooms. From each of the park's four corners, a broad walkway leads to the charming, round bandstand at its center. Pass through a major intersection at Petaluma Boulevard South.

Consider a visit to Steamer Landing Park (on a section of the Ridge Trail's long-term route) by heading north on D Street after First Street. Stay on the southern sidewalk if walking, go over the Petaluma River drawbridge, and after a long block take a right into the park. There is a large landscaped parking lot, benches at the edge of the water, and an information panel about the slough. A decomposed granite walkway on the park's east side ends at the railroad track and Hopper Street. Eventually the Ridge Trail will continue along the Petaluma River, through Shollenberger Park, along the Adobe Creek Trail, and to Petaluma State Historic Park.

Back to the main route, take a left from D Street onto First Street. A PGE transmission site is on your right with a whimsical gigantic electrical outlet sculpture mounted on the building's exterior. Cross C Street, take a left and then a right through the bollards into the public walkway, lined on the right by redwoods. The paved path exits near the abandoned railroad tracks and the Petaluma River at Water Street and Western Avenue, a bustling area that has restaurants and shops and is a fun place to explore. The path continues between the river and cobblestoned Water Street.

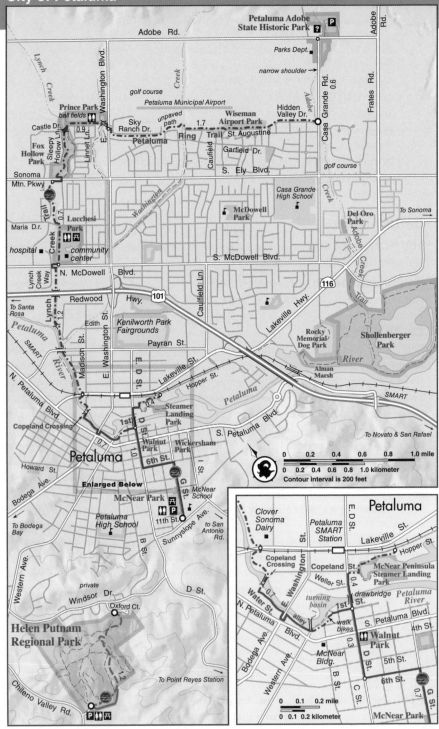

Side Trip to the McNear Building

An optional two-block detour to the historic McNear Building heads north along South Petaluma Boulevard from the east side of Walnut Park. Petaluma's downtown has numerous historic buildings. The McNear Building's graceful iron front is typical of the sheet- or cast-iron facades popular here in the 1880s and 1890s; they were pre-fabricated in San Francisco and shipped here by boat along the Petaluma River. The Petaluma River was an important commerce route for other goods as well, beginning with the gold rush, when it was used to ship supplies for 49ers. Until 1950, grain and farm products were transported downriver to San Pablo Bay and San Francisco.

You reach Washington Street, a major boulevard; the easiest way across is to go left and up to the crosswalk and then back down to North Water Street. Head down the street through the refurbished warehouse area to the informal parking area at the end and you see the trail going over the bridge to your right. After crossing the bridge, the trail runs along the east side of the river through a light industrial area. The trail comes up to Lakeville Street, passes over a crosswalk, and then heads back down to the river again.

This river stretch is an especially scenic part of trail where you feel like you are miles away from the city. From Lakeville Street, the path crosses a bridge at Lynch Creek after 0.6 mile, then starts heading toward US 101 between the creek and a huge field. You pass underneath US 101 and come to North McDowell Boulevard. Take a left, cross the boulevard at Lynch Creek Way, and head right to get on the Lynch Creek Trail, to your left.

The Ridge Trail passes through the 30-acre Lucchesi Park, which has the Petaluma Community Center, a lake and playground, multiuse fields, picnic areas, tennis courts, and restrooms. At the end of the park at Maria Drive, take the crosswalk and join the Lynch Creek Trail again on the other side. The creek is now on your right and a residential neighborhood is on your left across Flanigan Way. When you reach Sonoma Mountain Parkway, head right, cross at Monroe Street, and then take a left to continue on the trail into Fox Hollow Park, which has fields and a playground. After you enter the park, when you get to an intersection, go left instead of heading over the bridge. The trail then parallels Sleepy Hollow Lane.

When you reach Castle Drive take a right over the bridge and then a left. This takes you into Prince Park, with multiuse fields and restrooms. The trail runs parallel to Noriel Lane, with houses on one side. You cross over a bridge in the Washington Creek Riparian Area and come out onto East Washington Boulevard. Take a right and then use the crosswalk to the entrance of the Petaluma Municipal Airport. This trail, called the Petaluma Ring Trail, heads down along the edge of Sky Ranch Drive. At the end of the road you reach the Petaluma Municipal Area Walk, a dirt path through a field that turns into a paved path as it enters another residential neighborhood and runs between Wiseman Airport Park and Caulfield Lane, and then Wiseman Park and St. Augustine Circle. The park has multiuse fields and a playground. The trail continues after the park and runs between huge fields on the left and Hidden Valley Drive on the right. You are now in rural Petaluma, with the hills in the distance. At Casa Grande Road the trail terminates.

The Ridge Trail follows the Petaluma River on an undeveloped section of the route.

The next leg of the Bay Area Ridge Trail starts in Jack London State Historic Park, near Glen Ellen on the other side of Sonoma Mountain, an 18-mile drive.

Jack London State Historic Park and East Slope Sonoma Mountain Ridge Trail

From Lake Trail to End of East Slope Sonoma Mountain Ridge Trail in Glen Ellen

LENGTH 5.5 miles one-way (plus 5.5 miles return to trailhead); includes 2.1-mile connector trail

ELEVATION GAIN/LOSS 1,495'/180' one-way

ACCESSIBILITY Hikers, equestrians, and mountain bikers

AGENCIES California State Parks, Valley of the Moon Natural History Association, and Sonoma County Agricultural Preservation and Open Space District

REGULATIONS State park has vehicle entrance fee and walk-in/bicycle fee. Park open 9:30 a.m.–5 p.m. Dogs prohibited on trail.

FACILITIES Large parking lots, water, bathrooms, picnic tables at trailheads

JOIN THE MAIN RIDGE TRAIL route from a 2.1-mile connector trail, starting in this engaging historic park. The Ridge Trail then travels south on the Sonoma Ridge Trail and

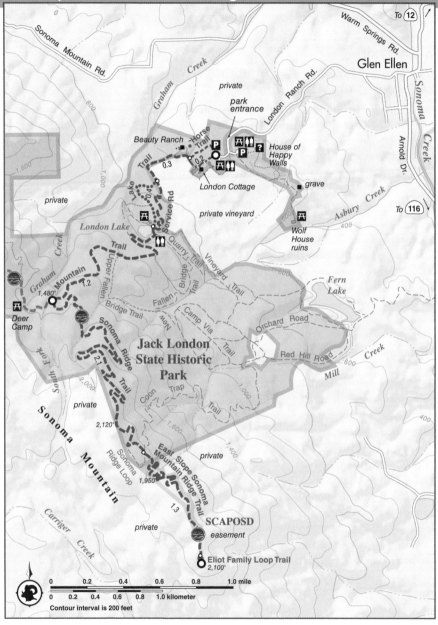

East Slope Sonoma Mountain Ridge Trail, terminating on the Eliot Family Loop Trail. The trail is routed along lively streams, through dense forests, and across grasslands on the eastern flanks of Sonoma Mountain. At the top of the ridge, enjoy scenic views of the Valley of the Moon and the bay.

Getting Started

TRAILHEAD Jack London State Historic Park, 2400 London Ranch Road, Glen Ellen. Trailhead at upper parking lot. (**GPS: N38° 21.380', W122° 32.700'**)

On the Trail

Jack London Trailhead to Mountain Trail and Sonoma Ridge Trail Junction

Because there is no trailhead at the southern end of the Bay Area Ridge Trail in this section, the first 2.1 miles of this trip follow connector trails (the Lake and Mountain Trails) to join the Ridge Trail route. **Hikers and mountain bikers** begin on the Lake Trail from the middle of the westernmost parking lot. **Equestrians** take the trail from the parking area's north corner and follow short paths through the trees to join the Lake Trail.

The multiuse Lake Trail skirts the edges of a private vineyard, which has lovely shades of red and tawny gold in the fall. Once the prized vineyard of Jack London, who laid it out on stepped terraces, it still produces wine today. After 0.5 mile on the service road, **hikers** can cut right onto a narrow trail through a redwood and fir forest and then at 0.9 mile rejoin **mountain bikers and equestrians** at a reed-rimmed lake, created by London in 1913 for swimming, fishing, and poolside partying. Today, the lake's curving stone dam offers park visitors a sunny place to rest on their trek up the mountain.

Beyond the lake, all users turn right (due west) to join the Mountain Trail; large black oaks and madrones line the road. Then the road swings south through a cool dark forest of redwoods and Douglas-firs. Tanoaks, madrones, and bigleaf maples fill the openings where large redwoods were cut long ago. After climbing steadily and passing the junction with the Fallen Bridge Trail, Mays Clearing lies before you at 1.3 miles, a wide meadow with fine views south over the valley and east to the mountains. A picnic table is nearby. In fall, look for the clear red berries that hang from long tendrils of native honeysuckle vine; in winter, white snowberries attract deer and birds but are poisonous to humans.

Stay uphill on the Mountain Trail, and as you pass the Upper Fallen Bridge Trail on the left, the trail swerves right to make a hairpin turn north and then south through lovely Pine Tree Meadows. Filled with many native flowers in spring, especially Douglas iris, pink checkerspot, and yellow buttercups, this meadow is a delight to behold. The trail gets steeper in the creek corridor's Douglas-fir forest before coming to the Sonoma Ridge Trail junction at 2.1 miles.

Sonoma Ridge Trail and East Slope Sonoma Mountain Ridge Trail

At the Sonoma Ridge Trail intersection, you have reached the Ridge Trail, an 8.7-mile-long segment on Sonoma Mountain. The southern section begins here and extends 3.4 miles south. There is no trailhead on the southern end, making it necessary to turn around; the trail description below is from north to south.

At the intersection of the Mountain and Sonoma Ridge Trails, you can view the park map on an information board. The Sonoma Ridge Trail heads up to the left as a singletrack trail. You pass through a forest of redwoods, bays, black oak, Oregon oak, bigleaf maple, and Douglas-firs that follows the contours along a gentle ascent. In just less than a mile you get a glimpse out to the Sonoma Valley.

When you reach the ridge on the East Slope Sonoma Mountain Trail, the woods open up to a scenic grass-and-oak landscape.

In about a mile, when the trail turns sharply and heads northwest, you begin to see the ridges of Sonoma Mountain, and then the trail turns sharply east after 0.3 mile. Two miles from the trail junction, you begin to emerge from the woods into grassland, walking under magnificent coast live oaks, valley oaks, and black oaks. It's a beautiful landscape, with views of the Sonoma Valley, the ridgeline between Napa and Sonoma Counties, the Napa River, the bay, and Mount Diablo in the distance. In spring, flowers bloom in the sunny meadows—deep blue lupine, purple-tufted brodiaea, and tiny pink linanthus.

Shortly you will pass the junction for the Coon Trap Trail, an alternative route back to the state park trailhead. Go right on the East Slope Trail; you will again be in the woods and arrive at the state park boundary. A sign displays an East Slope Trail map and reminds trail users to stay on the trail because portions of the trail cross private land.

Jack London's Beauty Ranch

No trip to this park is complete without a visit to Beauty Ranch, Jack London's cherished estate. By 1876, London had already achieved international fame for his adventure stories *The Call of the Wild* and *The Sea-Wolf.* Jack and his wife, Charmian, then moved to Sonoma Valley to escape busy city life, and he began work on Beauty Ranch. Over the remaining years of his life, he embarked on continual projects to improve the land and repair or construct buildings.

Trails in the state park lead to ranch buildings, the winery, the distillery, Wolf House, and the House of Happy Walls, built by Charmian London after Jack's death. Charmian lived at the ranch until her death at age 84, after which the House of Happy Walls became a museum with artifacts from the London family; today it is also the park visitor center. Jack London's gravesite and Wolf House can be accessed by trail from the House of Happy Walls. The handsome rock walls of Wolf House are all that remains of the Londons' dream house, which burned down in 1913 before they moved in.

Opened in 2015, the trail switchbacks in and out of a creek corridor in oak woodland and in 0.5 mile climbs to open grassland with fine views of the valley. You begin seeing coyote brush and buckeyes and Mount St. Helena to the north. After about a mile on the East Slope Trail, you reach the ridge at an elevation of 2,100 feet. Enjoy the expansive views looking south across San Pablo Bay.

If you continue down the hill you will reach the end of the Ridge Trail segment at the Eliot Family Loop Trail, a 0.1-mile loop under oaks that weaves through mossy rocks, routed on an easement donated by a local family.

Jack London State Historic Park and North Sonoma Mountain Regional Park and Open Space Preserve

see map on p. 93

From Lake Trail in Glen Ellen to North Sonoma Mountain Park Trailhead in Santa Rosa

LENGTH 7.4 miles one-way (includes 2.1-mile connector trail); car shuttle possible

ELEVATION GAIN/LOSS 1,695'/1,345' one-way

ACCESSIBILITY Hikers, equestrians, and mountain bikers (except bikes prohibited on a 0.7-mile section)

AGENCIES California State Parks, Valley of the Moon Natural History Association, Sonoma County Regional Parks

REGULATIONS State park has entrance fee and walk-in/bike fee; open 9:30 a.m.–5 p.m.; dogs prohibited on trail. North Sonoma Mountain Park has a parking fee; open 7 a.m.–sunset; dogs prohibited on trail.

FACILITIES Restrooms and picnic tables near trailheads; water in state park

JOIN THE MAIN RIDGE TRAIL route from a 2.1-mile connector trail through redwood and oak forests. The Ridge Trail then travels north on the Mountain Trail and North Sonoma Mountain Ridge Trail. It passes through forests and grasslands on the eastern and northern flanks of Sonoma Mountain; you'll travel on a fire road to reach lofty heights with grand views of the Sonoma Valley, then descend on a well-designed narrow trail through beautiful oak woodlands. For the first 2.1 miles of this trip, refer to "Jack London Trailhead to Mountain Trail and Sonoma Ridge Trail Junction" on page 88 of the previous section.

Getting Started

EAST TRAILHEAD Jack London State Historic Park, 2400 London Ranch Road, Glen Ellen. Trailhead at upper parking lot. (**GPS: N38° 21.380', W122° 32.700'**)

WEST TRAILHEAD North Sonoma Mountain Regional Park and Open Space Preserve, 5297 Sonoma Mountain Road, Santa Rosa (0.6-mile gravel/dirt entrance road). Large parking lot. (**GPS: N38° 21.808', W122° 36.297'**)

On the Trail

Mountain Trail to North Sonoma Mountain Park Trailhead

At the junction of the Sonoma Ridge and Mountain Trails, continue straight on the Mountain Trail. Shortly you cross South Graham Creek; in winter and spring it may overflow

The North Sonoma Mountain Ridge Trail rambles through gorgeous oak woodland.

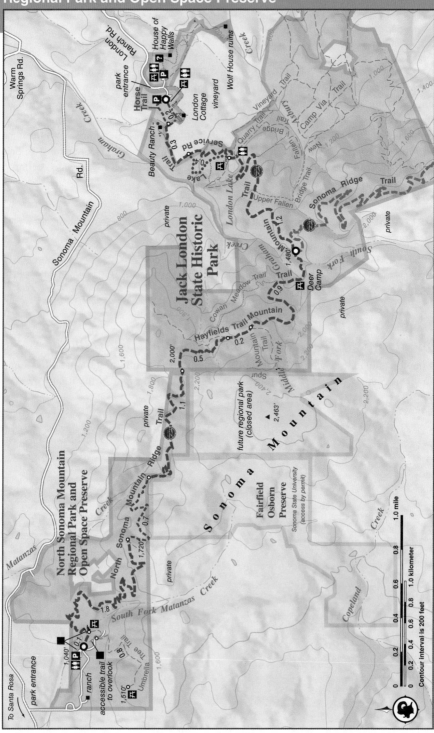

onto the road, but you can usually rock-hop across. In the rainy season, rushing water cascades over rocks in a moist, fern-clad canyon upstream. Then cross Middle Graham Creek, where you come to a rest area with a picnic table. Ferns grace the trail beneath large redwoods, and hazelnut leaves glow golden against the dark redwood trunks in fall.

After a third Graham Creek crossing, you reach the junction of Mountain and Cowan Meadow Trails. The multiuse Ridge Trail route stays on the Mountain Trail, swinging left and gaining more than 400 feet of elevation in 0.6 mile. Here, at 3 miles, you come to an expansive meadow below Sonoma Mountain. Take a detour up the 0.4-mile spur trail to get close to the summit for fabulous views overlooking the Sonoma Valley.

To continue on the Bay Area Ridge Trail, bear right onto the Hayfields Trail. After descending for 0.2 mile, with distant views to the north, you will reach a junction. Veer left on the North Sonoma Mountain Ridge Trail, built over many years before its dedication in 2015. Soon you come out of the woods and cross a large meadow with views of Sonoma Valley and San Pablo Bay.

At about 0.5 mile from the junction, you reach the state park boundary and cross into North Sonoma Mountain Regional Park and Open Space Preserve, managed by Sonoma County Regional Parks. The remaining 3.7-mile trail winds along the contours of the mountain's north slope, slowly descending almost 1,000 feet to the trailhead and crossing numerous creeks. Although mostly wooded until reaching the valley, several open sections offer scenic views.

From the park boundary you pass through beautiful Oregon white oak and bay forest, with some madrone, buckeye, Douglas-fir, black oak, and bigleaf maple. The oaks' sculptural, moss-covered trunks are stunning. In early spring you find abundant red larkspur on this section of the trail. In 0.2 mile from the park boundary, you reach one of the trail's two benches, where the trail takes a sharp turn. From the bench you get a framed view looking northeast through the trees to Bennett and Hood Mountains, where other Ridge Trail segments are located.

In another 0.2 mile, the trail crosses a private ranch road and takes a sharp turn to the left. Here, to your right, the view opens to the north and Bennett Valley. The trail then contours along the slope, makes a switchback, then turns north and begins descending. Around here begins a 0.7-mile stretch where bikes are not permitted on the trail. You begin passing under huge north–south transmission lines; turn left, cross under the lines, and again enjoy views to the valley below, as well as the Santa Rosa Plain, Coast Range, Mount St. Helena, and Bennett, Sugarloaf, and Hood Mountains. At 2.2 miles from the trail's end, you reach a trail junction for the Bennett Valley Overlook to your left. A short walk up the hill rewards you with unsurpassed views to the west, east, and north.

The trail then enters the forest again, passing through a meadow. After a long switchback, the trail descends in a series of switchbacks. When it straightens, the view extends out to the north as you contour the steep hillside. Around a bend, the trail heads northeast and you have a view of the nearby grasslands. A bench sits in the shade, about 250 feet before the trail takes a sharp left into the meadow, with wonderful views north. The next third of a mile winds through scenic open grasslands and small stock ponds; a vineyard is on the adjacent property to the north.

After entering coast live oaks and redwoods, the trail descends to a bridge over the South Fork of Matanzas Creek. On the other side of the creek, three picnic tables sit in the Redwood Grove Picnic Area and a trail leads down to the creek. To the left, the Umbrella Tree Trail leads to a picnic area in 0.7 mile. The last 0.1 mile of the Ridge Trail before the parking lot—wide, unpaved, and lined with bay and redwood—is ADA accessible.

In the future, proposed trails will connect this Bay Area Ridge Trail segment to Petaluma (to the south) and Trione-Annadel State Park (to the north). For now, the next segment begins 9 miles north in Spring Lake Regional Park.

Spring Lake Regional Park and Trione-Annadel State Park

From Spring Lake Regional Park in Santa Rosa to Trione-Annadel's East Gate at Lawndale Road in Kenwood

LENGTH 10.8 miles one-way; car shuttle possible

ELEVATION GAIN/LOSS 1,120'/955' one-way

ACCESSIBILITY Hikers, equestrians, and mountain bikers

AGENCIES Sonoma County Regional Parks and California State Parks

REGULATIONS Spring Lake Regional Park open 7 a.m.–sunset and charges an entrance fee; dogs must be leashed. Trione-Annadel State Park open 8 a.m.–sunset and prohibits dogs on trails.

FACILITIES Water, restrooms, and picnic tables at Oak Knolls Picnic Area in Spring Lake Regional Park

GRADUALLY CLIMB OVER GRASSY HILLSIDES and through oak woodlands and conifer forests on the east side of Bennett Mountain. This is an extremely popular mountain-biking route that travels along wide, rocky service roads and singletrack trails. Pass lush Ledson Marsh and descend through a conifer forest in the park's southeast corner. The west- and south-facing slopes can be hot in summer; north- and east-facing slopes are forested. The 2017 Nuns Fire burned through most of the trail corridor except for a few miles of the northernmost section.

Getting Started

NORTH TRAILHEAD Spring Lake Regional Park, south entrance at 5585 Newanga Ave., Santa Rosa. After entering park, go right to equestrian parking at south end of Oak Knolls Picnic Area. (**GPS: N38° 26.817', W122° 38.946'**)

EAST TRAILHEAD Lawndale Road, 1.1 miles southwest of CA 12, Kenwood. Dirt parking lot. (**GPS: N38 25.054', W122° 34.524'**)

On the Trail

Two local parks—Howarth Park and Spring Lake Regional Park—are connected by trail to 5,500-acre Trione-Annadel State Park. This trip begins in Spring Lake Regional Park

Spring Lake Regional Park and Trione-Annadel State Park

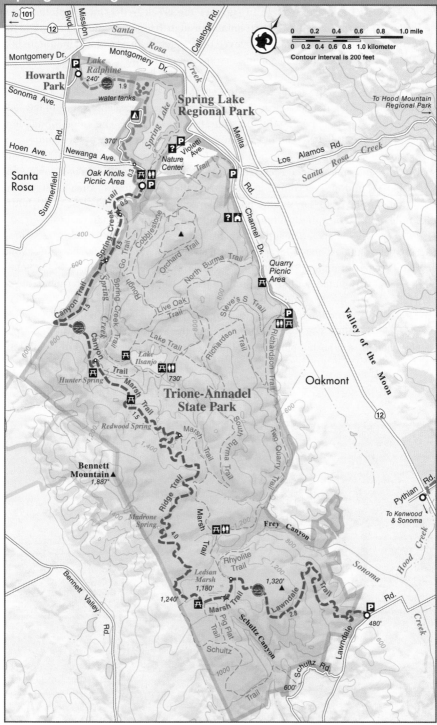

at the southern end of the Oak Knolls Picnic Area and follows a gravel road due south on the levee next to Spring Creek. In summer the creek is dry, but in winter water flows from the north side of Bennett Mountain through Trione-Annadel State Park to the flood-control basin of Spring Lake. The levee trail, much favored by local mountain bikers, hikers, and equestrians, runs along the base of a west-facing hillside, just outside the state park boundary.

After 0.5 mile, the trail crosses the creek and then shortly passes a concrete weir for Spring Creek flood control. The trail enters a narrow, scenic valley of bay–oak woodland, crossing into Trione-Annadel State Park at 0.8 mile. The stone foundations on your right are all that remain of a cabin built by a former owner of this land.

Continue on the wide trail and at 1 mile veer right over the bridge on the Canyon Trail. Ascend on a wooded rocky road with an understory of poison oak, toyon, and monkeyflower, and emerge into a gentle open valley at 1.6 miles. Ahead you see the low, rounded ridge of Taylor Mountain and a large house; as you get close to the house in 0.2 mile, make a hairpin turn to the left, and your ascent begins in earnest.

At 2 miles you enter a beautiful, expansive grassy hillside where you can see north to Spring Lake and beyond to Rincon Valley. On clear days, Mount St. Helena's long shoulder and its taller, prominent left hump are visible in the distant north. Looking south, you see Bennett Mountain's 1,887-foot summit just outside the park. Up to your right you begin to see where the 2017 Nuns Fire burned through the trees. If you come here in late March or early April, you may find the rare white fritillary blooming in moist grasslands.

After 2.5 miles, you reach a junction with the Marsh Trail. Here you find a picnic table, bench, and posted park map. Make a sharp right turn and continue climbing

The 2017 fire burned much of the spectacular oak woodland along the state park's Ridge Trail. Hood Mountain, which hosts a section of the Ridge Trail, is in the distance.

on the singletrack Marsh Trail. Along this trail you see splendid examples of northern oak woodlands comprised of Oregon white oaks, black oaks, coast live oaks, buckeyes, madrones, bays, bigleaf maples, and occasional manzanitas. Beautiful, lush stands of California fescue, a native gray-green bunchgrass with tall, graceful stalks and feathery flower heads, fill the spaces between rounded, moss-covered boulders on the forest floor. The Pomo people who used to live here collected fescue seeds for food.

Look down to the left over the expanse of the park to view scenic Lake Ilsanjo. The rocky trail keeps ascending, and you can take a break at a shaded picnic table at 3.3 miles. You begin to notice the blackened trees from the fire, and from here on out, most of the trail and surrounding park was burned in the 2017 Nuns Fire.

Shortly you reach the shade of redwoods and Douglas-firs, with soft duff underfoot, and cross the headwaters of Spring Creek. Here, where ferns drape the road banks and redwoods tower overhead, a quiet serenity prevails. You proceed through the forest and at 4 miles reach a junction with the well-designed singletrack Ridge Trail. Make a sharp right turn onto this trail to head south on a gentle uphill grade. A high forest canopy arches over skeletons of huge manzanitas, and in moist places, spring blooms of scarlet columbine stand between 1 and 3 feet tall.

You begin descending at 4.4 miles and enter a woodland of oaks, bays, and madrones; subsequently, you start to see more grassland. You emerge from the woods in another mile and look to the south over the burned landscape, where you can see Sonoma Mountain (which the Ridge Trail traverses), Mount Veeder, and Bismark Knob. Soon you arrive at a picnic table where the Ridge Trail makes a left turn. You begin passing through open meadows where grasses are golden in summer and vivid green in winter and spring. Fine specimens of manzanita grow here, and spring wildflowers and bunchgrasses fill the meadow after winter rains. Oregon white and California black oaks dot your route through the grasslands. Burned in the fire, some of these trees are over 200 years old. At 6.5 miles you cross a bridge over a huge open meadow.

Look northeast across the meadows and Ledson Marsh at 6.9 miles for unobstructed views to 2,730-foot Hood Mountain, named in honor of William Hood, who owned Rancho Los Guilicos for almost 30 years. Beyond lies 2,729-foot Bald Mountain. Lower Red Mountain, immediately west of Sugarloaf Ridge State Park on private property, is easily recognized by its unusual color.

The Ridge Trail turns left onto the Marsh Trail, a wide road, and heads toward Ledson Marsh at 7.3 miles. You pass a picnic table that offers fine views of the enormous reed-rimmed marsh. In fall, the reeds' gold and brown tones present a subdued contrast to the dark green woods. The Marsh Trail then passes the Pig Flat Trail junction, continues around the south side of the marsh, and crosses a bridge over the outlet stream where a low dam holds winter runoff from the surrounding hillsides. Continue up the east side of the marsh through coyote brush and manzanita to the Lawndale Trail junction at 8 miles.

The Lawndale Trail, burned in the 2017 fire, is a rocky road leading toward the park's east entrance. Look for piles of dark basalt rock, remains of late-nineteenth-century cobblestone quarrying. European immigrants chipped and shaped basalt rocks into paving stones here and sent them by barge and train to San Francisco. At 8.4 miles you reach a junction where transmission lines are overhead: veer right down the rocky singletrack trail. Soon you will enter a Douglas-fir and madrone forest where the slope drops steeply to your right.

The trail then ambles through a burned redwood-and-fir forest, following a gentle downhill slope. Nine months after the 2017 fire, the redwoods and bays were resprouting. You reach a picnic table on a grassy knoll after leaving the conifer forest, then descend a south-facing hillside through oak woodland and grassland to a residential neighborhood and the gate at the Lawndale Road Parking Area.

The next leg of the Bay Area Ridge Trail begins on CA 12, just southwest of Hood Mountain Regional Park, a 2-mile drive, ride, or walk.

Hood Mountain Regional Park and Open Space Preserve

From CA 12 to Hood Mountain Summit in Kenwood

LENGTH 5.5 miles one-way (plus 5.5-mile return to trailhead; alternative return route possible)

ELEVATION GAIN/LOSS 1,950'/200' one-way

ACCESSIBILITY Hikers, equestrians, and mountain bikers

AGENCY Sonoma County Regional Parks

REGULATIONS County charges a parking fee. Dogs must be leashed.

FACILITIES Historic Hood Mansion; equestrian-trailer parking at Eliza Road; kiosk at Pythian Road Trailhead parking lot with area maps, water, and toilet.

A VIGOROUS UPHILL TRIP begins at CA 12 and follows Hood Creek through forests and meadows, past several ponds, and then climbs to the top of 2,730-foot Hood Mountain for distant views. After the first mile, the 2017 Nuns Fire burned through most of the trail corridor.

Getting Started

TRAILHEAD North Pythian Road and CA 12 intersection, Kenwood. If starting here, use the parking lot at the corner of Los Guilicos Drive and North Pythian Road. To bypass hiking or riding on the entry road, head up North Pythian Road 1.1 miles to the parking area; stay to the right when the road forks. (**GPS: N38 26.121', W122° 34.688'**)

EQUESTRIAN TRAILHEAD Veer left off Pythian Road onto Eliza Way to equestrian parking near the Hood Mansion. (**GPS: N38° 26.571', W122° 34.765'**)

On the Trail

The trail up Hood Mountain starts on the southwest side of CA 12 and North Pythian Road. Cross the two crosswalks to get to the trail signs on the path running parallel to North Pythian Road. With Hood Mountain rising before you, start up the Lower Johnson Ridge Trail, a gravel trail elevated on rocks for 0.2 mile until it reaches Los Guilicos Drive.

Take the crosswalk and head straight on the paved trail. To your left is an extensive county government complex. The path parallels a road in the complex and at 0.5 mile enters an oak woodland. Follow the trail signs and shortly you cross Pythian Road,

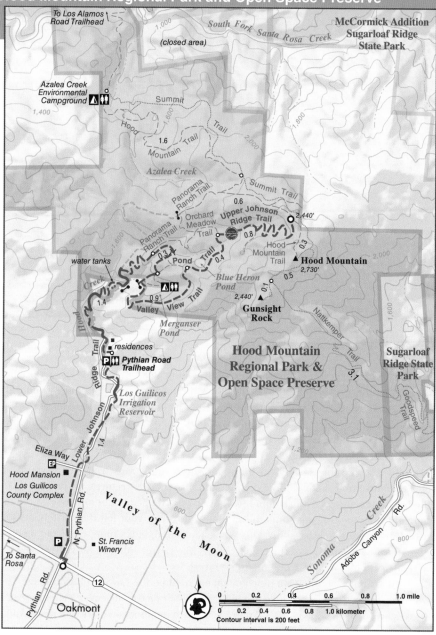

only to cross it again in 0.2 mile. Near Hood Creek and within a Douglas-fir forest, you begin to see the impact of the 2017 Nuns Fire. At 1 mile you come back to the road and go through the main gate. The Lower Johnson Ridge Trail then splits off onto a single-track trail and looks out over an old reservoir before coming to the parking lot for the Pythian Road Trailhead at 1.4 miles.

Manzanita surrounding Hood Mountain's summit burned in the 2017 fire, but the views to surrounding mountains are splendid.

The following mileages are from the Pythian Road Trailhead. From the kiosk at the parking area, take the trail that follows the upper side of the fence around the parking area. The Ridge Trail route follows the Lower Johnson Road Trail past a few houses, and shortly merges onto the park road. It goes up steeply with little shoulder, so listen for oncoming cars. Hood Creek flows far below in a narrow, wooded canyon; you can hear it on a calm day.

In 0.3 mile the trail leaves the road onto a singletrack trail where you again enter the burn area that continues to the summit. The trail returns to the road at 0.5 mile before reaching a trail sign and private driveways. Bear right and ascend the dirt road, following the trail sign onto the singletrack trail on your left that switchbacks up through the woods. You pass three big water tanks and, at 0.8 mile, come out again to the road, which soon crosses the creek. Shortly, the Lower Johnson Ridge Trail goes off the road again into a tanoak and madrone forest.

At 1.4 miles you reach a junction; take a right on the Lower Johnson Ridge Trail toward Merganser Pond. You come to a high-sided fiberglass bridge over a larger creek in a heavily wooded canyon, and at 1.7 miles you reach the junction of the Pond and Valley View Trails. Head downhill on the Valley View Trail, where you will glimpse Merganser Pond through the trees below you. When you emerge from the forest, you arrive at a point where the view merits the name of the trail. You make a sharp turn left around the point and then head across the middle of the densely forested mountainside. After about 0.25 mile, this route veers left and climbs back uphill to join the Pond Trail at 2.6 miles.

Take the Pond Trail and soon you pass Blue Heron Pond, a small, circular body of water surrounded by tall trees and a cool site for a hot summer day picnic—not far beyond, in a small clearing, is a picnic table. This route crosses many drainages lined with flat rocks, which are easily managed in summer and late fall. The going may be a little too wet after serious winter storms.

Rather abruptly you leave the forests and walk through a sloping meadow with widely spaced, large deciduous trees, called Orchard Meadow. Just beyond here, a RIDGE TRAIL sign directs you to the right on the Upper Johnson Ridge Trail at 3 miles. On your left you see the rock wall remains of the Hendrickson Historic Site.

Continuing on the Upper Johnson Ridge Trail, climb steadily on a dirt road through a forest of Douglas-fir, coast live oak, bay, madrone, and bigleaf maple. After 0.3 mile turn left up a singletrack trail that zigzags for more than 0.5 mile before emerging on a ridge. Here you have expansive views of the Santa Rosa Plain. This is the official end of the Ridge Trail, but turn right to continue to the summit (or take a quick detour a short ways down the road to the left for a view north). Head toward the summit and look left in about 200 feet for a great view of Mount St. Helena. The road then ascends very steeply to the summit. In 0.3 mile you reach the 2,730-foot summit: a wide, circular opening enclosed by tall manzanita shrubs burned in the 2017 fire.

Hood Mountain is the highest peak between the Sonoma and Napa Valleys in the Mayacamas Range. On a clear day, you can see the top of neighboring Bald Mountain in Sugarloaf Ridge State Park, Mount Veeder, Sonoma Mountain, and Mount Tamalpais in the far distance. If you have time, take the trail southeast to 2,440-foot Gunsight Rock for splendid views of the Sonoma Valley. Look at the return possibilities on a map if you're interested in an alternative route back to the trailhead.

The next segment of the Ridge Trail lies north in Bothe–Napa Valley State Park, a 21-mile drive.

Bothe–Napa Valley State Park

From Bothe–Napa Valley State Park Entrance Road to Traverso Homestead in Calistoga

see map on next page

LENGTH 3.4 miles one-way for hikers and equestrians, 2.2 miles one-way for mountain bikers (plus 3.4-mile or 2.2 mile return; alternative return possible)

ELEVATION GAIN/LOSS 1,120'/75' one-way

ACCESSIBILITY Hikers and equestrians; mountain bikers for first 2.2 miles

AGENCIES California State Parks and Napa County Regional Park and Open Space District

REGULATIONS Park hours 8 a.m.–sunset; day-use fee applies; dogs prohibited on trail

FACILITIES Visitor center, picnic tables, campground with yurt and cabin rentals, swimming pool, showers, and toilets

THIS RIDGE TRAIL SEGMENT, an excellent outing in hot weather, offers an opportunity to hike up Ritchey Canyon through the woods and alongside a scenic creek. The 1,900-acre park is the farthest-inland state park with coast redwoods. There are many route options for a return trip, so be sure to pick up a trail map when you enter the park.

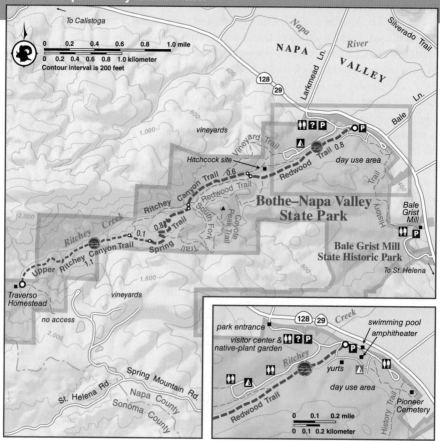

Getting Started

TRAILHEAD On park entry road, 0.3 mile from CA 29, Calistoga. (**GPS: N38° 33.098', W122° 31.258'**)

On the Trail

After entering the park, you can park near the visitor center and continue a short distance down the road to the trailhead across the creek on the right side of the road, or park a bit farther down the road at the information board and alternative trailhead. The Bay Area Ridge Trail follows the Redwood Trail up the canyon on Ritchey Creek, and begins in a woodland of bay, coast live oak, buckeye, and bigleaf maple. In about 400 feet, the two trails merge.

In 0.1 mile you begin seeing redwoods and soon enter a large grove with an inviting bench. When you pass the Ritchey Canyon Trail and Coyote Peak Trail intersections, stay on the Redwood Trail. The peaceful forest also has tanoak, Douglas-fir, madrones, manzanita, and ferns, including delicate maidenhair ferns. A stretch of the trail passes through lichen-covered deciduous oaks, elegant and sculptural in winter without their leaves.

At 0.8 mile take a right over the creek to the Ritchey Canyon Trail; then take a left up the dirt road. In 0.2 mile it will intersect the Vineyard Trail; take a left. Ascending, notice beauty of the forest and the buckeyes lining the road. At 1.4 miles, you reach an intersection; stay straight on the Spring Trail, which heads across the creek. The road begins climbing steeply and winds uphill, with the creek far below to your right, and you see more madrones and black oaks. At 2.2 miles the road reaches a turnaround; from here continue on the singletrack Upper Ritchey Canyon Trail, where bikes are prohibited.

The trail levels in the madrone, bay, and tanoak forest. Take a left when you come to an intersection and begin passing through towering redwoods and getting closer to the creek. At 3 miles the forest opens enough for you to get some glimpses of the drier hills across the canyon. You see a sign at 3.4 miles indicating the end of this Ridge Trail segment. Cross the creek just ahead and walk around the old Traverso Homestead site from the 1880s, which has a stone marker.

If time allows, the visitor center displays artifacts from the Wappo era (which goes back to 6,000 B.C.) and historical photos. The visitor center is located in a house originally built in 1858; these early residents are buried in the park cemetery. The park also has an American Indian garden.

◆ ◆ ◆

The next Ridge Trail segment is at the Lower Oat Hill Mine Trailhead, a 4.8-mile drive or bike ride.

Although much of the Ridge Trail in the state park is in a redwood forest, a section passes through oak woodland.

Robert Louis Stevenson State Park: Lower Oat Hill Mine Trail

From CA 29 to Palisades Trail in Calistoga

LENGTH 4.5 miles one-way (plus 4.5-mile return to trailhead or 6 miles to CA 29 and Table Rock Trailhead; see page 107)

ELEVATION GAIN 1,860' one-way

ACCESSIBILITY Hikers, equestrians, and mountain bikers

AGENCIES California State Parks and Napa County Regional Park and Open Space District

REGULATIONS Dogs must be leashed

FACILITIES None

THIS SEGMENT OF THE RIDGE TRAIL is a steady ascent from the Napa Valley floor to the striking volcanic formations at the ridge. The historic trail is rough and rocky but provides spectacular views of the Napa Valley, Mount St. Helena, and nearby mountain ranges. The trail follows a public easement over private land and passes through state land and Robert Louis Stevenson State Park. This is an advanced, technical trail for mountain bikers. The trail is mostly exposed, so start early in warmer weather.

Getting Started

TRAILHEAD Silverado Trail and CA 29 intersection, Calistoga. Parking along CA 29. (**GPS: N38° 35.363', W122° 34.646'**)

On the Trail

Between 1876 and the late 1960s, the Oat Hill Mine was one of the most productive cinnabar mines in the United States (cinnabar ore was used to produce quicksilver or mercury). The Oat Hill Mine Road was built over a 20-year period beginning in 1873 as a route from Calistoga to the mine, and heavy wagons used the road. The old mines, farther north from the trail, are closed to the public.

The trailhead has a bulletin board with trail information and maps. The trail immediately ascends on a rocky dirt road into a landscape of gray pine, coast live oak, black oak, manzanita, toyon, and poison oak. In 0.1 mile you already have scenic views down to the vineyards north of the trail and Calistoga. When the trail takes a turn south, you see lots of picturesque lichen-filled deciduous oaks and views of the Napa Valley. At 0.5 mile, take a break on the bench overlooking the vineyards and valley to the south. The trail then heads northeast into the trees, and you start seeing madrone, buckeyes, and Douglas-firs.

For the first 3 miles, the trail ascends through the woods with a number of open stretches offering expansive views of the valley. Rock outcroppings surround you, and after 2 miles, you see side valleys down below, ridges in the foreground between you and the valley, and peaks in the distance including Twin Sisters and Mount Diablo to the south and Bald Mountain to the west. The trail narrows at about 2.5 miles, and you see more outcroppings, as well as monkeyflower and lupine.

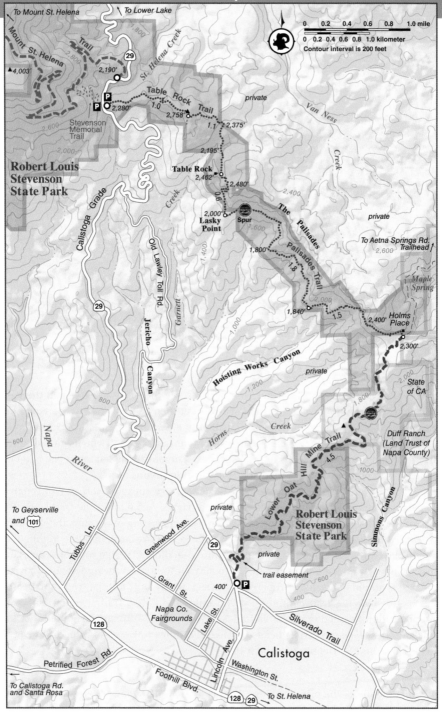

The Lower Oat Hill Mine Trail ascends to the base of the volcanic Palisades.

After the 3-mile trail marker, you begin to see the exposed ridge and the Palisades ahead when the deciduous oaks are without their leaves. Shortly you come out onto a broad grassy slope where you transition to a drier landscape. At 3.3 miles, you reach the ridge and enjoy expansive views of Mount St. Helena (which burned in the 2017 fire) and the volcanic cliffs of the Palisades. A detour to the left takes you to a fantastic lookout point over the jagged volcanic rock formations.

Head right up the Ridge Trail; it becomes very rocky as you pass through a chaparral of chamise and manzanita, with great views. At 3.6 miles the trail edges the base of the Palisades, a 4-mile long rock formation consisting of rhyolite and obsidian. Being next to this rock, with dramatic views ahead and to your left, is the highlight of the journey. After 4.3 miles the trail heads into a saddle and a sign indicates that land trust property is ahead and instructs you to stay on the trail, veering left. Just beyond this sign is an old homestead property from 1893, where only a stone wall remains.

Although the trail continues, at 4.5 miles the Ridge Trail segment comes to an end at the intersection of the Palisades Trail. A Ridge Trail spur beginning on the Palisades Trail (see next trail) heads northwest 6 miles to CA 29 and the trailhead to 4,343-foot Mount St. Helena (see page 109).

◆ ◆ ◆

The next section of the primary Ridge Trail is in Moore Creek Park (see page 112), an 18.5-mile drive or bike ride from the Lower Oat Hill Mine Trailhead.

Robert Louis Stevenson State Park: Table Rock and Palisades Trails Spur

From CA 29 to Oat Hill Mine Trail in Calistoga

see map on p. 105

LENGTH 6 miles one-way (10.5 miles one-way when combined with Lower Oat Hill Mine Trail); car shuttle possible

ELEVATION GAIN/LOSS 1,280'/1,410' one-way

ACCESSIBILITY Hikers only

AGENCY California State Parks

REGULATIONS Dogs prohibited

FACILITIES None

THIS SPUR TRAIL, used solely by hikers, is a challenging, often overgrown trail across steep, rocky terrain. The views are spectacular and it's a unique experience, particularly at Table Rock, to be up close to the volcanic mountains. Most trail users do a one-way trip from the CA 29 Trailhead near Mount St. Helena to the Lower Oat Hill Mine Trailhead instead of the reverse, because the 3,200-foot elevation change is far easier as a descent. Try to do this hike between April and June, when the wildflowers are blooming.

Getting Started

TRAILHEAD CA 29, 5.9 miles north of Tubbs Lane, Calistoga. Parking at pullout on east side of road. (**GPS: N38° 39.153', W12° 35.985'**) Trail ends at Lower Oat Hill Mine Trail.

On the Trail

The singletrack trail begins at the pullout off CA 29 and ascends through a tanoak, madrone, and Douglas-fir forest. Turn left when you intersect a dirt road; by 0.5 mile the forest opens, and you have fine distant views looking northeast into the hills of Lake County. Along the trail you also have your first views of massive, exposed Mount St. Helena. Continue through canyon oaks, black oaks, gray pines, toyon, California pitcher sage, yerba santa, chaparral pea, and manzanita. In some grassy stretches you can see far down to the Napa Valley, which may be covered in fog. You reach an intersection at 0.7 mile; follow the signs and turn right through a bay forest. By 1 mile you reach the Table Rock Overlook, where you have excellent views of surrounding mountains, including Sugarloaf Mountain.

The narrow, exposed trail is rocky and slippery as it descends steeply through chaparral and a gully. At 1.2 miles, you suddenly come out to a flat open area covered in volcanic-rock cairns created by hikers. The spot is starkly beautiful and feels quite remote; you have distant views of mountains to the east, and just ahead on the trail will find two large labyrinths built with the dark volcanic rocks.

Keep heading down the rocky trail into the trees and emerge into chaparral at 1.4 miles, where you begin seeing huge volcanic rocks, buckeyes, and the Palisades ahead. The trail can be overgrown as you head down to the creek corridor. Cross the creek, lush with vegetation, and head steeply up, continuing through huge rocks and a display of wildflowers in spring and summer. At 2.1 miles you reach the Palisades

Trail at Table Rock. Climb on the rock to look down over the valley; view the dramatic, immense volcanic formations below you, as well as Mount St. Helena to your right, and the challenging route you have just traveled.

The Palisades Trail ascends on a rocky pathway through chaparral and then levels right beneath the Palisades before descending. The trail is overgrown and progress is slow as you go through shrubs, Douglas-firs, and bays, sometimes steeply. You cross a steep meadow and get fabulous views of the valley below, arriving at Lasky Point at 2.7 miles. A plaque honors Moses Lasky, who helped create this trail.

From here the trail weaves in and out of coast live oaks and madrones and contours the steep grassy hillsides on a narrow trail, with excellent views of the Palisades. At 3.7 miles the trail enters an expanse of open grassland on steep slopes, but soon you pass through chaparral again, and then trees, before emerging to big views into side canyons. The trail becomes very exposed after 4.2 miles, and soon volcanic rocks are everywhere and the Palisades are even closer. Up ahead you see the Lower Oat Hill Mine Trail. The overgrown trail gets steep and the views get better and better before going into the bay trees. Heading downhill now, you are right against the rock overhangs; descend slowly down the steep, wooded trail to the endpoint at the Holms Place, a historic homestead, where you intersect the Lower Oat Hill Mine Trail at 6 miles.

◆ ◆ ◆

The next section of Ridge Trail is a spur to Mount St. Helena. The trailhead is 7 miles from the Lower Oat Hill Mine Trailhead, across from the Table Mountain Trailhead.

The scenery from Table Rock makes this challenging trek worth the effort.

Robert Louis Stevenson State Park: Mount St. Helena Spur

see map on next page

From CA 29 to Mount St. Helena Summit in Calistoga

LENGTH 5 miles one-way for hikers, 5.5 miles one-way for multiuse route (plus 5- or 5.5-mile return)

ELEVATION GAIN/LOSS 1,790'/15' one-way for hikers, 1,990'/15' one-way multiuse

ACCESSIBILITY Hikers, equestrians, and mountain bikers; hikers can take a hiker-only connector trail

AGENCY California State Parks

REGULATIONS Dogs prohibited

FACILITIES None

MOUNT ST. HELENA, the second-highest mountain in the Bay Area, is the northernmost point of the Ridge Trail. The summit is at 4,343 feet, and the views from the trail and at the top are spectacular. The dedicated Ridge Trail is the multiuse fire road, which has inadequate parking at the trailhead; extreme caution is advised along busy CA 29. It is recommended that hikers take the Stevenson Memorial Trail, the hiking-only connector from the main parking area (the Table Rock Trail is on the opposite side of CA 29). If taking this trip in the summer, start early to minimize sun exposure.

Getting Started

TRAILHEAD (HIKERS) CA 29, 5.9 miles north of Tubbs Lane, Calistoga. Parking at pullout on west side of road. (**GPS: N38° 39.153', W122° 35.985'**)

TRAILHEAD (MULTIUSE) CA 29, 6.2 miles north of Tubbs Lane, Calistoga. Very limited parking at pullout on east side of road, just south of fire road. (**GPS: N38° 39.315', W122° 35.836'**)

On the Trail

Although not officially dedicated as part of the Ridge Trail, the Stevenson Memorial Trail is the best trailhead for hikers to access Mount St. Helena because there is parking at the trailhead. The trail begins on the west side of CA 29; just above the parking area you pass through a level shaded area with picnic tables before the trail starts ascending and switchbacking through bigleaf maples, madrone, Douglas-fir, bays, tanoak, and coast live oak.

By 0.5 mile, the trail gets rocky and at 0.7 mile you reach a monument to Robert Louis Stevenson; this clearing is where he stayed in a cabin with his bride while writing *The Silverado Squatters* in 1880. From here the trail climbs 0.1 mile over steep rock, through a landscape of manzanita and knobcone pines, and then up a rocky gully until you reach the multiuse fire road, the official Ridge Trail.

The multiuse fire road begins on CA 29; parking is prohibited at the base of the road, but a pullout south on CA 29 can accommodate a few cars. Be extremely careful crossing the highway, as there are blind corners, the shoulder is narrow, and the traffic is moving fast. The dirt fire road is relatively smooth—for the first mile it passes through a mixed woodland similar to the forest along the hiking trail; some sections are more

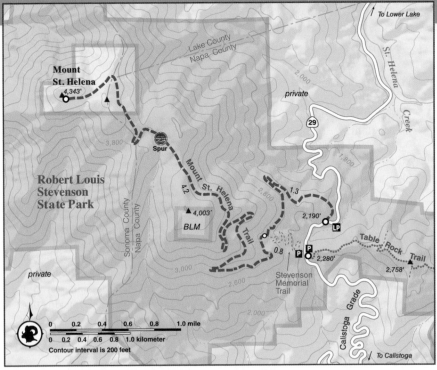

densely wooded than others. It reaches the junction with the Stevenson Memorial Trail in 1.3 miles.

At 0.2 mile past this junction, the trail curves to the west and the view out over the Napa Valley and surrounding mountains opens before you. It's a magnificent vista, and the great views continue as you travel up the road. At this point you also enter the extensive burn area from the 2017 Tubbs Fire, with the blackened skeletons of pine trees extending as far as you can see. Less than a year after the fire, bay trees and manzanita were resprouting.

In 0.5 mile the trail takes a 180-degree-turn east at an immense volcanic rock wall at the edge of the road. As you continue on the road and round the bend, heading north, you can see the road switchbacking up the mountain ahead, and you have views east to Table Rock and the Palisades Trail, another section of this Ridge Trail spur trail. In a mile, the road reaches the power lines and another switchback turn, where the fire did not burn to the north.

The road takes a sharp turn and heads southwest through an exposed chaparral landscape before making another switchback turn in 0.4 mile, heading north and crossing under the power lines into an unburned landscape. At 2.6 miles from the Stevenson Memorial Trail, you reach an unnamed junction. The road to the left leads to the summit of South Peak, a worthwhile detour to see views to the south. Stay straight on the Ridge Trail; to your right is a massive firebreak bulldozed during the 2017 fire, which continues to the summit.

You are now on a saddle and in a chaparral landscape of canyon oak, golden chinquapin, chamise, chaparral pea, and yerba santa. You then resume your climb to the summit and reach a ridge of volcanic outcroppings that extends out to your right at 3.8 miles beyond the Stevenson Memorial Trail. Here another road goes left to a communication tower but stay straight. At about 0.2 mile from the top you will begin climbing steeply.

The 4,343-foot summit, 5.5 miles up the fire road, has a communication tower and concrete-block building, and you can climb some rocks nearby to sit, rest, and enjoy the fantastic view. On clear days, you can see the Sierra Nevada, Mount Lassen, and Mount Shasta to the east and Mount Diablo and Mount Tamalpais to the south. You can also identify other local peaks on the Ridge Trail, including Hood Mountain and Sonoma Mountain. On your return, enjoy the distant views as you head downhill.

◆ ◆ ◆

The next section of the primary Ridge Trail is in Moore Creek Park, a 25.5-mile drive from the Mount St. Helena hiker trailhead.

In summer you may look out over a sea of fog when climbing Mount St. Helena. Most of the mountain burned in 2017.

Moore Creek Park

From Staging Area to End of Moore Creek Trail in St. Helena

LENGTH 4.9 miles one-way (plus minimum 4-mile return trip)

ELEVATION GAIN/LOSS 880'/450' one-way

ACCESSIBILITY Hikers, equestrians, and mountain bikers

AGENCY Napa County Regional Park and Open Space District

REGULATIONS Dogs prohibited

FACILITIES Toilet in parking lot. A large gravel parking lot contains space for horse trailers.

THE RIDGE TRAIL in remote Moore Creek Park climbs high onto the exposed east slopes of the Moore Creek canyon, offering sweeping views, then descends and heads up the shaded scenic creek corridor to a series of creek pools. The exposed Vista Valentine Trail is hot in summer, so hike early in the day or in cooler weather.

Getting Started

TRAILHEAD Moore Creek Park, 2602 Chiles Pope Valley Road, 1.3 miles north of Sage Canyon Road, St. Helena. Large parking lot. (**GPS: N38° 30.586', W122° 21.323'**)

On the Trail

The 700-acre secluded Moore Creek unit of Moore Creek Park was a private cattle ranch before the park district purchased the property in 2008 and built the Valentine Vista Trail. A bulletin board in the parking lot offers information about the park and brochures. Bring plenty of water!

The Ridge Trail starts on the Valentine Vista Trail, about 0.1 mile back up the entrance road from the parking lot. The singletrack trail immediately begins ascending, climbing up the east side of Moore Creek Canyon. The trail passes through a landscape of coast live oak, tanoak, Oregon oaks, buckeyes, digger pines, manzanita, toyon, chamise, and monkeyflower, and lichen hangs from the oaks. At 0.9 mile the trail enters an open grassland high up on the steep slopes and you begin to have long-distance views to western mountains—including Bald Mountain and Mount St. John.

The trail follows the contours, and after passing the 1-mile marker, look down into the canyon below and turn around for fabulous views of Lake Hennessey. The expansive Moore Creek canyon is absolutely beautiful; you are in a remote, quintessential California landscape. After the 2-mile marker, the trail heads away from the canyon. When it takes a bend to the west, look for a spur trail up to the right that takes you to a bench with an impressive view. Once back on the main trail, you wind steeply down into the canyon amid chamise chaparral and coast live oaks.

At 3.1 miles you reach the Moore Creek Trail, an unpaved road. Turn right up the hill (a park residence is below on your left). Before long, the creek will be on your left, with alders running along its length. From here, you are mostly in shade. In 0.3 mile from the road intersection, you reach a trail junction. Going right takes you on a new 0.6-mile singletrack bypass trail—the Dry Foot Trail—on the east side of the creek,

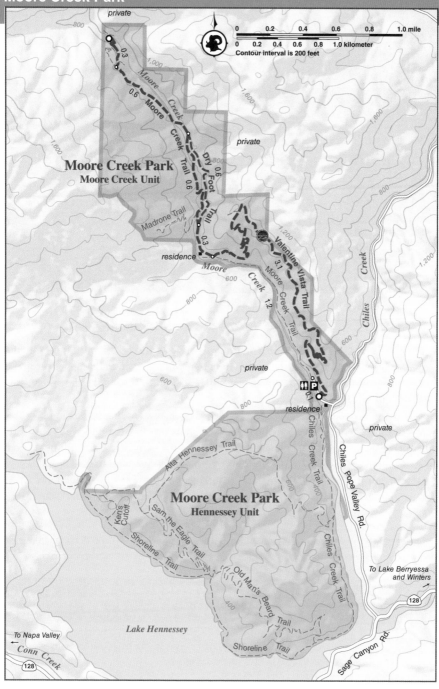

The Valentine Vista Trail rewards hikers with views into Moore Creek Canyon.

avoiding the creek crossings. Going left takes you over the creek and to the junction for the Madrone Trail, a proposed 4-mile loop that will take you to the upper portion of Moore Creek (in February 2018, it was a 2-mile dead end). If you take the creek route, you cross the creek four times.

At 4 miles you climb out of the creek corridor in a bay, madrone, and Douglas-fir forest and reach a sign indicating that the pools are in 0.3 mile. Walk out to the Andrea Overlook to sit on the bench and look down the canyon; then continue down to the scenic creek pools set among big rocks, ferns, buckeyes, and bays. This is the end of the trail. For the trip back to the parking lot, head all the way down the Moore Creek Trail, which turns into an unpaved road at the north end of the Valentine Vista Trail.

The next Ridge Trail segment is in Skyline Wilderness Park, a 24-mile drive or bike ride.

Skyline Wilderness Park and Napa Solano Ridge Trail

LENGTH 4.8 miles one-way for hikers, 4.9 miles one-way for multiuse route (plus 4.8 or 4.9-mile return; alternative return possible)

ELEVATION GAIN/LOSS 1,400'/550' one-way

ACCESSIBILITY Hikers, equestrians, and mountain bikers

AGENCIES Skyline Park Citizens Association and Napa County Regional Park and Open Space District

Skyline Wilderness Park and Napa Solano Ridge Trail

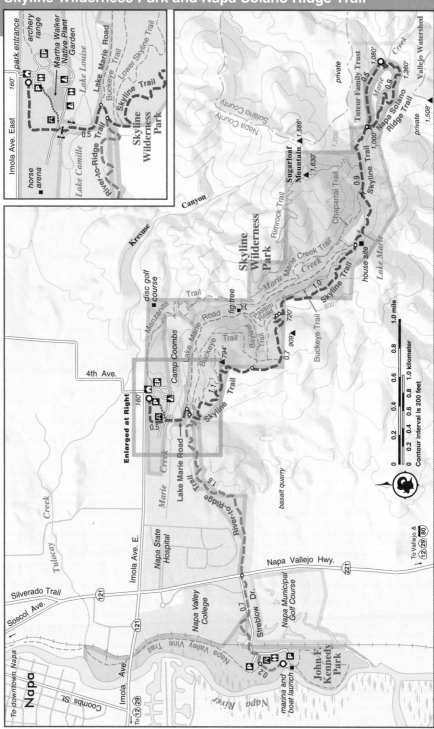

The Skyline Trail skirts the west side of the park, yielding views of the southern Napa Valley and San Pablo Bay.

REGULATIONS Park is open daily; an entrance fee applies. Park hours vary seasonally; call 707-252-0481 or check at skylinepark.org before you go. Dogs prohibited on trail. Swimming in the lake is prohibited, but fishing is allowed.

FACILITIES Restrooms and water at picnic area near park entrance; several picnic tables near Lake Marie, about 3.2 miles up the trail; horse arena, archery ranges, disc golf course, and Native Habitat Garden; tent camping and RV facilities.

EAST OF NAPA STATE HOSPITAL in the southern foothills of Napa Valley, this out-and-back trail is for hardy hikers and careful equestrians and mountain bikers; it is a narrow, often rocky trail. After a steep climb in the first mile, the trail ambles through oak forests and high grasslands to views of North Bay marshes and mountains and then continues beside a perennial stream to the far reaches of the park. In October 2017, the Atlas Fire burned through most of Skyline Wilderness Park, and fire damage surrounds the Ridge Trail. In the months following the fire, hundreds of damaged trees were removed. Start early, particularly on warm days, and take plenty of water.

Getting Started

TRAILHEAD 2201 Imola Ave., 1.4 miles east of Napa Vallejo Highway, Napa. Parking lot inside the park gate. (**GPS: N38° 16.737', W122° 14.968'**)

On the Trail

Skyline Wilderness Park was established in 1980 when the State of California declared 900 acres of the Napa State Hospital grounds as surplus property. A dedicated local group, wishing to preserve the beautiful Marie Creek Canyon and its surrounding watershed, formed the nonprofit Skyline Park Citizens Association. It leases the land from the state and county and manages these foothill forests and grasslands for public enjoyment. Today, many trails thread through the park, including one to its highest point, 1,630-foot Sugarloaf Peak. The Skyline Trail, designated as a section of the Bay Area Ridge Trail, is the most westerly and longest route in the park, reaching the southeastern park boundary near the Solano County line.

Hikers can start at the trailhead at the southwest corner of the main-entrance parking lot. The Martha Walker Native Habitat Garden, on your left, is worth a visit when you return from your hike. In 400 feet you come to a large grassy expanse. Go down the paved road, which then turns left onto unpaved Lake Marie Road; this is where you meet the multiuse trail.

All trail users can start the hike or ride on Lake Marie Road just north of the parking lot, which heads west and then south, intersecting with the hiking route in 0.3 mile. (All mileage notations apply to the hiking route.) Lake Marie Road heads south and crosses a fenced causeway between two ponds, Lake Louise and Lake Camille, which are still part of the Napa State Hospital grounds. Lake Marie Road bends left, and at 0.4 mile intersects the Skyline Trail. Take a right and in 0.1 mile the Ridge Trail heads left up a singletrack trail.

The Skyline Trail zigzags up a steep grassy hill studded with volcanic rock outcrops. As you gain elevation, you get distant views of the Napa Valley and peaks off to the north: Mount George, Atlas Peak, Bismark Knob, Mount Veeder, Bald Mountain, Mount St. John, and Mount St. Helena. At each western bend, the trail comes close to a low wall, built of rocks gathered in early ranching days. In spring, native wildflowers— bright orange, yellow, and blue—accent the green grasslands; in summer, golden oats contrast with the dark, lichen-covered rocks.

At 1.1 miles you enter an oak–buckeye woods where the trail straightens and levels a little, having gained over 600 feet in elevation. As the trail heads south, lovely views open to the Napa marshlands edging San Francisco Bay. Beyond lies majestic Mount Tamalpais. And below is the open jaw of an immense rock quarry, close to the park boundary. The trail parallels the rock wall on the right.

You pass several trail junctions but stay on the Skyline Trail, which is well marked. The trail veers east through chaparral shrubs, woodland, and ubiquitous poison oak, contours along the hillside, and heads down into a valley and a crossroads. Turn right and switchback up the Skyline Trail, climbing to the high grasslands at the western edge of the park. When the weather is clear, you can see chaparral-covered Mount George to the north and Mount Tamalpais to the southwest. Soon there is also an expansive view to the baylands. Hawks, scrub jays, woodpeckers, and towhees are just a few of the many birds a quiet hiker can observe in this wilderness park.

At about 2.7 miles, on a hill to your right, look for a bench where you can enjoy fantastic views north; farther up the hill is another bench facing the bay. The trail descends from here into bay woodland and at the trail junction at 2.9 miles, it turns

---

River-to-Ridge Connector

Another way to access the Ridge Trail in Skyline Wilderness Park is via the 2.5-mile multiuse River-to-Ridge Connector Trail. This trail starts next to the Napa River at the Napa Valley Vine Trail (the route of the San Francisco Bay Trail) in John F. Kennedy Park, a city park. From the parking lot at the end of Streblow Drive, go north on the paved Napa Valley Vine Trail 0.1 mile and turn right on the River-to-Ridge paved trail. As the trail heads east it parallels Streblow Drive and passes the Napa Golf Course and Napa Valley College until it crosses Napa–Vallejo Highway. The dirt trail then passes between an industrial site and the Napa State Hospital before entering an oak forest and a chaparral landscape, eventually intersecting the Skyline Trail (Bay Area Ridge Trail) in Skyline Wilderness Park.

---

right up a dirt road. Below, perennial Marie Creek cuts a deep valley between this hillside and 1,630-foot Sugarloaf Peak.

In a small clearing, you come upon the skeleton of a house—a tall chimney and stonework foundations. Although known as the Sea Captain's House, local historians claim that it was originally built for the gatekeeper who tended the dam at Lake Marie, just a few hundred feet below. When the state decided it no longer needed the gatekeeper, it took down the house. A trail turnoff just ahead goes down to the lake, but the Skyline Trail continues above it.

From here the trail follows an old roadbed, traversing the slope through dense bay forest with a fern understory. It then descends to cross the creek upstream of the lake. Continuing on the singletrack Skyline Trail, you follow the meandering creek, leaving it only to skirt a sloping meadow. Then you cross to the south side of Marie Creek and a tributary. On a gentle forest path, you soon reach a gate.

In 2005, the Tuteur Family Trust dedicated the next 1.4 miles of trail on their ranch as a segment of the Ridge Trail. Known as the Napa Solano Ridge Trail, it was the first section of the Ridge Trail to be built and managed by the Bay Area Ridge Trail Council, which raised the money to build the trail and oversaw the volunteers who maintained and patrolled it. In 2018, the council transferred management responsibility to the Napa County Regional Park & Open Space District.

On this trail you cross Marie Creek on a fiberglass bridge and climb high in the valley through chaparral and heritage oak trees. The trail zigzags back down to the creek and crosses a second trail bridge before looping back across grasslands into the park. To return to the trailhead, retrace your steps along the route you just followed or return by any of several other trails that lead to the park entrance.

◆ ◆ ◆

The next segment of the Bay Area Ridge Trail begins in the hills west of Fairfield at Rockville Regional Park, a 15.7-mile drive.

Rockville Hills Regional Park and Vintage Valley Trail

From Rockville Road to Antiquity Drive in Fairfield

LENGTH 4.2 miles one-way for hikers and mountain bikers, 0.8 mile one-way for equestrians; car shuttle possible

ELEVATION GAIN/LOSS 540'/580' one-way

ACCESSIBILITY Hikers and mountain bikers in Rockville Hills Regional Park; hikers, equestrians, and mountain bikers on Vintage Valley Trail

AGENCY City of Fairfield

REGULATIONS Park is open sunrise–sunset and charges an entrance fee. Dogs must be leashed. Horses prohibited in park.

FACILITIES Picnic tables along the Ridge Trail near the main gate and at Upper Lake. Restrooms on trail.

Getting Started

NORTH TRAILHEAD 2149 Rockville Hills Road, 0.8 mile west of Suisun Valley Road, Fairfield. Although the Bay Area Ridge Trail route begins 0.6 mile farther on Rockville Hills Road, use the parking at the main gate because this trailhead gate is locked and there is no off-road parking on either side of the road. (**GPS: N38° 14.916', W122° 07.965'**)

SOUTH TRAILHEAD Antiquity Drive and Mangels Boulevard intersection, Fairfield. Street parking. (**GPS: N38° 12.907', W122° 09.135'**)

CLIMB GENTLY THROUGH VOLCANIC HILLS to a remote, grassy valley with a splendid stand of blue oaks. Then ascend to a plateau with views of Mount Diablo, Elkhorn Peak, and the Twin Sisters. The trail then drops into and through a residential subdivision. This trip begins on a connector trail to the park's north entrance and then travels paved and unpaved service roads to a paved trail through the subdivision. Most trees in the park are deciduous, so on a winter day the trails can be comfortably sunny, yet in summer the blue-oak forest offers welcome shade.

On the Trail

From the Rockville Hills Regional Park's main gate on the park's eastern boundary, take the 0.5-mile Lower Quarry Trail that ascends north, paralleling Rockville Road, to join the main Bay Area Ridge Trail route on the park's north side. The Bay Area Ridge Trail route follows the wide, paved road from the upper gate, which ascends through a landscape of red-berried toyon, shiny-leafed manzanita, and shrubby coyote bush. Live oaks cling to steep hillsides above and below the trail, offering shade on warm days. In late spring, blue Douglas iris and orange sticky monkeyflower fill the road banks with color. Soon you have views south across the farmlands and wind farms to Suisun Bay and the Central Valley.

Continue beneath sizable deciduous oaks, their great branches arching over the trail to provide filtered shade. At the crest of the hill in 1 mile, take a moment to rest on the bench at the intersection with Old Ranch Road. Look west to see a high, rocky ridge topped by tall towers supporting ribbons of electric transmission lines. The park's

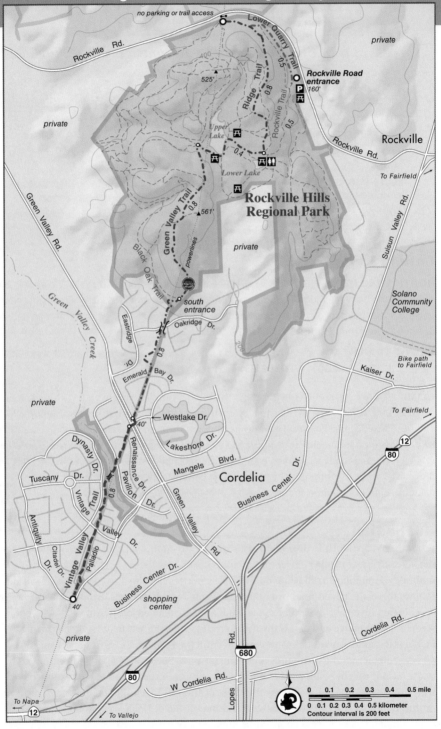

The Creation of a Park

Rockville Hills Regional Park was once part of a large cattle ranch owned by the Masons, a local ranching family. In the 1970s, the City of Fairfield bought these rocky, wooded highlands to build a golf course. The city laid out golf-cart paths on the hills and in the interior valleys and improved existing stock ponds for irrigation, but Fairfield citizens defeated a bond issue to fund further development of the golf course, and the land became a city park instead.

central valley lies between this ridge and your trail. In the distance you can see Elkhorn Peak and Twin Sisters.

As you descend past some very large specimens of manzanita, you look down at the lake nestled among beautiful stands of mature blue oaks. David Douglas, a botanist in the early days of Western-states plant collecting, first identified these blue oaks, a species that can withstand the high summer temperatures and scant rainfall of these Inner Coast Range foothills. When blue oaks begin to leaf out in late spring, their thick, slightly lobed leaves take on a blue-gray color.

About 1.3 miles from the trailhead, you meet the Rockville Trail, a 0.8-mile connector trail to the main parking area that joins your trail from the left. A kiosk has trail maps, information, and a bike repair station, and restrooms are just down the paved road. A picnic site in a nearby grove of blue oaks offers vistas over the surrounding plain. The Bay Area Ridge Trail route swings right from the junction and heads into grasslands on an unpaved trail. You pass close to Lower Lake and continue toward Upper Lake, your way brightened by spring wildflowers, including low-growing, daisy-like goldfields, bright yellow Johnny-jump-ups, and tall blue brodiaea.

At the top of Upper Lake's low dam, you may find tame, year-round resident ducks and geese. Migratory water birds, winter visitors only, are less sociable. Birds of the surrounding blue-oak woodland—acorn woodpeckers, flickers, and western bluebirds—will reward you with quick displays of color. A sign indicates that the city is working to bring back the Western pond turtle. Several picnic tables around the lake offer places to enjoy your lunch.

From the dam you can look across the lake to rocky cliffs that form the backbone of the park. This rock formation, known as Sonoma Volcanics, is made up of undifferentiated volcanic and sedimentary rocks, ash, basalt, and andesite, dating from the late Miocene and Pliocene epochs, some 2–10 million years ago. Rockville Hills Regional Park marks the southern end of a 40-mile-long band of Sonoma Volcanics.

Bear left at Upper Lake to follow the trail along the east side of the lake, pass one left-branching trail, and veer right around the south end of the lake. At a second trail intersection, turn left to follow the Ridge Trail route toward the Green Valley Trailhead.

After a short steep ascent, the trail reaches the ridgetop and levels off in a saddle. Stay straight at the intersection and at 2.2 miles you emerge onto a high, treeless plateau, where you look due south to I-680 heading toward Suisun Bay and the 3,849-foot summit of Mount Diablo rising prominently above the surrounding plain.

Overhead, hawks circle lazily, searching the grasslands for their prey of mice, voles, and gophers. With luck, you may spot a pair of black-shouldered kites, frequent visitors to this area, identifiable by their long white tails and sharply pointed wings.

The trail veers right and soon bends left across the scenic plateau. If you continue straight at this bend, you reach the edge of the plateau. From here, you have an unobstructed view of Green Valley's lush fields; the mountains that serve as a natural boundary between Napa and Solano Counties rise in the background. Twin-topped, 1,330-foot Elkhorn Peak, fringed with a thatch of trees, stands due west. Visually follow this line of mountains north along undulating, tree-cloaked slopes to the Twin Sisters, each more than 2,000 feet high.

Return to the main trail, rest on a bench for a view, and continue across the plateau into a grove of ancient evergreen oaks, their branches sculpted by prevailing northwest winds and their trunks 4–6 feet in diameter. Following the path through these widely spaced, venerable trees is like walking down a *grande allée* of some fabled estate of yesteryear.

Beyond the ridgetop, the wide trail descends a steep, east-facing hillside dotted with California buckeye trees, and a large residential subdivision lies below to your left. Then a short descent on a south-facing hillside takes you under power lines at about 2.7 miles to a wide, fenced corridor that leads through a gate to a finger of open land between houses. Descending steeply, the trail shortly arrives at the trailhead's information board.

Cross the pedestrian bridge over Oakridge Drive to a paved landscaped path between houses that passes underneath the power lines, and walk through a gate just before arriving at Emerald Bay Drive. After crossing Emerald Bay Drive again, you

Rockville Hills Regional Park features a fabulous blue-oak landscape.

come to Green Valley Road at 3.3 miles. This next section is not dedicated. Head left on Green Valley Road, cross Westlake Drive, and then cross busy but pleasant tree-lined Green Valley Road to the path on the other side. Take the path to Renaissance Drive for the beginning of the Vintage Valley Trail, the dedicated Ridge Trail section.

After crossing Renaissance Drive and Pavilion Drive, the Vintage Valley Trail veers left into a natural area with large majestic oaks. After a bridge over Green Valley Creek, the trail meets Dynasty Drive in a residential area. Turn left and the trail continues down a landscaped park median under the power lines. Cross Vintage Valley Drive and then Citadel Drive. Now the path parallels Palladio Way and comes to a large grassy park area on your right, just before ending at Antiquity Drive, the edge of the subdivision at 4.2 miles. The land beyond the end of the trail is undeveloped hillsides.

The next segment of the Bay Area Ridge Trail begins on McGary Road, a 2.7-mile drive.

Lynch Canyon Open Space and McGary Road

see map on next page

*From Redtop Road in Fairfield to
Hiddenbrooke Parkway in Vallejo*

LENGTH Lynch Canyon segment, 4.3 miles one-way (plus 4.3-mile return to trailhead); McGary Road segment, 3.5 miles one-way

ELEVATION GAIN/LOSS 665'/150' one-way (Lynch Canyon segment); 295' gain (McGary Road segment)

ACCESSIBILITY Hikers, equestrians, and mountain bikers

AGENCIES Solano County Parks and Solano Land Trust (Lynch Canyon)

REGULATIONS Park open Friday–Monday, 9 a.m.–5 p.m.; parking fee applies. Dogs and fishing prohibited.

FACILITIES Restroom at entrance parking lot

THE TRAIL IN LYNCH CANYON climbs and descends a series of grassy hilltops and offers stunning 360-degree views. An ideal time to visit is the spring, when dazzling arrays of wildflowers cover the hillsides and the creeks run full. A distinctive feature along the spine of the preserve is a loose aggregation of irregularly shaped rocks graced by wind-sculpted live oak and bay trees. The McGary Road segment is a bike lane that begins at Red Top Road, connecting to Lynch Canyon and the Hiddenbrooke Trail.

Getting Started

LYNCH CANYON TRAILHEAD End of Lynch Road, inside Lynch Canyon Open Space entrance, 0.2 mile west of McGary Road, Fairfield. Large parking lot. (**GPS: N38° 11.104', W122° 10.779'**)

McGARY ROAD TRAILHEAD North end at Redtop Road intersection, Fairfield. (**GPS: N38° 12.088', W122° 09.376"**) South end at Hiddenbrooke Parkway intersection, Vallejo. (**GPS: N38° 10.124', W122° 11.958'**)

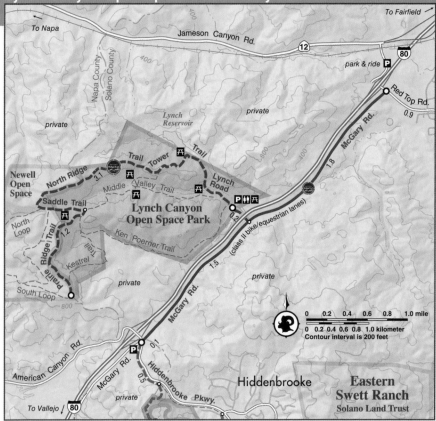

On the Trail

The 3.3-mile Ridge Trail segment on McGary Road is a Class II bike/equestrian lane, and the 0.2-mile Ridge Trail section connecting McGary Road and the Lynch Canyon Trailhead is a wide paved road for 440 feet, then a gravel entry road. McGary Road runs between I-80 and grassland–oak woodland.

Lynch Canyon lies along the northwest side of I-80 between Fairfield and Vallejo, and its major ridge is a scenic landmark for residents and travelers alike. Beginning in the early 1990s, residents of this area, along with the Solano Land Trust and local government agencies, worked to save this 1,039-acre site for public open space. The property has long been used for cattle grazing and farming, and the Suisun tribe once hunted game—deer, antelope, and elk—for food, clothing, and shelter.

After you pass through the trail gate at the staging area, your route on Lynch Road heads down a broad valley bordering Lynch Creek, which flows under a canopy of oaks, bigleaf maples, and willows. You pass the Middle Valley Trail turnoff on your left in 0.3 mile, where two forks of the creek converge, and then pass some corrals and picnic tables. You are now closer to the creek and see bay and buckeye trees, as well as many bird-nesting boxes. At 0.7 mile take a left on the Tower Trail. The road ascends a grassy hill; up to your left is an enormous tower and transmission line, and down to

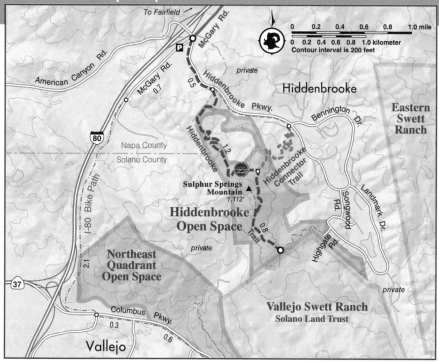

your right is a willow-lined scenic reservoir. Here, cows graze, frogs croak, and countless birds swoop over the lake to catch insects or take a quick drink.

At 0.8 mile, where a picnic table and bench overlook the valley, a trail heads down to Lynch Reservoir. The Ridge Trail keeps climbing on the Tower Trail with views of Elkhorn Peak, Twin Sisters, and Signal Hill in the distance. You pass two more benches before getting to the trail junction at 1.2 mile, with picnic tables and views into pastoral Middle Valley.

Bear right on the North Ridge Trail, and make your way across the rolling grasslands toward a saddle in the hills marked by an umbrella of live and valley oaks. On the way you pass more benches and a picnic table; as you go up, down, and then up again, turn around to see the Central Valley, and look east to the next Ridge Trail segment at Sulphur Springs Mountain. At 2.1 miles you reach a ridge with phenomenal views and a picnic table to rest on. You are at the Solano and Napa Counties boundary with expansive views of the vast Napa marshlands, San Pablo Bay, Mount Veeder, Sonoma Mountain, Mount Tamalpais, and Mount Diablo.

Your trail heads downhill and at 2.8 miles takes a left on the Saddle Trail, a level road. Pass a pond and enter a wide valley with clumps of eucalyptus ahead. When you reach the picnic table, the trail goes up to your right and joins the Prairie Ridge Trail at 3.1 miles. Turn right and ascend the steep road. At the ridge you are once again on the county line with magnificent views; you can look ahead to a ridge dotted with oaks and large boulders that seem like sentinels guarding the valley below. There are a number

From these ridges, the Solano County hills extend in all directions.

of picnic tables, and at 3.5 miles interpretive panels provide information about the pre-serve, cattle grazing, and common raptors of Solano County.

The Prairie Ridge Trail turns to singletrack and passes through a unique area of windswept bays and oaks growing amid rocks. When you intersect the Kestrel Trail at 4 miles, keep straight, headed toward Mount Diablo and I-80. The trail veers south, with views opening up of the East Bay Hills. When you reach a fence at 4.3 miles, with views west down to American Canyon, you're at the end of this Ridge Trail segment. To return to the trailhead via a loop, you can take the Kestrel Trail back down from the ridge and then either the Middle Valley Trail or Ken Poerner Trail.

After returning to the trailhead and heading down McGary Road, the next segment of the Bay Area Ridge Trail begins at McGary Road and the Hiddenbrooke Trail.

Hiddenbrooke Open Space

see map on p. 125

From McGary Road to Trail's Southern Terminus in Vallejo

LENGTH 2.5 miles one-way (plus 2.5-mile return to trailhead)

ELEVATION GAIN/LOSS 530'/190' one-way

ACCESSIBILITY Hikers, equestrians, and mountain bikers

AGENCY Hiddenbrooke Estates

REGULATIONS Trail hours are 6 a.m.–sunset; dogs prohibited

FACILITIES None

THESE ROLLING GRASSLANDS offer expansive views of San Francisco, San Pablo and Suisun Bays, and the mountains that encircle them, from Mount Tamalpais to Mount Diablo. You have short steep climbs along this exposed trail, and you must return to

Hiddenbrooke Parkway. During summer, take this trip on cool mornings; some spots are muddy after heavy rains.

Getting Started

TRAILHEAD Hiddenbrooke Parkway and McGary Road intersection, Vallejo. Parking on west side of McGary Road just south of Hiddenbrooke Parkway. (**GPS: N38° 10.124', W122° 11.958'**)

On the Trail

Your trip begins by ascending a paved trail between the landscaped border of Hidden-brooke Parkway and the fenced property line. At 0.5 mile, the dirt Bay Area Ridge Trail veers off to your right, marked by a sign and a bulletin board with trail information. You pass graceful gray-green olive trees and then turn right to climb through the grassland. The parkway and extensive Hiddenbrooke residential development are below to your left and Sulphur Springs Mountain is ahead of you.

The trail climbs a steep hill near the fence to reach a ridge at 0.8 mile. On a clear day, you can see west across the community of American Canyon to the Napa River as it flows south past the former Mare Island Naval Shipyard. Slightly northwest of the island, the Napa-Sonoma Marshes Wildlife Area, fed by the Napa River, extends to the shores of San Pablo Bay. Across the water are the hills of Napa County and the taller peaks of the North Bay. Lynch Canyon is across the freeway, and in the distance are Solano County peaks: Twin Sisters, Elkhorn, and Signal Hill.

The trail turns left, descends along the fence line and county line, and then climbs again to a cattle gate at 1.2 miles. You drop into a small valley where clumps of oak and bay trees hug a rocky ridge just above the trail. Veined with red-brown ore, the rocks recall the mining days of this region, when mercury was extracted for processing

Mount Diablo and the Carquinez Strait seen from the slopes of Sulphur Springs Mountain

the gold found in the Sierra foothills. The mines are now closed and sealed, but one—St. Johns Mine—is the name of a nearby knoll on private property.

At 1.4 miles, the trail takes a sharp left and then rounds the north shoulder of Sulphur Springs Mountain. Wild artichoke surrounds the trail and rock outcrops cover the hill to the left. Continue to a gap in the hills, where you can see south to Suisun Bay and beyond to Mount Diablo. To the north lie the expansive green fairways and greens of the Hiddenbrooke Golf Course and the homes of Hiddenbrooke Estates. You reach a trail intersection here at 1.7 miles. To the left, the 1-mile Hiddenbrooke Connector Trail switchbacks down grassy hills to the Hiddenbrooke Parkway and Bennington Drive intersection. Take a right and climb steeply. The views down the long valley to the Carquinez Strait are fabulous. In early spring, you may see bright yellow tufts of hog fennel, a ground-hugging plant.

At 2 miles, you reach another junction; take a left and head downhill to a saddle and the Ridge Trail terminus at 2.3 miles, where you must turn around. If you go right at the junction, a short path leads uphill to 360-degree views of the Bay Area from the trip's highest point, 1,112-foot Sulphur Springs Mountain. After a winter storm has cleared the air, you will see east to the snowy Sierra peaks and west to the Golden Gate, spanned by the famous bridge. You can identify the prominent mountaintops around the bay and trace the circular Bay Area Ridge Trail on or nearby, beginning just north of the bridge with Mount Tamalpais and then to Mount Burdell, Sonoma Mountain, Mount St. Helena, Mission and Monument Peaks, Mount Madonna, Mount Umunhum, Black Mountain, Kings Mountain, and back to the bridge. You can also look south to a broad valley where a proposed route of the Ridge Trail would head toward McIntyre Ranch and the Ridge Trail in Blue Rock Springs Park.

The next segment of the Ridge Trail begins in Vallejo's Blue Rock Springs Park, a 4.6-mile drive from the Hiddenbrooke Trailhead.

Blue Rock Springs Park to Vallejo–Benicia Buffer

From Blue Rock Springs Park in Vallejo to Rose Drive in Benicia

LENGTH 5.5 miles one-way for hikers (plus a 0.4-mile return on a Blue Rock Springs Park trail extension); 3.1 miles one-way for equestrians; 5.1 miles one-way for mountain bikers (includes 0.1-mile gap); car shuttle possible

ELEVATION GAIN/LOSS 615'/1,070' one-way

ACCESSIBILITY Hikers, equestrians, and mountain bikers

AGENCIES Greater Vallejo Recreation District and City of Benicia

REGULATIONS Blue Rock Springs Park open 8 a.m.–sunset and charges an entrance fee; dogs prohibited. Buffer and Rollye Wiskerson Trails open sunrise–sunset; dogs must be leashed.

FACILITIES Water, restrooms, picnic tables, grills, and play areas at Blue Rock Springs Park

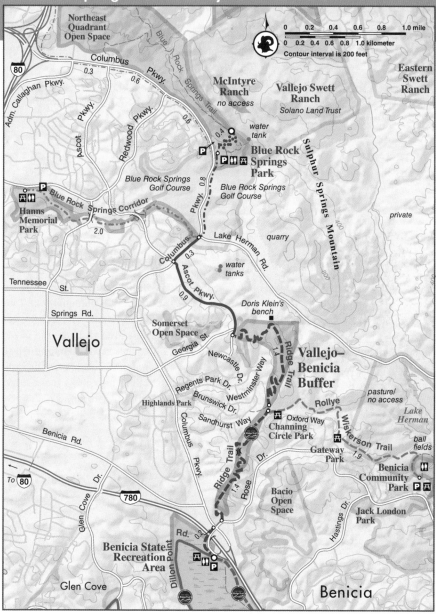

THIS TRIP BEGINS on a short round-trip to a rocky ridge and returns to the rolling green lawns and shady picnic areas of Blue Rock Springs Park. It then follows a paved path/sidewalk or bike lane for 2 miles to the Buffer Trail, which meanders 2.9 miles up and down hilly grasslands toward Benicia State Recreation Area. The last 0.3-mile section of trail is on city streets in Benicia, including a 0.1-mile undedicated section.

Getting Started

NORTH TRAILHEAD Blue Rock Springs Park, 650 Columbus Parkway, 0.7 mile south of Redwood Parkway, Vallejo. Large parking lot; use upper lot for northeast hillside trail. (**GPS: N38° 07.628', W122° 11.446'**)

SOUTH TRAILHEAD Rose Drive and Dillon Point Road intersection, Benicia. Park inside Benicia State Recreation Area (parking fee applies) or park on the street north of I-780. (**GPS: N38° 04.670', W122° 11.561'**)

On the Trail

This trip over General Mariano Vallejo's former lands begins in Blue Rock Springs Park, once the site of an elegant home and lavish gardens built by his son-in-law General Frisbie. It later became a popular picnic place and is now managed by the Greater Vallejo Recreation District; its green lawns, spring-fed pond, picnic tables, and big trees attract visitors year-round.

Northeast Extension

A short Bay Area Ridge Trail **hikers-only** section extends this segment 0.4 mile north toward the Hiddenbrooke Trail. On the planned Ridge Trail route, the Hiddenbrooke Trail will eventually connect to Blue Rock Springs Park via McIntyre Ranch. The trail begins on the park's north side; to reach it, park in the upper parking area and take the paved path through the green lawns to a grassy hillside. In 0.1 mile, look to your left for the trail on the other side of the fence ascending the hill. An information board is on your right before you go through the gate. Seven switchbacks climb to the summit of a rocky ridge. Along the way, benches offer the opportunity to pause and enjoy the North Bay ambience; you have fine views of the bay and surrounding hills, the golf course, and the residential

The Vallejo–Benicia Buffer Trail sits high above the vast Carquinez Strait.

subdivisions below. Uphill from these benches, a wall of huge rocks is reminiscent of ancient fortresses; on your left, these ragged outcrops top an adjacent hill. At 0.4 mile, you reach a fence and a gate; the trail continues but this is the end of the Ridge Trail segment. After you have enjoyed the views, retrace your steps to the parking area.

South to the Buffer Trail

To continue on the Ridge Trail route toward the Vallejo–Benicia Buffer, **hikers** return to the sidewalk and head south from the upper parking lot to join **mountain bikers.** Pass through the lower parking lot to find the unsigned paved trail near Columbus Parkway. The wide path runs parallel to the parkway, separated by a landscape buffer. The Blue Rock Springs Golf Course is on your left and extends to Lake Herman Road. Across Columbus Parkway, a 2-mile Bay Area Ridge Trail connector links to Hanns Memorial Park via the Blue Rock Springs Corridor, passing more of the previous golf course, another park, and a school.

Beyond Lake Herman Road, the path narrows and passes a grassy hill before coming into a residential neighborhood just before Ascot Parkway. Hikers take a left up the sidewalk and bicyclists use the bike lane. As you climb this street, extensive apartment complexes are on your left and mostly single-family houses are on your right. After the apartments, the road passes grassy hills on the left.

Buffer Trail

After passing Georgia Street, 0.9 mile up Ascot Parkway, look for a landscaped entry in front of a weathered-gray fence on the east side of the street. **Equestrians** join **hikers and mountain bikers** and turn left to begin the Buffer Trail, signed for the Ridge Trail route. Owned by the cities of Vallejo and Benicia, the trail is maintained by volunteers. Manzanita, toyon, coffeeberry, and blue lupine, all native California plants installed by volunteers, fill the space beside the trail for the first 50 feet.

The singletrack trail zigzags to the first of this trip's many hilltops. Rest on the bench. Before you is the long sweep of the greenway's undulating terrain that stretches almost to the shores of Southampton Bay on the Carquinez Strait. The homes that edge both sides of the Buffer highlight the importance of activists' persistent efforts to convince the cities of Vallejo and Benicia to create this linear open space.

Beyond the first hilltop, the trail heads north into a swale. It then goes uphill and has views north to an immense rock quarry. After a long traverse and switchback, it reaches its highest point on the trip at 700 feet, where it can be quite windy. Here a bench is dedicated to local outdoorswoman Doris Klein. You have views of impressive bodies of water from this vantage place: Due east is Lake Herman, the local water supply; below you to the south, a third of California's water surges through the Carquinez Strait, drained from the Sierra Nevada into the San Joaquin and Sacramento Rivers. Beyond the strait, San Francisco Bay spreads out over a vast expanse of tidelands, marshes, sloughs, and open waters. On a clear day you can see the towers of the Golden Gate Bridge, under which these waters flow to the Pacific.

For the next 0.5 mile, you follow a wide track south over the hilltops. You reach another knoll with a bench before descending. A RIDGE TRAIL sign directs you right on a narrower trail and you can see this trail extending far out in the distance. In spring, these rolling grasslands are ablaze with orange poppies and blue lupines. As the season progresses, yellow-flowered mule ears add their color to the hillsides. Heavenly blue brodiaea and lemon-yellow mariposa lilies are special floral treats that peek through the grasses in early June. The roasted bulbs of these plants were once the favorite foods of local American Indian tribes.

At 3.5 miles the trail reaches a low point and levels out, and the Rollye Wiskerson Trail joins your route from the east; built and named for the Solano County master trail-builder, it runs along the north edge of a residential neighborhood, connecting three community parks to the Buffer Trail.

Past the junction, your trail is again a wide track that undulates up and down along the fence line. At 4 miles it reaches another low point, crosses a bridge, and then climbs more switchbacks to the crest of another hilltop; from there you have good views of Southampton Bay and the Benicia State Recreation Area, where other legs of the Ridge Trail hug the waterfront. If the day is clear, you can see, and sometimes hear, ships on the fast-flowing waters of the Carquinez Strait. The trail descends along the fence line, with moderate undulations over the last hilltops, and finally descends steeply, going through a parking lot to Rose Drive in Benicia.

The short 0.1-mile section down Rose Drive to Columbus Parkway is not dedicated Ridge Trail because there is no official bike lane, but hikers can use the sidewalk. Cross the Columbus Parkway at the signal and use the 0.2-mile paved and separated path along the Rose Drive overpass that drops you on Dillon Point Road, the midpoint in the next Ridge Trail section and the beginning of the next trail segments.

Vallejo–Benicia Waterfront

From Dillon Point Road in Benicia to Waterview Terrace in Vallejo; From Dillon Point Road to East Fifth Street in Benicia

LENGTH 5.2 miles one-way for hikers, 4.5 miles one-way for mountain bikers, 3.2 miles one-way for equestrians, 4.6 miles one-way for hikers and mountain bikers, 0.8 mile one-way for equestrians; car shuttles possible

ELEVATION GAIN/LOSS 495'/225' one-way (from park entrance at Dillon Point Road to Carquinez Bridge Overlook); 90'/45' one-way (from park entrance at Dillon Point Road to Military East)

ACCESSIBILITY Hikers, equestrians, and mountain bikers (hikers only on Carquinez Overlook Trail); wheelchair users on state park waterfront trail and at Benicia Marina

AGENCIES California State Parks, Greater Vallejo Recreation District, and City of Benicia

REGULATIONS Benicia State Recreation Area open 8 a.m.–sunset; entrance fee applies, and dogs must be leashed. Bikes prohibited on Carquinez Overlook Trail. City of Benicia waterfront and City of Vallejo trails are open sunrise–sunset.

FACILITIES Water and restrooms at Benicia State Recreation Area; water and restrooms at Ninth Street Park

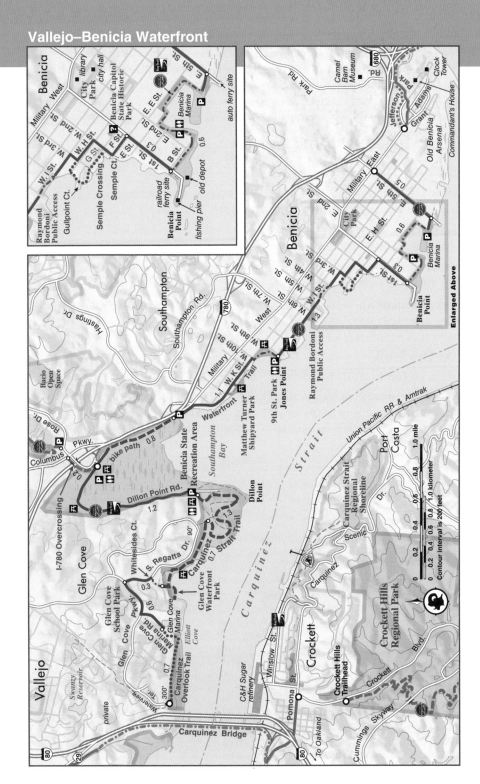

THIS IS WHERE THE BAY AREA RIDGE TRAIL splits and heads toward either the Carquinez Bridge or the Benicia–Martinez Bridge on the Carquinez Strait Scenic Loop Trail. Take a trip through Mexican and early-California history on these routes, which follow the waterfront through the thriving towns of Vallejo and Benicia. Enjoy brisk breezes and occasional fog as you watch the San Joaquin and Sacramento Rivers funnel into San Francisco Bay. This route travels mostly level trails, including sidewalks, paved and unpaved trails, and footpaths.

Getting Started

MIDDLE TRAILHEAD Dillon Point Road and Rose Drive intersection, Benicia. Street parking in park (fee applies). (**GPS: N38° 04.670', W122° 11.561'**)

WEST TRAILHEAD (HIKERS) South terminus of Waterview Terrace, Vallejo. Street parking. (**GPS: N38° 04.014', W122° 13.429'**)

WEST TRAILHEAD (MULTIUSE) Terminus of Glen Cove Marina Road, Vallejo. Street parking. (**GPS: N38° 04.080', W122° 12.849'**)

EAST TRAILHEAD Military East and East Fifth Street intersection, Benicia. Street parking. (**GPS: N38° 3.051', W122° 08.811'**)

On the Trail
West to the Carquinez Bridge Overlook

To take the waterfront trail west, **all trail users** begin at the entrance to Benicia State Recreation Area. Follow the paved park road (**hikers and equestrians** on the shoulder) as it skirts the marshes and western shore of Southampton Bay on its way to Dillon Point.

The Carquinez Overlook Trail edges a bluff high above the Carquinez Strait.

In 1.2 miles, take the paved road that goes right up the hill. In 185 feet, look for the RIDGE TRAIL sign and the dirt singletrack trail, and in 285 feet veer left to take the perimeter trail around the Dillon Point Peninsula. The trail gains elevation and traverses the slope, with views down to Southampton Bay and its wetlands, and the hills of the Vallejo–Benicia Buffer in the distance. As the trail turns west, views open of the Carquinez Strait and Mount Diablo. The trail loops north through a fennel-covered peninsula, and then heads south again, skirting a large transmission tower. Look due west from here for a view of the Carquinez Bridge and your route along the town of Vallejo's bluffs, high above the strait.

After 1.2 miles on the dirt trail, as it heads toward South Regatta Drive, look for a signed dirt trail to your left that heads west and parallels South Regatta Drive. In 0.3 mile you join a paved trail that takes you to Vallejo's Glen Cove Waterfront Park, the end of the off-street route for **equestrians**. A short Bay Area Ridge Trail section on the park waterfront has benches and picnic tables for enjoying the view. Then head uphill on Whitesides Drive through residential subdivisions, take a left on South Regatta Drive, and a left on Glen Cove Parkway. Follow the parkway for 0.3 mile, passing Glen Cove Park, and take a left on Glen Cove Marina Road. Go 0.3 mile steeply downhill to the west end of the Glen Cove Marina parking lot.

The Victorian yacht club at this marina once served as the residence for personnel at the Carquinez Strait Lighthouse and Life Saving Station, and was formerly situated just west of an early version of the Carquinez Bridge at the mouth of the Napa River. After the lighthouse was automated in 1955, the building was sold and barged to its present site at Elliot Cove in 1957. The three-story building now presides over the yacht basin.

Bicyclists end their trip here at the marina, and **hikers** follow a path from the parking lot through a small park, south between the houses and the marina, and then west along the shore. The trail then ascends rough steps and a grassy hill to a blufftop path above the strait, where you can look down on freighters, barges, naval vessels, and pleasure craft. On a foggy day, the horns of ships and the bells of buoys reverberate eerily from the strait's watery canyon. High above the water, the two bridges cross the strait.

Connecting trails from pocket parks in the adjoining subdivision intersect this segment of the Bay Trail and the Bay Area Ridge Trail. The trail ends at a dramatic vista point below the bridge, near Waterview Terrace. The swiftly moving waters of the strait join San Pablo Bay, with Mount Tamalpais and the Coast Ranges as a backdrop. Turn around to see the port communities of Vallejo, Benicia, and Martinez with Mount Diablo in the distance.

The next section of Ridge Trail is in Vallejo's Carquinez Park, a 5-mile drive.

East to Historic Benicia

Starting at the park entrance on Dillon Point Road, **all trail users** head southeast on the paved trail that skirts the marshlands around Southampton Bay. Eucalyptus lines one side of the trail, buffering the noise of I-780. Among the shorebirds and waterfowl that feed in the marshes, you may see the stately, 30-inch-tall white egret. You will certainly see many runners, strollers, and mountain bikers on this trail. Across Southampton Bay to the south, Dillon Point juts into the strait, named for a rancher who, in 1855, bought the 400 acres that now lie within the state recreation area.

Touring Historic Benicia

At First and G Streets stands the centerpiece of Benicia's attractions: an imposing redbrick building with white, two-story columns—California's third capitol. Although the legislature convened here only in 1853, the building is now faithfully restored and is a state historic park (707-745-3385, parks.ca.gov/?page_id=475). The **Fischer-Hanlon House,** part of the park complex, is next door and open for tours.

You are in the heart of Benicia's old town, where saloons, hotels, and the 1847 **Von Pfister Adobe** bring to life the years before and after the gold rush. If you continue down West First Street to Benicia Point, you see where 400-foot-long barges once ferried trains across to Port Costa. Cars were also ferried across the strait until the Benicia–Martinez Bridge was built. A 30-minute walk will take you to a group of 1850s military buildings: the **Benicia Arsenal,** the **Camel Barn Museum,** and the **Commandant's House** (visit beniciahistoricalmuseum.org for more information).

Today, Benicia bustles with activity that matches its lively past—huge ships unload Japanese cars at the port, and condominiums, shopping malls, and subdivisions line the hillsides and crowd its shores.

At 0.8 mile the path enters a parking lot, and an entrance road takes you to K Street. **Equestrians and wheelchair users** end this segment at the east boundary of the state recreation area, while **hikers and mountain bikers** go right and continue on the sidewalk or bike lane on K Street, the Waterfront Trail.

Take a detour and turn right on West 12th Street to the Matthew Turner Shipyard Park, where you have your first close-up view of the Carquinez Strait. In 1900, 169 ships were launched here; today you find benches, picnic tables, pretty gardens, and a historical marker. Across the strait lies Port Costa, once an important depot for transporting grain by barge, ship, and rail. The Southern Pacific Railroad still runs transcontinental freight, and Amtrak operates a fleet of passenger trains on waterfront tracks.

Now return to K Street, and at West 10th Street turn right, where a blufftop path runs diagonally across Ninth Street Park, home to a playground, volleyball courts, picnic tables, and benches. Jones Point is at the south end of the park: Commodore Thomas Jones was founder of the U.S. Naval Academy and commander of the Pacific Fleet in the 1840s. Southampton Bay is named for one of his supply ships. Jones feared war with Mexico and advocated for a port here in Benicia's deep offshore waters.

Follow I Street beyond the park, past houses with charming gardens. In the 1860s, two tanneries near here processed hides from vast inland cattle ranches. Each hide was marked with the ranch's unique brand. At I and West Sixth Streets, look out across Raymond Bordoni Public Access Beach for scenic views of the strait. At West Fifth Street, barriers exclude motor vehicles from I Street, but bikers and pedestrians can pass on a paved path above the bay. At West Fourth Street, picnic tables and children's play equipment sit above a small crescent-shaped bay.

Turn right on West Third Street. After one block, hikers have the option to turn right and, at the end of the block, go left on a paved path along the water and then join

Semple Crossing until converging with the main route at West Second Street. Alternatively, for the multiuse route, from West Third Street, take a left onto H Street, where you see older houses, and a then a right on West Second Street. After a block, use the path down the middle of the street to the shore. Take a left on West F Street to First Street, the main commercial street in Benicia.

Turn right and enjoy First Street, with its restaurants and storefronts; then take a left onto B Street just before Benicia Point, where there is a fishing pier, parking, and the old Southern Pacific Depot. Townhouses are on your left and a park on your right. At East Second Street, keep straight and then left on the path around the perimeter of the pleasant Benicia Marina, with housing on your left. The path will eventually exit into a parking lot at the end of East Fifth Street. The Ridge Trail continues up East Fifth, a wide residential street with some commercial uses, and ends at Military East.

The next Ridge Trail segment starts 0.4 mile east on Military East.

Benicia–Martinez Bridge

From Military East in Benicia to Mococo Road in Martinez

LENGTH 2.5 miles one-way; car shuttle possible.

ELEVATION GAIN/LOSS 170'/210' one-way

ACCESSIBILITY Hikers and bicyclists

AGENCIES City of Benicia, CalTrans, City of Martinez

REGULATIONS Dogs must be leashed

FACILITIES None

CROSSING ONE OF THE MAJOR BAY AREA BRIDGES is a not-to-be missed experience. This segment, a section of the Carquinez Strait Scenic Loop Trail, is especially fun as a bike ride because it is a paved route. Starting in Benicia, you have an opportunity to take a side trip and explore the historic Benicia Arsenal. Cross the Carquinez Strait from Solano County into Contra Costa County and see the maritime activity below. Be prepared for high winds on the bridge.

Getting Started

NORTH TRAILHEAD Military East and Adams Street intersection, Benicia. Street parking. (GPS: N38° 02.864', W122° 08.393')

SOUTH TRAILHEAD Mococo Road just east of Bridgehead Road intersection, at end of bike trail, Martinez. Limited street parking. (**GPS: N38° 01.557', W122° 06.870'**)

On the Trail

Begin this segment at the intersection of Military East and Adams Street. This section of Benicia is the historic Benicia Arsenal, which became a military reserve in 1847. Visit the Benicia Historical Museum on Camel Road for a complete history of the arsenal over the years. This military complex played a role in the Civil War, the Spanish-American

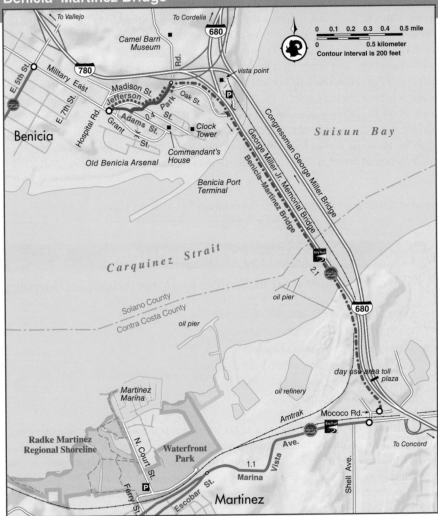

War, World Wars I and II, and the Korean War, and was deactivated in 1963. The one-time Command Post Headquarters, a Spanish-style building built in 1942, is located straight ahead, between Adams and Grant Streets.

There are alternative ways to get up to the bridge path entrance. **Cyclists** are advised to veer left on Adams Street and take the next left on Park Road, which ascends steeply for 0.3 mile until reaching the bridge bike path. Park Road has a bike lane as you ascend toward the bridge and a sidewalk on the opposite side. Alternatively, **pedestrians** can veer left up Jefferson Street on a sidewalk through a residential neighborhood for 0.2 mile, then take a left on Park Road and enter the bridge path in another 0.2 mile. The sidewalk on Jefferson Street is on the north side of the street.

You walk or ride under an I-780 overpass before turning right to enter the paved bridge path, clearly marked with BAY AREA RIDGE TRAIL and BAY TRAIL signs. After about 0.4 mile you will be on the bridge, and the path is separated from the roadway by concrete dividers topped with metal railings. Opened in 2009, the path is on the westernmost bridge with southbound traffic. The 1.2-mile George Miller Jr. Memorial Bridge opened in 1962 and was retrofitted to accommodate the bike/pedestrian lane. The bridge for northbound traffic opened in 2007, and the railroad bridge in between the two bridges opened in 1930.

Looking down to your right on the Benicia side you may see cargo ships at Benicia's port; on the opposite side of the Carquinez Strait you see the refineries of Martinez, and Mount Diablo to the southeast. On the east side of the bridge, in Benicia, view what remains of the Suisun Bay Reserve Fleet; hundreds of ships were parked here after WWII, but after deteriorating for decades, they were recycled or sold for scrap metal. When you reach the other side of the bridge you will continue alongside I-680 for 0.5 mile, even after you are no longer over water. The trail then drops down onto Mococo Road, where this official Ridge Trail segment ends.

The bridge segment is a critical link in the Carquinez Strait Scenic Loop Trail, shown on the interpretive panels installed on both sides of the bridge. On many sections of the loop trail, the Bay Area Ridge Trail and the San Francisco Bay Trail converge, including the routes across both bridges. In Contra Costa County, however, the regional trails split; the Bay Trail stays on the water and the Ridge Trail goes up the ridges.

◆ ◆ ◆

A gap exists between this Ridge Trail segment and the next one because there is no path along the road. To get to the next dedicated segment, take a right on Mococo, and carefully walk or ride along the shoulder. Take your first left over the train tracks and when you reach Marina Vista Avenue take a right to see the RIDGE TRAIL sign and a bike lane running along the north side of this street. This is the beginning of the next trail segment.

The Ridge Trail is on the western span of the three bridges that connect Benicia and Martinez.

Completed Ridge Trail
Proposed Corridor

Solano County

Vallejo

Carquinez Bridge
Rodeo
Crockett
Benicia
Benicia–Martinez Bridge

Suisun Bay

Sacramento River

San Pablo Bay

Crockett Hills Regional Park
Pinole
Fernández Ranch
El Sobrante
Martinez
San Joaquin River
Pittsburg
Antioch

John Muir National Historic Site

Mount Wanda 580'

Concord

BART

Sobrante Ridge Regional Preserve

EBMUD
Kennedy Grove
San Pablo Reservoir

Pleasant Hill

Black Diamond Mines Regional Preserve

Richmond

Briones Regional Park

Tilden Regional Park

Vollmer Peak 1,905'

UC Berkeley

Orinda

Lafayette

Walnut Creek

Contra Costa County

Mount Diablo

Berkeley

Round Top 1,763'

Moraga

Redwood Regional Park

Alamo

Mount Diablo State Park

Morgan Territory Regional Preserve

Oakland

Redwood Peak 1,619'

Danville

BART

Alameda

San Lorenzo Reservoir

EBMUD

Anthony Chabot Regional Park

San Leandro

San Ramon

Cull Canyon Regional Rec. Area

Dublin

Castro Valley

Five Canyons

Livermore

Hayward

Pleasanton Ridge Regional Park

Pleasanton

San Francisco Bay

CSU East Bay

Garin/Dry Creek Pioneer Regional Parks

Alameda County

Union City

Vargas Plateau

Sunol

San Antonio Reservoir

Coyote Hills Regional Park

Fremont

Ohlone College

Mission Peak 2,517'

Ohlone Wilderness Trail

Redwood City

Mission Peak Regional Preserve

Monument Peak 2,594'

Calaveras Reservoir

Don Edwards San Francisco Bay National Wildlife Refuge

Ed R. Levin County Park

San Mateo County

Palo Alto
Caltrain

Santa Clara County

Milpitas

0   2   4   6   8   10 miles
0   2   4   6   8   10 kilometers

Mountain View

EAST BAY

Carquinez Bridge and Crockett

Carquinez Park in Vallejo to Crockett Boulevard in Crockett

LENGTH 2.8 miles one-way; car shuttle possible

ELEVATION GAIN/LOSS 230'/260' one-way

ACCESSIBILITY Hikers and bicyclists

AGENCY Greater Vallejo Recreation District, CalTrans, and City of Crockett

REGULATIONS Dogs must be leashed on bridge; equestrians prohibited on bridge

FACILITIES Carquinez Park has picnic tables, restrooms, and parking. The bridge's south end has a parking lot adjacent to The Dead Fish restaurant (20050 San Pablo Ave.), which has many spaces available when the restaurant is closed.

JOIN STROLLERS, EXERCISE BUFFS, DOG WALKERS, and commuters on the west side of this high suspension bridge. Look out over the wide waters of the Carquinez Strait, where the Sacramento and San Joaquin Rivers flow into San Pablo Bay before entering San Francisco Bay. On the south side of the bridge, cross under I-80 and pass through downtown Crockett, famous for its C&H sugar refinery. This is also the route of the Bay Trail and Carquinez Strait Scenic Loop Trail.

Getting Started

NORTH TRAILHEAD Carquinez Park, northwest corner of Sonoma Boulevard and Sandy Beach Drive intersection, Vallejo. Parking lot in park. (**GPS: N38° 04.738', W122° 14.190'**)

SOUTH TRAILHEAD Crockett Boulevard and Pomona Street intersection, Crockett. Street parking. (**GPS: N38° 03.140', W122° 13.256'**)

On the Trail

Begin in Vallejo's Carquinez Park, a pleasant hillside area with rolling lawns, a playground, multiuse field, and picnic tables. From the parking area, go downhill on Adams Street, left on Sandy Beach Road, right on Sonoma Boulevard, and right on Maritime Academy Drive. At 0.4 mile look for the bridge trail entrance graced with native plants and marked by a large RIDGE TRAIL AND BAY TRAIL sign, a map of the trail, and a low blue metal bench. On the other side of the street is the campus of California State University Maritime Academy (aka Cal Maritime), a CSU training school for the U.S. Merchant Marine.

The wide bridge trail is separated from the noisy I-80 vehicular traffic by a 5-foot concrete wall topped by a black chain-link fence on each side of the trail. As you climb to the bridge, you can look far down to the campus below. Shortly, just west of the trail, you pass an open field flanked by tall eucalyptus trees that provide shade in the late afternoon. Then on your right is a high concrete wall incised with nautical themes.

Just before you get onto the bridge at 1.1 miles, take a detour to the vista point, where you can read interpretive panels about the Carquinez Strait, the San Francisco Bay, and the bridges. The bridge you will cross was opened in November 2003, replacing an earlier bridge. Look for the Alfred Zampa Memorial Bridge plaque, which tells the story of the Crockett native, an ironworker who worked on all the bridges that cross San

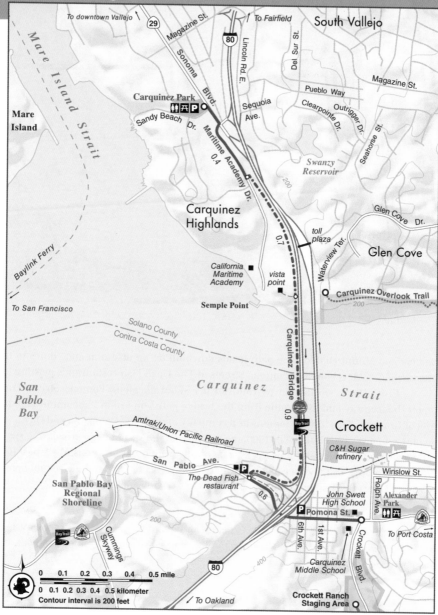

Francisco Bay. A survivor of a fall into the safety net during the building of the Golden Gate Bridge, he helped form the Halfway to Hell Club for bridge-building survivors.

Back on the Ridge Trail, start out across the bridge. About halfway across, you pass the sign that marks the watery boundary of Solano and Contra Costa Counties. The vehicle traffic roars by faster and noisier than the Carquinez Strait water below. You have an excellent view to the west of Mare Island and its wetlands, as well as views of

The bridge path is on the newer western span, the Alfred Zampa Memorial Bridge.

Benicia and Mount Diablo. The path heads downhill on an off-ramp and comes to the intersection of Merchant and Pomona Streets at The Dead Fish restaurant's parking lot.

Cross the I-80 off- and on-ramp to the sidewalk along Pomona Street. Walk under the freeway and in 0.3 mile from the bridge path you are in the commercial district of Crockett. This town is famous as a company town of the California and Hawaiian Sugar Company (C&H Sugar); in 1906, the refinery on the strait began processing sugar cane from Hawaii, but today it processes sugar only from other locations. Walk past four downtown blocks and another block between the high school and middle school before reaching Crockett Boulevard, the end of the Ridge Trail segment.

There is a 0.2-mile Ridge Trail gap on Crockett Boulevard before you reach the entrance to Crockett Hills Regional Park. This section of road lacks a bike lane or sidewalk but has a paved shoulder.

Crockett Hills Regional Park

From Crockett Ranch Staging Area in Crockett to Trail's End near CA 4 in Rodeo

LENGTH 5.4 miles one-way (plus 5.4-mile return to trailhead; shorter return route possible)
ELEVATION GAIN/LOSS 1,250'/1,000' one-way

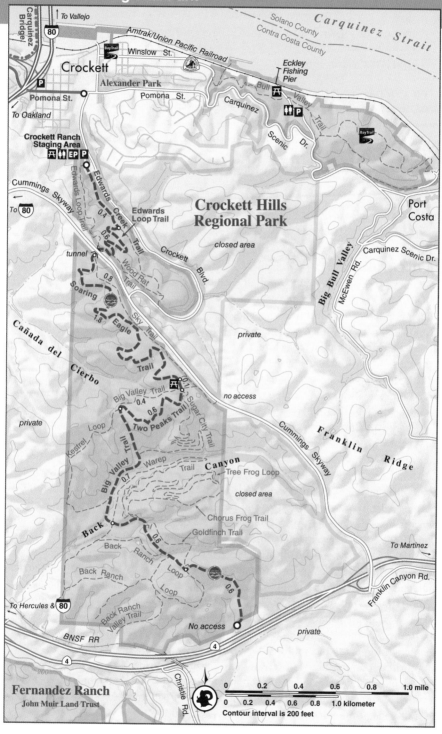

ACCESSIBILITY Hikers, equestrians, and mountain bikers

AGENCY East Bay Regional Park District

REGULATIONS Dogs must be leashed in developed areas (parking lot, picnic site) and under voice control elsewhere.

FACILITIES Water, restroom, and picnic table at staging area

CLIMB AND DESCEND HIGH, HILLY GRASSLANDS for scenic views southeast to Mount Diablo, west to Mount Tamalpais, and north to the Carquinez Strait. A section of the Carquinez Strait Scenic Loop Trail, the Bay Area Ridge Trail traverses exposed grassy hills south of Cummings Skyway and can be hot in summer. Watch for ticks on the narrow trails in spring!

Getting Started

TRAILHEAD Crockett Ranch Staging Area, Crockett Boulevard, 0.2 mile south of Pomona Street, Crockett. (**GPS: N38° 02.832', W122° 13.275'**)

On the Trail

From the staging area, go uphill through a gate and bear left on the wide Edwards Creek Trail. The trail runs parallel to Crockett Boulevard and a creek and then starts climbing at 0.3 mile, shaded by coast live oaks and edged by wild cucumber vines and tangles of poison oak. At 0.4 mile take a right on the Edwards Loop Trail, and after another turn, follow the contour through a bay forest, where in spring, cow parsnip and ferns flourish. Just before the trail intersection, where you turn right at the Edwards Loop Trail, you come out to an open landscape of coyote brush and poison oak. You start getting glimpses of the Carquinez Bridge and then have an unobstructed view just before you go through a low tunnel under Cummings Skyway at 1 mile (where equestrians should dismount).

After the tunnel, pass through a gate and enter open hilly grassland, green and dotted with wildflowers in spring and golden brown in summer. Veer right on the singletrack Soaring Eagle Trail; already you have views of the East Bay Hills, the bay, and Mount Tamalpais in the distance. This is a relatively new, narrow trail so watch for ticks in the spring. As the trail extends west around the contours, the views of the bay become more impressive. Cross an old ranch road at 2 miles and shortly pass under transmission lines, which you will cross under again in 0.5 mile after passing a stock pond. As the trail keeps changing direction, enjoy the varied distant views.

At 2.8 miles veer right toward a large, level, paved area with two picnic tables; it's very exposed but is a good place to rest and take in the views of Mount Diablo. Then head south and, when you cross the Big Valley Trail, look for an information board and a gate ahead. As you go through the gate, you feel the remoteness of your location, although you can see CA 4 in the distance. Pay attention, as the trails can be overgrown in the spring; take the Two Peaks Trail, which veers down to the right. It curves around and drops into the intersection of the Big Valley and Kestrel Loop Trails.

Go left on the Big Valley Trail, a fire road that descends steeply for 0.7 mile to cross an intermittent creek and the bottom of the canyon, and then climbs to regain lost elevation. Contouring along a hillside, you head southeastward for almost a mile. Here the trail ends at the park boundary near CA 4. Until the trail eventually crosses CA 4 and connects to Fernandez Ranch, you must turn around.

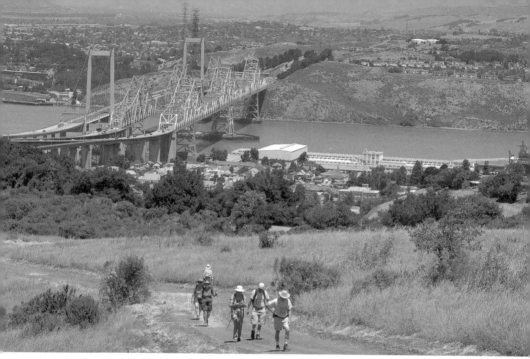

Once the park's trails ascend to the grasslands, views open of the Carquinez Bridge.

Retracing your outbound route, you can head down the Sky Trail, an alternative route. In the distance, tugboats and seagoing ships ply the strait's waters, which come from California's two great rivers—the San Joaquin and Sacramento—that drain the state's central valleys. You also see the big stacks of the California and Hawaiian Sugar Refinery, longtime landmarks in the town of Crockett. At the Crockett Ranch staging and picnic area, you can see the original barn, milk house, and corrals, reminders of earlier days.

The next segment of the Ridge Trail begins to the south across the Contra Costa hills in Fernandez Ranch, a 7.9-mile drive.

Fernandez Ranch

From Christie Road to Pinole Valley Watershed's Goat Road in Martinez

LENGTH 1.4 miles one-way (plus 1.4-mile return to trailhead). Car shuttle possible if combined with one leg of Ridge Trail in Pinole Valley Watershed (requires East Bay Municipal Utility District permit).

ELEVATION GAIN/LOSS 480'/20' one-way

ACCESSIBILITY Hikers, equestrians, and mountain bikers

AGENCY John Muir Land Trust

REGULATIONS Open sunrise–sunset. Dogs must be leashed in picnic areas but are allowed under voice control on trails.

FACILITIES Toilet, picnic tables, and benches at staging area

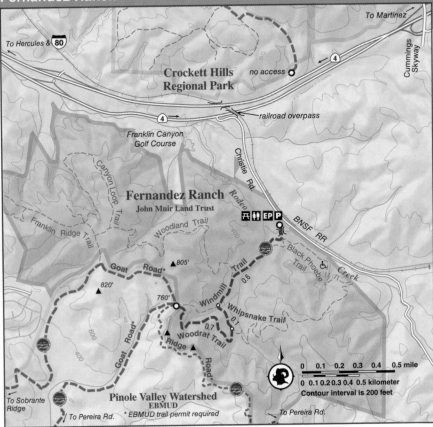

FERNANDEZ RANCH IS A QUINTESSENTIAL CALIFORNIA LANDSCAPE of open grassland and oak–bay woodland. The Ridge Trail, also a section of the Carquinez Strait Scenic Loop Trail, passes through varied habitats, and both sun and shade, before it reaches the Pinole Valley Watershed. Visit in the spring to see the green hills covered in poppies, lupine, and Mount Diablo sunflower.

Getting Started

TRAILHEAD Christie Road, 0.7 mile south of CA 4 junction, Martinez. Christie Road can be accessed only from eastbound CA 4; it is an unsigned road next to the railroad overpass, the exit after the Franklin Canyon Golf Course. Large parking lot with room for two horse trailers. (**GPS: N37° 59.935', W122° 12.291'**)

On the Trail

In 2005, the John Muir Land Trust began purchasing the 1,185-acre Fernandez Ranch from the Fernandez family, who had owned the property since 1882. The land had previously been part of the 17,000-acre property owned by Don Ignacio Martinez. After the land trust acquired the ranch, it installed more than 10,000 native plants and restored more than 1,000 feet of Rodeo Creek, which had severely eroded from road and railroad construction upstream. A large information board at the trailhead describes the land's history and all the trails in the preserve.

To access the trails, cross over Rodeo Creek on a 156-foot-long metal bridge, installed shortly before the preserve opened to the public in 2010. You reach an intersection shortly after crossing the bridge. To the left is a paddock that is used for the cattle operation. For the Bay Area Ridge Trail, stay straight on the Windmill Trail, an old ranch road in a landscape of open grassland and oaks. Just up the hill to the left, you come to two picnic tables at the Homestead Picnic Area. Foundations from the old farm buildings can be found here.

At 0.2 mile you reach a cattle gate and then start a gradual climb. You pass an old metal windmill to your right, a remnant from the dairy farm that occupied the property during the mid-20th century. Listen for the trains passing in the near distance.

At 0.6 mile take a left onto the Whipsnake Trail and enter woods of buckeyes, bays, and coast live oaks. The trail is named after the Alameda whipsnake—a threatened species found only in Alameda, Contra Costa, and Santa Clara Counties—because the grassland and oak woodland is the snake's preferred habitat. The narrow trail can be muddy in winter and spring.

In 0.1 mile go right on the Woodrat Trail. Woodrats, also known as pack rats, live in these bay forests and build large nests, several feet tall, of twigs and branches. You pass through woodlands and a few clearings as the trail gently ascends the hills. The trail enters a scenic steep meadow, under beautiful grand oaks, and then enters a bay woodland. In addition to coast live oaks, you will see black, Oregon, valley, and blue oaks in the preserve.

Fernandez Ranch is a beautiful landscape of grassland and bay–oak woodland.

You come to a gate at 1.4 miles; the East Bay Municipal Utility District (EBMUD) manages the adjacent Pinole Valley Watershed.

If you have an EBMUD permit, you can continue on this trail to the next Ridge Trail section (see Pinole Valley Watershed). This gate is the point where the two alternative Bay Area Ridge Trail routes crossing the Carquinez Strait merge: the one you are on is the route from the Carquinez Bridge, and the trail coming up from the south (to your left) on the Pinole Valley Watershed Ridge Trail is the route from the Benicia–Martinez Bridge. You can also turn around, either retracing your steps on the Woodrat Trail or taking the steep Windmill Trail downhill.

Martinez City Streets

From Mococo Road to Nejedly Staging Area in Martinez

LENGTH 2.2 miles one-way; car shuttle possible

ELEVATION GAIN/LOSS 130'/60' one-way

ACCESSIBILITY Hikers and bicyclists

AGENCIES City of Martinez and East Bay Regional Park District

REGULATIONS Radke Martinez Regional Shoreline, located north of the trail, is open 5 a.m.–10 p.m., unless otherwise posted.

FACILITIES Fishing pier, picnic tables, water, and restrooms at Radke Martinez Regional Shoreline. Picnic tables, water, and restrooms at Nejedly Staging Area.

TAKE A WALK OR BIKE RIDE near the Carquinez Strait shoreline in Martinez, the county seat, experiencing the town's industrial side, historic downtown, parks, and residential areas. This route, a section of the Carquinez Strait Scenic Loop Trail, follows sidewalks and bike lanes, and ends at the trailhead for the Carquinez Strait Regional Shoreline. A diversion to the Radke Martinez Regional Shoreline makes a pleasant stop.

Getting Started

EAST TRAILHEAD Marina Vista Avenue and Mococo Road intersection, Martinez. Street parking. (**GPS: N38° 01.524', W122° 06.925'**)

WEST TRAILHEAD Nejedly Staging Area, Carquinez Scenic Drive, 0.4 mile west of Talbart Street, Martinez. Large parking lot. (**GPS: N38° 01.066', W122° 08.866'**)

On the Trail

This Ridge Trail segment begins in the industrial side of Martinez, where its oil refineries are located. **Bicyclists** start the westward trip at Mococo Road on the Marina Vista Avenue bike lane. **Hikers** cross Marina Vista to use the paved sidewalk on the street's south side. The route parallels the railroad tracks and passes loaded freight trains and refineries. Huge pipes snake along the hillside and then form shiny, high bridges over the thoroughfare to reach storage tanks and railroad tank cars in rail yards. The sight of parked tanker

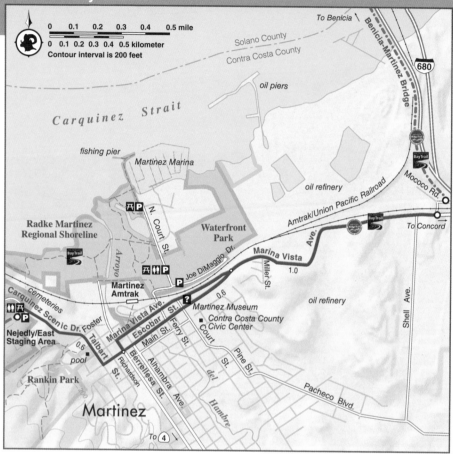

cars, the sound of switching engines, and the smell of oil refineries all create an ambience that's quite different than the sights, sounds, and smells of rural parkland trips.

In about 0.5 mile the route swings south, away from the tracks, and hugs the hillside below the refineries. In another 0.4 mile you enter a residential neighborhood. Just beyond Miller Avenue, tall eucalyptus masks the railroad view and Marina Vista becomes a one-way street going west. Bicyclists should stay on Marina Vista in the bike lane, but hikers may want to veer left down Escobar Street (a one-way street heading east, paralleling Marina Vista) to walk on a sidewalk. On a hillside to your left, the houses have broad views of the strait and the Benicia hills beyond.

At Pine Street you enter a commercial area that you stay on for the next five blocks. In a block you pass under the HISTORIC DOWNTOWN MARTINEZ sign on Marina Vista, and soon reach the busiest section of town, where county and city government buildings—courthouses, office buildings, and finance and postal departments—fill several square blocks. From Marina Vista or Escobar Street, turn north on Ferry Street to take a detour to the East Bay Regional Park District's Radke Martinez Regional Shoreline. Its picnic tables and shorefront benches offer attractive places to rest along your

The Radke Martinez Regional Shoreline, just off the Ridge Trail route, is an excellent resting spot.

Ridge Trail route and watch the waterfowl on the pond or the ships and pleasure boats that ply the swift waters of the Carquinez Strait.

When you leave this shoreline park, pass the old, wood-sided Southern Pacific Railroad station on Ferry Street and then the newly built Amtrak station off Marina Vista. You pass a park on your right at the corner of Marina Vista and Alhambra. Then turn left on Berrellesa and right on Escobar. Turn right again at Talbart Street after two more blocks, and ascend past an aquatic center and small homes of Victorian and early-20th-century vintage. Three blocks farther, at Foster Street, veer left onto Carquinez Scenic Drive, and pass cemeteries on your left and right. The road then heads downhill without a sidewalk: watch for the entrance to the East/Nejedly Staging Area of Carquinez Strait Regional Shoreline, where this segment of the Bay Area Ridge Trail ends.

◆ ◆ ◆

The next Bay Area Ridge Trail segment continues southeast from this staging area to the John Muir National Historic Site.

Historic Martinez

The **Martinez Museum** (925-228-8160, martinezhistory.org) is located in the Moore House, a charming white two-story structure with a covered veranda and double-gabled roof on the corner of Escobar and Ferry Streets. You can view artifacts from the town's long history and pick up a brochure for a walking tour of the historical buildings in Martinez. Learn about Don Ignacio Martinez, who received 17,000 acres in this valley for his military services to the Mexican government.

Martinez was the first city in present-day Contra Costa County. With the onset of the gold rush, it grew into a busy port and became the county seat in 1851. Oceangoing vessels carried grain grown in the Central Valley from Martinez docks to international ports. The completion of the transcontinental railroad through Martinez in 1876 brought the "iron horse" into Martinez. Shell Oil established its refineries and pipelines here in 1915. The city continues to be an important shipping and governmental center. It is also well known as the former home of famed conservationist John Muir (see next trip).

Carquinez Strait Regional Shoreline and John Muir National Historic Site

From Nejedly Staging Area to John Muir National Historic Site in Martinez

LENGTH 4.2 miles one-way (plus 1.1-mile return on Mount Wanda Trail); car shuttle possible

ELEVATION GAIN/LOSS 1,025'/485' one-way

ACCESSIBILITY Hikers, equestrians, and mountain bikers

AGENCIES East Bay Park Regional Park District and National Park Service

REGULATIONS Nejedly Staging Area open 8 a.m.–5 p.m. Dogs must be leashed in staging area and under voice control on the trail. Mount Wanda Trail open sunrise–sunset. Dogs must be leashed.

FACILITIES Restrooms and picnic tables at Nejedly Staging Area; water and restrooms at historic site visitor center

ROAM ROLLING RIDGELANDS in northern Contra Costa County following the old California Riding and Hiking Trail, a round-the-state trail system planned in the mid-20th century, and the Carquinez Strait Scenic Loop Trail. The route follows wide, unpaved service roads along the exposed ridge south of the Carquinez Strait to the Franklin Valley, and then enters the national historic site and climbs Mount Wanda, a hilltop that John Muir and his daughters often visited. Some short sections are steep, but the ridgetops offer terrific views in all directions.

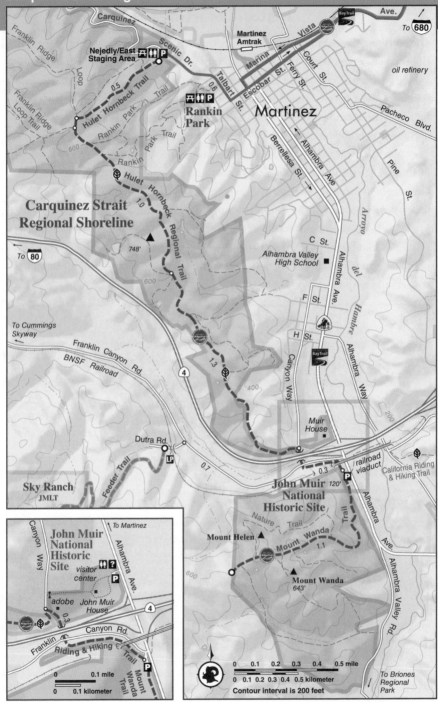

Getting Started

NORTH TRAILHEAD Nejedly Staging Area, Carquinez Scenic Drive, 0.3 mile west of Talbart Street, Martinez. Large parking lot. (**GPS: N38° 01.066', W122° 08.866'**)

SOUTH TRAILHEAD The southernmost point of the trail is a dead end, so the trail user must return to the trailhead and parking lot on the west side of Alhambra Avenue, just south of the Franklin Canyon Road junction in Martinez. (**GPS: N37° 59.350', W122° 07.774'**)

On the Trail

Hikers, equestrians, and mountain bikers begin this trip at the Nejedly Staging Area. From the upper parking lot, head uphill toward the green gate with a RIDGE TRAIL sign. The trail is named for longtime East Bay Regional Park District planner and trail enthusiast Hulet Hornbeck. The path cuts across a wide flat with an interpretive panel about Hornbeck and the trail. You soon enter a glade of bay, oak, and buckeye trees, where toyon and poison oak grow in the understory.

You begin a steady ascent, and beside a seasonal creek, gain more than 500 feet in elevation in less than 0.5 mile. You enter grasslands on a couple of switchbacks but soon return to shaded woodland. At 0.5 mile you emerge from the woods onto an open grassy slope and shortly intersect the Franklin Ridge Loop Trail fire road on the ridge. Pause here to look down on the Carquinez Strait, the wetlands in Martinez, the Benicia–Martinez Bridge, and the wind farms beyond in the Montezuma Hills. On a clear day you can see the Sierra Nevada. Turn left on the Hulet Hornbeck Trail, and at the next fork, turn left (the Franklin Ridge Loop Trail goes to the right) and ascend the hill.

From the Hulet Hornbeck Trail, view rolling hills, the Benicia–Martinez Bridge, and the communities across the Carquinez Strait.

John Muir National Historic Site

To learn more about the life of the man often called the father of the country's national parks, stop at the John Muir National Historic Site at 4202 Alhambra Ave. (925-228-8860, nps.gov/jomu). At the visitor center, you can watch a video about his life, from his childhood in Wisconsin to his trip in Yosemite with President Theodore Roosevelt. You can visit the Muir family Victorian house and grounds, with orchards, barns, and the old Vicente Martinez Adobe. The historic site is open 10 a.m.–5 p.m. every day except Thanksgiving, December 25, and January 1.

Although John Muir's real love was the Sierra Nevada, he often wandered these hills with his daughters, Wanda and Helen. From the desk in his study, Muir wrote many of the books and articles that inspired political action to save wild lands. He helped establish a national conservation policy, reflected today in environmental legislation and in the excellent national park system.

Up on the ridge you begin to get views of Mount Diablo and the city of Concord, and of Franklin Canyon on your right. To your left Martinez and its refineries are in full view. Coyote brush covers the hillside as you climb; before going through a cattle gate, rest at a bench at 0.9 mile and view the Benicia foothills rising across the strait, crossed by the Vallejo–Benicia Buffer leg of the Ridge Trail.

The view of Mount Diablo and Diablo Valley gets even better as you head southeast. When you reach the cattle shed on the ridge at 1.2 miles, pause to take in the views before descending. Kestrels may flutter overhead, while red-tailed and northern harrier hawks ride the updrafts, each bird searching for prey. Orange poppies and blue-eyed grass brighten the trail in spring.

When you reach the next gate, you can see the trail undulating over a succession of gently rounded hills. Take a minute to rest on the bench at about 1.7 miles for exceptional views of Mount Diablo. You may see the train make its way through Franklin Canyon. Franklin Ridge tops the canyon, both named after Edward Franklin, who lived here from 1853 to 1875, when he bought a portion of the Ignacio Martinez estate.

At the next gate at 2.4 miles, you're on an old paved road for a short stretch. Where the paving veers right near picnic tables and cattle pens, continue straight ahead on a dirt trail; you begin to hear traffic from CA 4 below. After going through another gate in 0.2 mile, you make a steep descent, above and parallel to CA 4, into the Franklin Valley. At the bottom, the trail enters the trees and then intersects a paved path at 2.8 miles. Go left to the John Muir National Historic Site buildings, but to stay on the Ridge Trail, turn right.

The Ridge Trail passes through a tunnel under CA 4 and comes out on Franklin Canyon Road. Cross the road and look for a wide, uphill dirt trail on your left. The trail heads east and then turns south under the railroad tracks before arriving at the Mount Wanda Trailhead at 3.1 miles.

Begin climbing the dirt road in the John Muir National Historic Site. It parallels Alhambra Avenue as it ascends along the park's eastern edge. As you climb, you have intermittent views of this neighborhood and of Mount Diablo. Dense growth of bay, buckeye, and oak trees overarch the trail. In spring, blue brodiaea bloom above patches of dainty white woodland stars. In sunny openings, look for bright, shiny-faced, yellow buttercups amid patches of low-growing, yellow-flowering pineapple plant, the latter of which is often considered a weed. At 3.7 miles you reach the junction for a loop trail, a resting spot with a picnic table. You are in an open landscape now with blue and valley oaks. The trail flattens out after the next hill; at 4 miles, veer right at the junction. If you turned left you'd reach Mount Wanda, named after one of John Muir's two daughters.

Look to the right for panoramic views of the Carquinez Strait and its surrounding cities, Benicia and Martinez. From these hilltops you will also be able to see the expanse of the Diablo Valley. The trail starts heading downhill and passes the other end of the loop trail, and to the right is Mount Helen, which Muir named for his other daughter. The trail then ascends and ends at a gate at 4.2 miles, with barns on the other side of the fence. Turn around to return, and consider taking the loop trail as an alternative route.

The next leg of the Ridge Trail begins on the Contra Costa Feeder Trail #1, a 1.1-mile drive or ride.

Contra Costa Feeder Trail #1

From Dutra Road to Ferndale Road in Martinez

see map on next page

LENGTH 3.3 miles one-way (includes 0.9-mile segment on connector trail); car shuttle possible

ELEVATION GAIN/LOSS 995'/440' one-way

ACCESSIBILITY Hikers, equestrians, and mountain bikers

AGENCY East Bay Regional Park District (EBRPD) and John Muir Land Trust

PARKS EBRPD easement, Sky Ranch, and Dutra Ranch

REGULATIONS Dogs must be under voice control

FACILITIES None

CLIMB THROUGH OAK AND BAY WOODLAND to open grassland and experience expansive views to Mount Diablo, the Carquinez Strait, and beyond. This trail, a section of the Carquinez Strait Scenic Loop Trail, takes you through two John Muir Land Trust preserves—Sky Ranch and Dutra Ranch—and along the length of the currently accessible historic Contra Costa Feeder Trail #1. The route ends at a ranch on Ferndale Road.

Getting Started

EAST TRAILHEAD Dutra Road, 0.1 mile west of Franklin Canyon Road, Martinez. Street parking for several cars on left side of trailhead. (**GPS: N37° 59.430', W122° 08.788'**)

WEST TRAILHEAD Ferndale Road, 0.6 mile north of Alhambra Valley Road, Martinez. Very limited parking on Ferndale Road. (**GPS: N37° 58.480', W122° 10.892'**)

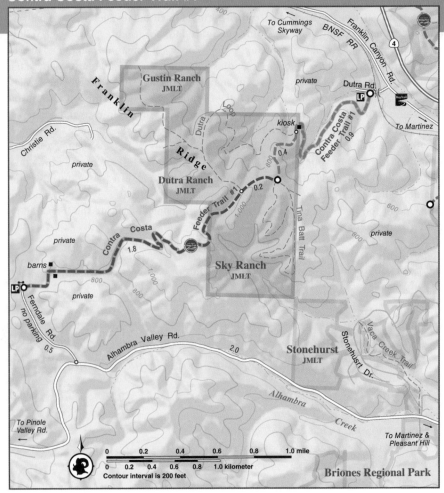

On the Trail

The Contra Costa Feeder Trail #1 was once a stagecoach trail between Martinez and Richmond, dating back to 1895. Never paved, it was named in the 1950s as part of a network of trails feeding into the proposed California State Riding and Hiking Trail. The East Bay Regional Park District acquired the public right-of-way easement in 2010. This segment of the feeder trail will eventually connect with the John Muir National Historic Site to the east, and with the Pinole Valley Watershed Ridge Trail to the west.

To access this stretch of the Ridge Trail from the east, you must take a connector trail (a section of the Contra Costa Feeder Trail #1) up to Sky Ranch. The trail begins at a green gate on Dutra Road: look for the sign that says SKY RANCH, DUTRA RANCH, AND GUSTIN PUBLIC OPEN SPACE 1 MILE AHEAD.

As you start on the trail, Franklin Canyon Stables will be on your right, and a storage facility on your left. The fire road begins climbing right away. You pass through a landscape of coast live oak, buckeye, bay, monkeyflower, and coyote brush. These hilly properties also host blue oak, valley oak, and California black oak. As you ascend, you can begin to see the CA 4 corridor to your right and then the refineries in Martinez and the wind farms beyond in Solano County. At 0.9 mile you pass a large private home on your right, and the trail veers to the left (follow the signage for the Feeder Trail). Soon you will arrive at the entrance gate for Sky Ranch.

The John Muir Land Trust acquired the 242-acre Sky Ranch in 1997. You can find preserve information here at the entrance kiosk. After crossing into the ranch, you enter expansive grassland with views of Mount Diablo. Continue straight up the hill, but remember to turn around to take in the fabulous views of the Carquinez Strait and the hills beyond. As you climb, the views continue off to your left. In another 0.4 mile you come to a junction with the Tina Batt Trail. To your left is a plaque commemorating the Sky Ranch dedication in 1999, as well as a bench overlooking the fine view. At just over 1,000 feet, this is the highest point of the trail.

This ridgetop intersection is the start of the Bay Area Ridge Trail. Take a right at the junction and in 0.2 mile you come to another gate and a sign announcing your entry to the John Muir Land Trust's 158-acre Dutra Ranch, a 2004 acquisition. Shortly you reach a junction: take the Feeder Trail to your left. (Going straight on the Dutra Loop will take you to an interpretive sign explaining the land's cattle ranching history in the 1800s.) The trail crosses a large open meadow in its own small valley, which was overgrown in the spring. On the other side of the open grassland you reach a gate, the far edge of Dutra Ranch.

After passing through the gate, you are on a less frequently used section of the Feeder Trail. The fire road climbs and passes through coast live oak habitat and, after 0.2 mile, enters an open landscape. On your left is a private home, and on your right are

Mount Diablo is a prominent landmark from Contra Costa Feeder Trail #1.

panoramic views of the Carquinez Hills, Mount Tamalpais, and San Pablo Bay. The trail begins heading downhill to the northwest and turns sharply to the left at about 2.3 miles, descending into the shade of oaks and bays. Also overgrown, this section continues downhill for about 0.5 mile, with the creek below on your right, until you reach a gate.

After another 0.1 mile of downhill, the trail opens into a large swale. Veer to the right where the road is graded (but pocked by cattle). You notice the telephone lines up ahead, which you begin walking under in this large grassland area. Up ahead is a ranch and soon you come into the barnyard, where a brown trail sign directs you left. The next part is confusing, but stay straight along the fence line to the left of the orchard. At the fence corner, a small RIDGE TRAIL sign directs you to take a sharp right turn. Stay along the edge of the orchard, drop into and out of the riparian area, and enter another orchard. Stay left along the fence line and you can see the gate up ahead. When you pass through the gate to Ferndale Road, this trail segment ends. The Feeder Trail is impassable beyond this point, but the Ridge Trail will eventually continue on the old Feeder Trail to the Pinole Valley Watershed.

The next section of Ridge Trail begins at the Pinole Valley Watershed Trailhead at Pereira Road, a 2.5-mile drive or ride.

Pinole Valley Watershed

From Pereira Road in Martinez to
Pinole Valley Road in El Sobrante

LENGTH 6.5 miles one-way for hikers and equestrians, 6.9 miles one-way for multiuse route; car shuttle possible

ELEVATION GAIN/LOSS 1,195'/1,175' one-way for hikers and equestrians, 821'/975' one-way for mountain bikers

ACCESSIBILITY Hikers, equestrians, and mountain bikers with trail-use permits

AGENCY East Bay Municipal Utility District (EBMUD)

REGULATIONS Trail permit required (go to ebmud.com and click "Trail Permits" on the right side of the page). Trails close at sunset. Bicycles use alternative route until junction with Fernandez Ranch trail. Dogs prohibited.

FACILITIES None

THESE INFREQUENTLY USED TRAILS provide views of the Pinole Valley Watershed and the Bay Area landscape beyond. Covering 3,681 acres, the watershed lands were purchased in the 1950s for a potential reservoir site. The open grassland offers much scenery, but the ranch roads can be steep in places. The first section up to Fernandez Ranch is part of the Carquinez Strait Scenic Loop Trail. There is little shade, so take the hike or ride in cooler weather.

Getting Started

EAST TRAILHEAD Pereira Road and Alhambra Valley Road intersection, Martinez. Park on Pereira Road. (**GPS: N37° 57.812', W122° 12.043'**)

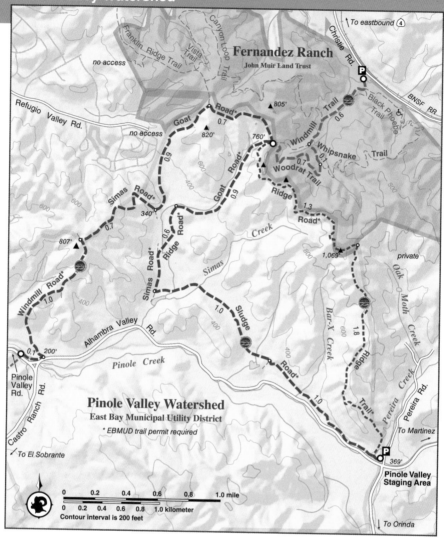

WEST TRAILHEAD Pinole Valley Road, 0.1 mile northwest of Alhambra Valley Road, El Sobrante. Park on Pinole Valley Road. (**GPS: N37° 58.296', W122° 14.692'**)

On the Trail

Hikers, equestrians, and mountain bikers begin on the west side of Pereira Road, near Alhambra Road. Between here and Fernandez Ranch, hikers and equestrians take a different route than mountain bikers; the hiker route travels over the hills on mostly a singletrack trail, and the biker route is primarily on dirt roads on the valley floor. Be sure to have your trail permit; there is a sign-in register at the trailhead.

Begin by crossing a meadow, where the trail is mowed in the spring; cross over a bridge and soon you come to a cattle gate; **hikers and equestrians** turn right and head uphill. In the spring the trail is a bit overgrown so watch for ticks. As you head uphill you see a farm complex in the valley to your right, and valley oaks and buckeyes on the hills above you. At 0.6 mile you reach a bench under the oaks and the view opens to the west out over Alhambra Valley and beyond to the bay. Just down the trail the view extends north, where you see the entire watershed and the trail making its way up the hills. In the spring you begin to see yellow mule-ears, and before long you're on the ridge with more open grassland and expansive views.

At 1 mile you come to another cattle gate. As you climb, you get better views of the bay and Mount Tamalpais in the distance, and at 1.3 miles you reach another bench overlooking the watershed and Alhambra Valley to the west. After this point you pass under some coast live oaks and have a few opportunities for shade.

You pass through a large meadow at 1.6 miles until you reach a RIDGE TRAIL sign. The trail goes left up an extremely steep old ranch road. As you climb you start to see CA 4 in the distance to your right. When the trail reaches the top it then descends steeply, just to ascend and descend steeply again. You start getting great views of San Pablo Bay and the mountains in the distance.

At 2.7 miles you reach a junction. Keep heading straight onto the singletrack trail, where you get some shade, and in the spring, see poppies, mustard, and milkweed. At 3.1 miles you reach the trail junction to Fernandez Ranch, where another segment of the Ridge Trail comes in from the right (this route passes over the Carquinez Bridge and through Crockett) and from the left (the mountain-biker route). The hiker/equestrian trail you have just traveled and the Ridge Trail in Fernandez Ranch are also part of the long-term route of the Carquinez Strait Scenic Loop Trail.

Mountain bikers split from hikers and equestrians 430 feet from the trailhead. Bikers take a left and ride parallel to Alhambra Valley Road in loose dirt. Follow the

The Pinole Valley Watershed extends across thousands of acres of rolling hills.

arrows, and the trail veers off the plowed perimeter at 0.2 mile; ride under the towering transmission lines and then the trail is on the grass until you cross a creek. Along this route, bikers will pass through many cattle gates (all open at the time of the field visit). The trail then turns into a wide dirt road in a huge expanse of flat grassland, with purple chicory and white bindweed blooming in summer.

You pass a large dilapidated barn at 1 mile; stay straight and at 1.5 miles stay straight again when a wide road goes off to the right near a large old metal tank. At 1.8 miles you merge with a gravel road; stay left as you ride through fields of nonnative European Harding grass. At 2 miles take a right at the T-junction, where the hills are now on your left; then veer right at the next junction and cross the creek, passing a metal barn and then a picnic table. At 2.6 miles take a right at the T-junction, following the creek, which is lined with coast live oaks.

After passing under transmission lines again and a road that goes up to your right, stay along the creek. The road begins ascending at 3 miles under tree cover. It gets very steep before leveling out in the open grassland and intersecting the hiker and equestrian route on the ridge at 3.5 miles.

After the Fernandez Ranch junction, **hikers, equestrians, and mountain bikers** continue on a ranch road that heads uphill. In another 0.3 mile the road starts to flatten and the views open. This 0.5-mile section is the highlight of the Pinole Valley Watershed, with panoramic views south and east over the entire watershed, East Bay Hills, Franklin Hills, and Mount Diablo; north to Solano County; and west to the bay and beyond.

In 0.7 mile from the Fernandez Ranch junction, you reach another junction— follow the RIDGE TRAIL signs and turn left down the ranch road (the road straight ahead is private). In a few hundred feet the road starts descending steeply through a saddle in the hills. Look ahead to see the road go up and down the hills ahead of you, and Sobrante Ridge is to your right. At 4.4 miles (bikers add 0.4 mile to these distances), you pass under large transmission lines and soon go through an open gate, entering an expansive open meadow. On the right side of the meadow is the edge of a large residential subdivision off Refugio Valley Road.

At the end of the meadow, you go though another gate and then begin to walk along a wooded creek corridor. The Ridge Trail road takes a right just ahead, passes through a cattle gate, and climbs the hill. After another gate, there is a junction at the top of the ridge. Here you get a long-distance view out across the bay to Mount Tamalpais and Sonoma Mountain, and to the south and east can view the entire relatively untouched watershed, and the valley and hills beyond. Take a left and soon the road descends steeply. The canyon on your right is full of buckeyes, bays, oaks, willows, and coyote brush.

At 5.6 miles you reach a gate; then you take a right at another junction. It's level for a short distance before heading downhill steeply again. You can see the intersection of Alhambra Valley Road, Pinole Valley Road, and Castro Ranch Road out ahead and will reach the gate to Alhambra Valley Road at 6.5 miles.

To get to the beginning of the next segment, take a right down the north shoulder of Alhambra Valley Road, cross the bridge, take a right on Pinole Valley Road, and in 0.1 mile you see the East Bay Municipal Utility District (EBMUD) trail entrance on the other side of the road.

◆ ◆ ◆

Mountain bikers are not permitted on the next section of EBMUD trail to Sobrante Ridge Regional Preserve; instead, they must ride down Castro Ranch Road and through the Carriage Hills subdivision to the preserve trailhead.

Pinole Valley Watershed West and Sobrante Ridge Regional Preserve

From Pinole Valley Road to Conestoga Way in El Sobrante

LENGTH 2.7 miles one-way for hikers and equestrians, 1.3 miles one-way for mountain bikers (plus 1.3-mile return to second trailhead below); car shuttle possible

ELEVATION GAIN/LOSS 585'/495' one-way

ACCESSIBILITY Hikers and equestrians with trail-use permits in watershed; hikers, equestrians, and mountain bikers in regional park

AGENCIES East Bay Municipal Utility District (EBMUD) and East Bay Regional Park District

REGULATIONS Trail permit required in watershed (go to ebmud.com and click "Trail Permits" on the right side of the page); bicycles prohibited. Trail closes at sunset. Bikes prohibited on 0.7-mile section of the Sobrante Ridge Trail from Conestoga Way. Dogs prohibited in watershed and must be under voice control in preserve.

FACILITIES None

THIS SEGMENT BEGINS in the western Pinole Valley Watershed and climbs to the ridge over hilly grassland, entering the regional preserve after 1 mile. The preserve's route is partially shaded, providing remarkable views of the mountains that ring the bay.

Getting Started

NORTH TRAILHEAD Pinole Valley Road, 0.1 mile northwest of Alhambra Valley Road, El Sobrante. Park on the road. Hikers and equestrians only. (**GPS: N37° 58.296', W122° 14.692'**)

MOUNTAIN BIKER TRAILHEAD Sobrante Ridge Regional Preserve, north end of Coach Drive, 0.3 mile north of Carriage Drive, El Sobrante. Parking lot. (**GPS: N37° 58.195', W122° 15.561'**)

SOUTH TRAILHEAD (HIKERS AND EQUESTRIANS) Conestoga Way, 160 feet north of Castro Ranch Road, El Sobrante. Street parking. (**GPS: N37° 57.825', W122° 15.348'**)

On the Trail

The gate to the Ridge Trail is on the west side of Pinole Valley Road; look for the EBMUD sign. The dirt Sobrante Ridge Road begins in a level field, which can be overgrown in spring. As you head west, an unmarked trail goes up the hill to the right, but stay straight and shortly the road curves uphill to the right. In 0.3 mile you reach a junction but stay straight; the fire roads, where public access is prohibited, are clearly marked. You are in open grassland with some coyote brush, and the hills have groves of coast live oak, bay, and buckeyes. Poppies cover the hills in the spring.

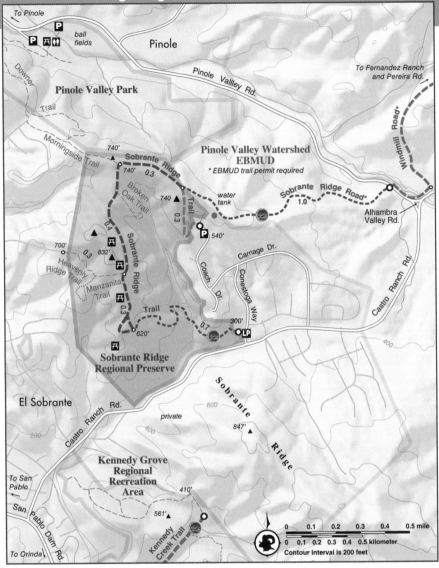

As you climb, look down to the grassy hills in the Pinole Valley Road corridor and turn around to see the scenic Alhambra Valley stretch out to the east. You can also view the hills where the previous section of the Ridge Trail passes through the Pinole Valley Watershed. As you get higher, the view gets more expansive. In another 0.1 mile, the road reaches a junction. Go left and head uphill; take another left in 0.25 mile when you reach the next junction.

As you approach the ridge, you begin seeing the extensive Carriage Hills residential subdivision below to the south. You pass by a cell tower and a large water tank (Castro Reservoir); then you go under a transmission line before coming to the gate for the Sobrante Ridge Regional Preserve, where the views are stellar. After passing through the gate at 1 mile, you see up ahead the Sobrante Ridge Trail, a fire road, where you take a right. Going left on the trail takes you on a connector trail to the Coach Drive Trailhead, the access point for mountain bikers.

The Sobrante Ridge Trail runs northwest along the ridge. On your right are oak and bay woodland, and on your left are views into the canyon and the ridge you'll be traversing. In 0.3 mile you reach the intersection with the Morningside Trail, which heads north to Pinole Valley Park. Here the views open to the northwest, across the bay. If it's clear, you can see many of the peaks the Ridge Trail traverses: Mount Tamalpais, Loma Alta, Mount Burdell, Sonoma Mountain, Sulphur Springs Mountain, and Vollmer Peak.

The Sobrante Ridge Trail veers left and south; in 440 feet, on your right, are picnic tables with superb views to the west, and to your left is the 0.25-mile Broken Oak Trail, which leads to picnic tables in a high canopy of majestic oaks.

The Sobrante Ridge Trail gently undulates over the grasslands; clearings along the way bring ever more expansive views of the North Bay, and more picnic tables along the trail attest to the popularity of this ridge. As you round the east side of the preserve's highest point (an unnamed 832-foot knoll), elderberry and toyon bushes and oak trees shade your route. Soon you pass the Manzanita Trail, which leads to a loop trail and a residential neighborhood. Take a detour on the loop trail to see the rare and endangered Alameda (pallid) manzanita. Despite the steep slope and the poor soil, the plant thrives on this west-facing slope because of the frequent fog that blows in from the bay.

On the main trail, the double summits of Mount Diablo are visible in the east, behind the nearer Oursan Ridge covered in tight rows of houses. The trail trends

Climb the Sobrante Ridge Road Trail through grazing land.

downhill and, in 0.2 mile, goes into oak woodland. Veer right at the fork and shortly you reach an intersection; follow the RIDGE TRAIL signs and take a left. In 310 feet, at the transmission tower, **mountain bikers** are prohibited on the next section of trail and must turn around. Pause first to enjoy the views out over the subdivision and the hills beyond.

Hikers and equestrians descend the 0.7-mile trail across an open slope, and when the trail narrows, turn right and descend steeply, paralleling a shady ravine under a canopy of oak and bay trees. The trail goes in and out of the trees and drops into the willow-filled creekbed that drains into the wildlife refuge pond on the preserve's southeast corner. Climb out of this canyon and descend to the short paved trail that leads to Conestoga Way, the end of the trail segment.

◆ ◆ ◆

The next leg of the Bay Area Ridge Trail starts in Kennedy Grove, a 2.2-mile drive or ride.

Kennedy Grove Regional Recreation Area to Tilden Regional Park

From Kennedy Grove in El Sobrante to Inspiration Point in Orinda

LENGTH 5.7 miles one-way (includes 1-mile round-trip on Laurel Loop and Kennedy Creek Trails); car shuttle possible

ELEVATION GAIN/LOSS 1,045'/270' one-way

ACCESSIBILITY Hikers, equestrians, and mountain bikers. Wheelchair users can access Nimitz Way.

AGENCIES East Bay Municipal Utility District (EBMUD) and East Bay Regional Park District (EBRPD)

PARKS Kennedy Grove Regional Recreation Area, EBMUD Watershed, Wildcat Canyon Regional Park, Tilden Regional Park

REGULATIONS Kennedy Grove Regional Recreation Area charges an entrance fee and opens at 8 a.m., and Wildcat Canyon opens at 7:30 a.m.; both parks have closing hours that vary by season. Tilden open 5 a.m.–10 p.m. (or as posted). In EBRPD parks, dogs must be on leash in parking lots, at picnic sites, on lawns, and on Nimitz Way but can be off-leash in open space. Kennedy Grove charges a fee for dogs and parking. The reservoir recreation area is open sunrise–1 hour before sunset; swimming is prohibited. EBMUD permit is required for the Eagle's Nest Trail; trail is open sunrise–sunset, and dogs are prohibited.

FACILITIES Water, restrooms, and picnic tables at Kennedy Grove; restrooms at Inspiration Point

WITHIN THREE PARKS AND A WATERSHED PROPERTY, this route passes through diverse landscapes and takes in far-flung views of the Bay Area. It starts in a shady eucalyptus grove, skirts San Pablo Reservoir, climbs a wide watershed trail through grasslands to San Pablo Ridge, and then follows a paved ridgecrest trail to Inspiration Point. This is the beginning of a 46-mile contiguous stretch of the Bay Area Ridge Trail to Garin Regional Park.

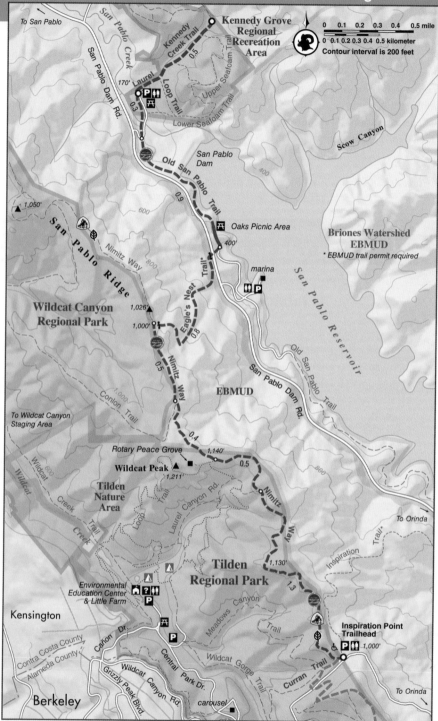

California and Nevada Railroad

The California and Nevada Railroad, a narrow-gauge wood-burning train, ran through the San Pablo Dam Road valley in the 1890s. The train introduced picnickers and vacationers to recreation sites along San Pablo Creek. Plagued by washouts in winter, dust in summer, and continual financial problems, the railroad never reached Nevada. Today's picnickers can see the wide swath of the train's former roadbed between the rows of eucalyptus trees in Kennedy Grove. The one-third-mile Kennedy Loop Trail, which encircles the upper lawn, passes picnic sites named for stops on this historic railroad.

Getting Started

NORTH TRAILHEAD Kennedy Grove Regional Recreation Area, 6531 San Pablo Dam Road, El Sobrante, north end of parking lot. (**GPS: N37° 56.862', W122° 15.968'**)

SOUTH TRAILHEAD Inspiration Point, Wildcat Canyon Road, 2.4 miles west of San Pablo Dam Road, Orinda. Large parking lot. (**GPS: N37° 54.293', W122° 14.693'**)

On the Trail

From the northwest parking area in Kennedy Grove, look for the Laurel Loop Trail heading into the eucalyptus and picnic area. After 0.2 mile veer right up the Kennedy Creek Trail for 0.3 mile, beyond the Upper Sea Foam Trail, until you reach a trail heading off to your right in open grassland. This is as far as the Ridge Trail extends now and is your turnaround point. Heading back, the dirt road goes downhill and then passes through a creek corridor with willow, coast live oak, and bays. Retrace your path to the Laurel Loop Trail.

At 1 mile cross the parking lot, veer right, and look for the BAY AREA RIDGE TRAIL sign. The singletrack trail descends into bays, eucalyptus, oaks, and redwoods, and crosses San Pablo Creek, easily forded, except after heavy rains. Then bear left and reach Kennedy Grove's entrance road at 1.3 miles. Across the road, go through a gate and enter EBMUD land; a permit is not required in this section. Veer right on a dirt road up the Old San Pablo Dam Road to the west side of San Pablo Dam. At 1.6 miles you get to the paved EBMUD entrance road and then the reservoir.

Continue on Old San Pablo Dam Road, which becomes unpaved again, along the reservoir edge. You have glimpses of the water and Sobrante Ridge above. The road becomes paved again and passes the Oaks Picnic Area. Look for the 0.9-mile Eagle's Nest Trail going uphill into the woods on your right at 2.2 miles. A short distance up the hill, you reach a crosswalk on San Pablo Dam Road. Be careful crossing here as the traffic is moving at highway speeds.

Head up the road, where a gate leads into EBMUD watershed lands; a permit is needed for this trail, and dogs are prohibited. The road passes through thick eucalyptus groves and transitions to grassland in 0.3 mile. The eucalyptus trees were planted here and all over the Berkeley and Oakland hills around 1910. Originally planted for use as building material, the soft wood of eucalyptus proved useless for lumber, and the trees were never harvested.

The road begins to ascend steeply and reaches a junction at 2.8 miles. Turn right and look to the right for expansive views of San Pablo Reservoir and Mount Diablo in the distance. When you reach the ridgetop, go through a gate into Wildcat Canyon Regional Park. Turn left (south) on Nimitz Way, named for Chester Nimitz, the World War II admiral who walked here daily in his retirement and scattered wildflower seeds. It runs for 4 miles along the crest of San Pablo Ridge, from a former Nike site northwest of here, to Inspiration Point. This paved multiuse trail is also part of the 31-mile East Bay Skyline National Recreation Trail and the Juan Bautista de Anza Trail.

You have remarkable views from this trail: San Francisco lies directly west across the bay; Mount Tamalpais rises north of the Golden Gate; the Richmond–San Rafael Bridge crosses the northern bay, joining Marin and the East Bay; Pinole and Hercules peaks lie in the northwest; and due east, Mount Diablo's 3,849-foot summit rises above the surrounding plain.

Continue south along Nimitz Way and veer left in 0.5 mile when you reach the Conlon Trail, an uphill gravel road. You have views of the East Bay Hills to your left and at 3.8 miles reach Tilden Regional Park. After the trail passes through a eucalyptus grove, you begin getting excellent views of San Francisco. Benches along the route offer an opportunity to take in the vistas. The trail passes through a grove of Monterey pines and a redwood grove that the Berkeley Hiking Club planted in the 1960s.

On the last 0.5 mile of your trip on Nimitz Way, as you near Inspiration Point, you are in the company of casual walkers, hikers, bicyclists, in-line skaters, neighbors walking their dogs, and parents pushing strollers. Soon you skirt the stone pillars at the end of Nimitz Way and reach the Inspiration Point viewpoint and parking area, the end of this trail segment.

San Pablo Dam

Built to create a water supply for the growing population in Berkeley and surrounding areas, San Pablo Dam impounds the waters of San Pablo Creek. Anthony Chabot constructed it by using hydraulic mining techniques to whittle away hillside rock and soil and sluice it to the dam site. The dam project began in 1916 and was completed in 1921, although the reservoir stood empty during many drought years. It wasn't until an aqueduct brought water from the Mokelumne River in 1936 that the reservoir reached capacity; it now stretches southeast for 3 miles.

In the 1970s, the reservoir was drained to rebuild the dam according to modern earthquake standards. Archaeologists found American Indian artifacts in shell mounds and graves, clues to native settlements in the San Pablo Creek Valley. (By 1810, most indigenous people from this area had been relocated to Mission San José; the few who remained to work on the Castro ranch died of pneumonia in 1850.) Archaeologists also found former farm sites of early American settlers.

Mount Diablo from the Eagle's Nest Trail

The next Bay Area Ridge Trail segment begins here at Inspiration Point.

Tilden Regional Park to Redwood Regional Park

see maps on p. 172 and p. 175

From Inspiration Point in Orinda to Skyline Gate in Oakland

LENGTH 9.3 miles one-way for hikers and equestrians, 4.3 noncontiguous miles one-way for mountain bikers; car shuttle possible

ELEVATION GAIN/LOSS 1,785'/1,520' one-way (hikers and equestrians)

ACCESSIBILITY Hikers, equestrians, and mountain bikers (bikers prohibited on EBMUD section and some EBRPD sections)

AGENCIES East Bay Municipal Utility District (EBMUD) and East Bay Regional Park District (EBRPD)

PARKS Tilden Regional Park, EBMUD Watershed, Sibley Volcanic Regional Preserve, Huckleberry Botanic Regional Preserve, Redwood Regional Park

REGULATIONS Tilden, Huckleberry, and Redwood Regional Parks open 5 a.m.– 10 p.m. Sibley opens at 7 a.m.; closing times vary by season. EBRPD dog rules apply (permitted off-leash in open space), but dogs must be on leash from Sibley's north boundary to its main staging area. EBMUD manages the trail between Tilden and Sibley; it prohibits dogs and bikes but does not require a trail permit for this section.

FACILITIES Restrooms at Inspiration Point; water and restrooms at steam trains and Sibley's staging areas; water and restrooms at Redwood's Skyline Gate

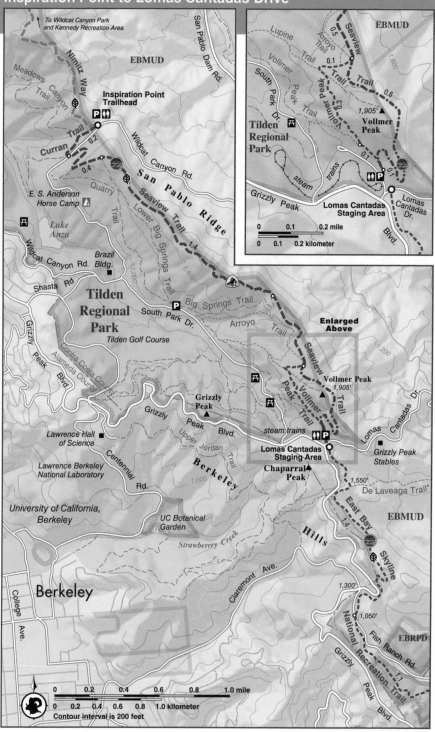

To Wildcat Canyon Park
and Kennedy Recreation Area

EBMUD

Nimitz Way

Meadows Canyon Trail

Inspiration Point Trailhead

P

San Pablo Dam Rd.

Curran Trail

0.2

0.6

0.4

Wildcat Canyon Rd.

San Pablo Ridge

Seaview Trail

Quarry Trail

E. S. Anderson
Horse Camp

Lake
Anza

Brazil
Bldg.

Wildcat Canyon Rd.

Shasta Rd.

Lower Big Springs Trail

1,000'

1.4

1,500'

Big Springs Trail

**Tilden
Regional
Park**

South Park Dr.

P

Arroyo Trail

Tilden Golf Course

Grizzly Peak Blvd.

Contra Costa County
Alameda County

**Grizzly
Peak**

Grizzly Peak Blvd.

**Enlarged
Above**

Seaview Trail

Vollmer Peak
1,905'

Vollmer Peak Trail

1,200'

**Lawrence Hall
of Science**

Upper Jordan Trail

steam trains

**Lawrence Berkeley
National Laboratory**

Centennial Rd.

1,000'

Berkeley

**Lomas Cantadas
Staging Area**

P

Lomas Cantadas Dr.

**Grizzly Peak
Stables**

**University of California,
Berkeley**

UC Botanical
Garden

**Chaparral
Peak**

1,550'

De Laveaga Trail

EBMUD

Strawberry Creek

Hills

East Bay Skyline

1.4

Claremont Ave.

1,300'

Berkeley

College Ave.

1,050'

National Recreation Trail

Fish Ranch Rd.

1.1

EBRPD

Grizzly Peak Blvd.

0 0.2 0.4 0.6 0.8 1.0 mile

0 0.2 0.4 0.6 0.8 1.0 kilometer

Contour interval is 200 feet

Inset (upper right):

EBMUD

Lupine Trail

0.5

Seaview Trail

0.1

Arroyo Trail

1,800'

South Park Dr.

Vollmer Peak Trail

0.3

0.1

Trail

0.6

1,905'

**Vollmer
Peak**

**Tilden
Regional
Park**

steam trains

0.1

0.1

P

Grizzly Peak

**Lomas Cantadas
Staging Area**

Lomas
Cantadas
Dr.

Blvd.

0 0.1 0.2 mile

0 0.1 0.2 kilometer

CLIMB TO DRAMATIC VIEWS on San Pablo Ridge, descend to wooded streamsides, and traverse open grasslands. This trip along the spine of the East Bay Hills crosses varied landscapes on trails that range from wide and rocky service roads to duff-covered narrow paths. You gain and lose considerable elevation in short stretches: a 920-foot gain in Tilden Regional Park and a 600-foot loss in Robert Sibley Volcanic Regional Preserve. This long segment can also be completed in shorter sections.

Getting Started

NORTH TRAILHEAD Inspiration Point, Wildcat Canyon Road, 2.4 miles west of San Pablo Dam Road, Orinda. Large parking lot. (**GPS: N37° 54.293', W122° 14.693'**)

SOUTH TRAILHEAD Skyline Gate Staging Area, 8490 Skyline Boulevard at Pine Hills Drive, Oakland. Large parking lot. (**GPS: N37° 49.889', W122° 11.116'**)

On the Trail

This 9.5-mile section of the Ridge Trail is part of the 31-mile East Bay Skyline National Recreation Trail, also known as the Skyline Trail, which forms the backbone of a vast trail network in the East Bay. The Skyline Trail traverses EBRPD and EBMUD lands, from Wildcat Canyon Regional Park in Richmond to Cull Canyon Regional Recreation Area in Castro Valley. This section is also part of the 1,200-mile Juan Bautista de Anza Trail, the route traveled by Anza and colonists in 1775 and 1776 from Mexico to the San Francisco Bay Area. In addition, the Seaview Trail follows the route of the American Discovery Trail and Mokelumne Coast to Crest Trail.

Two trailheads en route make it possible to divide this 9.5-mile trip into shorter sections by ending at Lomas Cantadas Drive near the steam trains (3.2 miles from Inspiration Point), Robert Sibley Volcanic Regional Preserve Staging Area (3.4 miles from Lomas Cantadas Drive), and Skyline Staging Area (2.9 miles from Sibley Staging Area).

Inspiration Point to Lomas Cantadas Drive (see map opposite)

From the trailhead at Inspiration Point, trail users have impressive views of rolling hills and San Pablo and Briones Reservoirs. Begin this trip from the west side of the parking area by passing through the stone gates on Nimitz Way and immediately turning left onto the Curran Trail. Pass the Meadows Canyon Trail on the right, and then turn left on a narrow trail that leads uphill to Wildcat Canyon Road at 0.2 mile.

Cross the road and pick up the broad, multiuse Seaview Trail, which climbs steadily up San Pablo Ridge through bays, eucalyptus, and Monterey pines to reach the vistas that its name promises. Panoramic views unfold at every step (if the day is clear) and by 0.7 mile you can see San Francisco Bay and its surrounding cities, and through the Golden Gate to the sea. The trail is intermittently open and edged by trees.

At 1.1 miles you have terrific views of the San Pablo and Briones Reservoirs to your east, and at 1.5 miles look for a short path up the hill to your right that leads to two benches and a picnic table and phenomenal views, including views east to Mount Diablo. Along the route you pass three trail junctions before reaching the Lupine Trail junction at 2.5 miles, the route for **hikers and equestrians.**

Mountain bikers continue straight on the Seaview Trail. At the trail's highest point, look east across the ridges and valleys of Contra Costa County to Mount Diablo, which dominates the landscape. At 2.6 miles, the trail becomes a paved road. Continue around the northeast side of 1,905-foot Vollmer Peak (or take a detour to the summit) and then descend to the parking lot, and just beyond, to the intersection of Lomas Cantadas and Grizzly Peak Boulevard, the end of the signed Ridge Trail route for bicyclists.

At the junction of the Seaview and Lupine Trails, **hikers and equestrians** turn right on the Lupine Trail (be sure not to make a sharp right on the Arroyo Trail, which goes north from this junction.) Continue along a coyote bush-wild blackberry-tangled hillside below Vollmer Peak to a junction with the Vollmer Peak Trail, where you make a very sharp left turn uphill. Climb 200 feet on this rocky path, and then veer right; your narrow trail follows the contour of the steep hillside, through grasslands dotted with purple lupine and yellow mule ears in spring, and offers views west over Tilden Park. Beyond pines, eucalyptus, and then bays, you emerge at the Steam Trains Overflow Parking Area. Pass through the parking area and meet the paved service road, where **bikers** rejoin the route; continue straight to reach Lomas Cantadas Drive.

Lomas Cantadas Drive to Sibley Preserve (see map opposite)

The second segment of this trip, for **hikers and equestrians** for the first 2.5 miles, extends from Lomas Cantadas Drive to the Sibley preserve, a 3.4-mile trip. A narrow trail begins on the south side of the road and leads to a gate into EBMUD lands. The trail descends through chaparral before reaching a bay–oak woodland, with plenty of poison oak on the trail's edge. Soon you see views east of the Contra Costa hills and to Orinda. At 3.5 miles, you pass the De Laveaga Trail, which descends east to Orinda, and the trail turns into a fire road. Veer right and shortly you pass though a gate and cross a fire road to get on a narrow trail again. The trail picks up bay woodland on the left and then eucalyptus on both sides, but many eucalyptus trees have been removed. Soon you get views east to Mount Diablo; in this peaceful scene of ranches nestled in valleys and cows grazing on hillsides, you can easily forget the proximity of nearby urban centers.

At 4.1 miles you come to a water tank and picnic table in a clearing where the trail starts descending and soon makes a zigzag descent to Grizzly Peak Boulevard and Fish Ranch Road. Carefully cross the road at 4.7 miles and pass through the gate to the well-marked Skyline Trail. Masses of poison oak and thistles border the narrow trail in some places, and fragrant sticky monkeyflower and cow parsnip blossom in spring and summer. Then you pass through coyote brush and bay–oak woodland. As you head uphill to cross over the Caldecott Tunnel at 5.4 miles, you can hear the traffic on CA 24 below, but near the top you will find a quiet, peaceful rest stop at a rustic bench in a mature oak woodland. Then the trail descends and at 5.7 miles comes to Old Tunnel Road, a staging area in Robert Sibley Volcanic Regional Preserve with restrooms. **Mountain bikers** can take this next 0.9-mile section to the Sibley Staging Area.

Go through the gate. The trail parallels and crosses Round Top Creek a number of times under a canopy of large evergreen oaks, multitrunked bays, and tall bigleaf maples. Then you climb a steep eroded section of trail for 0.4 mile to reach the Sibley Staging Area, picnic area, and visitor center at 6.6 miles.

Sibley Preserve to Skyline Gate (see map opposite)

The third segment of this Ridge Trail route, 2.9 miles, starts at the entrance to the Sibley preserve. **Hikers and equestrians** take the narrow Skyline Trail that begins just to the left

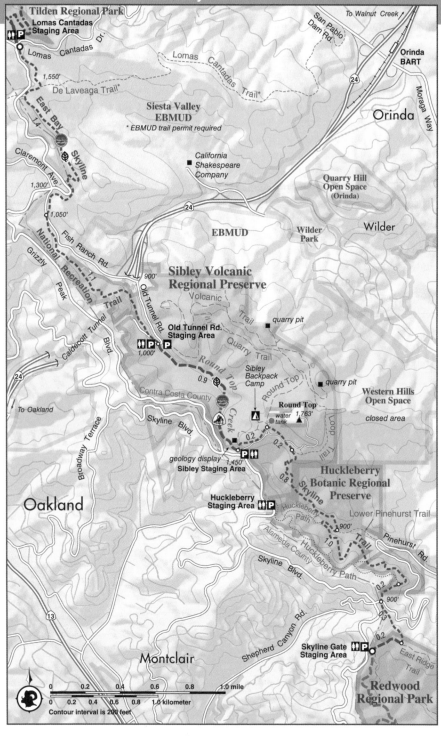

of the visitor center. Follow it 0.2 mile through pine forests and eucalyptus to a junction with a gated road on your left. A side trip on the Round Top Loop Trail begins through this gate. Round Top is an extinct volcano that last erupted more than 10 million years ago. Deposits from this volcano underlie some of the ridges you traveled over along this Ridge Trail route. Pick up an explanatory brochure at the visitor center to learn about the exposed volcanic rocks in Sibley preserve.

To continue on the Ridge Trail route along the Skyline Trail, cross the Round Top Loop Trail and the paved road to the water tank, and follow a narrow trail 0.2 mile through a fragrant pine forest. Then cross another paved road, which leads to Round Top's 1,763-foot summit, and arrive at the top of a steep, rocky hillside, where the other end of the Loop Trail comes in from the east. You descend a rugged, precipitous, south-facing hillside, where you may see pallid (or Alameda) manzanitas, an endangered plant naturally occurring only here and near the Ridge Trail on Sobrante Ridge in Contra Costa County.

At the bottom, you reach San Leandro Creek Canyon and enter the EBRPD's Huckleberry Botanic Regional Preserve. At 7.8 miles cross the creek on a defunct dam, then make a sharp right turn and start uphill on the north-facing slope. You pass a huge slide and then take a sharp left (the Huckleberry Staging Area is to the right).

Continue through this delightfully verdant section on a well-designed trail with a lush understory of ferns, ocean spray, and huckleberry. This preserve receives heavy winter rainfall and dense summer fogs. In the wet season, you may be crossing full-flowing rivulets coursing down the ravines. The trail follows the contour of the hillside through a damp oak–bay forest and then climbs steeply up and around the head of a ravine. When you reach some openings, turn around to see Round Top to the north. Stay left when you

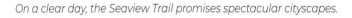

On a clear day, the Seaview Trail promises spectacular cityscapes.

reach a junction with the Huckleberry Preserve Nature Trail and cross warmer slopes in an oak–madrone forest, where you have a few expansive views out toward Mount Diablo.

At 9 miles you reach Pinehurst Road at its junction with Skyline Boulevard. Cross Pinehurst; the trail veers left behind the houses on Skyline Boulevard. Climb steeply through a eucalyptus grove, and continue over the hilltop to the junction with the East Ridge Trail in Redwood Regional Park. Turn right on the East Ridge Trail, also called the Skyline Trail, a broad dirt service road. Continue 0.2 mile to the Skyline Gate and the end of your trip.

The next leg of the Bay Area Ridge Trail continues here through Redwood Regional Park to Bort Meadow in Anthony Chabot Regional Park.

Redwood and Anthony Chabot Regional Parks

From Skyline Gate to Bort Meadow in Oakland

LENGTH 7.5 miles one-way for hikers and equestrians, 7.7 miles one-way for multiuse route; car shuttle possible

ELEVATION GAIN/LOSS 810'/1,375' one-way

ACCESSIBILITY Hikers, equestrians, and mountain bikers

AGENCY East Bay Regional Park District (EBRPD)

REGULATIONS Redwood and Anthony Chabot Regional Parks open 5 a.m.–10 p.m. (or as posted). EBRPD dog regulations apply (permitted off-leash in open space).

FACILITIES Water and restrooms at Skyline and Redwood Gates; group camping available at Bort Meadow and the Anthony Chabot family campgrounds by reservation

FOLLOW THE EAST BAY Skyline National Recreation Trail along the ridgeline of the East Bay Hills to a broad valley, taking in views of rolling Contra Costa County ridges. You travel wide trails through second-growth redwoods, descend into a wooded canyon, and climb to open grasslands. Forested segments provide relief from warm sun or fog on open ridgetops.

Getting Started

NORTH TRAILHEAD Skyline Gate Staging Area, 8490 Skyline Boulevard at Pine Hills Drive, Oakland. Large parking lot. (**GPS: N37° 49.889', W122° 11.116'**)

SOUTH TRAILHEAD Bort Meadow Staging Area, Redwood Road, 1.9 miles south of Pinehurst Road, Oakland. Large parking lot. (**GPS: N37° 46.665', W122° 07.531'**)

On the Trail

This segment of the Bay Area Ridge Trail route continues southeast on the EBRPD's 31-mile East Bay Skyline National Recreation Trail. It is possible to do the route in two sections: a 5-mile stretch from Skyline Gate to the MacDonald Staging Area, and a 2.7-mile leg from the MacDonald Staging Area to Bort Meadow.

Redwood and Anthony Chabot Regional Parks

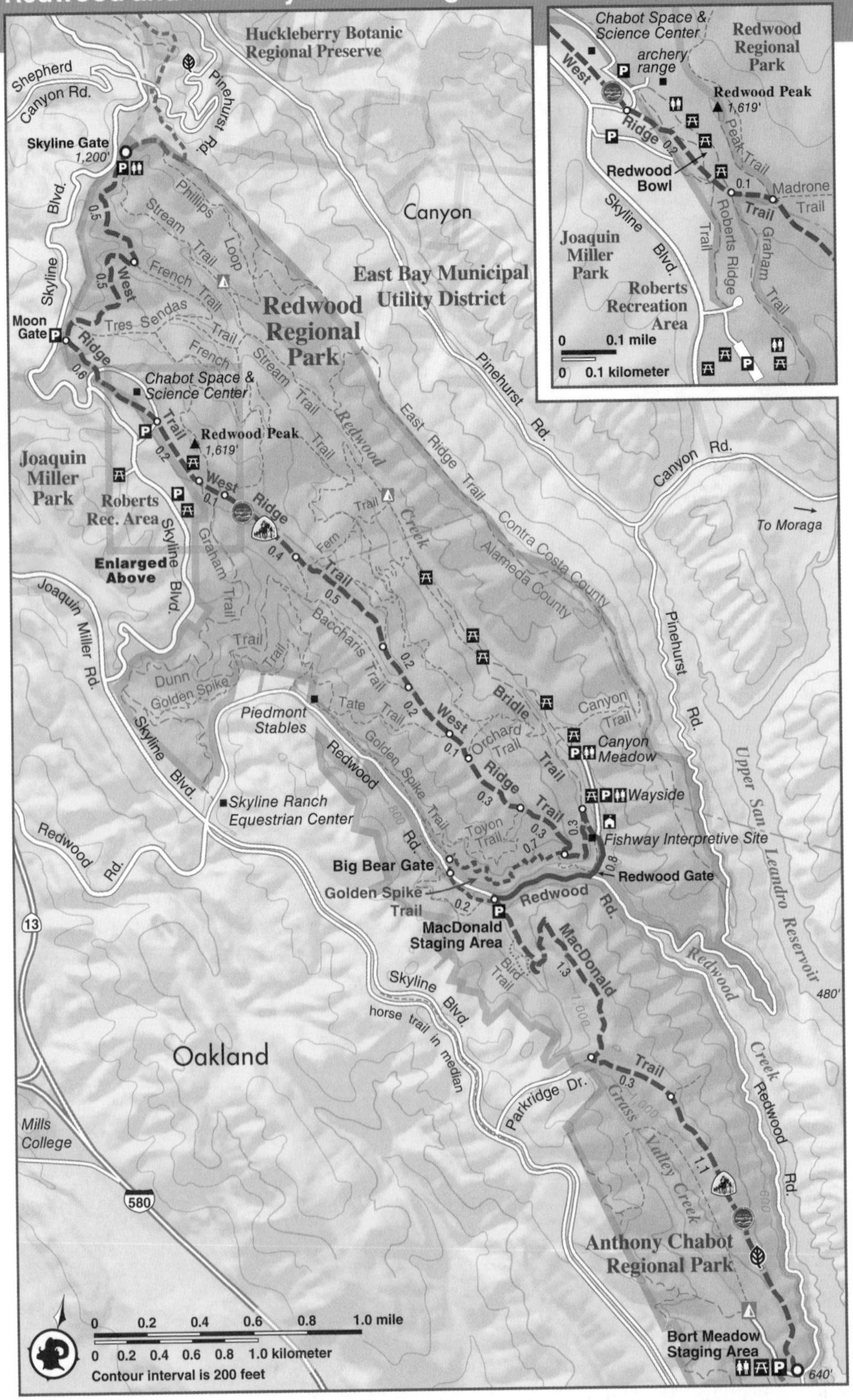

Inset (top right):

Chabot Space &
Science Center

Redwood
Regional
Park

archery
range

West

Redwood Peak
▲ 1,619'

Ridge 0.2

Redwood
Bowl

Peak Trail

0.1

Madrone
Trail

Skyline Blvd

Joaquin
Miller
Park

Roberts
Recreation
Area

Roberts Ridge

Graham Trail

0   0.1 mile

0   0.1 kilometer

Main map:

Shepherd
Canyon Rd.

Pinehurst Rd.

Huckleberry Botanic
Regional Preserve

Skyline Gate
1,200'

Phillips Loop

Canyon

Skyline Blvd.

0.5

West

French Trail

0.5

Stream Trail

Tres Sendas Trail

French Trail

East Bay Municipal
Utility District

Redwood
Regional
Park

Moon
Gate

Ridge

0.6

Trail

Stream Trail

Chabot Space &
Science Center

Redwood Peak
▲ 1,619'

Redwood Creek

West

0.7

Ridge

Joaquin
Miller
Park

Roberts
Rec. Area

Skyline Blvd.

Graham Trail

Enlarged
Above

0.4

Trail

0.5

Fern Trail

East Ridge Trail

Contra Costa County

Alameda County

Pinehurst Rd.

Canyon Rd.

To Moraga

Joaquin Miller Rd.

Skyline Blvd.

Redwood Rd.

Baccharis Trail

Dunn Trail

Golden Spike Trail

Piedmont
Stables

Tate Trail

0.2

Golden Spike Trail

0.2

West

0.1

Ridge

Orchard Trail

0.3

Bridle

Canyon Trail

Trail

Canyon
Meadow

Wayside

Fishway Interpretive Site

Upper San Leandro Reservoir

Skyline Ranch
Equestrian Center

Redwood Rd.

Toyon Trail

0.3

0.7

0.3

0.8

Redwood Gate

13

Big Bear Gate

Golden Spike
Trail

0.2

MacDonald
Staging Area

Redwood

Rd.

MacDonald

Bort Trail

1.3

Loop Trail

480'

Oakland

Skyline Blvd.

horse trail in median

Parkridge Dr.

Grass Valley Creek

Trail

0.3

Redwood Creek

Redwood Rd.

Mills
College

580

1.1

Anthony Chabot
Regional Park

0   0.2   0.4   0.6   0.8   1.0 mile

0   0.2 0.4 0.6 0.8   1.0 kilometer

Contour interval is 200 feet

Bort Meadow
Staging Area

640'

California's Biggest Redwoods

Redwood Regional Park was once the site of a magnificent redwood forest; some trees measured more than 20 feet in diameter, larger than the greatest redwood of the North Coast. Ships that entered the Golden Gate, 16 miles away, are said to have used two of the tallest trees as navigation to steer their course across San Francisco Bay.

This majestic redwood forest was part of early-19th-century Spanish land grants. Sadly, between 1840 and 1860, with the rapid growth of Bay Area cities—San Francisco, Oakland, Benicia, and Martinez—it was felled to the last tree; even the tree stumps were rooted out for firewood. After the 1906 earthquake, young redwoods that had sprouted from the remaining stumps were cut to rebuild devastated buildings. Today, although some redwoods in the park tower above the ridges, reaching 100-foot heights, all of them are second or third growth. Former mill sites for the logging operations serve as picnic areas in the park.

Hikers, equestrians, and mountain bikers begin this trip from Skyline Gate on the West Ridge Trail. The wide, level dirt path is frequented by a variety of trail users: strollers, bicyclists, runners, and local residents escorting their toddlers or walking their dogs. The trail is relatively exposed, although oaks, madrones, pines, and eucalyptus cover the hills sloping into the canyon below.

After passing a few trail junctions, at 1.2 miles you intersect a short spur on your right that leads to Moon Gate at Skyline Boulevard, and begin a steady climb around the flank of a hill dominated by communications equipment and a water tank. At the outer edge of the flank is a bench overlooking some of the park's 1,830 acres, as well as peaks north of Mount Diablo.

The trail passes through an extensive eucalyptus forest where some native plants spring up in the tangle of litter. You see robust toyon bushes on the hillside and wild huckleberry bushes in damp ravines. You can recognize the huckleberries by their small, shiny, green, oblong leaves on long, graceful branches; in late summer, you may see their blue-black berries, much favored by deer and Steller's jays. You pass seven maple trees to the right of the trail, planted on Arbor Day in 1986, to commemorate the seven astronauts lost in the *Challenger* disaster. A wooden plaque marks the site.

Cross a back entrance road to the Chabot Space and Science Center at 1.4 miles and continue on the West Ridge Trail below the impressive center. You start walking or riding under redwoods, as well as bays and madrones, then cross the center's entrance road at 1.8 miles and shortly reach inviting picnic facilities at Redwood Bowl, an open expanse on your left.

At the far end of Redwood Bowl, you meet the Graham Trail and bear left to stay on the West Ridge Trail. In 500 feet the Peak Trail branches left on a 0.2-mile climb to 1,619-foot Redwood Peak, the highest point in Redwood Regional Park. Continue on the Bay Area Ridge Trail route, still on the long ridge on the west side of the park. Following the ridgeline on a bare sandstone surface, this wide trail marks the limits of chaparral on the west and forest on the east.

At 2.1 miles, as you head downhill, you pass eucalyptus and cypress, then acacia and coyote brush. Over the course of the next 2 miles, you pass a number of trails intersecting with the main West Ridge Trail. At 2.9 miles take in the stellar views of many East Bay peaks: Mount Diablo, Eagle Peak, Los Trampas, Rampage Peak, Sunol Peak, Mount Hamilton, and Monument Peak. Before long, the chaparral slopes give way to a dense mixed woodland of oak, madrone, bay, and the occasional redwood.

Hikers and equestrians leave the West Ridge Trail at 4.1 miles and turn right on a short spur trail, just before the West Ridge Trail makes a wide arc to the left. The spur trail joins the narrow Golden Spike Trail for a pretty trip through the woods, across a rivulet, and down the hillside to the Golden Spike Trail. Here you swing left and emerge in a clearing (probably the site of a former settler's home), marked by exotic plantings, several sizable redwood trees, and a plank bridge across Redwood Creek. Cross Redwood Road and veer left on the lovely, shady Big Bear Trail through Redwood Canyon; you are now in Anthony Chabot Regional Park. In spring, white plum blossoms glow among the dark conifers at the creekside. In summer, their deep purple leaves contrast with the various greens of maples, sycamores, and bay laurels.

Mountain bikers stay on the multiuse West Ridge Trail, pass the hiker/equestrian spur trail, descend steeply through the redwoods down to the creek, and then take a sharp right on the creekside Bridle Trail. The trail ends at 4.4 miles at the stone bridge and the Fishway Interpretive Site; you then ride out the paved entrance road. Turn right on Redwood Road, and continue about 0.4 mile to the MacDonald Staging Area.

Hikers, equestrians, and bikers meet again at the MacDonald Staging Area to begin the second half of this trip, through 3,314-acre Anthony Chabot Regional Park. The park was named for a Californian pioneer who built an earth-fill dam across San Leandro Creek to form Lake Chabot. Long before Chabot's time, the Ohlone people

The view opens on the southern section of the MacDonald Trail.

Redwood's Native Trout

Explanatory plaques at the Fishway Interpretive Site tell the story of a unique species of rainbow trout, *Salmo iridia*. Descendants of the pure native strain of the original rainbow trout, these fish are found only in Redwood Creek. They migrate from a downstream reservoir up the creek to the park; a Denil fishway near the park's Redwood Road entrance helps the trout reach their spawning grounds farther upstream. Because the fish are the subject of scientific studies, fishing is not permitted anywhere in Redwood Creek.

lived in these hills, fished the streams, hunted small game, gathered acorns, and dug up many types of bulbs for food.

Begin your 2.7-mile trip through Anthony Chabot Park on the MacDonald Trail and climb steeply on the wide dirt park service road through oak woodlands to the park's central ridge; pause to look back northwest into wooded Redwood Canyon and over the vast public lands you have traversed. At 5.9 miles, up on the ridge on your left, look for two benches where you can rest after the steep climb. From the shady spot you have a distant view of the hills to the east. At 6.3 miles the trail passes a junction with the Parkridge Trail, a short trail up to Parkridge Drive and a housing development. The Parkridge Trail begins at the park's west boundary and crosses a narrow transverse ridge that divides two drainages; the eastern one feeds Chabot Park's Grass Valley Creek.

Bear left on the MacDonald Trail and round a small knoll graced by a few oak trees and many wildflowers in spring. In the open grassland you have wonderful views out ahead of the East Bay Hills, including Monument Peak, Sunol Peak, and Mount Hamilton. The trail continues downhill for another 1.2 miles along the southwest-facing ridge with little tree cover, so plan to take it in the cool hours. About a mile before the trail's end, you begin to see the grassy valley and tall trees of Bort Meadow.

You pass the junction for the next section of the Ridge Trail (at the Buckeye Trail) just before arriving at the Bort Meadow parking lot.

Anthony Chabot Regional Park

From Bort Meadow in Oakland to
Chabot Staging Area in Castro Valley

see map on next page

LENGTH 6.6 miles one-way for hikers and equestrians, 6.7 miles one-way for multiuse route; car shuttle possible

ELEVATION GAIN/LOSS 546'/870' one-way

ACCESSIBILITY Hikers, equestrians, and mountain bikers

AGENCY East Bay Regional Park District (EBRPD)

REGULATIONS Park open 5 a.m.–10 p.m. (or as posted). EBRPD dog regulations apply (dogs may be off-leash in open space).

Bort Meadow
Staging Area
640'
1.1
Grass Valley Trail
Brandon Trail
Goldenrod Trail
Skyline Blvd.
570'
Grass Valley
0.5
Redtail Trail
Stone
Bridge
440'
0.4
Cottontail Trail
Marciel
Staging
Area
460'

East Bay Municipal
Utility District
* EBMUD trail permit required

800

Creek
0.5
Brandon
0.4
Trail
0.5
Escondido Trail
Cascade Trail

Oakland Zoo

Golf Links Rd.
Goldenrod Trail

Oakland

Anthony Chabot
Regional Park

Loggers Loop
0.6
Marciel Rd.
Redwood Rd.
800
800

Lake Chabot
Municipal
Golf Course

700'
0.4
Mirador Trail
Two Rocks Trail
0.4

To Dinosaur Ridge
& Cull Canyon
Recreation Area

Cove Trail
Columbine Trail

Lost Ridge
Trail
Rd.
Live Oak Trail
0.1
Brandon Trail
0.6
1.1
300'

Willow View Trail

275'
Chabot
Staging
Area

Lakeview
Honker Bay
Trail
800
1.1

Willow Creek
Golf Course

Bass
235'
To City Park

Lake Chabot Rd.
To Estudillo Ave. & 580
West Lake Chabot
Shore Trail

Cameron
Loop
240'

East Shore Trail
520'
Ten Hills Trail
Proctor Trail

Fairmont Dr.
Lake Chabot Rd.
marina

San Leandro
To 580

Castro Valley
0.1
300'
Proctor
Staging
Area
400'
Redwood Rd.

To Castro Valley BART

0 0.2 0.4 0.6 0.8 1.0 mile
0 0.2 0.4 0.6 0.8 1.0 kilometer
Contour interval is 200 feet

FACILITIES Water and restrooms at Bort Meadow, restrooms at Marciel Staging Area and Chabot Staging Area, group camping available at Bort Meadow by reservation

EXPLORE THE 3,314-ACRE Anthony Chabot Regional Park along a trail that runs through a long, grassy valley and beside a willow-lined creek, then climbs gradually through eucalyptus forests to the ridgetop. Take in sweeping views; then descend into a valley through grassland and oak woodland. Mostly on wide service trails, this route offers half sun and half shade.

Getting Started

NORTH TRAILHEAD Bort Meadow Staging Area, Redwood Road, 1.9 miles south of Pinehurst Road, Oakland. Large parking lot. (**GPS: N37° 46.665', W122° 07.531'**)

SOUTH TRAILHEAD (HIKERS AND EQUESTRIANS) Chabot Staging Area, Redwood Road, 3.2 miles north of Castro Valley Boulevard, Castro Valley. Large parking lot. (**GPS: N37° 44.311', W122° 04.502'**)

SOUTH TRAILHEAD (MOUNTAIN BIKERS) Proctor Staging Area, Redwood Road, 1.9 miles north of Castro Valley Boulevard, Castro Valley. Parking lot. (**GPS: N37° 43.293', W122° 04.600'**)

On the Trail

From the Bort Meadow Staging Area, **hikers, equestrians, and mountain bikers** head north on the MacDonald Trail for 225 feet, take a left down the hill on a narrow trail toward the Grass Valley Trail, and at 550 feet turn left on the Grass Valley Trail. Shortly you come to a gravel road and an intersection with the service road that descends from the parking area. To visit the Bort Meadow camping area, you can go right about 0.25 mile; otherwise the Bay Area Ridge Trail route goes straight through Grass Valley on the Grass Valley Trail, a segment of the East Bay Skyline National Recreation Trail.

Pass through a cattle gate into a long meadow. For the next mile, the fire road traverses the east side of the valley, bordered by willow-lined Grass Valley Creek and chaparral slopes. Across the creek, the Brandon Trail runs parallel to the Grass Valley Trail. On the eastern ridge, power-line towers are used as perches for indigenous creatures: red-tailed hawks, which search the grasslands for rodents on broad, flat wings; and turkey vultures, whose wide, V-shaped wings and wobbly flight distinguish them from the hawks.

After you pass the Redtail Trail on the left at 1.1 miles, the valley narrows and your trail edges closer to the creek in an oak woodland; then you enter a eucalyptus grove, where coyote brush and young redwoods grow among the trees. The Peoples Water Company in Oakland planted the eucalyptus forests in the 1910s; the trees spread rapidly and greatly altered the ecology of the hills.

Soon the Grass Valley and Brandon Trails meet at the stone bridge, where the Grass Valley Trail terminates and the Brandon Trail crosses to the east side of the valley. Take a moment to walk out on the bridge to admire its huge sandstone block construction. Downstream from the bridge, Grass Valley Creek courses southeast through a tight canyon to reach Lake Chabot.

Now Ridge Trail users follow the Brandon Trail uphill as it gently climbs into the heads of ravines and around bends through the eucalyptus forest. This wide park service road is part of the well-traveled Lake Chabot Bicycle Loop. In about 0.25 mile, you pass an old trail that takes off left, but you continue on the broad Brandon Trail. In spite of the eucalyptus's dominance, the trail is edged with blackberries, ferns, and seasonal blossoms—inconspicuous creamy white miner's lettuce and white, four-petaled milkmaids early in spring. In sunny areas, you may see the white clusters of Fremont lilies atop their long stalks and the vibrant orange hues of California poppies. Ubiquitous poison oak plants explode each spring with shiny, green, three-lobed leaves. In fall, you can easily recognize poison oak by its brilliant red and orange leaves.

The trail intersects other trails, curving into canyons and rounding shoulders of the hillside as it continues through the eucalyptus forest. At 3 miles look off to your right for an impressive view of downtown San Francisco over the extensive eucalyptus forest in the foreground. In almost a mile, you emerge from the shade of the eucalyptus groves to a south-facing, sloping grassland. Head downhill past more trail intersections and into the trees. Just after another clearing covered in coyote brush, at 4.8 miles you arrive at Marciel Road, where you find a parking area and restrooms across the road.

Continue straight on the Brandon Trail; in 0.2 mile, at the intersection of the Towhee Trail, you have expansive views over the bay and the Santa Cruz Mountains in the distance. The bench here is a perfect place for a lunch stop. Look northeast across two canyons to Dinosaur Ridge, the highest point of the next Ridge Trail segment. Beyond is an impressive vista of the East Bay's seemingly endless succession of rugged ridges.

When it's time to move on, start down the ridgetop trail flanked by evergreen oaks, toyon, and coyote brush. At 5.5 miles look for the Willow View Trail and a bench on your left when the road curves to the right at a viewpoint over the valley. This is the turnoff for **hikers and equestrians**. Descending into the woods on the east side of the ridge, you wind under oaks and madrones and pass huge sandstone outcrops decorated with feathery moss and high trail banks festooned with ferns. At 5.9 miles you cross a little tributary of San Leandro Creek and follow it downstream for a ways. A canopy of

The southern section of the Brandon Trail passes under a canopy of oaks.

From Ranchland to Parkland

Once the 525-acre Grass Valley Ranch, this area was purchased by the EBRPD in 1951 and named Grass Valley Park. Today it is part of Anthony Chabot Regional Park. Later additions to today's park included the lands of Don Luis Maria Peralta and Don Guillermo Castro, who raised cattle to sell the hides for leather. In the 1860s, Don Castro's accumulated gambling debts led to the sale of his lands, which were later subdivided and sold to American beef cattle ranchers. As the Bay Area population grew, these lands became valuable watershed and were eventually consolidated into the East Bay Municipal Utility District (EBMUD). The EBRPD now leases the Lake Chabot area from EBMUD and makes it available for public recreation.

bushes and trees shields the trail from Redwood Road, which runs along the bank above this section of trail. For a short section you can watch the golfers on adjacent Willow Park Golf Course. Continue through a damp, woodsy flat; in early spring, a fabulous garden of three-petaled trillium flowers blossom in shades of pink, mauve, and burgundy. The Bay Area Ridge Trail arcs right at a fork in the trail (after heavy rains, take the left trail out to Redwood Road), goes under Redwood Road, crosses the creek, and ends at the Chabot Staging Area.

Back up on the Brandon Trail, **bicyclists** stay straight on the fire road, where hikers and equestrians turn left down the Willow View Trail. The road descends the exposed ridge with views to the valley and golf course below. Just before the clubhouse, the trail rounds the hill and then descends adjacent to the parking lot. Ride out the entrance road and follow the path parallel to Redwood Road to the Proctor Staging Area, the end of the Ridge Trail route for bicyclists.

The next Bay Area Ridge Trail segment, for hikers and equestrians, continues from the Chabot Staging Area. Bicyclists are permitted again at Independent Elementary School in Castro Valley.

East Bay Municipal Utility District Lands and Cull Canyon Regional Recreation Area

From Chabot Staging Area to Cull Canyon Regional Recreation Area in Castro Valley

LENGTH 6.6 miles one-way; car shuttle possible

ELEVATION GAIN/LOSS 1,050'/1,170' one-way

ACCESSIBILITY Hikers and equestrians

AGENCIES East Bay Municipal Utility District (EBMUD) and East Bay Regional Park District (EBRPD)

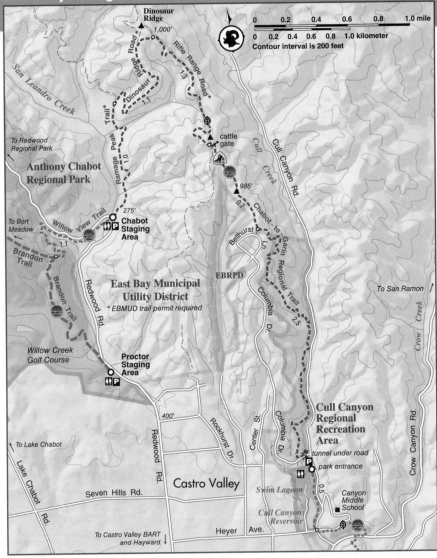

REGULATIONS Dogs and bikes prohibited on EBMUD trails; EBMUD permit required (ebmud.com). EBRPD trail through Cull Canyon Regional Recreation Area open 5 a.m.–10 p.m., permits dogs under voice control (except for the section through private lands), and prohibits bikes.

FACILITIES Restrooms at Chabot Staging Area and restrooms and water at Cull Canyon Regional Recreation Area

A LONG RAMBLE THROUGH ROLLING GRASSLANDS and wooded canyons arrives at a popular swimming, fishing, and picnicking site. This route begins with a steady 2-mile, 920-foot ascent to Dinosaur Ridge and its 360-degree views, then follows wide service

---

Side Trip to Dinosaur Ridge

The 0.2-mile alternative route via the summit of Dinosaur Ridge is a worthwhile detour that reveals the derivation of the ridge's name. The jagged protrusions indeed look like the protective plates or fins of a giant dinosaur; a closer look discloses white seashell fossils embedded in the rocks. Probably uplifted from the ocean floor during some ancient folding/faulting process, these rocks remained when softer materials eroded away.

From the top of Dinosaur Ridge you have around-the-compass views of the Bay Area: west to the Golden Gate, guarded by Mount Tamalpais; north to Mount St. Helena; east to ridge after ridge of open-space lands capped by Mount Diablo; and south to Mount Umunhum and Loma Prieta. To the southeast, your trail undulates along the ridgetops toward Cull Canyon.

---

roads along a rolling ridgetop, passes through cattle-grazed lands with little shade, and then descends on a narrow canyon trail to Cull Creek. More than half of the route is open grassland with some oak woodland, and can be hot in summer.

Getting Started

NORTH TRAILHEAD Chabot Staging Area, Redwood Road, 3.2 miles north of Castro Valley Boulevard, Castro Valley. Large parking lot. (**GPS: N37° 44.311', W122° 04.502'**)

SOUTH TRAILHEAD Cull Canyon Regional Recreation Area, 18627 Cull Canyon Road, 0.4 mile north of Heyer Avenue, Castro Valley. Large parking lot. (**GPS: N37° 42.608', W122° 03.321'**)

On the Trail

Hikers and equestrians leave the Chabot Staging Area and go a few paces along a graveled road to EBMUD's Ramage Peak Trail entrance on the right. Here you must sign in with your trail permit number. This path leads into a shady glade and then winds uphill through oak woodlands on the east side of San Leandro Creek canyon. For 0.3 mile the large Castro Valley Christmas Tree Farm is on your left until you head up the creek corridor then descend steeply into a redwood canyon. At 0.8 mile views open to the secluded valley and its immense fields, a luscious green in winter and spring.

You start climbing at 1 mile where the Bay Area Ridge Trail route veers right on Dinosaur Ridge Road, a wide ranch road. After a couple of zigzags under the power lines, the trail heads straight up the nose of a grassy hillside with some coast live oaks, madrones, bays, coffeeberry, and monkeyflower. An elevation gain of 480 feet in less than 0.5 mile promotes frequent stops to enjoy views back across San Leandro Creek canyon and the forested ridges of Anthony Chabot Regional Park and out to San Francisco Bay.

Partway up, the trail curves around a knoll and levels off; it then dips into a saddle before beginning another ascent. Looking ahead to the heights of Dinosaur Ridge, you see large white protrusions on the rounded mountaintop; regularly spaced and jagged, they stretch across the summit.

About 2 miles in, at a trail junction just below the summit, the Bay Area Ridge Trail avoids an old ranch road that leads directly uphill and turns right on Rifle Range Road. Consider taking a short detour up the steep road to Dinosaur Ridge to see the rock outcroppings and phenomenal views (see sidebar). After Dinosaur Ridge you head south. Although oak and bay trees fill the canyons below the trail, only a few offer shelter on this exposed west-facing slope. However, wildflowers—including lupine, wild cucumber, and Indian paintbrush—bloom in an extravagant display of color in springtime.

At 3.4 miles turn left where the Bay Area Ridge Trail leaves Rifle Range Road, and follow a short trail uphill to a green cattle gate. For 0.7 mile you are on an easement through private land. Your views extend eastward of steep-sided ridges clothed in spring green or summer gold, canyons filled with dark green oak and bay trees, and Mount Diablo's pyramid in the distance. You pass through another gate into an open area with a water tank and troughs. In 2018 an extensive grassy area had been rooted by wild boars. The trail turns into an old ranch road over the grassland then comes to a gate at 4 miles. After passing through the gate, you suddenly enter a residential neighborhood, a surprise after being in the remote hills for so many miles.

This is the EBRPD boundary and the north end of Cull Canyon Regional Recreation Area. Take a left, cross the clearing, and descend into a beautiful forest on the narrow Chabot-to-Garin Regional Trail. Wide-branched, symmetrically shaped specimen oaks stand at several switchbacks, immense bay trees grow around sandstone boulders, and shady stream canyons indent the steep hillside. On warm days, you will be pleased to plunge into these east-facing woods. Trailside gardens of blue hounds' tongue, blood-red trillium, and white milkmaids are early spring treats. Later in the

On top of Dinosaur Ridge, jagged rocks resemble a prehistoric creature's fins.

year wild roses show their pink blossoms, and in the fall, white snowberries hang on bare-branched shrubs.

At 4.7 miles you step out onto a knoll with views over Cull Canyon. Here the trail becomes a wide bare path through a pygmy forest of coyote bush. On a grassy shoulder between two forested canyons, you can find sunny picnic places or sheltered rest stops under wide-spreading oaks. You also find yellow suncups, blue-eyed grass, and blue brodiaea blooming beside and along the trail when in season. You then plunge back into the forest and zigzag down the mountain to steep-sided Cull Creek and the sounds of frogs croaking and birds singing. The creek is easily forded on rocks at low water, but it may be more difficult to cross in the wet season.

The trail gently undulates along Cull Creek for about a mile, up and down its high, fern-draped banks, back into ravines to cross intermittent streambeds, through a flowery meadow, and again into the woods. You reach a trail intersection; if you veer left, the trail will take you down to the creek and through a huge culvert under Columbia Drive. You then head toward the parking lot at the entrance to the swim lagoon, the end of this Ridge Trail segment. Cull Canyon provides opportunities to swim and fish in the lake, and to picnic.

◆ ◆ ◆

The next Ridge Trail segment begins here at the park information board.

Cull Canyon Regional Recreation Area to Five Canyons Parkway

see map on next page

From Cull Canyon Regional Recreation Area to Five Canyons Parkway in Castro Valley

LENGTH 2.6 miles one-way for hikers, 1.3 noncontiguous miles one-way for equestrians, 1.4 miles one-way for mountain bikers; car shuttle possible

ELEVATION GAIN/LOSS 310'/210' one-way for hikers

ACCESSIBILITY Hikers, equestrians, and mountain bikers (equestrians prohibited in hiker-only section, and mountain bikers only allowed south of Independent Elementary School)

AGENCY East Bay Regional Park District (EBRPD)

PARKS Cull Canyon Regional Recreation Area and Don Castro Regional Recreation Area

REGULATIONS Cull Canyon Regional Recreation Area open 5 a.m.–10 p.m.; bikes prohibited on the Ridge Trail. Don Castro Regional Recreation Area open 8 a.m.–10 p.m. (until 8 p.m. in winter). EBRPD dog regulations apply (permitted off-leash in open space but prohibited in swimming areas).

FACILITIES Restrooms, water, and picnic area at Cull Canyon and Don Castro Regional Recreation Areas

THIS SEGMENT CONNECTS two regional recreation areas and crosses urbanized Castro Valley, as well as the I-580 freeway. Follow creekside and woodland paths and city streets, passing schools and residential neighborhoods. This is an opportunity to get to know sections of Castro Valley.

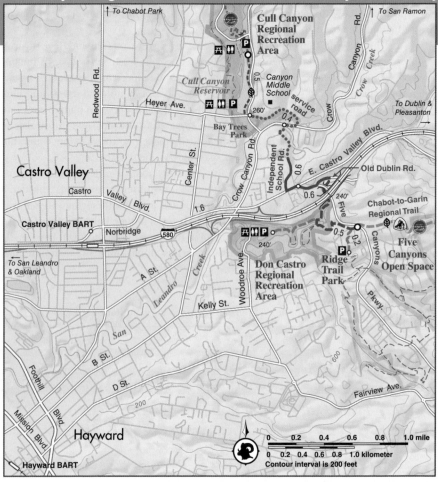

Getting Started

NORTH TRAILHEAD Cull Canyon Regional Recreation Area, 18627 Cull Canyon Road, 0.4 mile north of Heyer Avenue, Castro Valley. Large parking lot. (**GPS: N37° 42.608', W122° 03.321'**)

SOUTH TRAILHEAD Ridge Trail Park, Rancho Palomares Drive, 0.1 mile north of Boulder Canyon Drive, Castro Valley. Park on street; trailhead is 0.1 mile down unnamed paved road to Five Canyons Parkway, up the parkway 230 feet, and across the street. (**GPS: N37° 41.567', W122° 02.444'**)

On the Trail

Hikers and equestrians begin this segment at the information board in the Cull Canyon Regional Recreation Area parking lot, at the entrance to the swim lagoon. Follow the Bay Area Ridge Trail south along the edge of the parking lot. The trail then heads into the woods between Cull Creek and Cull Canyon Road. You pass picnic tables and to your right, the dry lakebed of the Cull Canyon Reservoir. Veer up to Cull Canyon Road and **hikers** cross at Heyer Avenue (this is the end of the equestrian route). On the north sidewalk, walk uphill on Heyer Avenue until you get to the parking lot for Canyon Middle School.

Look for the BAY AREA RIDGE TRAIL sign at the top of the hill and cross the street to descend on an asphalt service road to Crow Canyon Road. Turn right on Crow Canyon Road and head downhill to a stoplight. Cross the road and bear right; cross Crow Creek Road and in a few paces enter a signed woodland trail on your left. Under arching oaks, and bays and buckeyes, this trail ascends the sheer side of the fern-draped canyon of Crow Creek.

As the trail climbs steadily, the woodland thins out. Now you see straight down to homes along the creek and above to fences, some quite elaborate, enclosing manicured gardens of an adjoining subdivision. After a last little rise, you walk under eucalyptus and the trail edges Independent Elementary School's fenced playground and emerges at a cul-de-sac on Independent School Road.

Hikers join **mountain bikers** and head down the hill on Independent School Road to East Castro Valley Boulevard. Turn left; then, after crossing Jensen Road, cross East Castro Valley Boulevard at the stoplight, and start downhill on Five Canyons Parkway. Shortly veer left onto Old Dublin Road and, after a 0.1-mile descent along this narrow, paved road, look for a trail sign on the right, and head down a paved private drive to the pedestrian bridge next to a house.

Swollen by Eden and Palomares Creeks, Lorenzo Creek flows full and swift in winter but becomes a gentle trickle in summer. Turn right on the other side of the bridge and go under the high, arched span of noisy I-580. Continue above the creek on a narrow paved road under the shade of willows and oaks to a second bridge, beyond which your quiet route on a dirt road runs adjacent to, but below, I-580.

You've now entered Don Castro Regional Recreation Area. **Hikers, equestrians, and mountain bikers** descend the wide steep trail that bends along San Lorenzo Creek.

Picnic areas at Cull Canyon Regional Recreation Area offer a place to rest and snack.

Turn left to cross the third and last bridge (stay straight for the connector trail to parking, picnic tables, water, restrooms, fishing, and swimming at Don Castro Recreation Area). After crossing the bridge, go left uphill on a wide, rocky trail under a canopy of oaks, bays, and eucalyptus. When you reach a paved road, go left and watch for a trail entrance on the right. This narrow trail climbs switchbacks up a steep grassy hillside dotted with spring wildflowers. You pass under transmission lines before meeting Five Canyons Parkway.

Continue uphill on the sidewalk (equestrians use the gravel path next to the sidewalk); the next segment starts on the other side of the crosswalk 0.1 mile up the parkway. If you've done a car shuttle and are retrieving a car at Ridge Trail Park, take a right on the paved trail 440 feet up the parkway, which connects to the park and street parking in 0.1 mile.

Five Canyons Parkway to Garin/ Dry Creek Pioneer Regional Parks

From Five Canyons Parkway in Castro Valley to Garin Regional Park in Hayward or Dry Creek Pioneer Regional Park in Union City

LENGTH 10.6 or 11.2 miles one-way (includes a 0.2-mile connector on northern end and a 2.9- or 3.5-mile connector on southern end); car shuttle possible

ELEVATION GAIN/LOSS 1,470'/1,520' to Garin or 1,470'/1,875' to Dry Creek

ACCESSIBILITY Hikers, equestrians, and mountain bikers

AGENCY/OWNER East Bay Regional Park District (EBRPD) and Stonebrae Ltd.

PARKS Five Canyons Open Space, Garin and Dry Creek Pioneer Regional Parks

REGULATIONS Trail curfew 10 p.m.–5 a.m. in regional parks. Dogs must be leashed in Stonebrae and under voice control on trails in regional parks.

FACILITIES Water at Ridge Trail Park; water, restrooms, and picnic tables at Garin Regional Park Trailhead, restrooms and water at Dry Creek Regional Park Trailhead

THIS LONG STRETCH OF TRAIL is primarily on old ranch roads along the main ridge above Castro Valley, Hayward, and Union City. Mostly on open grassland, the trail offers unparalleled views of the bay and its surrounding mountains, as well as views out to the east. This section is best done as a car shuttle as it's about 11 miles one-way. Two miles of the trail's midsection pass through the Stonebrae Country Club on golf paths and roads. Because Stonebrae is a gated housing development, it cannot serve as a trailhead for the general public.

Getting Started

NORTH TRAILHEAD Ridge Trail Park, Rancho Palomares Drive, 0.1 mile north of Boulder Canyon Drive. Park on street; trailhead is 0.1 mile down unnamed paved road to Five Canyons Parkway, up the parkway 230 feet, and across the street. (GPS: N37° 41.567', W122° 02.444')

SOUTH TRAILHEAD Garin Regional Park at eastern end of Garin Avenue, Hayward, **or** Dry Creek Pioneer Regional Park at eastern end of May Road, Union City. Large parking lots. (GPS: Garin, N37° 37.745', W122° 01.755'; Dry Creek, N37° 36.482', W122° 01.063')

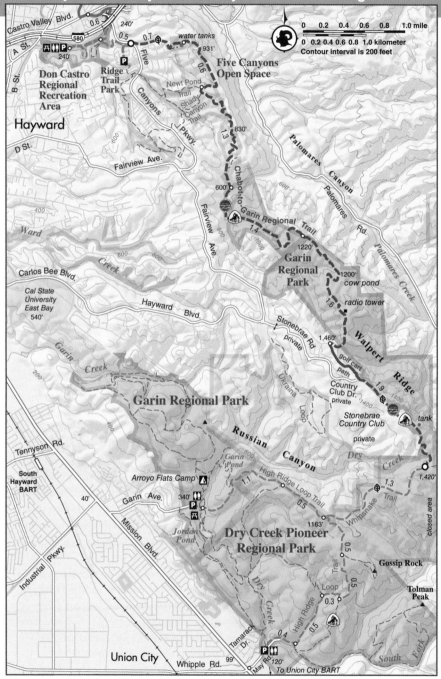

On the Trail

The easiest place to start this trail segment is at Ridge Trail Park, where there is ample street parking in a residential neighborhood. This Hayward Area Recreation and Park District park sits under transmission lines and has volleyball and basketball courts, benches, a playground, and water fountain. From the northwest corner of Rancho Palomares Drive, there is an unnamed paved road that connects to Five Canyons Parkway. Travel down this short stretch of road and when you reach the parkway turn right on the sidewalk. You can see the crosswalk up ahead to get to the trailhead on the other side of the parkway. The trailhead is clearly marked as the Chabot-to-Garin Trail and Bay Area Ridge Trail. It is also the route of the Juan Bautista de Anza Trail, the 1,200-mile trail that marks the route traveled by Anza and colonists in 1775 and 1776.

The trail begins as a road and heads through a valley of eucalyptus and coyote brush, with a housing subdivision above to the right. It gradually heads uphill, getting steeper. At 0.2 mile you reach a bridge over a culvert where you turn left up a narrow trail that ascends steeply, and in springtime is festooned with blossoms of lupines and poppies. In another 0.1 mile, the trail levels and runs parallel to the subdivision below. Look out to your right to the sea of houses, and the view of the bay and Coast Range beyond.

You come to another culvert bridge before turning to go through a gate at 0.4 mile. This takes you out to an East Bay Municipal Utility District paved road accessed from Boulder Canyon Drive in the subdivision. Two large water tanks are here; the road ascends very steeply to the next set of water tanks at 0.7 mile. Take the gravel road up to the left, and in 0.1 mile you'll be at the gate into Five Canyons Open Space, a cattle-grazing area.

Five Canyons Open Space and Garin Regional Park

You are now up on the ridge and a bench offers the opportunity to sit and enjoy the phenomenal view. You can see not only I-580 and the flatlands and hills of the East Bay, but also San Francisco, Oakland, and Mount Tamalpais. The fire road heads down from here into open grassland, where you also have views to the east into Palomares Canyon. Eventually you see more coast live oaks, bays, and sycamores, as well as willows and buckeyes when you pass a pond at 1.3 miles. Just past this, you come to the junction of the Newt Pond Trail. Stay left on the Shady Canyon Trail, and just ahead, near a large water trough, veer left (the Shady Canyon Trail turns right). At 1.5 miles go through an open road gate, passing a row of eucalyptus trees and transmission lines running east–west. This is where the trail ended until 2010, when the EBRPD opened the next 2.6 miles of Ridge Trail into Garin Regional Park.

Pass a wooded creek corridor below, and in another 0.3 mile when you turn the corner you can see the trail extending out ahead along the contours of the grassy hills. It's an open landscape with coyote brush and occasional rock outcroppings and oaks. Just after two miles, a landslide covers the road in several places and requires a careful crossing. Then the trail heads downhill into a valley, passes an old corral, and crosses a private road near Fairview Avenue. A trail sign directs you to stay straight.

At 2.6 miles you start descending into a riparian corridor of oak–bay woodland. Heading down, the trail veers sharply to the left and then to the right. In the canyon, at about 3 miles, you are in dense woodland and pass through an open road gate. In fall, the bigleaf maples are gorgeous as they change color. Coming out of the woods with

The trail heading down to Dry Creek showcases expansive South Bay scenery.

the creek to your right, you start ascending steeply. In about 0.5 mile, you climb out of the woods and into open grassland.

At 4 miles you reach the saddle of the ridge with spectacular views. This section is one of the highlights of the journey, as it feels remote yet a huge expanse of the Bay Area is in view. In another 0.25 mile you reach a gate, which was the end of the trail until 2015 when the EBRPD opened another 1.6-mile section on property it received through a donation from Stonebrae Ltd.

The ranch road continues across relatively level open grassland with scattered coyote brush. You see Sunol Ridge in the foreground and Mission Peak in the distance, and the bay and Mount Tamalpais to the north. At 4.8 miles the road takes a sharp turn to the right and ascends. As you climb, the views expand to include Mount Diablo, San Francisco, and Oakland, and the road you've hiked or ridden on for miles to the north. You see the flatlands of the East Bay and at about 5 miles start seeing the upscale Stonebrae subdivision and golf course to the west. The hill brings you up to the top of Walpert Ridge and the communications tower, as well as a number of rock piles where you can take in the fabulous view of the mountains to the east. The road edges the eastern perimeter of the fenced tower and comes to a paved road at 5.5 miles that heads down to Stonebrae. Pause to look out over the fantastic view of the bay and its bridges, the baylands, and the Santa Cruz Mountains.

Stonebrae and Garin Regional Park

A RIDGE TRAIL sign directs you left down the paved road, and in 0.3 mile you pass through a gate and under transmission lines onto the Stonebrae property. The next 1.3 miles of trail are in this gated community; the developers were required to set aside this trail corridor as a condition of development, and Stonebrae additionally granted the EBRPD 990 acres. The road turns to gravel and shortly intersects the paved golf path. Signs direct you left and you pass through the golf course until you reach the road in 0.5 mile.

The driving range is on your right and the country club up ahead on your right. The Ridge Trail is routed on the east side of the road until you reach the tennis courts at 6.4 miles. Then you will continue south on a service road for 0.7 mile with views on both sides; the golf course is on your right, and you pass service yards, all in an open landscape with transmission lines above you paralleling the road. At the water tank, the road turns to gravel, goes down the hill to a cattle gate and to the Garin Regional Park entrance at 7.1 miles. This next section of trail, all the way to Dry Creek Pioneer Regional Park, is on property that was part of the landholdings that Stonebrae donated.

You are on a ranch road that starts out relatively level on the contours of the grassy slopes. Open views look down on the bay, where you can see Coyote Hills Regional Park in Fremont. You pass a creek corridor with bays and buckeyes and at 7.7 miles get to the junction of the Whipsnake Trail. This is the end of the official Ridge Trail route. The future trail will eventually turn left and stay up on the ridge, continuing down to Vallejo Mill Historical Park on Niles Canyon Road. The future 7-mile Ridge Trail section will cross private lands on an EBRPD easement.

Connector Trails

To keep going on the connector trail, stay straight on the Whipsnake Trail. You are on an open plateau with spectacular views to the bay, as well as to Mission Peak and Mount Umunhum, other Ridge Trail destinations. The road begins descending with west-facing views along the entire route. Coast live oaks, bays, rock outcroppings, and stock ponds are situated along the route. In 0.5 mile the road passes through a wide valley and up to the right you can see the dense Stonebrae development on the ridge. At 9 miles you reach the gate passing into Dry Creek Pioneer Regional Park, an area with abundant rock piles. Just beyond the gate is the intersection of the High Ridge Loop Trail, where the views out to the Bay Area are spectacular.

At the High Ridge Loop Trail, you can turn left or right, depending on which trailhead you head toward. To end at Garin Regional Park, turn right. As you head down the ridge on the ranch road, you see panoramic views of San Francisco and Oakland, the Bay Bridge, and Mount Tamalpais on a clear day. In 0.5 mile you pass the Meyers Ranch Trail heading downhill to the left, and in 1 mile you reach the gate passing into Garin Regional Park. Just beyond this, you can walk out onto a knoll at the Newt Pond Trail to soak in the views. As you descend, look down into a steep canyon to your left with sycamores, willows, oaks and bays—the sycamores are a vibrant yellow in late fall. Your steep descent takes you to the trailhead, 10.6 miles later, at Garin Barn Visitor Center, where you can look at local farming and ranching artifacts if the center is open. The parking area also has displays of old ranching and farming equipment. The large staging area, shaded with sycamores, has picnic tables, restrooms, an apple orchard, and ample parking. Scenic Jordan Pond offers fishing.

If you turn left on the High Ridge Loop Trail, the road stays on the ridge for 0.5 mile, where it intersects a loop trail to Gossip Rock. This section is a beautiful expanse with views to Mission Peak. Then the trail descends steeply with views south to Fremont and the South Bay. In another 0.5 mile, the High Ridge Trail turns right at the intersection with the F.D. 143 Trail. This takes you down steeply into a canyon of bay–oak woodland, where you reach a cattle gate in 0.25 mile and intersect the Pioneer Trail. Stay left in the woodland for 0.5 mile until you emerge into grassland; ahead is a scenic pond filled with ducks, and numerous sycamores nearby, where the route turns right onto a gravel road. In 0.3 mile, go left on May Road to pass through another cattle gate and get to the trailhead at 11.2 miles. While you are here, walk into the Meyers Dry Creek Garden if open, where a ranger lives in the historic cottage surrounded by lovely gardens. The Meyers sisters, whose family donated 1,200 acres in 1978 to form this regional park, once owned the house and garden.

◆ ◆ ◆

The next section of the Ridge Trail at Vargas Plateau Regional Park is about a 13-mile drive from Garin Regional Park or Dry Creek Pioneer Regional Park.

Vargas Plateau Regional Park

From Vargas Plateau Staging Area to Upper Ranch Trail in Fremont

LENGTH 2 miles one-way (plus 1.8-mile return to trailhead)

ELEVATION GAIN/LOSS 190'/200' one-way

ACCESSIBILITY Hikers, equestrians, and mountain bikers

AGENCY East Bay Regional Park District

REGULATIONS Gate to parking lot opens at 8 a.m.; closing hours vary by season. Park closed 10 p.m.–5 a.m. Dogs allowed off-leash in open space.

FACILITIES Restroom and picnic tables

VARGAS PLATEAU SITS HIGH ON GRASSY HILLS overlooking the South Bay. The Ridge Trail, with moderate ascents and descents, runs north–south along the upper ridges of the park and offers sweeping views in all directions. The scenic park is a refreshing escape from the urban sprawl below. Visit in the spring, when the green hills are covered in poppies.

Getting Started

TRAILHEAD Vargas Plateau Regional Park, 2536 Upper Morrison Canyon Road, 0.4 mile north of Vargas Road, Fremont. Large parking lot. (**GPS: N37° 34.486', W121° 55.961'**)

On the Trail

Opened in 2016, this pastoral 1,249-acre park is named after the Vargas family, who owned the land during most of the 20th century for sheep and cattle ranching and dryland farming. The entrance and staging area has remnants of the old ranch, with the old barn still intact.

The trail starts near the information board and takes you up to a cattle gate. Here, you enter an open landscape of steep rolling grassy hills and coast live oaks on the Golden Eagle Trail, an old ranch road. To the left are sweeping views across the hills in the foreground to the expanse of the South Bay. As you continue on the trail, be sure to turn around and view the East Bay Hills and Mission Peak.

In 0.2 mile the trail crosses a riparian corridor with shade from eucalyptus and oaks. Shortly, there is another cattle gate and the trail begins to climb more steeply as

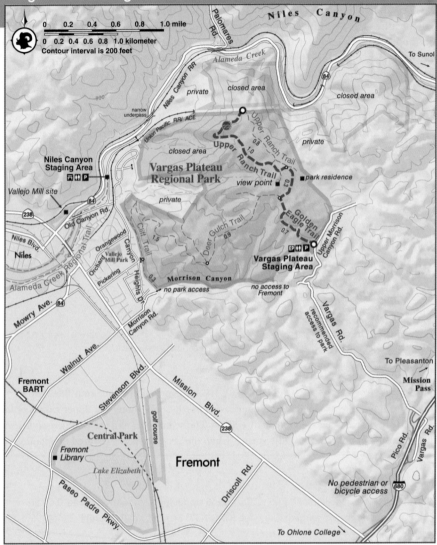

it veers east and passes rock outcroppings. At 0.5 mile the trail levels when it is almost on top of the ridge. The views of the bay off to the left are magnificent. At 0.7 mile you reach an intersection where the Ridge Trail turns right on the Upper Ranch Trail, another ranch road. Pass through another cattle gate and then head inland with views of the mountains to the east, including Mount Sunol, and a ranch in the valley below to your right.

After 0.3 mile you reach an intersection. The Ridge Trail heads left to the west through a bowl in the grassy landscape—take a short side trip up to the viewpoint for spectacular 360-degree views. Stay on the Upper Ranch Trail; steep wooded canyons of

Mission Peak dominates the view south from the Golden Eagle Trail.

bays and oaks are visible to the left, and at 1.2 miles the trail levels into a small, peaceful valley. At 1.4 miles the views open out to the bay and Niles Canyon, the route of the Niles Canyon Railway and Union Pacific Railroad. The trail starts descending, first slowly and then steeply.

At 1.6 miles the road takes a sharp turn and heads east, traversing the slopes above Niles Canyon. You pass through shade and by a pond, begin ascending, and at the trail's very northernmost point, the Ridge Trail segment terminates at 2 miles. At this time there is no connection to the north, so continue on the loop trail. The trail keeps climbing, now heading southeast, and levels off, crossing expansive grassland. The rest of the loop is 0.8 mile and returns you to the intersection where you can head back to the trailhead.

The park's inner coastal landscape is home to golden eagles, hawks, deer, bobcats, frogs, and snakes, and the ponds provide habitat for the threatened California red-legged frog and Alameda whipsnake, and for the federally threatened California tiger salamander.

◆ ◆ ◆

The next section of Ridge Trail is a 4.5-mile drive to the Mission Peak Trailhead at Ohlone College.

Mission Peak Regional Preserve and Ed R. Levin County Park

From Ohlone College in Fremont to Sandy Wool Lake in Milpitas

LENGTH 9.9 miles one-way; car shuttle possible

ELEVATION GAIN/LOSS 2,190'/2,030' one-way

ACCESSIBILITY Hikers, equestrians, and mountain bikers

AGENCY East Bay Regional Park District (EBRPD) and Santa Clara County Parks

REGULATIONS Mission Peak Regional Preserve open 6 a.m.–10 p.m. (or as posted); dogs allowed off-leash in open space. Ed R. Levin County Park open 8 a.m.–sunset; an entrance fee applies, and dogs must be leashed.

FACILITIES Drinking water and toilet at Eagle Spring Backpack Camp; toilet at junction of Hidden Valley and Peak Trails; water, restrooms, and picnic tables in Ed R. Levin County Park.

CLIMB THROUGH HIGH GRASSLANDS past three lofty peaks that top a rugged ridgeline. You have views of rippling hills, tree-filled canyons, and bayshore marshlands from these exposed and often windy trails. You encounter some very steep segments in the final 4-mile descent to a pretty lake in a quiet valley. The side trip to Mission Peak's summit is on a narrow, steep, and rocky trail; expect to see many people on their way to and from Mission Peak. Get an early start to do the climb before the day warms.

Getting Started

NORTH TRAILHEAD Ohlone College, Anza Pine Road, 0.3 mile east of Mission Boulevard, Fremont. Park in the parking structure or in Lot D, E or H and obtain a parking permit for a small fee at the vending machines. (**GPS: N37° 31.635', W121° 54.752'**)

SOUTH TRAILHEAD Ed R. Levin County Park, Downing Road, 0.6 mile north of Old Calaveras Road, Milpitas. The trailhead is near the hang-glider landing zone across from the parking area. The equestrian staging area is near Sandy Wool Lake. (**GPS: N37° 27.404', W121° 51.984'**)

On the Trail

Hikers, mountain bikers, and equestrians begin this trip on Anza Pine Road on the Ohlone College campus, where the trailhead has an information board about Mission Peak. The wide trail starts ascending the grassy hills, running parallel to Anza Pine Road, and passes through two gates.

After the second gate, take a sharp right and climb steadily up the Peak Trail, a wide service road with stellar views of the South Bay. Continue uphill past a small cave carved into the limestone bank, and bend north around the shoulder of the hill above a tree-canopied creek canyon where you will find a little shade at 0.6 mile. Then, for the next 0.5 mile, you climb through a narrow pass between high, rounded hills (stay on the Peak Trail); in early spring, masses of shiny, yellow-faced buttercups and luminous purple lupines cover these grasslands. In a basin at the top of the rise, a seasonal cattle pond sits among three hills where you might see swallows and red-winged blackbirds.

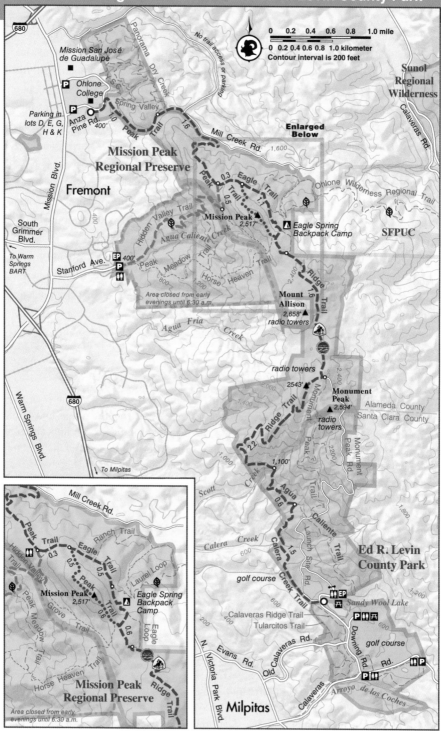

Mission San José de Guadalupe

This entire trip takes place on lands that were once part of Mission San José de Guadalupe. In 1797, Spanish colonizers established the mission at the base of Mission Peak, near the site of an American Indian village, Oroysom. At its height, the mission held lands from Oakland to Coyote Hills and from the bay to Mount Diablo.

Originally built of wood with thatched roofs, the mission church and outbuildings were later reconstructed with adobe walls and tile-covered, hewn redwood roof beams. Orchards, vegetable gardens, and promenades surrounded the mission, and extensive vineyards flourished at 400–500 feet on the rolling hills. On the upper hills, large herds of cattle ranged, said to number some 12,000 head. After the Mexican government took over Alta California, and following the arrival of the Anglos in 1849, the mission complex fell into disrepair; an earthquake further damaged the buildings in 1868.

Today, the refurbished mission church and a museum lie just north of Ohlone College, and the campus occupies some of the former mission gardens, promenades, and orchards. Mission Boulevard approximates the trail that the Spanish explorers and mission padres traveled between the Santa Clara and San José Missions. Some of the gnarled, gray-leafed olive trees lining the route remain from the mission plantings.

Bear right at 1.2 miles under evergreen oak and bay trees to follow the Peak Trail, which parallels Mill Creek Road to the left. When you emerge from the woods in 0.4 mile, a large house sits on the hill to your left and your vista takes in the grassy hills and tree-filled canyons that form the drainage of Mission Creek, which once powered the grist mill at Mission San José. Walk through a scenic meadow and take a U-turn up a gravelly road.

You begin a climb up the north shoulder of Mission Peak with views east to Sunol and Brushy Peaks. In springtime, watch for the hairy, curled necks of white phacelia peeking out of narrow crevices in a jumble of lichen-splashed rocks. Masses of yellow fiddlenecks crowd the surrounding fields. As the trail ascends the ridge, the shear, scarred west face of Mission Peak appears above you, dropping abruptly to the valley below.

The Peak Trail meets the Hidden Valley Trail in an open saddle at 2.6 miles, where there is a toilet. The 2.4-mile Hidden Valley Trail begins from the Stanford Avenue Staging Area. Drainage from Mission Peak and the surrounding high plateau flows into Agua Caliente Creek, which runs down the east side of Hidden Valley. In the Spanish era, an aqueduct carried warm water from this creek to Mission San José for laundering and bathing.

Veer left at the junction of the Hidden Valley and Peak Trails and ascend 0.25 mile to the Eagle Trail. Stay on the Eagle Trail around the peak's east side, and take in the spectacular views of the East Bay Hills. You reach the intersection for the trail up to Mission Peak, but the Bay Area Ridge Trail stays straight on the Eagle Trail (see page 205 for Mission Peak detour). The fire road undulates over the beautiful rolling hills;

most hikers take the trail up to the peak so now you're only sharing the hillsides with the cattle.

At 3.4 miles you reach the EBRPD Eagle Spring Backpack Camp, where you can get water and use a picnic table and toilet. Keep climbing, and in 0.2 mile you'll crest the ridge to the south of Mission Peak. Take a rest here to enjoy the awesome view of the bay and Coast Range. Keep traveling south along the open ridge and pass though a gate where the Eagle Loop Trail intersects the Bay Area Ridge Trail at 4 miles.

The road veers to the left, and on a gradual climb through grassland, it passes remnants of rock walls. These hills contain many rock walls that archaeologists are now mapping, and the debate continues over when they were built and who built them. The Spanish recorded that the hills "abounded in rocks which could be easily transported" to building sites. Here, too, lie some of the springs that the Spanish reported.

At 4.3 miles you come to a junction; veer left and, in 0.2 mile, cross a paved road, heading toward Monument Peak. You curve around the east side of 2,658-foot Mount Allison, the highest point on this three-peak trip. To the east, you may see the Ohlone Wilderness Trail on the west face of 3,817-foot Rose Peak on Valpe Ridge. It feels remote in this section, with the panorama of hills and mountains to your east.

For more than a mile, you travel through a high valley between Mount Allison and Monument Peak, both bristling with tall communication towers. Serpentine outcrops are scattered here. The trail surmounts a small rise and at 5.5 miles comes to a gravel road. Turning left takes you up to Monument Peak, but to stay on the Ridge Trail turn right on the Agua Caliente Trail, and take the gravel road toward the communication tower on the ridge.

In 0.2 mile you reach the Ridge Trail junction, but before you descend take in the view of the bay and Santa Clara Valley below. In the South Bay, you see the salt

Hikers descend the Eagle Trail after summiting Mission Peak.

ponds, tinged shades of blue-green to rosy lavender, and the marshes, sloughs, mud flats, and open waters of Don Edwards San Francisco Bay National Wildlife Refuge. Due west, Jarvis Landing, an important grain and hide shipping port in the 1800s, was located on the shoreline. The expanding communities of Fremont, Milpitas, and Newark stretch from the foothills to the bay.

Start down the trail, a mowed ranch road, and enjoy the views. It descends steeply, and over the next 4 miles, you lose more than 2,000 feet in elevation. Caught between the Hayward and Calaveras faults, these hills were uplifted through the eons by fault movement. Rocky knobs dotting the hillsides are the remains of sedimentary deposits formed as the Pacific Plate slid northward along the edge of North America some 15 million years ago.

A multitrunked bay tree grows in a heap of boulders at a wide switchback, casting welcome shade on a southwest-facing slope. Although the steepness of the trail requires your close attention, pause occasionally to glance skyward for turkey vultures and red-tailed hawks wheeling on the updrafts, or for the golden eagles known to soar over these still-wild lands.

Spring wildflowers bloom in rainbow hues, from magenta redmaids and frilly pink checkerblooms to yellow buttercups, tiny baby blue eyes, and tall purple brodiaea. Great swaths of orange California poppies glow on south-facing hillsides. By early summer, the drying grasses turn golden, contrasting with the dark-green oaks that fill the lower canyons, nourished by Agua Fria, Toroges, Scott, Calera, and other small, unnamed creeks. At 7 miles you pass through fields of invasive milk thistle.

Continue to descend the rounded shoulders of the hills and reach the wooded banks of Scott Creek, the Alameda–Santa Clara County boundary and the entrance to Ed

A group of adventurers gathers at Mission Peak.

Hiker Side Trip to Mission Peak

Hikers have two options for a short detour to the summit of 2,517-foot Mission Peak; whichever one you choose, be sure to make the less-than-0.5-mile ascent. From the junction of the Eagle and Peak Trails, hikers can stay on the Peak Trail to climb the eroded, rocky flank of Mission Peak. The other option is to follow the Eagle Trail around the peak's east side and veer right at the second junction of the Eagle and Peak Trails to ascend the peak's south flank.

If the day is clear, you have views of prominent peaks around the Bay Area—west to Loma Prieta, north to Mount Tamalpais, east to Mount Diablo, and south to Mount Hamilton. On a tall post a few feet north of the summit, directional sighting holes point to other important Bay Area landmarks.

R. Levin County Park. In Levin Park, the Bay Area Ridge Trail follows the Agua Caliente Trail then turns right at Calera Creek onto the Calera Creek Trail. Below are ranch buildings and a catch basin for watering cattle. The road descends steeply and then parallels Calera Creek. Lofty sycamore trees line the creekside, their gray-and-white-patterned bark mimicking the shades of the limestone deposits for which this creek is named. The Spaniards, and later the Mexican settlers, burned this stone in kilns to make mortar and whitewash for their adobes.

Now on a less-precipitous route, you cross Calera Creek and stay close enough to its banks to hear the rushing water and to appreciate the afternoon shade from trees along the trail. You leave the main creek and enter fields filled with brilliant yellow mustard in spring. At 9 miles pass a service road but stay straight; shortly you pass through a gate, and then the trail follows the fence before veering right toward large homes in the Milpitas hills. The trail passes above a golf course and comes to a paved road at 9.5 miles. Stay left on the road and come to a gate at Launch Site Road. Once through the gate, go right and head toward the parking lot. You skirt a landing field where, especially on weekends, brightly colored hang-gliders alight after their flight from the hills above. Just beyond are the picnic tables and greensward beside the blue waters of Sandy Wool Lake, a cool, refreshing finishing point. The trail segment ends at the parking lot after 9.9 miles.

The next Bay Area Ridge Trail segment begins about 8 miles south at the Penitencia Creek Trail in San José.

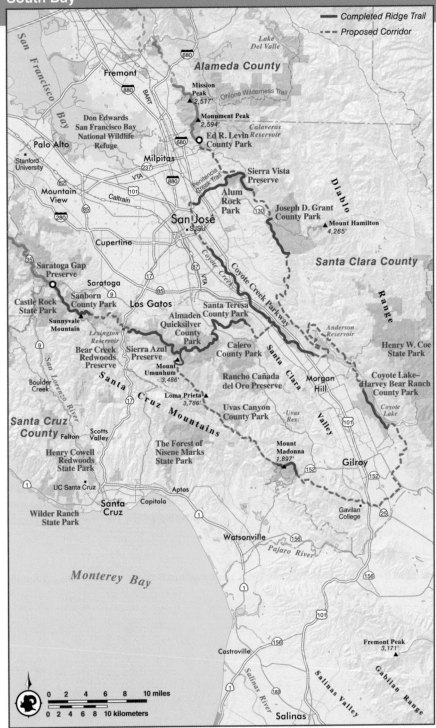

SOUTH BAY

Penitencia Creek

From North King Road to Rock Canyon Circle in San José

LENGTH 3.7 miles one-way (3.9 miles from Berryessa/North San José BART station, scheduled to open in 2019); car shuttle possible

ELEVATION GAIN 180' one-way

ACCESSIBILITY Hikers, equestrians, and mountain hikers

AGENCIES County of Santa Clara, City of San José, Santa Clara Valley Water District

PARKS Penitencia Creek Parkway, Penitencia Creek Gardens, Penitencia Creek Park

REGULATIONS Penitencia Creek Park open 8 a.m.–sunset.; dogs must be leashed

FACILITIES Restrooms and picnic tables in Penitencia Creek Gardens and Penitencia Creek Park

THIS 3.7-MILE LINEAR PARKWAY TRAIL crosses San José neighborhoods and ends at the eastern edge of the Santa Clara Valley. Mostly paved, the trail follows Penitencia Creek, a tributary of Coyote Creek, which flows down from Sierra Vista Open Space Preserve and Alum Rock Park. In total, Penitencia Creek Parkway covers 134 acres and passes through two sizable parks: Penitencia Creek Gardens and Penitencia Creek Park. It makes an excellent bike ride through urban San José.

Getting Started

WEST TRAILHEAD North King Road, about 400 feet south of Commodore Drive, San José. Street parking. (**GPS: N37° 22.211', W121° 52.286'**) *Fall 2019 and thereafter:* Berryessa/North San José BART Station, 1620 Berryessa Road, San José. BART station parking. (**GPS: N37° 22.230', W121° 52.452'**)

EAST TRAILHEAD Penitencia Creek Road and Rock Canyon Circle intersection, San José. Street parking. (**GPS: N37° 23.696', W121° 49.723'**)

On the Trail

The Penitencia Creek Parkway was dedicated as Ridge Trail in 2008 after several decades of planning and construction. The trail begins at the Berryessa/North San José BART station and heads west for 0.2 mile to North King Road; this short section, however, is scheduled to open with the station in fall 2019. So until then, start at North King Road and enter through the stone pillars at the parkway entrance. The dirt trail runs on the right side of the creek, with an undeveloped lot on the right. Halfway to Mabury Road, you pass a residential complex on your right and, in 0.3 mile, you reach Mabury Road, a major thoroughfare. Take a left and head down the sidewalk.

In another 0.3 mile, you reach the entrance to Penitencia Creek Gardens, a park completed in the early 1990s. Take a left into the park and go straight, following the outer loop trail and RIDGE TRAIL signs. The paved path follows the creek and passes picnic tables, benches, mature trees, and a large pond, a stop on the migratory flyway for a number of species. At the intersection where the restrooms and interpretive panels are located, stay left on the paved path that heads out of the park.

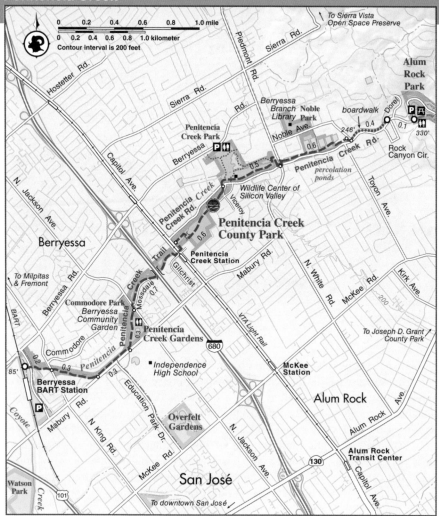

At Jackson Avenue, take a left at the sidewalk and cross at the crosswalk. Look for the RIDGE TRAIL sign at the Mossdale entrance to Penitencia Creek County Park. As you travel down the paved trail, which parallels Mossdale Way, the creek is on your left, lined with walnut and eucalyptus trees. The trail veers to the left at Gateview Drive and with a low clearance, passes under I-680. The trail then follows the creek in an undeveloped oak woodland; it veers right when you get to Capitol Avenue, a major street. The Penitencia Creek VTA Light Rail Station is located here. Go right and cross at Gilchrist Drive; then take a left to get back to the trail.

At 1.6 miles you're at the corner of Capitol Avenue and Penitencia Creek Road. The trail turns right just before Penitencia Creek Road—this is where the landscape opens with an expansive field to your right and a view of the Diablo Range in front of you. After crossing a bridge, the field continues with the creek on your left, edged by

Penitencia Creek Parkway feels more rural east of Capitol Avenue.

willows, eucalyptus, oaks, and walnut trees. This stretch is a welcome relief from the subdivisions you've passed through, yet there are more subdivisions up ahead. The trail comes to Viceroy Way: turn left and when you reach Penitencia Creek Road, cross to Penitencia Creek Park, and then stay right on the Penitencia Creek Trail. From the trail you can see the park's large open field, and you can use the restrooms and picnic tables.

The trail skirts the southern edge of the park, paralleling the creek and passing by buckeyes, oaks, sycamores, and pines, as well as the Wildlife Center of Silicon Valley. You come into a large open field and then go back into the trees, where you pass an old house leased by Santa Clara County Parks. At 2.6 miles you reach Piedmont Road, a major street. Cross the road and follow the sign for the creek trail. You're on a gravel path with fences on either side. After crossing a bridge, look for percolation ponds on your left. You are getting close to the eastern edge of the Santa Clara Valley, with the hills ahead. Keep veering right and you reach Noble Avenue. Take a right and then a left on the paved path running along Penitencia Creek Road. Pass over stretches of boardwalk (bicyclists must dismount), and under sycamores, willows, walnuts, and buckeyes, and head uphill. The Ridge Trail ends at Rock Canyon Circle, where you can read interpretive panels and rest on a bench.

◆ ◆ ◆

There is a short 0.1-mile Ridge Trail gap on Penitencia Creek Road before you reach the next segment in Alum Rock Park.

Alum Rock Park and Sierra Vista Open Space Preserve

see map on next page

From Alum Rock Entrance to Sierra Road Staging Area in San José

LENGTH 3.9 miles one-way; car shuttle possible

ELEVATION GAIN/LOSS 1,775'/205' one-way

ACCESSIBILITY Hikers, equestrians, and mountain bikers

AGENCIES City of San José and Santa Clara Valley Open Space Authority

REGULATIONS Alum Rock Park and Sierra Vista Open Space Preserve open 8 a.m.–30 minutes after sunset daily. Dogs prohibited. Alum Rock charges an entrance fee.

FACILITIES Water and restrooms at Alum Rock Park

BEGIN IN A CREEK CORRIDOR and climb to high ridges on the east side of the Santa Clara Valley for a bird's-eye view of nearby San José, the South Bay, and the Peninsula. The steep trail winds up a grassy, southwest-facing hillside. Because of the sun exposure, the trip is best done with an early start on cool spring days or midday in winter, when skies are clear after rains.

Getting Started

WEST TRAILHEAD Alum Rock Park, Penitencia Creek Road, 0.2 mile east of Dorel Drive, San José. Park in lot to left of road before gate. (**GPS: N37° 23.724', W121° 49.517'**)

EAST TRAILHEAD Sierra Road Staging Area, Sierra Road, 3.7 miles east of Piedmont Road, San José. Large parking lot. (**GPS: N37° 24.528', W121° 48.057'**)

On the Trail

All trail users start on the Creek Trail in Alum Rock Park, which begins steeply on a wide trail, then narrows and levels as it travels through the wooded Penitencia Creek corridor. In 0.6 mile it enters the Quail Hollow Creek Picnic Area then crosses the creek into a parking lot. Look for the Ridge Trail on the other side of the road. Head up this trail 0.1 mile, take a sharp left on the Lariat Trail, and then a sharp right on the North Rim Trail.

As you ascend the wide North Rim Trail, the grassy mountaintops in Sierra Vista Open Space Preserve rise ahead and the wooded Alum Rock Canyon is to your right below. In spring the hills are green and yellow, covered in yellow mustard. At 1.1 miles veer right; then turn right at the trail junction and descend for a short section—passing two picnic tables—and at 1.4 miles take a left at the Todd Quick Trail.

On the way up, enjoy views to downtown San José and the Santa Cruz Mountains. You pass through palm and pepper trees, and evidence of a recent fire. Switchbacking up the hill, the trail narrows to a singletrack. At the Todd Quick Rest Area, 0.6 mile from the junction, enjoy a rest at the picnic table under the eucalyptus trees; then go through the green gate to the wide Boccardo Loop Trail.

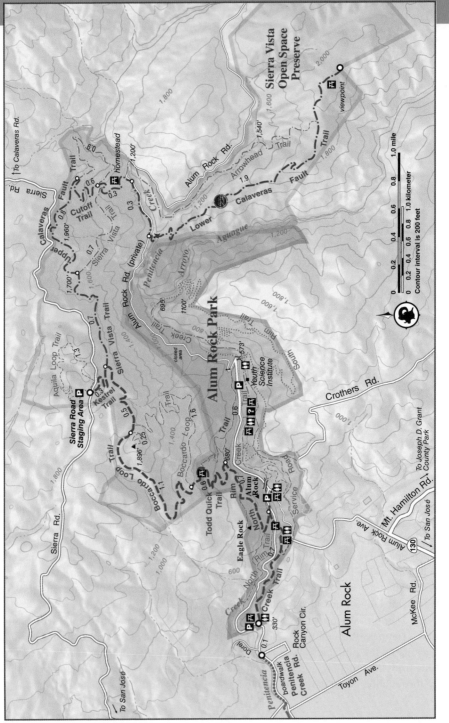

You are now in the Sierra Vista Open Space Preserve, where you'll find an information board about the preserve. Note the sandstone boulder that is embedded with a dedication to the Boccardo family, who helped fund the purchase of this beautiful open ranchland. Look to the left for fabulous views of the Santa Clara Valley. In spring, you may hear the cheery, lilting song of red-winged blackbirds calling to their mates from perches on the mustard. Listen, too, for the meadowlarks' trilling song from their nests hidden in the grass.

The trail heads uphill through grassland, and plenty of milk thistle, and reaches the Boccardo Loop intersection at 2 miles. The Ridge Trail route goes straight and widens to a ranch road, rising steeply. In 0.2 mile, when rounding a bend, you traverse a south-facing shoulder of the hill for a fantastic view of the South Bay, and a direct view to downtown San José. In another 0.2 mile, as you curve around the top of a west-facing prominence on a long, rounded ridge, you get even wider views where you can see farther north. Sit on the bench to determine where the Ridge Trail route travels in the South Bay, including Joseph D. Grant County Park, Mount Madonna County Park, Santa Teresa County Park, and Almaden Quicksilver County Park.

The trail turns east and you begin a steady uphill climb up the ridge. On your left, a sheer bank clothed with trees drops into a tight ravine. Spring wildflowers bloom in abundance on either side of the trail. Golden poppies and yellow mule ears stand tall and bright, but you may need to search for the reddish-purple tomcat clover among the grasses; lupine and blue-eyed grass complete the show. Later in spring, you may find yellow mariposa lilies waving on tall stems, intermixed with deep blue brodiaea. In summer and fall, this route is redolent with the fragrance of California sagebrush, which covers the slope down the canyon.

After passing through an open field, you enter an oak, bay, and buckeye forest, forming a veritable tunnel for a brief stretch. Then you emerge in a small valley where, in early spring, shiny buttercups paint the hills yellow. Off to your left, a carpet of brilliant orange poppies covers a west-facing slope. At 3.1 miles take the 0.25-mile spur to the hill's summit as a side trip. From the top you can see north to San Francisco with Mount Tamalpais rising beyond it, and south to Mount Hamilton topped by its observatories. West lie the Santa Cruz Mountains surmounted by Loma Prieta and Mount Umunhum. At your feet is the trail you just climbed and the tree-filled canyon of Alum Rock Park. On the broad bay plain, the sprawling metropolis of San José stretches south to Coyote Valley and north to the edge of San Francisco Bay.

The strong winds that often sweep this hill offer challenges to raptors. Updrafts provide the loft these big birds need to glide on their 3- to 6-foot wingspan. You can identify a red-tailed hawk by its rusty-red tail feathers. Other "frequent flyers" include turkey vultures and red-shouldered hawks; an occasional golden eagle also soars here.

After savoring the summit views, head back down to the Ridge Trail. Just ahead is the intersection for the Sierra Vista Trail and a view of Mount Hamilton. Here you can look into the steep, rugged canyons of Penitencia Creek and Arroyo Aguague. Penitencia Creek begins in the hills east of Alum Rock Park, and Arroyo Aguague flows north from the heights of Joseph D. Grant County Park to join Penitencia Creek at the northeast end of Alum Rock's Penitencia Creek Trail.

The Boccardo Loop Trail heads down to the right; turn left up the Sierra Vista Trail and pass though a gate. Now on a well-designed, relatively level singletrack trail,

The North Rim Trail in Alum Rock Park heads toward Sierra Vista Open Space Preserve.

keep turning around for beautiful views of the Boccardo Loop Trail descending the grassy hillsides. You pass rock outcroppings and see the next segment of the Ridge Trail up on the ridges in front of you. Notice the old rock walls running up the hill perpendicular to the trail. At 3.6 miles you reach the intersection of the Kestrel Trail; the Sierra Road Staging Area is another 0.25 mile up the hill. You can end your hike at the Sierra Road Staging Area if you did a car shuttle, stay on the Sierra Vista Trail for a ways, or make your way back to the Alum Rock Trailhead.

In Alum Rock Park, consider stopping at the visitor center farther up the road from the Ridge Trail to see photos of the park's heyday: mineral baths, an indoor swimming pool, a tea garden, a grand restaurant, and even a dance pavilion made this a popular recreation area in the early 20th century. The Alum Rock Steam Railroad, which operated from 1890 until heavy floods destroyed it in 1911, ferried passengers between downtown San José and Alum Rock Park.

The next segment of the Ridge Trail begins here at the intersection of the Kestrel and Sierra Vista Trails, or up the Kestrel Trail at the parking lot on Sierra Road.

Sierra Vista Open Space Preserve

see map on p. 212

From Sierra Road Staging Area to
Lower Calaveras Fault Trail Vista Point in San José

LENGTH 4.9 miles one-way (plus a 4.2-mile alternative return route)
ELEVATION GAIN/LOSS 1,290'/1,210' one-way
ACCESSIBILITY Hikers and mountain bikers

AGENCY Santa Clara Valley Open Space Authority

REGULATIONS Open 8 a.m.–30 minutes after sunset. No parking along Sierra Road. Dogs prohibited.

FACILITIES None

THE SIERRA VISTA TRAIL opened in 2011, connecting the Ridge Trail at the lower elevations with the Upper and Lower Calaveras Fault Trails, and creating a long 8.9-mile Ridge Trail segment. This upper Ridge Trail section starts high up on the grassy ridge, with spectacular views of the Santa Clara Valley, and then follows the contours of the steep Alum Rock Canyon before dropping down to Penitencia Creek and climbing out to another ridgetop to the southeast. The end point has sweeping vistas of the valley below and the hills to the east. This is a very exposed trail for much of the route, so start early on hot days.

Getting Started

TRAILHEAD Sierra Road Staging Area, Sierra Road, 3.7 miles east of Piedmont Road, San José. Large parking lot. (**GPS: N37° 24.528', W121° 48.057'**)

On the Trail

The connector to the main Ridge Trail starts at the Sierra Road Staging Area; both the Kestrel Trail connector and parking area opened in 2014. Benches along the edge of the parking lot look out over the phenomenal view, and an interpretive panel shows many of the visible landmarks, including Loma Prieta, Mount Umunhum, downtown San José, San Francisco Bay, and San Bruno Mountain. You can get trail maps and other preserve information here before starting your journey.

From the Kestrel Trail, the hills drop into the Santa Clara Valley.

The Kestrel Trail, a singletrack trail, begins at the end of the parking lot, passes through a cattle gate, and immediately begins descending and winding down the hill. Look straight ahead to see Mount Hamilton in the distance. An old rock wall heads straight down the hill near the trail. At 0.25 mile you reach the intersection where the previous Ridge Trail section ends (to your right); turn left up the Sierra Vista Trail. *Note:* Horses are prohibited on this trail.

The singletrack trail begins along the contours of the steep canyon that descends to Upper Penitencia Creek on your right. Crumbly sandstone, a sedimentary rock, forms the banks to your left. The trail heads back into the hills in open grassland, and in the spring, colorful wildflowers edge the trail: the unique yellow-flowered Lindley's blazing star, lupine, and poppies. The trail begins gradually descending at 0.6 mile and just before a sharp turn to the left you can rest on a bench overlooking the canyon and the tree-filled north-facing slopes. Continuing down the trail, you pass through welcome shade on a hot day under deciduous oaks and buckeyes.

You reach a bridge at 0.9 mile and then ascend to a cattle gate. Just beyond the gate is a trail junction at 1 mile; take a left on the Upper Calaveras Fault Trail. This trail and the Lower Calaveras Fault Trail are named for the earthquake fault that runs through the park; in 2007, a 5.6-magnitude earthquake originated in Alum Rock Park and was felt around the Bay Area.

The trail ascends and, at about 1.2 miles, gets fairly steep after it passes under the transmission lines. Look up to see some houses off Sierra Road; at 1.5 miles you'll reach the junction with Sierra Road. Turn right and head downhill on the Upper Calaveras Fault Trail, a gravel road. The road turns into a dirt road and, at 1.8 miles, comes to the Cutoff Trail intersection; take this trail by turning sharply right. Now you head into some coast live oaks for a bit as you wind steeply downhill. The chaparral landscape features coyote brush, poison oak, toyon, and California sage.

You merge again with the Calaveras Fault Trail; veer right and keep heading downhill until you reach the junction with the Sierra Vista Trail at 2.4 miles. On your way back, take this Sierra Vista Trail for a shorter return route. Take a left here and you are on the Lower Calaveras Fault Trail. Just down the road you walk by the Furtado family's old ranch homestead—a corrugated-metal barn, a boarded-up house with a picnic table in front, and an orchard. Just below here, walk through another gate, keep straight, and you will come to a paved road at 2.7 miles, where you may encounter occasional vehicles.

The road parallels sycamore-lined Upper Penitencia Creek on your left. At 3 miles the trail turns left, passes madrones and bigleaf maples, and crosses the creek on a wide bridge. This next section of trail is a mowed road and begins climbing steeply after it crosses the creek. This uphill section has intermittent shade under oaks and some gray pines, which you will appreciate on a hot day. You reach your first meadow at 3.6 miles and will come to another one shortly. Turn around in the meadow to see where you started on the ridge far across the canyon. After ascending a corridor of coyote brush, poison oak, and monkey flower, you enter a huge expanse of grassland on the ridge at 4.2 miles, and begin seeing the Santa Clara Valley and Coast Range beyond.

The trail flattens out as you walk or ride in the open along the edge of the preserve. After a bit more uphill, you reach the transmission lines and turn right to access the viewpoint and the end of the trail. You will be relieved to see a picnic table to rest on. Here you have panoramic views of the valley and mountains on the Ridge Trail route, including Mount Umunhum, Black Mountain, and Mount Allison. Behind you are Mount Day and Mount Hamilton.

After your rest at the end of the trail, head back and, after passing the ranch buildings, take a left on the Sierra Vista Trail for a shorter return trip up through the open grassland.

◆ ◆ ◆

The next Ridge Trail segment begins in Joseph D. Grant County Park, a 13-mile drive or ride southeast via Mt. Hamilton Road.

see map on next page

Joseph D. Grant County Park

From Edwards Trail Gate on Mt. Hamilton Road to
Dutch Flat Trail Gate at Southwest Park Boundary in San José

LENGTH 5.9 miles one-way (plus a minimum 2.8 miles from Ridge Trail terminus to main parking area if doing car shuttle)

ELEVATION GAIN/LOSS 950'/980' one-way

ACCESSIBILITY Hikers, equestrians, and mountain bikers

AGENCY Santa Clara County Parks

REGULATIONS Park open 8 a.m.–sunset year-round; an entrance fee applies. Dogs must be leashed.

FACILITIES Water and restrooms at main entrance

THIS SEGMENT TRACES THE WESTERN BOUNDARY of 10,822-acre Joseph D. Grant County Park on a broad trail. Traverse grasslands, remote oak woodlands, and an ancient bay-tree forest to reach a 2,457-foot vista point with outstanding views of the Coast Range high peaks, the Santa Clara Valley, and Halls Valley to the east. Much of the route is in sun, so plan for an early start and carry plenty of water.

Getting Started

NORTHERN EDWARDS LOOP TRAILHEAD Mt. Hamilton Road, 0.9 mile north of Quimby Road, San José. Look for trailhead on west side of road. A small roadside pullout is just south of the trailhead. (**GPS: N37° 21.044', W121° 43.968'**)

On the Trail

From the trailhead on Mt. Hamilton Road, **hikers, equestrians, and mountain bikers** pass through a gate and begin a fairly steady climb on the Edwards Loop Trail, an old ranch road. In spring, the trail may be overgrown and you may meet grazing cattle. Occasional deciduous oaks shade your route, and blue lupine, large yellow mule ears, stork's bill, clover, and poppies bloom in spring. At one of several wide switchbacks you can look back over Halls Valley to the buildings of Joseph D. Grant's former ranch house complex. Beyond, the park's steep eastern hills rise from the valley, and the white domes of Lick Observatory on Mount Hamilton glisten in the sun.

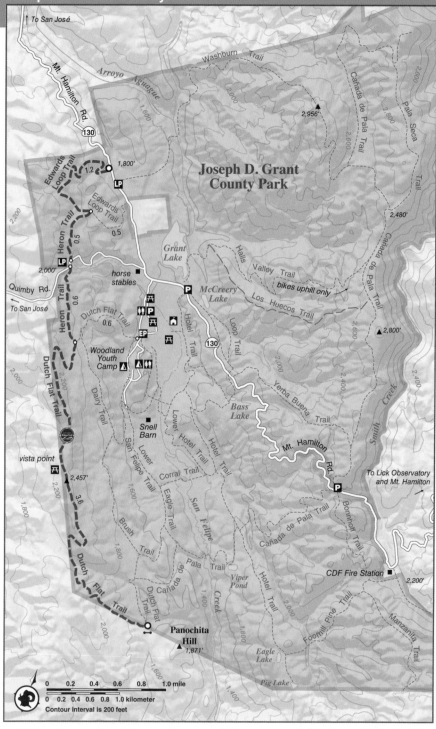

At 0.6 mile you cross under transmission lines and soon pass a scenic pond on your right, the highest point of this first leg, before heading downhill to intersect the Heron Trail at 1.2 miles. Turn right and head uphill, proceeding under the power lines. In 0.4 mile you head down again, into the woods and through the green gate to Quimby Road at 1.7 miles. Cross the road, head uphill, and you see the trail through a gate.

The undulating Heron Trail continues beyond Quimby Road under the power lines; huge oaks arch over the trail, and bay trees and willows grow in shaded ravines. Quite unexpectedly, you dip into a dense cool grove of very large and mature bay trees; one has 14 trunks growing from its central bole. In the open grassland you see vast Halls Valley, the centerpiece of this park. Grant Lake shimmers in the sunlight, and the park's many trails meander down the valley and up grassy hillsides indented by streamlets that nourish stands of oaks and sycamores.

The Heron Trail ends at a junction at 2.3 miles; turn right and continue your route to the south end of the park on the Dutch Flat Trail. You're in a chaparral landscape, and after a wide swing to the right, your climb begins in earnest through a fine stand of black oaks—deciduous in winter, bronze-red in spring when they get their new leaves, and tawny-gold and orange in fall. In spring, an abundance of blooming yarrow and monkeyflower edge the trail.

At 3 miles the trail levels out on a ridge and then enters a large, scenic meadow. Just a bit farther down the trail, you get your first glimpse of the Santa Clara Valley below you. This is a quintessential Ridge Trail hike, with fantastic views to the west and east.

Continue along the ridge and at 3.4 miles you reach the 2,457-foot vista point. Across Coyote Valley, Mount Umunhum and Loma Prieta dominate the western skyline, their summits often backed or obscured by fog. Sit at the picnic table or bench and note how well the two arms of the Coast Range enclose the Santa Clara Valley. Then view the panorama of the Outer Coast Range, from the dominant southern peaks to Black Mountain, San Bruno Mountain, and Mount Tamalpais to the north. In the eastern hills, Mount Misery is just to your south.

You begin your descent on the Dutch Flat Trail through an avenue of deciduous black and valley oaks. In fall, the spent oak leaves carpet the trail and hillsides, their acorns crunch underfoot, and mistletoe hangs from branches. These magnificent trees are long-lived, but you may see a fallen giant lying beside the trail, its bark riddled with woodpecker holes and its undersides inhabited by ground-burrowing creatures. The trail descends steeply through the woodland with a tangled understory of toyon, poison oak, and wild rose.

You come into a swale at 3.7 miles and climb out; then you're right up against an old wooden fence at the western property line. Your views continue for more than 0.5 mile as you descend. Going through a gate, curve down to the west to picturesque stock ponds in the gorgeous oak landscape. The trail undulates, with views to Mount Hamilton, but mostly heads downhill. At 5.7 miles cross under the power lines and continue downhill through oaks and bays. The Ridge Trail segment ends when the trail takes a sharp turn to the left at the bottom of the hill.

For an easier route back, hikers and equestrians can go through the valley via the Brush Trail and Dairy Trail across the vast meadows to the Dutch Flat Trail and Heron Trail. If, however, you did a car shuttle and left a car near the main entrance,

The Edwards Loop Trail sits above Halls Valley and across from Mount Hamilton.

you have different route options. **Hikers and equestrians** can take the Brush Trail to the Dairy Trail and then go right instead of left on the Dutch Flat Trail to the main parking lot.

For an alternative return, **mountain bikers** can turn right off the Dutch Flat Trail on the Canada de Pala Trail and head north on the Eagle Trail, Lower San Felipe Trail, and Snell Trail to the parking area.

The next Bay Area Ridge Trail segment begins at Coyote Creek Parkway North, a 9-mile drive west.

Coyote Creek Parkway North

From Tully Road to Metcalf Park in San José

LENGTH 9.3 miles one-way

ELEVATION GAIN/LOSS 145'/80' one-way

ACCESSIBILITY Hikers, equestrians, and bicyclists; wheelchair users on most of trail

AGENCIES Santa Clara County Parks and City of San José

REGULATIONS Stonegate, Shady Oaks, and Metcalf Parks open sunrise–1 hour after sunset. Hellyer County Park open 8 a.m.–sunset; an entrance fee applies. Dogs must be leashed.

FACILITIES Restrooms at Hellyer and Metcalf Parks and Silver Creek Staging Area

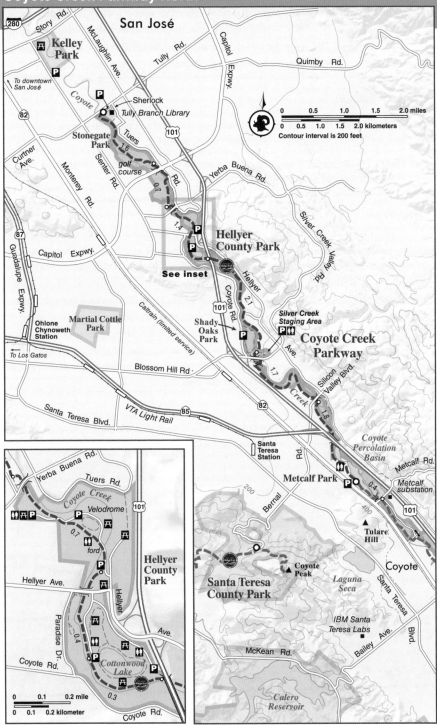

COYOTE CREEK TRAVELS 31 MILES from the Diablo Range to San Francisco Bay. On this trail segment, follow the creekbed through shady riparian cover, parks, developed areas, and open fields to Metcalf Park's freshwater lagoons, the habitat for many year-round and migratory bird species. The wide paved trail travels a nearly level course and is an excellent bike ride, popular with families on bicycles, especially on weekends.

Getting Started

NORTH TRAILHEAD Parking lot on southeast side of Tully Road between Kenoga Drive and La Ragione Avenue, San José. (**GPS: N37° 18.620', W121° 50.611'**)

SOUTH TRAILHEAD Metcalf Park Parking Area, Monterey Street, 0.4 mile northwest of Metcalf Road, San José. (**GPS: N37° 13.788', W121° 45.397'**)

On the Trail

From the parking lot at Tully Road start at the paved circle southwest of the parking lot. As you head south, Coyote Creek is below on your right and baseball diamonds are on your left before you enter the trees. In 0.3 mile you might see skateboarders trying daring leaps at a skateboard park or children playing at Stonegate Park, where there are also numerous picnic tables. You also see Los Lagos Golf Course on your left before entering the woods again. A dense forest of red ironwood eucalyptus, cottonwood, and live oak trees shade the creek, and poison oak is ubiquitous. Although chain-link fencing runs along the top of the bank, you can see the creek and hear it, especially after heavy rains. Pass the driving range before going under the Capitol Expressway at 1.6 miles. Now the creek is closer to the level of the trail.

Coyote Creek Parkway North gets close to the hills on the east side of US 101.

Coyote Creek

The longest creek in Santa Clara County, Coyote Creek begins in the steep, rugged ridges of Henry W. Coe State Park and flows north through the eastern foothills into the Santa Clara Valley. The 63-mile-long creek is joined and enlarged by many tributaries, including Silver, Penitencia, and Berryessa Creeks, as it makes its way through a corridor of riparian vegetation to the salty waters of San Francisco Bay. The creek's fresh water empties into the complex system of sloughs and marshes in the Don Edwards San Francisco Bay National Wildlife Refuge.

Before European settlers arrived in the Santa Clara Valley, the Ohlone used paths along the Coyote and other creeks to reach settlements of other tribes, with whom they traded shells, salt, cinnabar, arrowheads, and stone knife blades. Spanish explorers also followed the creek along Ohlone routes, keeping to high ground above the water's edge. Early settlers in the valley built houses along Coyote Creek and used its water for their homes, farms, and orchards. Periodic floods destroyed many settlers' homes and inundated their croplands.

In the 1930s, the Santa Clara Valley Water District dammed the valley's major streams—the Guadalupe, Los Gatos, Stevens, Calero, Los Alamitos, and Coyote—to provide drinking and irrigation water and to reduce ground subsidence, and they built percolation ponds along some watercourses to recharge the groundwater supply. Today, Coyote Creek's broad, tree-lined course provides a recreation corridor for the residents of urbanized Santa Clara Valley, as well as food, shelter, and a travel route for wildlife.

At 1.9 miles, when you reach a T-intersection, take a right and follow the trail along the creek: you're now on the west side of the creek. The trail climbs, and to your right, on the other side of a chain-link fence, is a huge open field, a rare site in the middle of San José. At the far end of the field you're near a residential neighborhood on your right. At 2.3 miles the trail goes under Yerba Buena Road and enters Hellyer County Park.

In the park, the trail passes under a leafy canopy of cottonwood, sycamore, and oak trees. A veil of poison oak vines and elderberry bushes shields the creek here, but you can frequently peek through the vegetation to see the creekbed. In summer, very little water flows through the creekbed, but during winter storms, it can be a raging torrent. You see inviting picnic tables and lawns; you then pass bathrooms and the velodrome at 2.8 miles and a field of solar panels on your right. The trail then travels through the riparian corridor; at 3.1 miles you see parking areas, open lawns, and pretty Cottonwood Lake. The trail curves east near the southern perimeter of the lake and dips under noisy US 101 at 3.8 miles, leaving the park.

The other side of the highway takes you through a rural landscape. Soon the trail rises to the bluffs high above the creek, where venerable oaks shade the way. These ancient oaks send their roots deep to tap the creek's underground moisture. White-barked, big-leafed sycamore trees and cottonwoods, whose roots prefer a streamside location, grow closer to the water. You will probably see swallows and blue jays flitting in and out of the trees and hear mourning doves and quail calling.

At 4.5 miles you enter a large business park on your left and notice housing developments across the creek. On your right, at 5.2 miles, a wide wooden plank bridge arches over the creek. Take a detour to cross it to the City of San José's Shady Oaks Park, a pleasant place under the oak and pepper trees. This neighborhood park offers acres of invitingly green turf, basketball courts, and young children's play equipment. In the creekbed, tall reeds, cattails, and grassy thickets make good nesting sites for migratory and resident ducks and grebes.

Return to the trail to meander under wide-spreading oaks. Just before you go under the large Silver Creek Valley Road bridge at 5.9 miles, you pass a Coyote Creek Trail staging area to your left with restrooms. After passing under the road, take a sharp right at the junction, cross over a bridge, and you now have the creek on your left. Ride parallel to US 101 as you continue near the business park. Then, at 6.8 miles, the trail veers east and enters an immense field with the eastern hills ahead of you. After turning south, the trail begins paralleling Eden Park Place as it skirts the business park again. Go under Silicon Valley Boulevard at 7.5 miles; then you're in a natural area until you pass under US 101 again in 0.8 mile.

Soon you see the first of the percolation ponds on your left and a housing development on your right. These ponds are the largest freshwater lagoons in the county, harboring many year-round and migratory bird species. Look for white egrets and terns, black cormorants, and blue-gray kingfishers as you travel the last part of this trail. You will find some magnificent ancient oak trees that still border the lakes and shade the Coyote Creek Trail as it meanders through Metcalf Park. Pass basketball courts, play structures, and picnic tables, and more percolation ponds before seeing the parking area to the right at the south end of Metcalf Park.

At 9.3 miles, this is the end of the Coyote Creek Parkway North segment and the starting point for the Coyote Creek Parkway South section.

Coyote Creek Parkway South

From Metcalf Park in San José to Anderson Lake Visitor Center in Morgan Hill

LENGTH 9.2 miles one-way; car shuttle possible

ELEVATION GAIN 150' one-way

ACCESSIBILITY Hikers, bicyclists, equestrians, and wheelchair users. Equestrians use alternative marked trail.

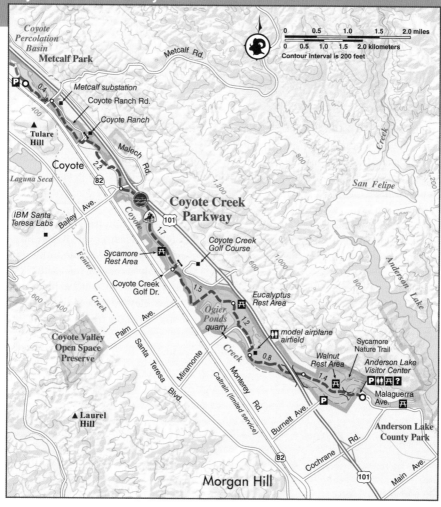

AGENCIES Santa Clara County Parks, City of San José, and Santa Clara Valley Water District

REGULATIONS Metcalf Park and Anderson Lake County Park open 8 a.m.–sunset. Dogs must be leashed.

FACILITIES Water and restrooms at Metcalf Park, model airplane airfield at Anderson Lake County Park

TAKE A CREEKSIDE STROLL or ride through the undeveloped broad Coyote Creek floodplain. Enjoy pleasant rest stops under large shade trees and awesome views of the nearby Coast Range. The trail provides an opportunity to appreciate what the Santa Clara Valley looked like before it was developed. The entire route follows a level paved trail (with a separate unpaved path for horses). Much of the trail is in the sun, so plan the trip for cooler weather.

Getting Started

NORTH TRAILHEAD Metcalf Park Parking Area, Monterey Street, 0.4 mile northwest of Metcalf Road, San José. (**GPS: N37° 13.788', W121° 45.397'**)

SOUTH TRAILHEAD Anderson Lake Visitor Center, northwest end of Malaguerra Avenue, Morgan Hill. Large parking lot with space for horse trailers. (**GPS: N37° 09.923', W121° 38.824"**)

On the Trail

All trail users head south from the parking area at Metcalf Road, between percolation ponds and the old Monterey Highway and railroad tracks. In 0.3 mile the trail turns left to cross a pedestrian and bicycle bridge, then turns right onto Metcalf Road. Cross the road and continue south. The immense PG&E transmission substation is on your left, with power lines overhead. Then, on the other side of Monterey Road, you see another industrial complex.

In an open landscape with occasional sycamore and walnut trees, the trail follows the willow- and blackberry-bordered creek closely. You reach Coyote Ranch Road at 1.3 miles; turn left, and at the entrance to the historic Coyote Ranch, the trail turns right and parallels the east side of Coyote Ranch Road before crossing the road at 1.6 miles and heading toward the creek. Pass ponds on your left, and agricultural fields and the hills to your west. It feels like the rural Santa Clara Valley from decades ago. You pass ranches and barns, and begin hearing freeway noise when the trail turns east and begins its course closer to US 101.

At 2.6 miles the trail dips under Bailey Avenue and then continues near the freeway, passing through some oaks and eucalyptus. You are farther from the creek,

Coyote Creek Parkway South passes several large, scenic ponds.

but you have expansive views up to the Santa Cruz Mountains. At 3.3 miles the Coyote Creek Golf Course is on your left, and the trail gets close to the creek again. At 4.1 miles you reach the Sycamore Rest Area, the first of three shady, attractive stops with picnic tables. This is a delightful lunch place where you can enjoy the lush creekside environment. As the name implies, tall, white-barked, big-leaved sycamores provide welcome shade on a hot summer day. These deciduous trees are shorn of their leaves in fall, offering dappled sunlight as the weather cools.

You merge with Coyote Creek Golf Drive for a short distance at 4.2 miles: look for the trail just ahead on the left. You have the creek and its trees on your left for almost 0.5 mile before the trail enters an open grassland. At 5 miles cross another pedestrian/bike bridge, and begin passing scenic large ponds in an old quarry before reaching the next rest area in a grove of eucalyptus trees at 5.8 miles. In the open grassland and near the quarry lakes, you're in a beautiful pastoral setting.

At 7 miles you reach a mini airport for model planes that you might be able to watch take off and land. After the "airport," the trail gets close to the creek and heads toward US 101, passing under the freeway at 7.8 miles. The hills are just to your left and the creek is tumbling downhill toward the bay. At 8.5 miles the trail turns left at the Walnut Rest Area, where picnic tables sit under a canopy of oak trees; it's a popular spot for anglers trying their luck in the rushing waters below the Anderson Dam outflow. You're at the edge of an old walnut orchard where an interesting old farm structure remains in the field.

Stay on the trail, veer right at the intersection, cross the creek and a large field, and you come to the Anderson Lake Visitor Center at 9 miles. The Coyote Creek Trail extends to Morning Sun Drive for another 0.2 mile. If you have time, take the park road into Anderson Lake, the largest reservoir in Santa Clara County, or check out the exhibits in the visitor center.

The next section of the Bay Area Ridge Trail starts in Coyote Lake–Harvey Bear Ranch County Park, a 20-mile drive.

Coyote Lake–Harvey Bear Ranch County Park

From Harvey Bear Trailhead at Coyote Dam in Morgan Hill to Mendoza Ranch Trailhead in Gilroy

see map on next page

LENGTH 5.6 miles one-way (includes 0.9 mile on Harvey Bear Trail, a connector trail); car shuttle possible

ELEVATION GAIN/LOSS 500'/490' one-way

ACCESSIBILITY Hikers, equestrians, and mountain bikers

AGENCY Santa Clara County Parks

REGULATIONS Trail open sunrise–sunset. Dogs must be leashed. A camping and boating fee is required at Coyote Lake.

FACILITIES Parking, camping, picnic tables, and restrooms available on Coyote Lake Road

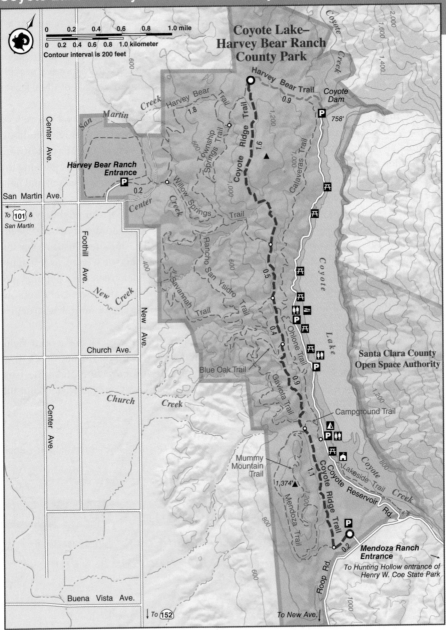

After a short connector trail, this route heads south on a relatively level trail high up in the hills with splendid views of Coyote Lake, the surrounding foothills, the Santa Clara Valley, and the Coast Range. This hike or ride can be combined with a picnic or camping next to Coyote Lake. The trail is mostly in sun, so plan the trip in cooler weather or early in the day.

Getting Started

NORTH TRAILHEAD Coyote Lake–Harvey Bear Ranch County Park, Coyote Dam parking lot, end of Coyote Lake Road, Morgan Hill. (**GPS: N37° 07.056', W121° 33.106'**)

SOUTH TRAILHEAD Coyote Lake–Harvey Bear Ranch County Park, Mendoza Ranch Entrance, Roop Road, 0.9 mile north of Leavesley Road, Gilroy. Parking lot. (**GPS: N37° 04.229', W121° 31.370'**)

On the Trail

In springtime the hills at this county park are a vibrant green, the birds sing in the trees, hawks call out en route to unwary prey, and wildflowers extravagantly clothe the trailside with rainbow hues. This is the ideal time to visit. Coyote Creek, which the Ridge Trail follows in San José, runs in and out of Coyote Lake.

Hikers and riders use the Harvey Bear Trail to connect to the northern end of the Bay Area Ridge Trail. There are two trailhead options: from Coyote Dam (0.9 mile) and from the Harvey Bear Ranch Trailhead (2.5 miles). This trail description starts from the shorter connector trail at Coyote Dam. The trailhead can be accessed from the Coyote Lake entrance, after driving the length of Coyote Lake, and passing the campground, numerous picnic areas, and parking areas along the lake. A large dirt parking area is at the trailhead at the end of the road.

Start on the Harvey Bear Trail by ascending a dirt ranch road through an oak–bay woodland. Pass through a gate and, in 0.2 mile, emerge onto the open grassy hills with occasional coast live and deciduous valley oaks. At the first trail junction, veer right and stay on the Harvey Bear Trail. When you get to the Ridge Trail junction at 0.9 mile, take a left up the hill on the Coyote Ridge Trail. Here, at 1,100 feet, you can see across the valley to other parks on the Ridge Trail route: Almaden Quicksilver, Sierra Azul, and Mount Madonna.

On the Coyote Ridge Trail, the Bay Area Ridge Trail route traverses the length of the old Harvey Bear and Mendoza Ranches. It has gentle ascents and descents, making this a pleasant hike. The grassy road has wonderful views of the southern Santa Clara Valley, and from this high perch, the valley looks quiet and pastoral. In the spring, the yellow mustard provides a delightful contrast to the green hills. After passing a cattle gate at 1.6 miles, you climb to a point where the view to the south opens and you see the undulating hills below you descend to the valley.

By 2.1 miles, you have views of scenic Coyote Lake, which is generally placid, except when large numbers of motorboats ply its waters. You then pick up some trees and shade for a short stretch. Many trails intersect the Coyote Ridge Trail, but stay on this trail. Continuing south, you have fine views of the lake and Santa Clara Valley as you amble up and down over small hills.

At 3 miles you come to a gate and a wooden fence; on the other side is a perfectly placed bench overlooking the valley. Within the next mile you pass another bench before descending into the woods at 4 miles. In 0.2 mile come out of the woods to overlook a gorgeous meadow high above the south end of the lake. Passing another bench and another gate, the trail ascends a meadow edged in trees and at 5 miles reaches benches and a memorial plaque for four people killed in a 2005 airplane crash in the area. Shortly, the trail enters open grassland and you can see the trailhead in the distance to your left. Turn left at the intersection at 5.4 miles. The end of the trail is just ahead at the parking lot.

The hills and southern Santa Clara Valley from the Coyote Ridge Trail.

The next leg of the Ridge Trail, an 18-mile drive, lies in Mount Madonna County Park, across the Santa Clara Valley in the Outer Coast Range.

Mount Madonna County Park

From Sprig Recreation Area Entrance to Old Mt. Madonna Road in Gilroy

LENGTH 3.5 miles one-way; car shuttle possible

ELEVATION GAIN/LOSS 1,150'/160' one-way

ACCESSIBILITY Hikers and equestrians

AGENCY Santa Clara County Parks

REGULATIONS Mount Madonna County Park open 8 a.m.–sunset and prohibits bicycles. Dogs must be leashed.

FACILITIES Restrooms at Sprig Recreation Area entrance; water and restrooms at campgrounds

ON AN UPHILL TRIP from the Sprig Recreation Area Trailhead to Mt. Madonna Road, you take in excellent views of southern Santa Clara County and the Inner Coast Range. The wide service road skirts an intermittent creek, crosses boulder-strewn grasslands, swings through chaparral and scrub-oak forest, and finishes in a cool, steep-sided redwood canyon. This is the southernmost segment of the Ridge Trail.

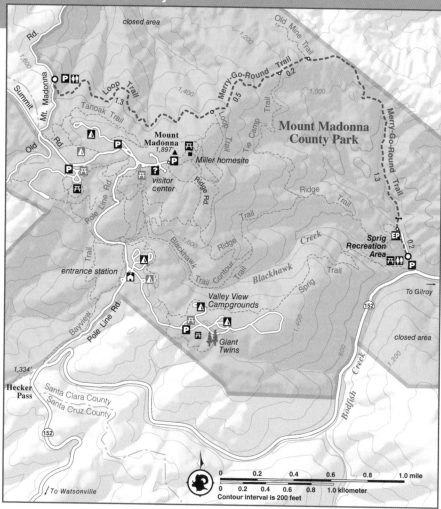

Getting Started

EAST TRAILHEAD Sprig Recreation Area, CA 152 and Blackhawk Canyon Road intersection, 7 miles west of US 101, Gilroy. Car and horse-trailer parking. (**GPS: N37° 00.305', W121° 40.904'**)

WEST TRAILHEAD Mt. Madonna Road, 0.2 mile north of Pole Line Road, Gilroy. A few cars can park on Mt. Madonna Road near here. (**GPS: N37° 01.073', W121° 43.016'**)

On the Trail

Starting from the Sprig Recreation Area, **hikers and equestrians** head up the Merry-Go-Round Trail, a wide dirt road, beside an unnamed tributary to Blackhawk Creek. Under a shady canopy of tall oaks, bays, buckeyes, and bigleaf maples, you can glimpse the small creek bouncing over its rocky bed through the tangled undergrowth well below the left side of the trail. On the right, perennial streams have cut deep canyons on a forested ridge.

231

After 0.2 mile you come to a fork in the road where you turn right on the Merry-Go-Round Trail, pass some picnic tables, and go in and out of the trees. Oaks and buckeyes predominate, but tall madrones search for sunlight and offer climbing posts for persistent poison oak and occasional native honeysuckle vines. The road starts climbing more steeply at 0.4 mile and soon you enter stands of tall second-growth redwoods; moss-covered rocks, old tree stumps, and lush redwood sorrel complete this patch of coastal redwood community.

At 1.1 miles the Merry-Go-Round Trail enters an oak grassland and ascends steeply, and you begin to get views off to your left of ridges in the distance. When you turn the corner, at 1.4 miles, you're up on top of the ridge's plateau with views in all directions. Turn around to see the mountains on the east side of the Santa Clara Valley, including Pacheco Peak. Large boulders dot the serpentine grasslands, accented by a springtime riot of orange poppies, yellow mule ears, and blue lupine. To the west, near the terminus of the Ridge Trail, rises the Mount Madonna summit, the southernmost high point of the Santa Cruz Mountains. Pass the right-branching Old Mine Trail at 1.5 miles.

You start climbing from the plateau, and after 1.7 miles on the Merry-Go-Round Trail, the Tie Camp Trail branches left. Indeed, a tie camp was once situated along this trail, where redwoods were cut and shaped to form railroad ties. Continue on the Merry-Go-Round Trail and as you ascend steadily with little shade, you realize the importance of starting early on a summer day.

The chaparral plants found here—manzanita, artemisia, sticky monkeyflower, toyon, and honeysuckle—offer good forage for the birds whose calls you may hear. Before long, the trail narrows a little, and live oaks reach over the chaparral plants. At 2 miles you begin to see redwoods again; shortly the Merry-Go-Round Trail ends and the Loop Trail forks straight ahead and left. To continue on the Ridge Trail route, go straight on the Loop Trail.

Spring wildflowers abound in the serpentine grasslands off the Merry-Go-Round Trail.

Beneath the shade of oaks, tanoaks, bays, and madrones, this 1.3-mile old logging road is pleasantly cool. The trail levels off and then, in a dramatic change of terrain and vegetation, descends slightly into a second-growth redwood forest. Note the horizontal ax cuts on huge redwood stumps. Loggers inserted boards into these cuts and then placed cross boards on top. Two hardy men stood on the cross boards, 8–10 feet above the ground, and used a long, two-handled saw to cut through the gigantic trees. They always felled the tree uphill because it might have splintered in the longer fall.

As you follow the trail along a shelf cut into a high, steep, north-facing mountainside, you hear the sound of water, sometimes just rivulets, falling over sandstone boulders in the still forest. The moisture from rain and fog-drip promotes the growth of these second- and third-growth redwoods into a healthy forest. Scattered eucalyptus trees have grown exceedingly tall along the road in the forest's dense shade.

The trail heads into deep ravines cut by intermittent streams and then swings out around the shoulders of the mountain. Drooping branches of wild roses and several kinds of ferns grace the hillsides above the trail. A few immense sandstone boulders accent the steep hillside, and others form jumbled streambeds for tumbling, intermittent creeks.

Shortly, look for a small shed on your left, backed by a 15-foot-high, moss-covered rock wall; another lower wall is on the other side of a lively stream. Henry Miller, a 19th-century cattle baron who once owned today's parkland, built these walls to protect his underground water tank and pumphouse; a steam engine pumped water hundreds of feet uphill to his mountaintop home. Today, the water serves as a backup supply for fire suppression.

A few minutes beyond the water tank you reach Old Mt. Madonna Road, the end of this segment of the Ridge Trail. To return to the Sprig Recreation Area parking by trail, take the Bay Area Ridge Trail in reverse (downhill most of the way), or head up Mt. Madonna Road to other trails that loop back to the trailhead.

The next segment of the Ridge Trail is in Santa Teresa County Park, a 25-mile drive north.

Santa Teresa County Park and Calero Creek/Los Alamitos Creek Trails

From Pueblo Day Use Area to McKean Road in San José

LENGTH 6.3 miles one-way (plus 1.1-mile return trip from Coyote Peak); car shuttle possible

ELEVATION GAIN/LOSS 805'/1,020' (includes round-trip to Coyote Peak)

ACCESSIBILITY Hikers, equestrians, and mountain bikers; wheelchair users can use Calero Creek and Los Alamitos Creek Trails.

AGENCIES Santa Clara County Parks and City of San José

REGULATIONS County park open 8 a.m.–sunset. Dogs must be leashed.

FACILITIES Water and restrooms at Pueblo Group Picnic Area in Santa Teresa County Park

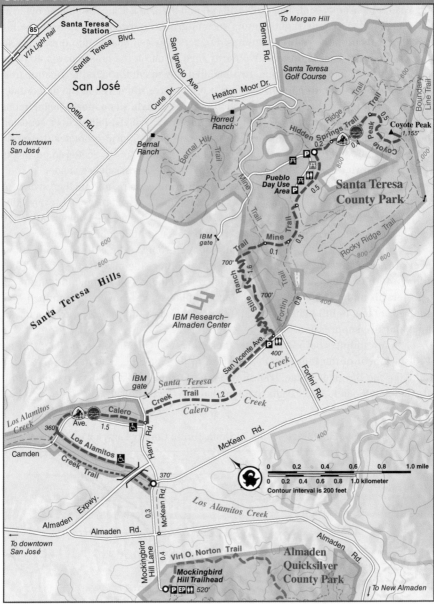

THE RIDGE TRAIL ROUTE BRANCHES EAST and west through Santa Teresa County Park. Take a round-trip trail east through high, oak-studded grasslands to Coyote Peak. Then head west on well-graded, exposed paths, past spring wildflower displays, serpentine outcrops, and Coast Range views. Listen to the sound of running water on the tree-lined Calero Creek Trail, and finish on the wide, paved, partially shaded Los Alamitos Creek Trail. The trail through Santa Teresa County Park is exposed and can be hot in summer and early fall.

Getting Started

EAST TRAILHEAD Pueblo Day Use Area, Santa Teresa County Park, Bernal Road, 2.7 miles west of CA 85, San José. The trailhead is near the first large parking lot. (**GPS: N37° 12.838', W121° 47.133'**)

WEST TRAILHEAD Calero Creek/Los Alamitos Creek Trails, McKean Road and Harry Road intersection, San José. Street parking. (**GPS: N37° 12.102', W121° 49.731'**)

MIDDLE TRAILHEAD Santa Teresa County Park, west end of Stile Ranch Trail, San Vicente Avenue, 0.1 mile west of Fortini Road, San José. Parking lot. (**GPS: N37° 12.200', W121° 48.354'**)

On the Trail

The 2.2-mile round-trip to 1,155-foot Coyote Peak, the highest point in Santa Teresa County Park, begins at the Pueblo Day Use Area. Look for the Hidden Springs Trail on the eastern side of the parking area, where you see information boards. The old ranch road ascends in grassland with broad-branched oaks and buckeye trees along the route. You have extensive views to San José, the Santa Clara Valley, and the Diablo Range. The trail becomes steep as you pass the park's own Ridge Trail on the left at 0.2 mile. As you climb, you lose the trees and begin to see the Outer Coast Range and the southern Santa Clara Valley.

At 0.6 mile you reach a junction and a cattle gate; stay straight on the Coyote Peak Trail, which climbs steeply under the transmission lines. For the next 0.4 mile, you follow the hillside up to and around the peak, with westward views to the wooded heights of the Santa Cruz Mountains. When the trail swings around to the south slope of the peak, where the view opens to the south and west, you reach a four-way intersection; take a left turn to reach the summit in 0.1 mile, rest on a bench, and see sweeping panoramas of the Santa Clara Valley (an interpretive panel shows the landmarks in your view).

The Stile Ranch Trail heads into Almaden Valley.

Now retrace your steps to the Pueblo Day Use Area, and begin the next leg of your Ridge Trail trip. At the trailhead, turn left up the Mine Trail and head west on the ranch road. In 0.2 mile you reach the restrooms and then walk between the parking lot and equestrian arena. On the far side of the arena, bear left on the Mine Trail, which descends gently to Santa Teresa Creek, the small stream that drains the park's lush central meadow.

With views up to Mount Umunhum, descend through a little valley, along the west side of the stream, bordered by a few oaks and many bay trees. The south-facing hillsides, punctuated by lichen-encrusted igneous rocks interspersed with gray sage bushes, come alive with blue brodiaea, orange poppies, and magenta clarkia after winter rains. Among the rocks you may see gray-green serpentine, the California state rock.

In 0.5 mile (mile notations are from trailhead), veer right at the trail junction up the Mine Trail. Curve north, away from the creek, and climb to a ridgetop where a clump of gnarled oak trees with small, leathery, dull-green leaves stands beyond the fence on your left. This native California tree, mostly found on serpentine soil, is known as the leather oak. You will see other specimens of leather oak as you traverse sections of this trail cut through serpentine rock.

The trail descends into a quiet, grassy swale, sprinkled with fine old valley oaks and pierced by an intermittent stream. After you cross the stream, go left on the Stile Ranch Trail at 0.9 mile; the Mine Trail continues right. The Stile Ranch Trail weaves through the sloping sagebrush grasslands at a very manageable grade, eventually narrowing. You cross a bridge where teasel fills the riparian area, and you will notice the large IBM complex on the hill above.

Then you follow well-graded switchbacks uphill; this section of trail—after the fence to the Stile Ranch Trailhead—lies on an easement-protected IBM property built by volunteers. As you climb the ridge through rock outcroppings you can see Coyote Peak and the Diablo Range. At 1.3 miles, at the top of the ridge, you have unobstructed views south and west.

As the rocky trail dips into another valley among clumps of bunchgrass, light-pink-flowered buckwheat, and white yarrow, a couple of switchbacks take you to a plank bridge across a wash (dry in summer). Then you begin ascending an east-facing ridge, a veritable Persian carpet of multicolored wildflowers in spring. Even in July, this hillside glows with the magenta haze of clarkia blossoms. A few oaks and an occasional bay tree offer shade in the late afternoon. When you reach a switchback, look east to see the white domes of the Lick Observatory atop Mount Hamilton in the Diablo Range.

At 1.8 miles the trail levels at the top of the ridge and passes a couple of 6-foot-high sentinel rocks splashed with orange and red lichen. You have a panoramic vista west of the Santa Cruz Mountains: Loma Prieta, the tallest mountain in this range, lies south of Mount Umunhum, which you can identify by the tall structure on its summit. In the pastoral Almaden Valley below, subdivisions and ranchettes are replacing the vineyards and orchards of yesteryear.

As you descend in the grassland, note a fine old rock wall that undulates uphill and down, defining an early boundary. The rocky trail makes its final switchback descent through California and black sage. When you reach the bottom of the hill you intersect the Fortini Trail and have an opportunity to sit at a shaded picnic table just before the San Vicente Avenue Trailhead.

Calero Creek and Los Alamitos Creek Trails

At the parking area, take a right and head west down the trail paralleling San Vicente Avenue. You pass by a few houses before coming to a fence opening in 625 feet. Now on the City of San José's Calero Creek Trail, proceed along the base of the slope on a bumpy dirt trail past wide fields, planted or plowed according to the season.

In 0.6 mile from the San Vicente Trailhead, the trail turns left and dips down into the channel of intermittent Santa Teresa Creek, which drains from the county park. This stream course is a cool damp place under a tall canopy of trees—delightful on a hot day but potentially difficult to cross after heavy rains.

After you cross the stream, the trail is fenced on both sides; a well-kept walnut orchard is on the right and a small model-plane landing strip on the left. When you reach the next line of trees, veer right and follow a wide track for 0.5 mile beside Calero Creek. Accompanied by the sounds of running water, leaves rustling in the breeze, and birds singing in the trees, you wander along the creek bank sheltered by tall, white-barked sycamores and broad-branched oaks. Through openings in the understory of elderberry, poison oak, and wild roses, you can see the creek flowing toward its confluence with Los Alamitos Creek.

Your creekside ramble continues to Harry Road, where you cross the road, jog left on the bridge over the creek, and then turn right on the paved trail that meanders through a wide swath between the creek and Camden Avenue. Although the creek is completely hidden from view, its wooded corridor adds charm to the residential community.

Wheelchair users can join others on the paved creekside trail. About 0.7 mile from Harry Road, Camden Avenue crosses Los Alamitos Creek, which joins Calero Creek just beyond. On the other side of the creek the City of San José's Los Alamitos Creek Trail extends 3.3 miles to Almaden Lake, a water sports and picnic park, from which a trail will someday follow the Guadalupe River to San Francisco Bay.

However, to continue on the Bay Area Ridge Trail from Camden Avenue, cross the street and take the path just before Los Alamitos Creek, which runs south along the creek (there is another path on the other side of the creek). These wide paths are built on raised levees between the generous creekbed and adjoining subdivision roads, and meander upstream for nearly a mile, shaded by oaks, sycamores, and cottonwoods. **Equestrians** use the unpaved trail on the west side.

Continue on the creek trail as it dips under the broad span of the Almaden Expressway bridge. The Ridge Trail segment terminates at the intersection of McKean and Harry Roads.

◆ ◆ ◆

The next segment of the Bay Area Ridge Trail is in nearby Almaden Quicksilver County Park, only 0.7 mile down McKean Road and Mockingbird Hill Lane.

Almaden Quicksilver County Park

From Mockingbird Hill Trailhead to Jacques Ridge Parking Area in San José

LENGTH 4.6 miles one-way; car shuttle possible

ELEVATION GAIN/LOSS 1,160'/345' one-way

ACCESSIBILITY Hikers, equestrians, mountain bikers, and horse-cart drivers

AGENCY Santa Clara County Parks

REGULATIONS Park open 8 a.m.–sunset. Dogs must be leashed.

FACILITIES Picnic areas, restrooms, potable water, equestrian staging area, and horse trough at Mockingbird Hill Lane entrance; toilet at Jacques Ridge Parking Area

A STEADY CLIMB TO THE SLOPES of Mount Umunhum takes you through a beautiful landscape once actively mined for quicksilver. The Ridge Trail follows old mining roads over these hills, where you can imagine New Almaden Mine's heyday. Historic buildings and interpretive panels tell the story of the community that once occupied these hills. Superb views look out over the Santa Clara Valley and Santa Cruz Mountains. Much of this route is exposed and can be hot in summer—plan accordingly.

Getting Started

EAST TRAILHEAD Almaden Quicksilver County Park, Mockingbird Hill Lane, 0.4 mile southwest of Almaden Road, San José. Large parking lot. (**GPS: N37° 11.622', W121° 50.176'**)

WEST TRAILHEAD Sierra Azul Open Space Preserve, Jacques Ridge Parking Area, Hicks Road and Mount Umunhum Road intersection, San José. A larger parking lot with equestrian parking is across Hicks Road. (**GPS: N37° 10.521', W121° 51.863'**)

On the Trail

Hikers, equestrians, and mountain bikers start on the Virl O. Norton Trail on the east side of the parking lot. The dirt road goes in and out of an oak and bay woodland, roughly following the northeastern boundary of the park. In the open grassland, you soon have views of the Diablo Range, and when the trail veers south it begins to climb steeply. Along the trail you see poison oak, coyote brush, toyon, and sagebrush, as well as a range of oak species here and throughout the park: blue, interior live, coast live, valley, black, California scrub, and leather oaks. As you climb you can see the Ridge Trail in Santa Teresa County Park, and the ridges it follows in the Diablo Range, including Mission Peak.

At 1.2 miles your route turns right on the Hacienda Trail (a bench here overlooks Loma Prieta) and heads for Cape Horn Pass, which you reach in 0.4 mile and take a left. Here you are up on the ridge with fabulous views of the Almaden Valley and downtown San José. After heading downhill and passing two picnic tables, turn right at the three-way junction on the middle trail: the Mine Hill Trail. Contouring up the north-facing slope, you have some shade. Stay left at a junction at 2.5 miles where bigleaf maples lean out over the road. You are now on the Castillero Trail, which takes you to the historic site of Englishtown. From the 1860s to the early 1900s, it was home to as many as 1,000

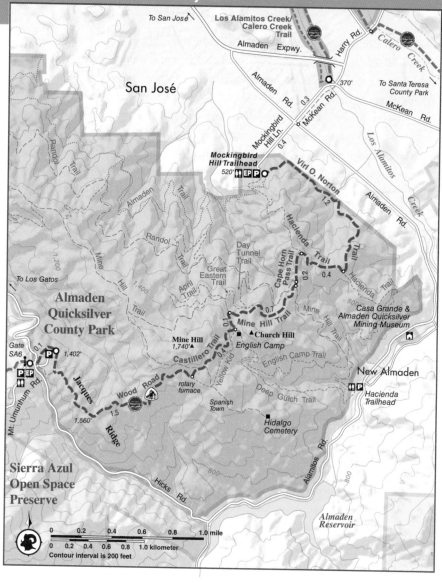

people, and from 1933 to 1939, the Civilian Conservation Corps (CCC) moved here. At this site you find a barn, picnic tables, interpretive panels, and a monument to the CCC.

The trail veers right and, just before a major junction at 3 miles, you get far-reaching views to San Martin and Morgan Hill. Look for picnic tables near eucalyptus trees and a dilapidated building. At the junction, take in the stunning view to the Santa Cruz Mountains and Mount Umunhum; then veer left down Wood Road. At the bottom of the hill, take a few minutes to look at the old mining buildings and rotary furnace, and to read the interpretive exhibits.

Quicksilver Mining

These parklands once contained the most productive quicksilver mine in the Western world. The mercury-producing cinnabar was highly valued for its use in the reduction of gold, and became important to gold miners after gold was discovered in the California hills.

Miles of tunnels pierced the hills and more than 500 houses were clustered on the ridge. Today, the mine tunnels and shafts are closed off, and the furnaces of the New Almaden Quicksilver Mining Company have long since been dismantled. English Town, Spanish Town, and a Chinese camp where miners lived are gone. Mining began in 1847 and by 1870 production at the mine had peaked, but under a new manager, James Randol, mining methods were improved, and some new bodies of ore were found. After Randol left in 1892, the fortunes of the company declined, and by 1912 it had declared bankruptcy.

Then, in an effort to reduce hazards from the mercury-producing process, the U.S. Army Corps of Engineers demolished nearly all the early structures, the miners' cottages, and two churches on Mine Hill. However, the entrance to the San Cristobal Mine has been reconstructed so that visitors can look into the tunnel. New Almaden is listed as a National Historic Landmark district and the community of New Almaden retains the integrity of this old village.

At present, historical markers and interpretive plaques tell the story of cinnabar, a term derived from an ancient Persian word meaning "dragon's blood." The county's New Almaden Quicksilver Mining Museum, located in the Casa Grande building at 21350 Almaden Road, has displays of mining equipment, models, maps, and photographs, all of which give you some grasp of the astounding scale of mining operations at New Almaden.

Long before Europeans settled in the Santa Clara Valley, Ohlone Indians traveled upstream along Los Alamitos Creek to gather cinnabar in the hills of today's Almaden Quicksilver Park. They crushed the rock to make the red pigment with which they decorated their bodies.

Residual mercury in the soil and streams is highly toxic. Some areas of the abandoned Almaden Quicksilver mines are closed to the public, and prominent signs along the trails warn that fish in the creek are contaminated with mercury and should not be eaten.

On the exposed Wood Road, you cross Jacques Ridge on a long reach through grasslands and oak woodland. The road heads gradually downhill and, at 3.6 miles, enters an expansive open field. On the opposite side of the field you enter an oak woodland habitat until you reach the large Hicks Road parking lot. Head through the parking lot and down the entrance road until you reach the intersection of Hicks and Mount

Brilliant green oaks line the Hacienda Trail in Almaden Quicksilver County Park.

Umunhum Roads. Crossing Hicks Road, walk or ride along Mount Umunhum Road until you get to the small Jacques Ridge Parking Area at 4.6 miles.

This marks the end of the Almaden Quicksilver County Park segment and the beginning of the next segment in Sierra Azul Open Space Preserve.

Sierra Azul Open Space Preserve and Lexington Reservoir County Park

*From Jacques Ridge Parking Area in San José
to Lexington Reservoir in Los Gatos*

LENGTH 11.7 miles one-way; car shuttle possible

ELEVATION GAIN/LOSS 1,830'/2,460' one-way

ACCESSIBILITY Hikers, equestrians, and mountain bikers

AGENCIES Midpeninsula Regional Open Space District and Santa Clara County Parks

REGULATIONS Preserve open sunrise–30 minutes after sunset. Dogs prohibited on the Woods Trail but leashed dogs allowed on the Priest Rock, Kennedy, and Lime-kiln Trails. Lexington Reservoir County Park open 8 a.m.–sunset.

FACILITIES Toilet located at Jacques Ridge; equestrian parking at Hicks Road Parking Area; restrooms at boat launch and Miller Point at Lexington Reservoir

YOU ARE REWARDED WITH PANORAMIC VIEWS of Mount Umunhum, the Santa Clara Valley, and the Inner and Outer Coast Ranges on this long trek through the Midpeninsula Regional Open Space District's largest preserve. Beginning along the lower wooded slopes of Mount Umunhum, the trail climbs to a chaparral landscape up Mount El Sombroso. The remainder of the route undulates northwest over rugged hills and makes a long 3.9-mile descent to Lexington Reservoir. Choose a cool day to hike or ride this exposed fire road.

Getting Started

EAST TRAILHEAD Jacques Ridge Parking Area, Hicks Road and Mount Umunhum Road intersection, Gate SA6, San José. (**GPS: N37° 10.521', W121° 51.863'**)

WEST TRAILHEAD Alma Bridge Road, 2.5 miles east of CA 17, Gate SA21, Los Gatos. Parking on west side of road. (**GPS: N37° 11.789', W121° 59.040'**)

On the Trail

Prepare for this trip with plenty of water, lunch, snacks, weather-appropriate clothes, and an early start. Go through the gate at the Woods Trail entrance on Mount Umunhum Road and the fire road soon enters the woods. The trail winds for miles around the contours of lower Mount Umunhum in the Guadalupe Creek watershed. On north-facing slopes, you pass under canyon and coast live oaks, bays, tanoaks, madrones, bigleaf maples, and buckeyes.

At 0.5 mile you walk under transmission lines for the first of many times on this journey. Look up ahead for your first unobstructed view of the impressive 3,486-foot Mount Umunhum. Topping this mountain is an immense structure built for a U.S. Air Force station early-warning radar network and in use from 1957 to 1980.

As you cross many creek drainages, some openings in the trees give you distant views of the Santa Clara Valley and the road you will be traversing ahead; then at 1.7 miles after you have curved to the north, pass through open areas where you can look back at the road you've traveled. A 2.8 miles you pass Barlow Road, the route up to Mount Umunhum (see next section), but stay straight.

The road gains elevation gradually at 3.3 miles and ascends steeply by 4 miles. In less than 1 mile, you're in an exposed chaparral landscape and for the rest of the journey will see many species line the road: California pitcher sage, toyon, manzanita, chaparral pea, chamise, monkeyflower, coyote brush, coffeeberry, California yerba santa, leather oak, scrub oak, poison oak, and deerweed.

By 5 miles, you can see Loma Prieta and all of Mount Umunhum, as well as many peaks toward the east in the Diablo Range, especially Mount Day. Almaden Quicksilver County Park is below, which the Ridge Trail crosses. Here the trail takes a sharp left as it climbs the flanks of Mount El Sombroso. Shortly before you reach the unmarked turnoff for Mount El Sombroso at 5.8 miles, you are up on the ridge with your first views west to the Santa Cruz Mountains. In the summer, you may see fog toward the coast. The 2,999-foot Mount El Sombroso summit, marked by a transmission tower, is a short distance up the road. On clear days you can see Monterey Bay glistening in the sunshine.

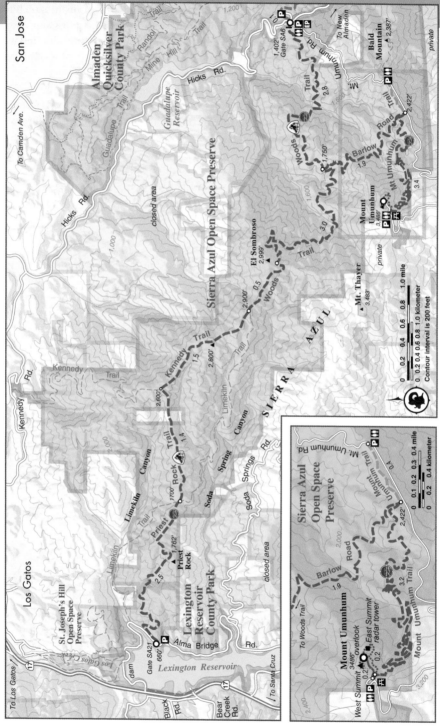

San Jose

Almaden Quicksilver County Park

To New Almaden

Gate SA6
1,402'
P
P
EP

Bald Mountain
2,387'

Randol Trail

Hicks Rd.

Mine Hill Trail

Guadalupe Trail

Guadalupe Reservoir

To Camden Ave.

Woods Trail

1,750'

Mt. Umunhum Rd.
2.8

2,422'
P

Sierra Azul Open Space Preserve

1,200

1,000

closed area

1,600

Barlow
1.9

Mt Umunhum Road Trail

3.4

private

El Sombroso
2,999'
0.5

Woods Trail
3.0

Mount Umunhum
3,486'
P
P

Mt. Thayer
3,483'

private

Kennedy Trail

Kennedy Rd.

2,600'

1.5

2,800'

Limekiln Canyon Trail

Limekiln Trail

Spring Canyon

Soda Springs Rd.

Soda Springs Rd.

closed area

1.4

Rock Trail
1,700'

Priest Rock
1,762'

2.5

SIERRA AZUL

0 0.2 0.4 0.6 0.8 1.0 mile
0 0.2 0.4 0.6 0.8 1.0 kilometer
Contour interval is 200 feet

Sierra Azul Open Space Preserve

Mt. Umunhum Rd.
P

Mount Trail
0.4

2,422'

Barlow
1.9

Mount Umunhum Road

3.2

Mount Umunhum Trail

To Woods Trail

Mount Umunhum
3,486'
West Summit overlook
East Summit radar tower
0.2
0.2
P
P

0 0.1 0.2 0.3 0.4 mile
0 0.2 0.4 kilometer

St. Joseph's Hill Open Space Preserve

Los Gatos

Lexington Reservoir County Park

Priest Rock Trail

Gate SA21
660'
P
Alma Bridge Rd.

dam

Lexington Reservoir

To Los Gatos

17

Black Rd.

Bear Creek Rd.

To Santa Cruz

Los Gatos Creek

Back on the Ridge Trail, you now have splendid views to your right to San José and the urbanized Santa Clara Valley. You are on the ridge, under the transmission line, and the slopes drop steeply to the foothills above the valley. After 6.3 miles you reach the end of Woods Road. The Limekiln Trail goes left, and the Ridge Trail route follows the Kennedy Trail to the right. In spring and summer you may see a profusion of purple Clarkia and lupine here just beyond the junction.

The trail undulates, ascending and descending steeply, with some views of the valley. At 7.3 miles you have a distant view of the fire road going up and down a series of hills far out in front of you, preparing you for the topography ahead. Just before you reach the junction to the Priest Rock Trail at 7.8 miles, a short trail goes off to your left to a west-facing overlook.

Take a left on the Priest Rock Trail (the Kennedy Trail goes north on a downhill route to the lower reaches of Los Gatos). The road is rocky and begins descending steeply right away. In about 0.5 mile, the road levels some but the Priest Rock Trail descends more than 1,800 feet in just under 4 miles to the trail's end. At 9 miles you begin to see north to the communities at the base of the Santa Cruz Mountains, the closest being Los Gatos.

At 9.2 miles you intersect the Limekiln Trail, and the Ridge Trail route stays straight. Pass in and out of the transmission lines again; houses and vineyards are on nearby slopes. Finally, at 10.7 miles, you find your first bench under an enormous eucalyptus tree, and shortly you have your first glimpse of scenic Lexington

Mount Umunhum from the Woods Trail

Reservoir. As you head down to the lake, you pass under more trees—oaks, bays, and eucalyptus—and finally drop to the paved road above the lake, your ending point, at 11.7 miles.

◆ ◆ ◆

The next Ridge Trail segment climbs to the summit of Mount Umunhum; it can be accessed from Woods Road or from the Bald Mountain Staging Area on Mount Umunhum Road.

Sierra Azul Open Space Preserve: Mount Umunhum

From Jacques Ridge Parking Area or Bald Mountain Parking Area to Mount Umunhum Summit in San José

see map on p. 243

LENGTH 8.1 miles one-way (Jacques Ridge Parking Area to summit) or 3.8 miles one-way (Bald Mountain Parking Area to summit); car shuttle possible

ELEVATION GAIN/LOSS 2,435'/385' one-way (from Jacques Ridge) or 1,150-foot gain one-way (from Bald Mountain)

ACCESSIBILITY Hikers, equestrians, and mountain bikers

AGENCY Midpeninsula Regional Open Space District

REGULATIONS Preserve open 30 minutes before sunrise–30 minutes after sunset. Summit open 7 a.m.–half hour after sunset. Dogs prohibited.

FACILITIES Toilets at Jacques Ridge, Bald Mountain, and Mount Umunhum parking lots. Picnic tables and shelter at summit.

THE MOUNT UMUNHUM TRAIL PROVIDES AN OPPORTUNITY to experience the mountain's ecosystem before arriving at the 3,456-foot summit. Most of the well-graded uphill trail is in a bay, oak, and madrone woodland with sections opening up to fantastic views of the Santa Clara Valley. The summit provides unparalleled views of the Bay Area and the ocean, and an opportunity to learn about the mountain's cultural and natural history through numerous interpretive panels. Be prepared for extreme temperatures and wind on the summit! Starting from the Jacques Ridge parking lot is a much longer and more challenging route.

Getting Started

EAST TRAILHEAD Jacques Ridge Parking Area, Hicks Road and Mount Umunhum Road intersection, San José.**(GPS: N37° 10.521', W121° 51.863')**

ALTERNATIVE TRAILHEAD Bald Mountain Parking Area, Mount Umunhum Road, 1.7 miles southwest of Hicks Road, San José. **(GPS: N37° 09.561', W121° 52.553')**

WEST TRAILHEAD Mount Umunhum summit, San José. Parking lot is 0.2 mile below summit. **(GPS: N37° 09.631', W121° 53.881')**

On the Trail

The trail, the Bald Mountain and summit parking areas, and the summit facilities opened in 2017. Mount Umunhum is where the central Santa Clara County Ridge Trail route will meet the planned southern Santa Clara County Ridge Trail route from Mount Madonna. If you choose the longer route up to the summit, start at the Jacques Ridge Parking Area, the same starting point for the previous Sierra Azul Ridge Trail segment. See the previous trail description for the first 2.8 miles of Woods Trail to its intersection with Barlow Road.

Barlow Road

From the Bay Area Ridge Trail on Woods Road, the climb to the summit of Mount Umunhum begins on Barlow Road. This 1.9-mile road (marked as 1.5 miles on the trail signs) connects you to the Mount Umunhum Trail. The Barlow fire road is accessed through an open gate, and it begins an immediate steep ascent out of the canyon. The route passes in and out of a woodland of bay, oak, madrone, tanoak, and buckeye, as well as an understory of toyon, holly, yerba santa, and monkeyflower.

At 0.3 mile you have good views of Mount El Sombroso to the north, which the Ridge Trail traverses. In another 0.3 mile, you reach a ridge where you can see southwest to Mount Umunhum Road and Loma Prieta, the highest peak in the Santa Cruz Mountains. To your left in the distance are Mount Hamilton and the Diablo Range. The road descends here and then ascends at the mile point, getting steep. When you emerge from the trees at 1.6 miles, you also see Mission Peak, a Ridge Trail destination in Alameda County, and Mount Diablo in the far distance. At 1.9 miles you reach the junction

The Summit's Long History

The fourth-highest peak in the Santa Cruz Mountains, Mount Umunhum is the second-highest point on the Bay Area Ridge Trail after Mount St. Helena. The mountain was a sacred place to the Ohlone and Amah Mutson peoples (*Umunhum* means "resting place of the hummingbird" in the Ohlone language). As early as the 1850s, settlers inhabited the mountain, which was part of the first legal mining claim filed in California.

The summit is primarily known as the site of the Almaden Air Force Station during the Cold War, from 1957 to 1980, when the eight-story concrete structure, or "cube," served as a radar station. During this two-decade period, hundreds of people lived in military housing on the mountain. Then the station's technology became obsolete, leading to the site's closure. The Midpeninsula Regional Open Space District acquired the property in 1986 and undertook the enormous project of removing hazardous materials and more than 13,000 tons of concrete, asphalt, wood, and other materials, as well as recontouring the mountain to a more natural state.

The Santa Clara Valley and Diablo Range from Mount Umunhum's summit

of the Mount Umunhum Trail: the connector trail to the Bald Mountain parking lot is on your left and the trail to the summit on your right.

Mount Umunhum Trail

The Mount Umunhum Trail can be accessed from the Bald Mountain parking lot, which has kiosks, brochures, and restrooms. To get to the trail, cross the road and follow the signs. The 0.4-mile connector passes in and out of a bay, madrone, and oak forest, with many trees covered in beautiful dendroalsia moss.

When the connector trail reaches Barlow Road, turn left to cross the road and head up the Ridge Trail route on the Mount Umunhum Trail, a singletrack trail (mileage notations are from this point). The trail begins in a bay forest, offering views through the trees up to the summit. You also see canyon live oak farther down the trail and then impressive big berry Manzanita plants, abundant along most of the trail corridor. At about 0.3 mile from Barlow Road, a dirt road merges with the trail and the view opens to the right but the trail soon narrows down again. You start seeing knobcone and foothill pines as the trail ascends; at 0.7 mile you cross a bridge. As you climb you are mostly in a forest of bays, oaks, and Pacific madrones; the mountain's serpentine soils provide a habitat for many rare native plants.

Reach the turnoff for the Guadalupe Overlook in 1 mile; it is a short distance down to the right and provides outstanding views of Sierra Azul Open Space Preserve in the foreground, Santa Clara Valley in the middle ground, and Mount Diablo and the Diablo Range in the distance, with Mount Umunhum rising steeply to your left. An interpretive panel about the Guadalupe watershed explains how water quality had been contaminated from historic mercury mining; the headwaters of Guadalupe Creek begin in the canyon below.

Heading back up the trail, at 1.3 miles you enter a chaparral landscape with views to Loma Prieta, Crystal Peak, Mount Chual, and the southern Santa Clara Valley—Morgan Hill, San Martin, and Pacheco Peak near Gilroy. At 1.7 miles, after crossing a bridge, you reach remnants of a cabin built in the first half of the 20th century. An interpretive panel mentions the Austrian and German refugees who settled on Mount Umunhum in the 1870s and the many people who settled in Santa Clara County to work in the mining, cannery, and railroad industries in the early 1900s.

After crossing the next bridge, you have intermittent views up to the summit and at 3 miles you see an enormous metal sphere on the mountain above. This is the National Weather Service's main radar for the greater Bay Area. In another 0.3 mile, you reach the intersection for the 0.2-mile Ridge Trail hiking route to the summit. This trail has a long set of stairs at it gets closer to the summit. An alternative route is to turn left at this junction, which leads to the road and parking area. Just before the road is a sheltered picnic area with interpretive panels, and below is a hitching post and nonpotable water for horses. From the parking lot, you can access the summit via 159 stairs. Bicyclists can cycle up the last 0.2 mile of Mount Umunhum Road.

From different sections of the summit, you have outstanding 360-degree views of the region, including San Francisco, the Pacific Ocean, and Monterey Bay. You can see all the of the Bay Area's prominent peaks: Mount Tamalpais, Mount Diablo, and Mount Hamilton, as well as the other open-space preserves along the ridges of the Coast Range to the north. Next to the massive radar concrete fortress, the district built an attractive shelter and cantilevered deck overlooking the Santa Clara Valley, a perfect place to rest and enjoy the view. Many interpretive panels summarize the site's cultural, military, and natural history. On the west summit, a ceremonial circle provides a place for American Indians to pray and dance; the Amah Mutson Tribal Band worked closely with the open space district to protect the sacred site.

The next Bay Area Ridge Trail segment is in Sanborn County Park; the Sunnyvale Mountain Trailhead is a 24-mile drive from the summit of Mount Umunhum.

Sanborn County Park: John Nicholas Trail

From Lake Ranch Reservoir to
Sunnyvale Mountain Staging Area in Saratoga

LENGTH 3.5 miles one-way (plus 0.5 mile via Lake Ranch Trail from Sanborn Road or 1.9 miles via John Nicholas Trail from Black Road); car shuttle possible

ELEVATION GAIN/LOSS 1,160'/190' one-way, east–west (1,550' gain from Sanborn Road Trailhead; 1,200' gain from Black Road Trailhead)

ACCESSIBILITY Hikers, equestrians, and mountain bikers

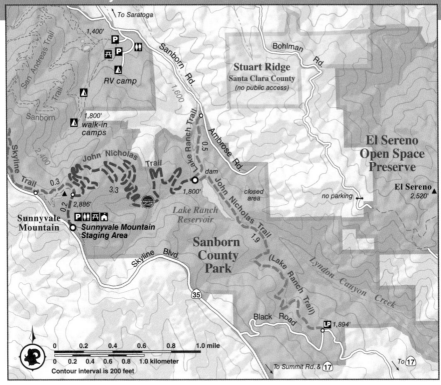

AGENCY Santa Clara County Parks

REGULATIONS Trail open sunrise–sunset. Dogs must be leashed.

FACILITIES Toilet and picnic tables at Sunnyvale Mountain; picnic tables at Lake Ranch Reservoir

OPENED IN 2014, this well-designed singletrack wooded trail is a popular mountain biking route with a significant ascent or descent. Lake County Reservoir provides a scenic resting spot. Parking at the ends of both connector trails is extremely limited, so consider doing this route as a round-trip from the Sunnyvale Mountain Staging Area.

Getting Started

WEST TRAILHEAD Sunnyvale Mountain Staging Area, Skyline Boulevard, 360 feet north of Las Cumbres Road, Saratoga. Parking lot. (**GPS: N37° 13.025', W122° 04.177'**)

EAST TRAILHEAD Lake Ranch Trail connector trail, Sanborn Road, 1.9 miles south of Congress Springs Road (CA 9), Saratoga. A few pullouts provide limited parking. (**GPS: N37° 13.652', W122° 03.163'**)

SOUTH TRAILHEAD John Nicholas Trail, Black Road, 1 mile east of Skyline Boulevard, Saratoga. Limited parking. (**GPS: N37° 12.348', W122° 02.253'**)

The John Nicholas Trail, with its massive sandstone rocks, is a popular biking route.

On the Trail

When the John Nicholas Trail opened in 2014, it created a 22-mile-long contiguous Ridge Trail segment north to Russian Ridge Open Space Preserve. The trail was named in honor of the late John Nicholas, who cofounded the Park Management Program at West Valley College in Saratoga, and forged a partnership between the college and Santa Clara County Parks. On weekends, expect to see many mountain bikers enjoying the trail's numerous turns and smooth, well-graded trail.

Parking is limited at the trailheads for the connector trails, Lake Ranch Trail and John Nicholas Trail at Black Road, so another option is to do this hike or ride as a round-trip from Skyline Boulevard. The following route description, however, is written starting from Lake Ranch Reservoir. The Ridge Trail starts at this location because in the future the trail will connect to El Sereno Open Space Preserve to the east, continuing across CA 17 to connect to the Ridge Trail in Lexington Reservoir County Park.

From Sanborn Road, the Lake Ranch Trail is a dirt road that ascends steeply through a bay woodland for 0.5 mile before intersecting with the John Nicholas Trail. The John Nicholas Trail from Black Road is a relatively level 1.9-mile wooded route. At the north end of scenic Lake Ranch Reservoir, sit at the picnic table under the grand bigleaf maples and enjoy the beautiful mountain setting. You are sitting where the San Andreas Fault cuts diagonally through the park.

The Bay Area Ridge Trail starts at the junction of the Lake Ranch Trail and the John Nicholas Trail. Head west on the John Nicholas Trail and shortly you will be in the trees for the remainder of the route on a wide singletrack trail. The tree canopy is very high, due to the density of the trees, mostly bays and Douglas-firs. In 0.2 mile you come to the first of three bridges in close proximity that cross the creek, and a bench to rest on. Impressive, huge sandstone rocks sit right at the edge of the trail.

After the bridges, the trail ascends more steeply. This is where the trail starts its long switchbacks. You pass by madrones, California black oaks, coast live oaks, and tanoaks. The trail alternates between climbing and following the contours, but it's a constant ascent. After about 1.4 miles from the Lake Ranch Trail intersection, you enter a Douglas-fir forest where you can peer through the trees to the Santa Clara Valley beyond, but soon it is more of a mixed forest again. In about a mile you come to a beautifully built stone retaining wall against the culvert for a creek crossing and a bench on the trail.

A bit farther down the trail, as you come around the bend, stands an enormous 40-foot tall tafoni sandstone outcropping. It's a fantastic feature on the trail, worth a stop, with a bench to rest on. Immediately after this unique landmark, the trail ascends in tight switchbacks through black oak woodland. At 2.8 miles up the trail from the lake, you start to get a clear view of the Santa Clara Valley; then, in another 0.2 mile, you reach an official viewpoint with a number of benches on which to rest and take it all in. The view looks northeast to the hills in the foreground, the valley and bay, and Mount Diablo in the distance.

In another 0.3 mile, you reach the junction with the Skyline Trail. Take a left to reach the Sunnyvale Mountain Staging Area in 0.2 mile, or take a right to start on the next Ridge Trail segment (see next trip).

Sanborn County Park and Castle Rock State Park

see map on p. 253

From Sunnyvale Mountain Staging Area to Saratoga Gap in Saratoga

LENGTH 6 miles one-way; car shuttle possible

ELEVATION GAIN/LOSS 560'/850' one-way

ACCESSIBILITY Hikers, equestrians, and mountain bikers

AGENCIES California State Parks and Santa Clara County Parks

REGULATIONS County park open 8 a.m.–sunset; trails open sunrise–sunset. State park hours sunrise–sunset. Dogs must be leashed in county park. Dogs prohibited on trail in state park.

FACILITIES Picnic tables and toilet at Sunnyvale Mountain

FOLLOW THE SKYLINE TRAIL along the wooded ridgeline of two vast parks: Sanborn County Park and Castle Rock State Park. On the route of old Summit Road, you wind along the protected east side of the crest of the Santa Cruz Mountains through forests of Douglas-fir, oak, and madrone; you pass immense sandstone outcrops and vestiges of early homesteaders' orchards and dwellings. This fairly level trip, entirely in shade, is ideal for warm days.

Getting Started

SOUTH TRAILHEAD Sunnyvale Mountain Staging Area, Skyline Boulevard, 360 feet north of Las Cumbres Road, Saratoga. Large parking lot. (**GPS: N37° 13.025', W122° 04.177'**)

NORTH TRAILHEAD Saratoga Gap Staging Area, Skyline Boulevard and CA 9 intersection, Saratoga. Large parking lot at southeast corner of intersection. (**GPS: N37° 15.500', W122° 07.289'**)

On the Trail

From the north side of the Sunnyvale Mountain Staging Area, follow the Bay Area Ridge Trail as it skirts the edge of an overgrown orchard and heads northward on a wide old farm road. Stay left at a fork in the trail and in 0.2 mile you reach the intersection of the John Nicholas Trail, a section of the Ridge Trail that heads down to Lake Ranch Reservoir (see previous segment description). Pass the junction and climb gently under a canopy of mature Douglas-firs, bays, oaks, and bigleaf maples.

You soon pass the first of several wind- and water-eroded sandstone outcrops, uplifted over the millennia by folding and faulting along the San Andreas Rift Zone. At 0.6 mile the trail parallels Skyline Boulevard and passes more outcroppings. It heads east, descending and reaching a trail junction at 1.3 miles. Going right takes you down to camping and picnic sites, but to follow the Ridge Trail, take a sharp left uphill. Beyond here, the trail narrows and continues through a dense forest, into and around steep-sided canyons, the headwaters of streams named for early settlers: Todd, McElroy, and Bonjetti.

Madrones and tanoaks intersperse the Douglas-fir forest, and you have occasional glimpses of the Santa Clara Valley. At 2.9 miles, when the trail comes to Skyline Boulevard, a massive moss-covered sandstone outcrop is on your right, where a huge oak has grown into the rock. A larger sandstone outcrop, Indian Rock, lies 0.2 mile uphill. Rock climbers and casual hikers clamber up Indian Rock, set among gnarled oaks and madrones, for eastern and southern views over the Santa Clara Valley to the high points of the South Bay: Mount Hamilton and Mission Peak. The dramatic drop-off on the east side of the rock is a breathtaking 150 feet.

On the Ridge Trail, just past the Indian Rock junction, a cluster of sculptural sandstone outcrops extends down the hill. Continuing north on the Skyline Trail, you pass the south end of the Summit Rock Loop Trail, which descends into Bonjetti Creek canyon. Then, at 3.9 miles, the north end of the loop trail, after curving around a settler's homesite, joins the main trail. A side trip on this 1.8-mile loop takes you to huge

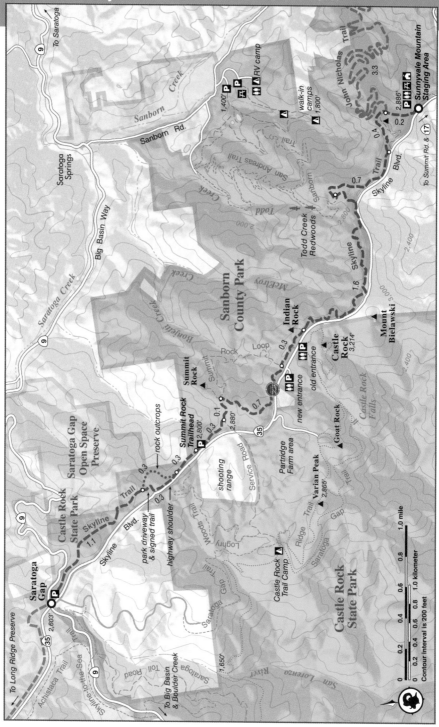

The Ridge Trail through Sanborn and Castle Rock Parks is heavily wooded.

sandstone outcrops, one of which lures climbers to the top, but the trail may be closed to protect the peregrine falcon habitat.

Bear left at the second junction of the Summit Rock Loop Trail, and follow the wide old roadbed northwest past some big mahogany-barked, broad-branched madrones. Within 0.4 mile the trail parallels Skyline Boulevard and soon crosses over into the 120 acres of Castle Rock State Park on the east side of Skyline Ridge. The hiking trails in this 5,150-acre state park, mostly on the steep west face of the Santa Cruz Mountains, lead to waterfalls, shady forests, extensive sandstone outcrops, and a backpack trail camp.

Shortly, when you pass between two boulders marking the trail entrance from a parking area near Skyline Boulevard at 4.6 miles, **hikers** can veer right, staying on a narrow ridge until joining the old Summit Road going north. **Equestrians and bikers** must go left, staying close to Skyline Boulevard before rejoining hikers 0.3 mile north. Before this junction, pause to look out over the valley to Mount Hamilton.

Early Skyline Settlers

In the late 1800s, immigrants from mountainous regions of Europe settled these hillsides, set out orchards and vineyards, and built wineries. But the 1906 earthquake struck hard here, causing landslides and severe property damage. Eventually, most of the hillside farms were abandoned. After Santa Clara County bought the parklands in the 1970s, the dwellings were removed, but some exotic plantings remain. As you follow the route of the old road joining their farms, imagine the hard work and tenacity required to carve out an existence on these steep hillsides far from the fertile Santa Clara Valley.

Skirting a fenced, private inholding, the trail continues north with tall, fragrant firs overhead, soft forest duff underfoot, and trailside moss-covered rocks. Fern fronds and clumps of iris edge the trail, while fine-leafed ocean spray and hazelnut bushes often overhang it. In springtime you may find blue hound's tongue blooming on tall stalks.

The trail drops you into the Saratoga Gap parking lot at 6 miles; walk to the north end of the lot to begin the next segment.

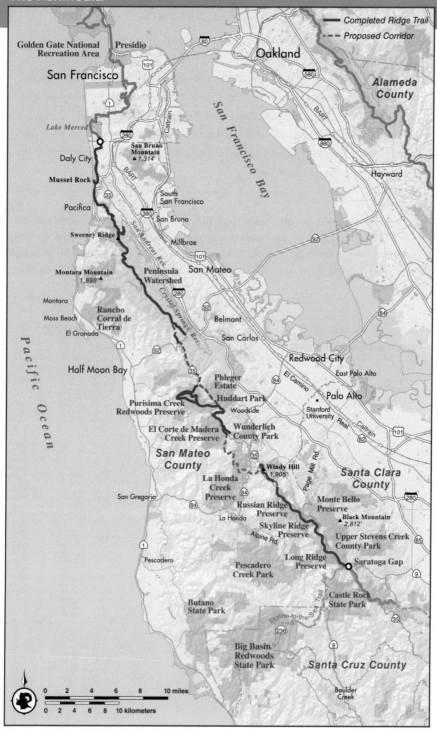

Golden Gate National Recreation Area

Presidio

80

Oakland

San Francisco

101

San Francisco Bay

Alameda County

580

BART

Lake Merced

280

Caltrain

880

Daly City

San Bruno Mountain
▲1,314'

Hayward

Mussel Rock

BART

Pacifica

San Andreas Res.

380

San Bruno

South San Francisco

Completed Ridge Trail
Proposed Corridor

35

Sweeney Ridge

Millbrae

92

Montara Mountain
1,898'▲

Peninsula Watershed

101

San Mateo

Crystal Springs Res.

Montara

280

Moss Beach

Rancho Corral de Tierra

92

Belmont

El Granada

1

San Carlos

84

Redwood City

East Palo Alto

Half Moon Bay

92

35

Phleger Estate

El Camino

Palo Alto

Pacific Ocean

Huddart Park

84

Stanford University

Purisima Creek Redwoods Preserve

Woodside

El Real

Caltrain

82

101

El Corte de Madera Creek Preserve

Wunderlich County Park

San Mateo County

35

Windy Hill
1,905'

Page Mill Rd.

Santa Clara County

280

La Honda Creek Preserve

San Gregorio

84

Russian Ridge Preserve

Monte Bello Preserve

Black Mountain
▲2,812'

85

La Honda

Skyline Ridge Preserve

1

Alpine Rd.

Upper Stevens Creek County Park

Pescadero

Long Ridge Preserve

Saratoga Gap

9

Pescadero Creek Park

Castle Rock State Park

35

Butano State Park

Skyline-to-the-Sea Trail

236

9

Big Basin Redwoods State Park

Santa Cruz County

Boulder Creek

0   2   4   6   8   10 miles

0   2   4   6   8   10 kilometers

THE PENINSULA

Saratoga Gap Open Space Preserve to Skyline Ridge Open Space Preserve

From Saratoga Gap in Saratoga to Horseshoe Lake Trailhead in La Honda

LENGTH 8.1 miles one-way for hikers, 7.8 miles one-way for multiuse route; car shuttle possible

ELEVATION GAIN/LOSS 665'/1,280' one-way

ACCESSIBILITY Hikers, equestrians, and mountain bikers; wheelchair users at Horseshoe Lake

AGENCIES Midpeninsula Regional Open Space District and Santa Clara County Parks

PARKS Saratoga Gap Open Space Preserve, Long Ridge Open Space Preserve, Upper Stevens Creek County Park, Skyline Ridge Open Space Preserve

REGULATIONS Preserves open 30 minutes before sunrise–30 minutes after sunset. Dogs prohibited except for a designated area of Long Ridge Open Space Preserve just north of the Grizzly Flat Parking Area. Upper Stevens Creek County Park open 8 a.m.–sunset; dogs must be leashed.

FACILITIES No water on route; restrooms at Horseshoe Lake Parking Area in Skyline Ridge Preserve; water at Saratoga Summit Cal Fire Station (0.7 mile north of Saratoga Gap on west side of Skyline Boulevard)

TRAVEL THROUGH MOIST EVERGREEN FORESTS, oak–madrone woodlands, and high grasslands along the crest of the Santa Cruz Mountains. You experience stunning coastal mountain views on this route through three open-space preserves and one county park. Trail width and surface vary from narrow paths to wide roads—soft in forests and along creekbeds, firm and bare through grasslands. Be prepared for wind and fog on exposed ridgetops, and for heat on west- and south-facing slopes.

Getting Started

SOUTH TRAILHEAD Saratoga Gap Open Space Preserve, Skyline Boulevard and CA 9 intersection, Saratoga. Parking lot at southeast corner of intersection. (**GPS: N37° 15.500', W122° 07.289'**)

NORTH TRAILHEAD Skyline Ridge Open Space Preserve, Skyline Boulevard, 1 mile south of Page Mill Road, La Honda. Large parking lot. (**GPS: N37° 18.734', W122° 10.616'**)

On the Trail

The trail roughly follows old Summit Road, a wagon route used by early settlers before Skyline Boulevard was built. The Hickory Oak gate on Skyline Boulevard makes it easy to break this route into two trips—a shady, moderately level, 2-mile trip from Saratoga Gap to Long Ridge Open Space Preserve, and a 5.8-mile trip from there to the Horseshoe Lake Parking Area in Skyline Ridge Open Space Preserve.

Hikers, equestrians, and mountain bikers park at Saratoga Gap and must carefully cross CA 9 to enter Saratoga Gap Open Space Preserve. The Saratoga Gap Trail begins under a canopy of great oaks, and for the next 1.7 miles, you meander around bends and into hollows above a steep-sided canyon with Douglas-firs towering

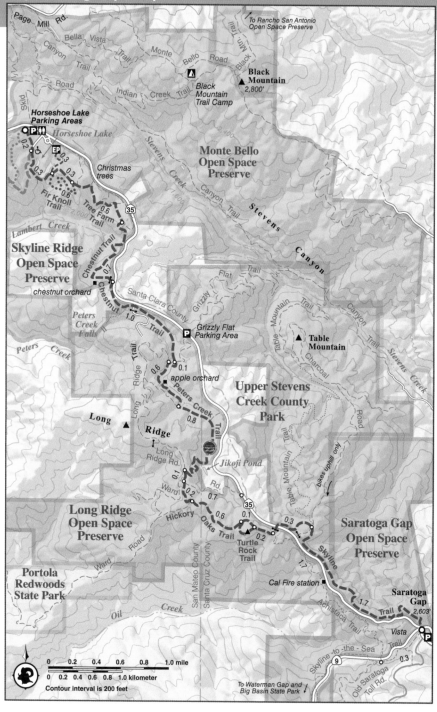

To Rancho San Antonio
Open Space Preserve

Page Mill Rd.

Bella Vista Trail

Canyon Trail

Road

Monte Bello Road

Black Mtn Trail

Black Mountain 2,800'

Indian Creek Trail

Black Mountain Trail Camp

Horseshoe Lake Parking Areas

Horseshoe Lake

0.2

EP

0.3

0.3

0.3

Christmas trees

Fir Knoll Trail

0.6

Tree Farm Trail

0.6

2,000'

35

Lambert Creek

Skyline Ridge Open Space Preserve

chestnut orchard

Chestnut Trail

0.7

Chestnut Trail

1.0

Santa Clara County

Monte Bello Open Space Preserve

Stevens Creek

Canyon Trail

Stevens Canyon

Grizzly Flat Trail

Flat Trail

Peters Creek Falls

Peters Creek

Long Ridge Trail

0.6

0.1

apple orchard

Peters Creek Trail

0.8

Grizzly Flat Parking Area

Table Mountain Trail

Table Mountain

Charcoal Road

Stevens Creek

Upper Stevens Creek County Park

Long ▲

Ridge

Long Ridge Rd.

0.1

Ward Rd.

0.2

Jikoji Pond

0.7

Rd.

35

Table Mountain Trail

bikes uphill only

Long Ridge Open Space Preserve

Hickory Oaks Trail

0.6

0.1

0.2

Turtle Rock Trail

0.3

Saratoga Gap Open Space Preserve

Ward Road

Portola Redwoods State Park

San Mateo County

Santa Cruz County

Oil Creek

Cal Fire station

Skyline Trail

1.7

Achistaca Trail

1.7

Saratoga Gap 2,603'

Vista Trail

Skyline - to - the - Sea Trail

9

Old Saratoga Toll Rd.

0.3

0   0.2   0.4   0.6   0.8   1.0 mile
0   0.2 0.4 0.6 0.8 1.0 kilometer
Contour interval is 200 feet

To Waterman Gap and Big Basin State Park

overhead. Many of the oaks, bays, and madrones in the forest are covered with beautiful Dendroalsia moss. Because the steep topography is too sheer for farming or cattle grazing, this mountainside has remained relatively untouched. The rather unusual California nutmeg tree, which you can recognize by the flat, prickly needles that distinguish it from Douglas-fir needles, is taking hold here.

In 1.2 miles you enter Upper Stevens Creek County Park and swing east, reaching a clearing and the unpaved Charcoal Road in 0.5 mile. This historic road, once used for hauling charcoal that was made from trees here, descends through second-growth forests to Stevens Creek in Monte Bello Open Space Preserve. Your trail, however, continues northwest toward Skyline Boulevard, through oak–madrone woodland.

At 2 miles carefully cross Skyline Boulevard to the Hickory Oak gate of Long Ridge Open Space Preserve, where you can pick up a brochure and read the information board. After a short rise to the ridgetop, you head north on the Hickory Oaks Trail, part of old Summit Road, through a forest of the area's namesake—mature, widely spaced hickory oaks, also called canyon live oaks, some at least 5 feet in diameter. You start getting distant views to the west through openings in the trees.

Beyond the woods, the main Bay Area Ridge Trail route continues along the road, but you can veer left over open grassland on a narrow trail to the preserve's 2,693-foot high point. Here more sandstone outcrops, lichen-splotched and weather-etched, stand near the lip of an abrupt decline into tree-filled Oil Creek canyon. At 2.3 miles rest on the bench where the trail juts out to the west. From this vantage point, the panorama—grassy hills creased by wooded stream canyons and successive forested ridges in the distance—is an uncluttered, pastoral scene to nourish your spirit.

This section of the Peters Creek Trail follows a wide path under towering trees.

Continue on the narrow trail around the shoulder of the knoll and zigzag down-hill through the hickory and live-oak woods to loop back to the main Bay Area Ridge Trail route on the wide Hickory Oaks Trail. Take a left. You make several descents into broad swales and subsequent climbs to grassy hilltop viewpoints. In spring and summer bright orange poppies nestle against boulders, and pink checkerblooms peek out from the grasses; in fall, vinegary-smelling blue curls add trailside touches of color to this spectacular trip.

At the next junction, at 2.9 miles, you ascend right on the narrow trail, around a shoulder of the ridge, but the Hickory Oaks Trail descends west to Portola Redwoods State Park on Pescadero Creek. Follow the Long Ridge Trail through open grassland and past another bench to a junction with the Peters Creek Trail at 3.2 miles. Turn right and descend switchbacks on a narrow trail through oak forest and a meadow to cross the earthen dam that holds back the waters of Peters Creek. Cross a bridge and on the dam's east side, turn left and follow the former wagon road, an avenue of welcome shade in summer and a moist trail under leafy arches in winter.

Past historic homesteaders' moss-covered fence posts and remnants of an apple orchard, you traverse a secluded valley where willow thickets mark the creek's course. Soon the trail and creek arc right into a tight little canyon with delicate fern fronds draping the hillsides and exposed, gnarled tree roots growing around moss-covered boulders. After crossing the bridge over Peters Creek at 4.7 miles, the Ridge Trail fol-lows the Chestnut Trail to the southern entrance of Skyline Ridge Open Space Preserve. This 1-mile trail travels through an open, narrow valley filled with poppies and lupine in the spring. You will cross two private roads and enter Skyline Ridge Open Space Preserve at Castanea Road.

At 5.7 miles the trail reaches a knoll overlooking a hillside orchard of widely spaced chestnut and walnut trees planted more than 100 years ago. If you come here in the fall, you can collect and buy chestnuts. The next leg of the Ridge Trail meanders downhill through the orchard, above a tributary of Lambert Creek, and under a canopy of overhanging trees. In spring, fronds of creamy Solomon's seal drape over moist, fern-clad banks, and heavenly blue and light yellow irises bloom.

You pass ancient oaks and bays, bigleaf maples, and madrones until you reach the dirt Tree Farm Trail. Take a sharp left and watch for RIDGE TRAIL signs that guide you up and down hills on a gravel road bordering a large Christmas-tree farm estab-lished in 1958. Straight, tight rows of conically pruned conifers lie on one side and a graceful, untamed native forest on the other. After a final uphill pitch on the graveled surface, pause to look east across Stevens Creek Canyon and the San Andreas Rift Zone to Monte Bello Ridge. Creased by tree-filled canyons, the rounded, grassy ridge is sur-mounted by 2,800-foot Black Mountain, its summit marked by tall antennae.

At 7 miles the 0.6-mile **hikers-only** route, the Fir Knoll Trail, angles left up to a ridgetop crowned by venerable, 3-foot-diameter Douglas-firs. Wend your way along the ridge under these magnificent trees; then abruptly descend switchbacks to Horseshoe Lake, the headwaters of East Lambert Creek, on a steep, oak-and-fir-forested, west-facing slope.

Equestrians and mountain bikers continue on the dirt road that curves around the northeast side of the ridge that the hiker's route traverses, and meet **hikers** on the east side of Horseshoe Lake.

Hikers and mountain bikers proceed southwest around Horseshoe Lake to the dam; to reach the Horseshoe Lake Parking Area from the dam, take the trail north, passing a trail junction, to the handicapped parking area. Proceed another 0.2 mile uphill on the road and cross a sloping meadow to the Horseshoe Lake North Parking Area at 7.8 miles (or 8.1 miles for hikers).

Equestrians leave the hiker, bicyclist, and equestrian junction on the east side of the lake and proceed north through woods to the equestrian parking area.

Before leaving Horseshoe Lake, note that the lake does indeed resemble an equine shoe, with arms wrapped around the base of a high, tree-thatched knoll. Home to red-winged blackbirds and several species of ducks, Horseshoe Lake is known to attract a pair of black-shouldered kites. Enjoy this scene by circling the lake on the foot trails that reach the picnic tables at the tip of the knoll above the lake.

From the handicapped parking area, **wheelchair users** can take the gently graded Ridge Trail route along the lake's reed-lined west shore, and cross the bridge over the dam to the junction of the Lambert Creek Trail.

The next leg of the Bay Area Ridge Trail continues northward from the Horseshoe Lake parking areas and connects to Russian Ridge Open Space Preserve.

Skyline Ridge and Russian Ridge Open Space Preserves

From Horseshoe Lake Trailhead to Rapley Ranch Road in La Honda

LENGTH 5.1 miles one-way for hikers, 5.3 miles one-way for multiuse route (includes 0.1 mile on Rapley Ranch Road); car shuttle possible

ELEVATION GAIN/LOSS 780'/810'

ACCESSIBILITY Hikers, equestrians, and mountain bikers. Wheelchair users have access to two lakeside trails around Horseshoe and Alpine Lakes.

AGENCY Midpeninsula Regional Open Space District

REGULATIONS Preserves open 30 minutes before sunrise–30 minutes after sunset. Dogs prohibited.

FACILITIES Water and toilets at Horseshoe Lake and Alpine Pond Parking Areas; toilets at junction of Skyline Boulevard and Alpine Road

ENJOY THE PENINSULA'S FINEST VIEWS and most spectacular spring wildflower displays on these ridgeline trails through Skyline Ridge and Russian Ridge Open Space Preserves. Climb through open grasslands to high knolls with gradual elevation gains and losses. The route has narrow hiking trails and wide ranch roads on duff-covered to gravelly or rocky surfaces. These exposed ridgetops can be foggy and windy; trails on south- and west-facing slopes offer only intermittent shade.

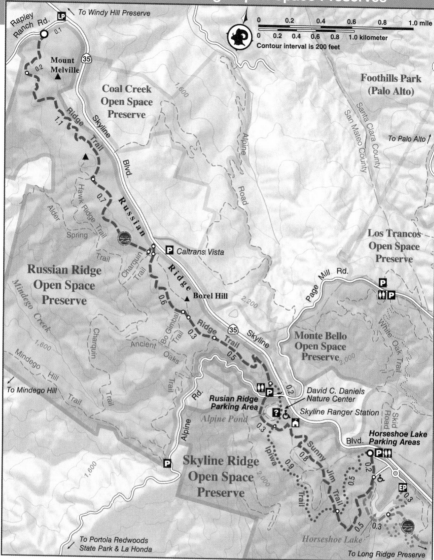

Getting Started

SOUTH TRAILHEAD Skyline Ridge Open Space Preserve, Horseshoe Lake Parking Lot, Skyline Boulevard, 1 mile south of Page Mill Road, La Honda. (**GPS: N37° 18.734', W122° 10.616'**)

NORTH TRAILHEAD Rapley Ranch Road, 0.1 mile west of Skyline Boulevard, La Honda. Roadside parking on west side of Skyline Boulevard at Rapley Ranch Road. (**GPS: N37° 20.389', W122° 13.320'**)

On the Trail

Wheelchair users can follow the gently graded trail around Horseshoe Lake's west shore to the bridge over the dam, and to the junction of the Lambert Creek Trail. The trail around Alpine Pond is also wheelchair accessible from the Alpine Road Parking Area.

Hikers begin this Ridge Trail segment on a different route from equestrians and mountain bikers. From the northwest parking area near Horseshoe Lake, make a long, gradual ascent southwest on a steep grassy hillside above East Lambert Creek on the Ipiwa Trail. In late spring, a striking display of lemon-yellow mariposa lilies and blue brodiaea rise above drying oat grass. The trail enters oak woodland before crossing the multiuse Ridge Trail (Sunny Jim Trail) in 0.5 mile. Then swing northwest through pungent chaparral punctuated by occasional small oaks. From a dramatic parapet chipped out of a sheer sandstone butte, a 180° sweep of forests, stream canyons, ridges, and grasslands unfolds below you. On clear days, you can see the ocean, and in almost any weather, you can find Butano Ridge, which forms the western rampart above Portola Redwoods State Park and Pescadero and Memorial County Parks. The trail bends into folds of the mountain and traverses sloping grasslands before entering a brief forested section, where great canyon live oaks flank the trail. Round the east side of reed-lined Alpine Pond, cross Alpine Road to the Russian Ridge Parking Area, and rejoin the mountain bikers and equestrians.

Mountain bikers and equestrians leave the Horseshoe Lake Parking Areas (mountain bikers use the northwest area, equestrians the northeast) and follow the marked routes down to the road above the handicapped parking area at Horseshoe

From the Ridge Trail in Russian Ridge Open Space Preserve, you have sweeping vistas of the Bay Area, including Stanford University, the Dumbarton Bridge, and Mount Diablo.

Lake. Here, you head out on the Monterey pine–lined road overlooking Horseshoe Lake. At 0.3 mile veer right onto the Sunny Jim Trail, and shortly start a steep climb out of the canyon above East Lambert Creek. You enter a grassland-and-chapparal land-scape and soon get fantastic views over the coastal mountains. Cross the hikers' route and continue uphill on an old, hard-surfaced farm road, with views out to the bay and Mount Diablo. At the Butano View Trail junction you enter an oak woodland and begin descending. As you come into a maintenance area, take a left at 1.4 miles and then an immediate right. At scenic Alpine Pond, use the trail on the west side, but consider a visit to the David C. Daniels Nature Center on the pond's east side. Take note of the beautiful rock outcroppings at the Old Page Mill Trail junction before crossing Alpine Road to the Russian Ridge Parking Area.

From the north side of the parking area, **hikers, equestrians, and mountain bikers** take the multiuse singletrack Ridge Trail route that zigzags up through grasslands toward 2,572-foot Borel Hill. Although this hill was named for former owner Antoine Borel, a San Francisco banker and Peninsula resident, the preserve's name commemo-rates a Russian immigrant who lived east of the ridge from 1920 to 1950.

In years of ample rain, this ridge in springtime is a wondrous wildflower sight. On both sides of the trail, as far as you can see, extravagant palettes of color sweep over the hillsides and knolls. Often, beginning in January, you will find perky Johnny-jump-ups turning their yellow-orange faces to the sun. Then goldfields, cream cups, orange poppies, pink checkerblooms, red maids, and blue lupines follow.

After 0.5 mile stay straight at the intersection and, in another 0.3 mile, just before you reach Borel Hill, veer left at the fork and follow the gently graded, multiuse Bay Area Ridge Trail route around the west side of the ridge. From this trail you can look past the preserve's boundary to Mindego Hill, an extinct ancient volcano. Beyond lies a succession of rounded, grassy hills creased by almost a dozen streams that join San Gregorio Creek on its way to the San Mateo Coast. The road goes over the ridge, and your view expands to the bay and the ridges ahead on your route. Descend to a cleft in the ridgeline to a junction with the Charquin Trail.

From the trail junction, a short steep climb to a 2,400-foot ridgetop will reward you with wonderful views of the Bay Area: To the north lie San Francisco and Mount Tamalpais. Across the bay is Mount Diablo, and farther south are Mission and Monu-ment Peaks, where another Bay Area Ridge Trail segment traverses East Bay ridgetops. Southeast beyond San José is Mount Hamilton. If you look due south on very clear days, you can see the Santa Lucia Mountains rising beyond Monterey Bay.

At 3.9 miles look right for a singletrack Ridge Trail turnoff—the Hawk Ridge Trail angles sharply left. The trail curves around the south and east sides of another 2,400-foot hill crowned by telephone-relay and electric-transmission-line towers. Abruptly you enter woods of tall oak trees that shade the low-growing shrubs of elder-berry, hazelnut, gooseberry, and thimbleberry. As the trail straightens out on the north side of the hill, you pass a wooden platform, a perfect picnic site.

Continue north on a long downhill switchback, under a canopy of broad-branch-ing oaks with lichen- and moss-covered trunks. A few more switchbacks carry you downhill, across a service road, and below a fascinating, glass-fronted, circular pri-vate home high above on the crest of the hill. Follow the contour of the trail around a few curves midway between the woods and the ridgecrest; you pass great boulders splattered with lichen and bedecked with healthy patches of poison oak. In late summer the pearly everlasting's tufted, creamy flowers edge the trail cut into a steep hillside.

After passing through a little woods nourished by an intermittent stream, you emerge onto a dirt road at 5 miles, which you follow 0.2 mile before reaching the preserve gate at Rapley Ranch Road. Turn right and head up the road for just 0.1 mile to roadside parking on Skyline Boulevard.

The next Bay Area Ridge Trail segment is in Windy Hill Open Space Preserve, 0.8 mile north on Skyline Boulevard.

Windy Hill Open Space Preserve

From Upper Razorback Ridge Trailhead to Spring Ridge Trailhead in Portola Valley

LENGTH 3.3 miles one-way for hikers, 3.1 miles one-way for equestrians, 0.5 mile one-way for mountain bikers; car shuttle possible

ELEVATION GAIN/LOSS 420'/550' one-way

ACCESSIBILITY Hikers, equestrians, and mountain bikers (bikers restricted to a short section)

AGENCY Midpeninsula Regional Open Space District

REGULATIONS Preserve open 30 minutes before sunrise–30 minutes after sunset. Dogs must be leashed and are prohibited on the Razorback Trail and a section of the Lost Trail. Mountain bikers allowed only on Fenceline Trail.

FACILITIES Restrooms at picnic area along Skyline Boulevard

FOLLOW THE WINDY HILL RIDGELINE through a sheltered forest and across rolling grasslands on a narrow footpath and broad wagon road. Enjoy sweeping views of the San Mateo Coast and Santa Clara Valley. True to the preserve's name, strong winds are possible here, as is coastal fog. Because this is a relatively short trip, hikers and equestrians may want to do the 6.6-mile round-trip. Bicycles are allowed only on a short 0.4-mile section.

Getting Started

SOUTH TRAILHEAD Windy Hill Open Space Preserve, Skyline Boulevard, Razorback Ridge Trailhead, 3.8 miles south of La Honda Road, Portola Valley. Limited parking. (**GPS: N37° 20.867', W122° 13.831'**)

NORTH TRAILHEAD Windy Hill Open Space Preserve, Skyline Boulevard, Spring Ridge Trailhead, 1.9 miles south of La Honda Road, Portola Valley. Ample off-road parking. (**GPS: N37° 22.004', W122° 14.846'**)

On the Trail

Hikers and equestrians begin at the Razorback Ridge Trailhead. Head downhill, leaving the whir of Skyline Boulevard traffic behind. Descend through a mixed woodland where feathery moss and clusters of lichen decorate the trees. After 0.4 mile and a couple

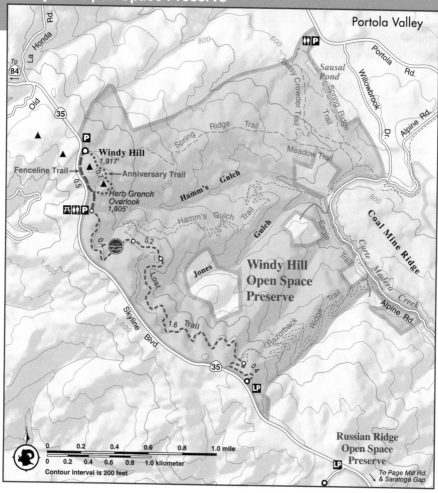

of zigzags on the steep hillside, bear left on the Lost Trail. Head northwest through a fir forest at an elevation of approximately 1,700 feet. Wind in and out of little ravines and cross headwaters of streams named for settlers who once farmed this mountainside. Water seeping from the hillside and onto the trail feeds the creeks that empty into perennial Corte Madera Creek on the lower east side of the preserve.

At 1.7 miles you skirt a chaparral-covered, south-facing flank of the mountain and then cross a dirt access road from Skyline Boulevard. Expansive views of the bay and the East Bay Hills open. Then, bending west toward Skyline, you tread an area that is fed by springs emptying into Hamm's Gulch. Where the trail that bears this settler's name turns right at 2 miles, you veer left along the edge of the gulch, where several immense Douglas-firs cling to the hillside. (The Hamm's Gulch Trail zigzags downhill for 2.6 miles to a stone bridge over Corte Madera Creek and the ornate iron gates of the former Lauriston estate.)

Continue north on the Lost Trail just off Skyline Boulevard in the chaparral and grassland. At 2.6 miles you reach the picnic area and bathrooms next to Skyline

267

Boulevard near the site of the pioneering Brown Ranch. Settlers Brown and his neighbor to the north, Orton, must have traversed the Lost Trail route you just followed. Until Skyline Boulevard was built in the 1920s, this old wagon road, known as the Ridge Road, stayed below the ridgecrest.

From the picnic area, begin the northbound leg of this trip on the Anniversary Trail. **Hikers** continue on this trail and gradually ascend the east side of the Windy Hill knobs. Take side trips to the Herb Grench Overlook or the summit of Windy Hill. These treeless protrusions above the long sweep of grasslands descending to Portola Valley are prominent landmarks on the Peninsula. On a clear day, they offer views of the entire Bay Area and the San Mateo Coast. On a day true to its name, the windy

You'll find ferns along forested sections of the Ridge Trail in Windy Hill.

Primeval Redwood Forest

As you travel through the forest, try to picture its former grandeur. Before the mid-19th century, redwood trees 8–10 feet in diameter covered the mountains above present-day Portola Valley and Woodside. These primeval redwood forests supplied the wood that built Mission Santa Clara and the Pueblo of San José. The heavy logging required to build gold-rush San Francisco in the 1850s, along with a disastrous fire in the 1860s, left hardly a tree standing here.

Today a second-growth forest of Douglas-firs and redwoods flourishes in the 1,130-acre Windy Hill Open Space Preserve. Some trees have grown to considerable girth, aided by natural springs, heavy rainfall, and coastal fogs.

1,917-foot summit can be a challenge to steady footing, yet a delight for kite flyers and model-glider enthusiasts. From the summit, it is a quick descent to the north parking area at the top of Spring Ridge, the end of this Bay Area Ridge Trail segment.

Mountain bikers' access to Windy Hill Preserve begins at the picnic area. **Equestrians and mountain bikers** leave the Anniversary Trail at the first swale and veer left on the Fenceline Trail. The wide dirt road, which heads north above Skyline Boulevard, offers splendid ocean views when the day is clear. They join hikers at the Spring Ridge Trailhead. This 0.5-mile section is the only place along the Ridge Trail at Windy Hill where bikes are allowed.

The next Ridge Trail segment begins in Wunderlich County Park, 6.4 miles north on Skyline Boulevard.

Wunderlich County Park to Huddart County Park

Skyline Trail from Wunderlich West Gate to Purisima Creek Trailhead in Woodside

see map on next page

LENGTH 5.9 miles one-way; car shuttle possible

ELEVATION GAIN/LOSS 715'/845' one-way

ACCESSIBILITY Hikers and equestrians

AGENCIES San Mateo County Parks, California Water Service Company, and Mid-peninsula Regional Open Space District

PARKS Wunderlich County Park, Bear Gulch Watershed, Teague Hill Open Space Preserve, and Huddart County Park

REGULATIONS County parks are open 8 a.m.–sunset and prohibit dogs and bicycles. Preserve is open 30 minutes before sunrise–30 minutes after sunset.

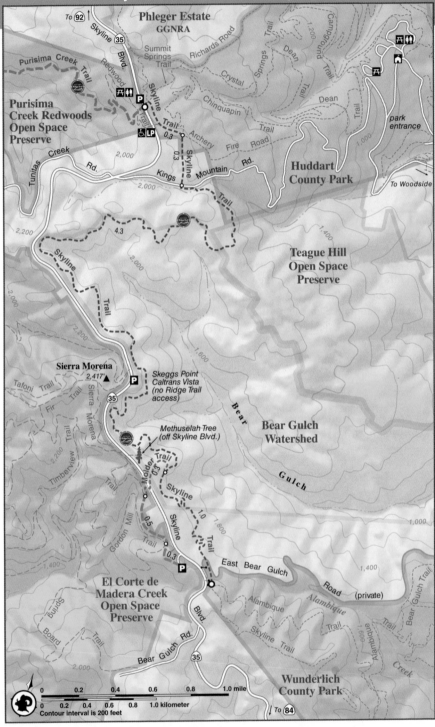

FACILITIES Water and restrooms at El Corte de Madera Open Space Preserve Staging Area, 0.2 mile north of south trailhead. Restrooms on Redwood Trail near Skyline Boulevard in Purisima Creek Redwoods Open Space Preserve.

FOLLOW THE GENTLY GRADED SKYLINE TRAIL through redwood and Douglas-fir forests just below the crest of the Santa Cruz Mountains. Discover unusual spring wildflowers along one of the few remaining segments of the old California Riding and Hiking Trail, a trail system established in 1954. Take this easy, shaded trail on a summer day when you need a retreat from the valley heat.

Getting Started

SOUTH TRAILHEAD Wunderlich County Park, Skyline Boulevard, 2.6 miles north of La Honda Road, Woodside. Parking is limited on the west side of Skyline Boulevard. (**GPS: N37° 23.943', W122° 17.594'**) Alternative parking at El Corte de Madera Open Space Preserve Staging Area, 0.2 mile north of trailhead. (**GPS: N37° 23.978', W122° 17.701'**)

NORTH TRAILHEAD Purisima Creek Redwoods Open Space Preserve, Skyline Boulevard, 6.4 miles south of CA 92, Woodside. Parking at the Purisima Creek Trailhead on west side of Skyline Boulevard. (**GPS: N37° 25.811', W122° 18.807'**)

On the Trail

Hikers and equestrians begin this trail from the northwest corner of Wunderlich County Park and quickly lose 100 feet in elevation on switchbacks through a redwood forest. In the spring, delicate fairybells carpet the forest floor, as well as forget-me-nots and ferns. In 0.2 mile cross private Bear Gulch Road (take a right and then a left), and head north above houses in the shade of redwoods and firs, grown tall since most logging ended here in the mid-1860s.

For the next 4 miles, you're on the upper slopes of the watershed of the California Water Service Company (formerly the Bear Gulch Water Company). You wind in and out of small ravines, hearing the calls of Steller's jays, the crested blue-black cousins of the blue (scrub) jays of the foothill woodlands. You begin ascending switchbacks at 0.7 mile and pass a large house; then you start to see more bay trees. At 1 mile you reach the junction with the Molder Trail. Taking a left here brings you to the El Corte de Madera Creek Open Space Preserve Staging Area in 1.1 miles (an alternative starting point for the hike), where you travel through Douglas-fir, madrone, and redwood forests. Stay right toward Huddart Park.

On clear days, you catch occasional glimpses through the trees of the valley below, though fog often shrouds the view. Tall Douglas-firs are part of the forest that has been taking hold here since the logging of the 1800s. Contrasting with the dark conifers are beautiful mature madrones and the light foliage of bigleaf maples growing in ravines. By the edge of the trail, blue hound's tongue blooms in early spring, followed by masses of Douglas iris in shades of lavender. In May you will find the bright, rose-red flower clusters of the uncommon Clintonia and the elegant, lacy-leafed, pink bleeding heart nestled in damp ravines.

After traveling 1.5 miles along the trail, you see old moss-covered stumps of the largest redwood trees, some 10 feet or more in diameter. These immense trees, some of which were 2,000 years old when they were cut down, flourished in the heavy rainfall—as much as 40 inches a year—along the ridge, with frequent fogs adding to the precipitation. Try to visit the nearby 1,700-year-old Methuselah Redwood just off Skyline Boulevard before or after this hike or ride.

At 3.3 miles the trail veers east, and you follow a south-facing ridge through oak woodland, which opens to chaparral at 4.6 miles. Then, as you enter Teague Hill Open Space Preserve, the trail passes under major power lines where the trees have been cleared. The trail turns northwest and stays near the power lines until about 5 miles, when you begin a gentle descent to Kings Mountain Road through a redwood forest with huge sandstone outcroppings.

You reach Kings Mountain Road at 5.3 miles. Follow the footpath beside the road to a marked pedestrian crossing leading to a private drive, and look for the trail on the left. The trail passes a large private home on a hill and enters redwood forest again at a Huddart Park crossroads. The Bay Area Ridge Trail route, also the Skyline Trail, turns west at 5.6 miles on a gravel service road through open woodland and continues to Skyline Boulevard. Walk parallel to the highway for 0.1 mile and then cross the road to the Purisima Creek Parking Area, the end of this Bay Area Ridge Trail segment.

The next segment of the Ridge Trail in Purisima Creek Redwoods Open Space Preserve begins here.

Forget-me-nots line the trail in shady Wunderlich County Park.

The Pulgas Redwoods

The size of the redwood stumps along this trail gives you an idea of the scale of the ancient forest. Known to the Spanish as the Pulgas Redwoods, the forest once covered the eastern slopes of the Santa Cruz Mountains above present-day Woodside and Portola Valley. This whole forest was cut to supply redwood to build gold-rush San Francisco. Oxen dragged the logs down the steep hills to sawmills; the wood was then taken to the port of Redwood City and sent up the bay on barges. So great was the demand for wood that by 1870 hardly a redwood remained standing on this mountainside. Logging finally ceased here because the water of Bear Gulch Creek, formerly used in the sawmills, was needed for other uses—first to supply a grist mill and then for the growing communities in the valley.

Purisima Creek Redwoods Open Space Preserve

see map on p. 275

From East Purisima Creek Trailhead to Preserve's Northeast Entrance in Woodside

LENGTH 5.8 miles one-way for hikers; 7.5 miles one-way for multiuse route; car shuttle possible

ELEVATION GAIN/LOSS 1,215'/1,290' one-way for hikers; 1,710'/1,675' one-way for equestrians and mountain bikers

ACCESSIBILITY Hikers, equestrians, and mountain bikers; wheelchair users can access a 0.3-mile trail

AGENCY Midpeninsula Regional Open Space District

REGULATIONS Preserve open 30 minutes before sunrise–30 minutes after sunset. Dogs prohibited.

FACILITIES Restrooms at both trailheads

FIVE TRAILS IN PURISIMA CREEK REDWOODS Open Space Preserve link for a challenging loop through forested canyons and over high ridges with ocean views. Hikers lose more than 1,000 feet of elevation in the first 2 miles but then regain it on a steady climb out of the canyon (bicyclists and equestrians experience a greater elevation loss and gain). The Craig Britton Trail for hikers is a relatively level trail through a majestic redwood forest. Summer fog sometimes bathes the forested areas, while the open, south-facing ridges may be hot.

Getting Started

SOUTH TRAILHEAD Purisima Creek Redwoods Open Space Preserve, Skyline Boulevard, 6.4 miles south of CA 92, Woodside. Limited parking near trailhead. (**GPS: N37° 25.811', W122° 18.807'**) Parking for wheelchair users is 360 feet farther south at the head of the Redwood Trail on west side of Skyline Boulevard. (**GPS: N37° 25.773', W122° 18.759'**)

NORTH TRAILHEAD Purisima Creek Redwoods Open Space Preserve, Skyline Boulevard, 4.4 miles south of CA 92, Woodside. Large parking area on the west side of road; parking also available for equestrian trailers. (**GPS: N37° 26.997', W122° 20.321'**)

On the Trail

Wheelchair users start at the head of the Redwood Trail and follow the well-graded path northwest through a beautiful redwood grove for 0.2 mile, where shade-loving wildflowers and shiny-leaved huckleberry shrubs thrive at trailside. Your path crosses the Purisima Creek Trail to a picnic table where you can rest and enjoy the forest view.

Hikers, equestrians, and mountain bikers descend into a deep canyon on the Purisima Creek Trail under tall, second-growth redwoods and tanoaks. The trees in this 2,511-acre preserve were heavily logged in the late 19th century. In fall, the brilliant yellow of bigleaf maples accents the forest greens. After 1.8 miles of steady downhill on the Purisima Creek Trail, **equestrians and mountain bikers** split from the **hikers** and continue downhill to the western terminus of the Purisima Creek Trail for another 2.4 miles, losing 1,710 feet in elevation, and then turn right on the Harkins Ridge Trail, riding uphill 2.1 miles before meeting the hiking trail.

Hikers turn right on the 2.6-mile, hiker-only Craig Britton Trail, named for the open space district's general manager who retired in 2008. The secluded entrance is on the right side of a hairpin turn. The beautiful trail follows the forested east side of No Name Gulch, where delicate springtime flowers, like trilliums and checker lilies, abound. Cross a bridge over a tributary and another over the main creek and then switch to the drier, south-facing slope. Tanoaks, cream bush, and even an evergreen oak or two flourish in this sunny zone.

You reach Soda Gulch and return to deep forest, where circles of second-growth trees surround redwood stumps 5–6 feet in diameter. One of the largest trees on the steep-sided trail is a towering, double-trunked redwood, whose scarred bark may indicate it was once used to anchor cables for hauling logs uphill.

At 3.1 miles a handsome wooden bridge crosses the upper reaches of Soda Gulch Creek, which is full in the spring but sometimes dry by the fall. Now more than halfway along the Craig Britton Trail, you again leave the moist redwood forest and begin to ascend open chaparral slopes with views to the west and the ocean. Look uphill to see the whole watershed as you climb through the open slopes.

Purisima in the 1800s

The forest scene in the 19th century was very different than what you see now: loggers felled redwoods by hand, several streamside mills cut the wood into shingles, and oxen teams pulled wagons loaded with logs up the steep mountainside. Logging continued sporadically into the 20th century, until the Midpeninsula Regional Open Space District completed its purchase of this land in 1984. Today, historic logging roads, linked by newly built footpaths, make fine trails. The wide openings in the forest were once used as landings for the logs and are now springtime gardens of blue ceanothus, scarlet columbine, and the yellow blossoms of invasive Scotch broom.

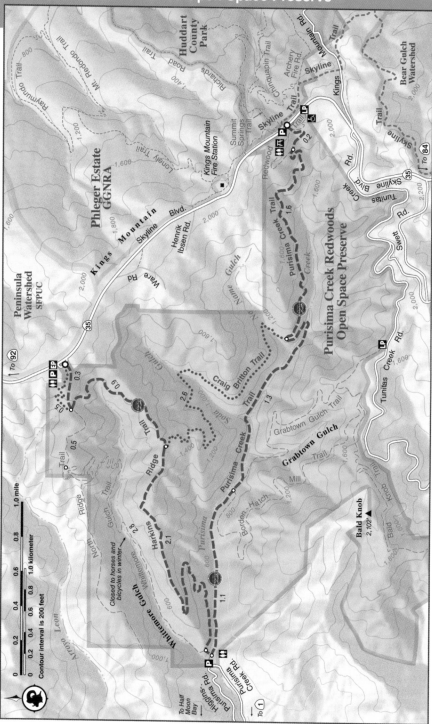

The Craig Britton Trail wends through a beautiful redwood forest.

When you reach the Harkins Ridge Trail junction at 4.4 miles, turn right and meet the equestrian/bicyclist route. **Hikers, equestrians, and mountain bikers** climb steeply on the wide Harkins Ridge Trail. Low chaparral and a scattering of trees line the trail, which veers left and levels off to cross over the headwall of Whittemore Gulch. Look west to the ocean to see breakers crashing on the beach near Half Moon Bay. Past sizable redwoods, clusters of Douglas-fir, and abundant seasonal flowers, you come to the North Ridge Trail junction at 5.3 miles.

Hikers cross the wide North Ridge Trail to a well-graded 0.5-mile footpath that zigzags up through a fir and tanoak forest. At one of the bends in the footpath, you can see other high points of the Santa Cruz Mountains to the northwest: Montara Mountain, Scarper Peak, and the long central Cahill Ridge in the San Francisco Peninsula Watershed. Soon you reach the parking area at the crest of the Skyline ridge, having regained the elevation you lost in Purisima Creek Canyon. **Equestrians and mountain bikers** veer right and follow the 0.3-mile North Ridge Trail to the parking area.

◆ ◆ ◆

The next Ridge Trail section at Skylawn Memorial Park is 4.5 miles north on CA 92, where Skyline Boulevard ends.

Skylawn Memorial Park

From CA 92 to end of Lifemark Road in San Mateo

see map on next page

LENGTH 1.1 miles one-way

ELEVATION GAIN/LOSS 235'/15' one-way

ACCESSIBILITY Hikers, equestrians, and bicyclists

AGENCY Skylawn Memorial Park

REGULATIONS Open 7 a.m.–6 p.m.

FACILITIES None

THIS IS THE ONLY SECTION of the Bay Area Ridge Trail that passes through a cemetery. The trail segment was dedicated so that it can eventually link future Ridge Trail from the south (near Skyline Boulevard) and the San Francisco Peninsula Watershed Trail. A short gap now exists between the cemetery and the watershed. Enjoy stunning views of the ocean and bay as you walk or ride the cemetery roads.

Getting Started

TRAILHEAD Lifemark Road and CA 92 intersection, San Mateo. Large dirt lot. Or park 0.4 mile into Skylawn Memorial Park at funeral home. (**GPS: N37° 29.775', W122° 22.076'**)

On the Trail

The Skylawn Ridge Trail segment begins on CA 92 between San Mateo and Half Moon Bay, at the entrance to Skylawn Memorial Park. There are no sidewalks along the entire route, but **hikers** can walk on the side of the road. About 0.2 mile up the road, take a right at the intersection. If you are driving into the cemetery, in another 0.2 mile take a left into the funeral home parking lot. A bulletin board in the parking lot has information about the Ridge Trail.

The Ridge Trail continues up Lifemark Road, with the cemetery to the west and an open chaparral landscape to the right, with views to the East Bay. Stay on this road for 0.3 mile, passing a Chinese section of the cemetery until you reach a junction; then take a right to stay on Lifemark Road. As you walk or ride along this next 0.4-mile stretch, you have a fine view out to the Pacific Ocean and Half Moon Bay. The road turns northeast, and the views extend into the San Francisco Peninsula Watershed, with its redwood forests on east-facing slopes. In this section of the cemetery, the infrastructure has been built for future burial sites.

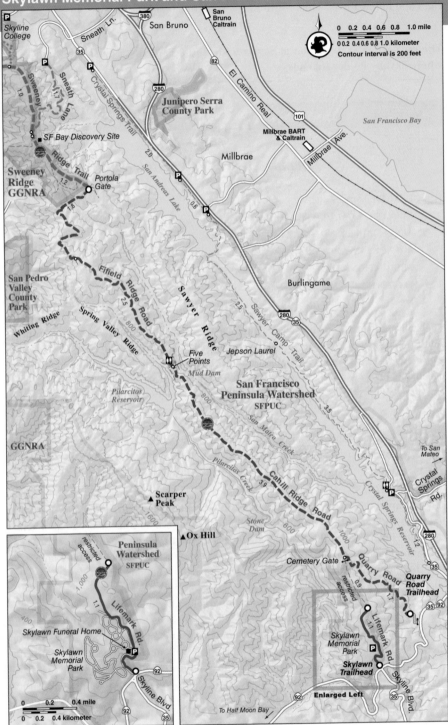

Skylawn Memorial Park and San Francisco Peninsula Watershed

Skyline College

San Bruno

San Bruno Caltrain

Sneath Ln.

Crystal Springs Trail

Sweeney Ridge Trail

SF Bay Discovery Site

Sweeney Ridge GGNRA

Portola Gate

Ridge Trail

El Camino Real

Junipero Serra County Park

Millbrae BART & Caltrain

Millbrae

Millbrae Ave.

San Francisco Bay

San Andreas Lake

Fifield Ridge Road

Sawyer Ridge

Burlingame

San Pedro Valley County Park

Whiting Ridge

Spring Valley Ridge

Five Points

Mud Dam

Jepson Laurel

Sawyer Camp Trail

Pilarcitos Reservoir

San Francisco Peninsula Watershed SFPUC

San Mateo Creek

GGNRA

Scarper Peak

Pilarcitos Creek

Cahill Ridge Road

To San Mateo

Crystal Springs Rd.

Peninsula Watershed SFPUC

restricted access

Lifemark Rd.

Skylawn Funeral Home

Skylawn Memorial Park

Skyline Blvd.

Ox Hill

Stone Dam

Cemetery Gate

Quarry Road

Quarry Road Trailhead

restricted access

Lifemark Rd.

Skylawn Memorial Park

Skylawn Trailhead

Skyline Blvd.

Enlarged Left

To Half Moon Bay

Contour interval is 200 feet

Half Moon Bay and the Pacific Ocean from Lifemark Road.

The Ridge Trail segment ends at the paved turnaround, but the road extends another 0.9 mile to the watershed entrance gate. Along this continuing road, the watershed lands lie on the east side of the fence, lined by pines and cypress. The Ridge Trail will eventually connect to the watershed's Fifield–Cahill Ridge Trail when the San Francisco Public Utilities Commission develops the 1-mile connector trail and new staging area. Until then, the next section of the Ridge Trail begins on Quarry Road, 1.2 miles east of the Skylawn Memorial Park entrance. It is a gated road and can only be accessed on a docent tour of the watershed.

San Francisco Peninsula Watershed

From Quarry Road in San Mateo to Sneath Lane in San Bruno

see map on facing page

LENGTH 12.8 miles one-way (includes 2.9 miles to Sneath Lane Trailhead); car shuttle possible

ELEVATION GAIN/LOSS 1,725'/1,490' one-way

ACCESSIBILITY Hikers, equestrians, and mountain bikers on guided trips only (shuttle return is arranged)

AGENCIES San Francisco Public Utilities Commission and National Park Service

REGULATIONS Trail open for docent-led group trips on Wednesdays, Saturdays, and Sundays during daylight hours (register at sfwater.org). Dogs prohibited in watershed but permitted on leash on Sweeney Ridge and Sneath Lane.

FACILITIES Restrooms at Quarry Road and Sweeney Ridge; also at 2-mile intervals along route in watershed. No water is available on the trail.

IN THIS REMOTE OPEN SPACE, dedicated volunteers will lead you through dense forests and over hilly grasslands with far-reaching views of the entire Bay Area. This trip is a unique opportunity to experience the 23,000-acre watershed, a state Fish and Game Refuge and home to the highest concentration of rare, threatened, and endangered species in the Bay Area. The pristine property contains Crystal Springs, Pilarcitos, and San Andreas Reservoirs.

Getting Started

SOUTH TRAILHEAD Quarry Road, CA 92, San Mateo. Shortly after crossing the causeway, heading west on CA 92, look for the Quarry Road entrance sign on the north side of the road. Gate is open only during docent-led tours. **(GPS: N37° 30.410', W122° 21.673')**

NORTH TRAILHEAD Sneath Lane, 1.1 miles west of Skyline Boulevard, San Bruno. Street parking. **(GPS: N37° 37.153', W122° 27.238')**

On the Trail

Currently the southern watershed trailhead is at Quarry Road, but plans are in the works to move the southern trailhead to Skylawn Memorial Park with a new staging area. Although 1.1 miles of Ridge Trail has been dedicated in the cemetery, a 0.9-mile gap remains between the cemetery and watershed lands. The previous segment description provides information on Skylawn's Ridge Trail section.

Montara Mountain and the Pacific Ocean from Fifield Ridge Road

Rift Zone Lakes

On clear days from the watershed trail, you can see long lakes that fill the linear valley at the east base of the ridge, San Andreas Lake and Crystal Springs Reservoir, from north to south. The linear valleys continue farther south, though they aren't dammed for water storage. On a visit to California in the 1890s, Andrew Lawson, a pioneering geologist, recognized these linear valleys as typical of a rift zone, and after the 1906 San Francisco earthquake, named the great California earthquake fault the San Andreas Fault for the valley containing the northernmost lake.

Water from the Hetch Hetchy Reservoir in Yosemite National Park is transported through huge pipes and stored in these lakes; this water, and water from other Bay Area watersheds, is then distributed to more than 2.7 million users. Local water runoff from the east side of Sweeney Ridge and those ridges to the south, Fifield and Cahill, also stored in these lakes, is a small percentage of the drinking water that the San Francisco Water Department supplies to its patrons.

Beginning at the quarry, you follow an old road up a steep hill, ascending 650 feet through woods and a chaparral landscape. At 1.7 miles you reach Cahill Ridge Road. To the left is the cemetery gate, which will eventually be the route of the Ridge Trail south through the cemetery. From here, the service road heads north along the middle ridge of the watershed lands (between the San Mateo Creek and Pilarcitos Creek watersheds) through a mature forest of tall Douglas-firs interspersed with coast live oaks and occasional redwood trees. Also growing along the route are occasional escaped plants from urban gardens, such as English holly and cotoneaster plants. For about 5.6 miles the route is primarily in the forest but passes through short stretches open to the sky.

You pass restrooms about every 2 miles, the first of which has some picnic tables nearby. At 4 miles, just beyond the restroom, is a perfect resting spot under the trees with plenty of seating for a group. Look for views off to your left at 5.2 miles, where you can see down to Pilarcitos Reservoir, the canyon of Pilarcitos Creek, and up to the heights of Scarper Peak. At 5.6 miles the road dips down to Five Points junction, the access point to the reservoir. Now on Fifield Ridge Road, the route ascends to the next restroom at mile point 5.8, where you can look back to scenic Pilarcitos Reservoir nestled in a deep canyon surrounded by wooded hillsides. Some of the docent-led tours turn around at this point.

The rest of the hike, high up on the ridge, is over an open chaparral landscape with occasional Douglas-firs on the road's edge. As you proceed up and down low hills with very little shade, low-growing shrubs permit very fine views of the bay and the mountains surrounding it. To the north lies Mount Tamalpais, east is Mount Diablo, and south lies Mount Hamilton. The near view takes in the full length of San Andreas Lake and Crystal Springs Reservoir and the curve of the San Francisco Bay shoreline beyond. At your feet in the spring are fields of glorious wildflowers covering the rolling grasslands.

Just after the restroom and picnic tables at 7.9 miles, you reach a bench where you can rest and take in the dramatic views down to Pacifica and the Pacific Ocean; Montara

Mountain rises 1,900 feet to your left. This next section of trail has fabulous views of the ocean and bay. The last 0.3 mile before the Portola Gate heads east, and when you reach the gate with your guide, the next 2.9 miles are in the Golden Gate National Recreation Area on Sweeney Ridge and Sneath Lane. The description for this Ridge Trail segment is in the next section (see the description between Sneath Lane and Portola Gate).

The next leg of the Bay Area Ridge Trail on Sweeney Ridge begins at the Portola Gate; however, the description is from north to south because the trailhead is at the northern end at Skyline College.

Sweeney Ridge

From Skyline College in Pacifica to Portola Gate in San Bruno

LENGTH 3.2 miles one-way for hikers; equestrians and mountain bikers take either the 1.7-mile Sneath Lane or 1.3-mile Mori Ridge connector trail instead of the 1-mile Notch Trail (additional 3.2-mile return for hikers or car shuttle at Sneath Lane or Mori Ridge Trailhead)

ELEVATION GAIN/LOSS 785'/300' one-way

ACCESSIBILITY Hikers, equestrians, and mountain bikers (hikers only on Notch Trail)

AGENCY National Park Service

PARK Golden Gate National Recreation Area (GGNRA)

REGULATIONS Dogs must be leashed and are prohibited on the Notch Trail. Skyline College open during school hours.

FACILITIES Toilet at Sneath Lane intersection on Sweeney Ridge

A TREK ALONG THIS 1,000-ACRE RIDGETOP visits the San Francisco Bay Discovery site, a former Nike missile site, and unique coastal plant communities. Offering sweeping views of the coast and bay, the trail is a combination of singletrack and unpaved and paved road. Because there is no trailhead on the southern end of the trail, this segment is described from north to south. The exposed ridge can be windy, foggy, or hot and is subject to sudden changes in weather.

Getting Started

HIKER TRAILHEAD Skyline College, Lot C, southeast corner, Pacifica. The lot is open on weekdays for a small permit fee, and if the parking gates are open on the weekend, parking is free. Several spaces are reserved for GGNRA trail use. (**GPS: N37° 37.702', W122° 27.902'**)

EQUESTRIAN AND MOUNTAIN BIKER TRAILHEAD From the east, street parking at Sneath Lane, 1.1 miles west of Skyline Boulevard, San Bruno. (**GPS: N37° 37.153', W122° 27.238'**) From the west, parking at Shelldance Nursery, Mori Ridge Road, 0.2 mile east of CA 1, Pacifica. (**GPS: N37° 37.039', W122° 28.994'**) From Sweeney Ridge Equestrian, 650 Cape Breton Drive, Pacifica, use the Sweeney Ridge Horse Trail up to the Sweeney Ridge Trail. (**GPS: N37° 35.735', W122° 27.536'**)

On the Trail

This segment of the Bay Area Ridge Trail can also be reached from the San Francisco Peninsula Watershed to the south, but watershed access is only allowed through docent

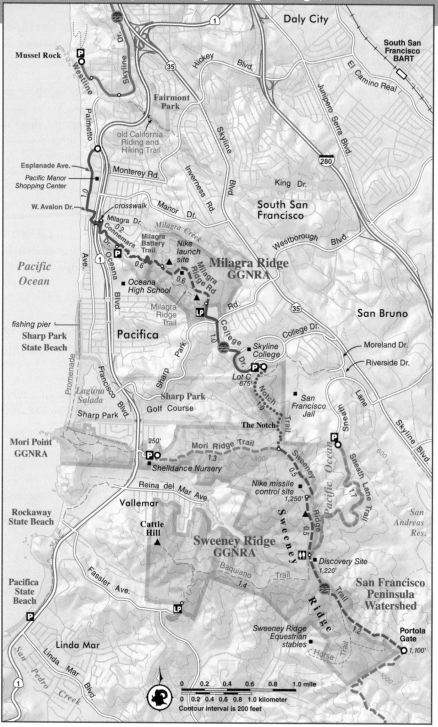

Mussel Rock
Daly City
South San Francisco BART

Esplanade Ave.
Pacific Manor Shopping Center

W. Avalon Dr.

Fairmont Park

old California Riding and Hiking Trail

Monterey Rd.

crosswalk

Milagra Dr.
Connemara
Dr.

Milagra Battery Trail

0.2
0.6

Nike launch site

Milagra Creek

Milagra Ridge Rd

Pacific Ocean

Oceana High School

0.6

Milagra Ridge Trail

LP

South San Francisco

Westborough Blvd.

Milagra Ridge GGNRA

San Bruno

fishing pier
Sharp Park State Beach

Pacifica

Sharp Park Golf Course

1.0

College Dr.

College Dr.

Skyline College

Lot C
675'

Moreland Dr.
Riverside Dr.

Laguna Salada

Promenade

Francisco Blvd.

The Notch

Notch Trail
1.0

San Francisco Jail

Sneath Lane

Skyline Blvd.

Mori Point GGNRA

250'

Mori Ridge Trail
1.3

Shelldance Nursery

Reina del Mar Ave.

800'

Sweeney Ridge

0.5

Nike missile control site
1,250'

Sneath Lane Trail
1.7

Pacific Ocean

San Andreas Res.

Rockaway State Beach

Vallemar

Cattle Hill

Baquiano Trail
1.4

Sweeney Ridge GGNRA

0.5

Discovery Site
1,220'

San Francisco Peninsula Watershed

Pacifica State Beach

Fassler Ave.

LP

Sweeney Ridge Equestrian stables

Sweeney Ridge Trail
1.2

Portola Gate
1,100'

Linda Mar

Linda Mar Blvd.

San Pedro Creek

Horse Trail

1000'

0   0.2   0.4   0.6   0.8   1.0 mile
0 0.2 0.4 0.6 0.8 1.0 kilometer
Contour interval is 200 feet

tours (see previous section). Prepare for a round-trip or one-way journey using the Notch Trail, Sneath Lane, or Mori Point Trailhead.

Long, rounded Sweeney Ridge, separating north Peninsula bayside and coastal communities, was slated to become I-380—the route from US 101 to CA 1—until the National Park Service purchased it in 1982.

For **hikers,** the Bay Area Ridge Trail segment begins by ascending steeply from the college parking lot through pine and cypress, coffeeberry and coyote brush. In 300 feet you reach the Notch Trail, where you head right on an unpaved road. You're out in the open headlands, and if the weather is clear, you already have expansive views up and down the coast. As you ascend, look down into Pacifica, and at 0.4 mile you can see sweeping views of the bay, Mount Diablo, Mount Tamalpais, and San Francisco.

At 0.6 mile you reach a graffiti-covered bunker before the trail heads downhill into a steep ravine known as the Notch. Signs indicate that you are in endangered Mission blue butterfly habitat. You go down many stairs in the sagebrush landscape, only to climb more stairs out of the ravine.

You reach the junction of the Mori Ridge and Sweeney Ridge Trails at 1 mile. The Mori Ridge Trail is an access point from Pacifica for **mountain bikers and equestrians** (see description following). The Sweeney Ridge Fire Road ascends the ridge through the chaparral landscape. Savor the views of the Marin Headlands, San Bruno Mountain, and the beautiful bay. Even when fog lies in the valleys, the peaks might be visible, giving you the feeling of overlooking a vast, misty sea pierced by isolated islands.

At 1.5 miles you reach the defunct buildings of a former Nike missile control site from the 1950s and 1960s—at 1,250 feet, this is the highest point on the ridge. The trail is now paved for 0.5 mile before reaching Sneath Lane, another connector trail for equestrians and mountain bikers (see below). Here you can rest on a bench or use the toilet.

Continue a short distance to the San Francisco Bay Discovery Site on a 1,200-foot knoll to your left. Two monuments commemorate the sighting of San Francisco

On Sweeney Ridge, you can look north across Pacifica, Daly City, and San Francisco to the Marin Headlands.

Bay on November 4, 1769, by Gaspar de Portolá's men. A bronze plaque on a weathered serpentine boulder states that the men first saw the bay while searching for a land route to Monterey Bay. On the south side of the knoll, a monument shows the outlines and names of the Bay Area's major peaks etched on a black granite cylinder. Among the mountain peaks shown are Tamalpais, Hamilton, Diablo, San Bruno, and Montara.

Continuing to the Portola Gate, you pass the horse trail that leads to Pacifica, as well as luxurious clumps of Douglas irises (which have beautiful blue or creamy-white blossoms in May) beside a few springs seeping from winter to early summer. You can locate the springs in summer by the patches of sedges and tall grasses that prosper in the damp soil of the seep. Toward the south end of the Sweeney Ridge Trail, crinkly-leaved ceanothus (California lilac) and orange-flowered twinberry have grown tall enough to provide a hedge and a modest but welcome windbreak. The vegetation soon opens in a clearing at the watershed boundary, and a high fence and restrictive signs at 3.2 miles bar travel beyond the Portola Gate. See the previous section for information on accessing the watershed.

Mountain bikers and equestrians must access the Ridge Trail from either Sneath Lane or Mori Ridge (**equestrians** can also come up the Sweeney Ridge Horse Trail). From Sneath Lane, go around the locked gate at the end of Sneath Lane and head up the paved road that climbs steeply through a dense growth of chaparral and coastal scrub. The trail curves into ravines and rounds shoulders of the ridge, offering great views of the Bay Area. A rich variety of native shrubs—red-berried toyon, cream-colored Queen Anne's lace, coyote brush, arroyo willows, elderberry bushes, and blue-blossomed California lilac—borders the route.

The Mori Ridge Trail climbs in a series of steep pitches that alternative with more gentle climbs. It offers magnificent views of the coast, from San Pedro Point in the south to the tip of the Point Reyes Peninsula in the north. Diverse species of coastal scrub cover the hillside along the Mori Ridge Trail, from pungent sage to aromatic coyote mint.

The next segment of the Ridge Trail begins at Skyline College's parking lot, where this route began.

Skyline College, Milagra Ridge, and Pacifica

From College Drive to Palmetto Avenue in Pacifica

see map on p. 283

LENGTH 3.4 miles one-way; car shuttle possible

ELEVATION GAIN/LOSS 115'/670' one-way

ACCESSIBILITY Hikers, equestrians, and mountain bikers

AGENCY National Park Service

PARK Golden Gate National Recreation Area (GGNRA)

REGULATIONS Dogs must be leashed on Milagra Ridge

FACILITIES Toilet on Milagra Ridge Road

THIS SEGMENT OFFERS A LOVELY STRETCH of open space along the bluffs and hillside of GGNRA's Milagra Ridge, with distant views over the Pacific. The route also follows streets within Skyline College and Pacifica, including a section along the oceanfront. The route is mostly level, with a downhill stretch from Milagra Ridge to Oceana Boulevard. Visit in March and April, when wildflowers are in bloom. Be prepared for fog in summer.

Getting Started

SOUTH TRAILHEAD Skyline College, Lot C, Pacifica. The lot is open on weekdays for a small permit fee, and if the parking gates are open on the weekend, parking is free. (**GPS: N37° 37.702', W122° 27.902'**)

NORTH TRAILHEAD Esplanade Avenue and Palmetto Avenue intersection, Pacifica. Street parking. (**GPS: N37° 39.288', W122° 29.498'**)

On the Trail

This Ridge Trail route begins at Skyline College's Lot C parking lot, where the Notch Trail connector begins. From here, head west out of the parking lot to College Road and turn left. **Hikers** can walk on the shoulder as the road circles around the west side of campus. View the 1906 earthquake centennial plaque at the visitor parking lot overlooking the ocean, which notes that the epicenter of the quake was a few miles offshore from Skyline College.

Access the sidewalk on the other side of the street; when you reach the entrance road to campus, College Road, use the crosswalk to turn left on this street. The sidewalk

Milagra Ridge is an inspiring place to look out over Pacifica and the Pacific Ocean.

A Habitat Island with a Unique History

Surrounded by development, Milagra Ridge is an island of coastal grasslands. Native Ohlone lived in these hills, livestock grazed here when the land was owned by the Spanish and Mexican rancheros, and artichokes were grown in the early 1900s. In the late 1930s, the United States Army purchased the ridge for defense. Initially the Army installed 6-inch shield guns to defend the underwater minefield outside the Golden Gate; then, in 1956, the military established Nike Missile Site SF-51, one of 11 sites in the Bay Area. At first the launch site was armed with conventional warheads, but by 1959 it contained nuclear warheads. The radar control tower was just south on Sweeney Ridge. The site was abandoned in 1974 and became part of GGNRA in 1987.

The ridge is habitat for the federally threatened red-legged frog, and the federally endangered San Bruno elfin and Mission blue butterflies. Milagra Ridge is one of the three locations in the Bay Area (in addition to the Marin Headlands and San Bruno Mountain) where the Mission blue butterflies are found.

is on the north side for 0.2 mile; then there's a short stretch without a sidewalk, after which you must cross to be on a sidewalk for the last 0.2 mile before Sharp Park Road. The entry road to Milagra Ridge is across the street. A sidewalk is on the east side of the Milagra Ridge entry road for over half the distance. In 0.2 mile you reach the gate into GGNRA, with information and interpretive panels. A limited amount of roadside parking accommodates about six cars.

The Ridge Trail follows Milagra Ridge Road. As you start, a North Coast County Water District Reservoir building is fenced off to your left. The open grassland and coyote brush–sagebrush landscape allows views of neighboring residential neighborhoods to your east and north, as well as the coast to the north when you come around the corner.

At about 0.3 mile from the gate, you reach a trail junction and composting toilet. Take the paved road to the right. You pass the intersection of the Summit Trail and Overlook Trail (worth the detour) and come to an interpretive panel about the historic Nike missile site. On a clear day, the expansive views out to the ocean and Pacifica are spectacular. You may, as a diversion, want to take the Milagra Ridge Trail (on your left), which goes out over the bluffs (a hiker-only trail splits off from the blufftop trail). After the Nike site, start heading downhill and follow the RIDGE TRAIL signs. A WWII gun battery is on your right, and at 1.7 mile you've reached the trail to the Connemara Trailhead.

The 0.6-mile Milagra Battery Trail, a singletrack trail that switchbacks down the hill, opened in 2016. This area was extensively restored with new native plantings, and much of the trail has cable railings. In July, buckwheat was blooming profusely along the trail. The trail ends in a recent subdivision at the trailhead parking lot, open 30 minutes before sunrise–30 minutes after sunset.

From this parking lot, it's about 0.2 mile down Connemara Drive—the sidewalk is on the south side—to Oceana Boulevard. Turn right and, in about 400 feet, you take the pedestrian and bicycle overpass that crosses CA 1. Cross Palmetto Avenue and in a block take a left on West Avalon Drive. In a residential area, you reach the ocean and Esplanade Drive in two blocks. The Esplanade Beach Overlook Trail extends for a long block along the bluff. If you're hungry, a sandwich shop is located along this street. Then head north, passing by many apartment buildings, including the area where apartment buildings were torn down in 2016 and 2017 due to the eroding cliffs. The Ridge Trail route extends along Esplanade Drive for 0.6 mile before ending at Palmetto Avenue.

The next Ridge Trail section is at Mussel Rock, a 0.9-mile drive, ride, or walk north. This 0.9-mile undedicated gap has no sidewalk, so use caution.

Mussel Rock to Lake Merced

From Mussel Rock in Daly City
to John Muir Drive in San Francisco

LENGTH 4.5 miles one-way; car shuttle possible

ELEVATION GAIN/LOSS 360'/475' one-way

ACCESSIBILITY Hikers, equestrians, and bicyclists

AGENCIES City of Daly City, San Francisco Recreation and Parks

PARKS Mussel Rock Open Space Preserve and Lake Merced Park

REGULATIONS Dogs must be leashed at Mussel Rock and Lake Merced. Horses prohibited when entering San Francisco at Lake Merced.

FACILITIES Restrooms at Lake Merced on John Muir Drive

TAKE IN IMPRESSIVE COASTAL VIEWS above Mussel Rock and then travel north on Daly City's residential and commercial streets to the south end of San Francisco's Lake Merced. The exposed route offers little shade and can be breezy and foggy.

Getting Started

SOUTH TRAILHEAD Mussel Rock Parking Area, north end of Westline Drive, 0.3 mile north of Skyline Drive, Daly City. (GPS: N37° 39.970', W122° 29.706')

NORTH TRAILHEAD Lake Merced Boulevard and John Muir Drive intersection, San Francisco. Parking lot on John Muir Drive, 0.3 mile north of intersection, or park along John Muir Drive. (**GPS: N37° 42.512', W122° 29.149'**)

On the Trail

Before you set off from the vista point above Mussel Rock, take in the panoramic view. The largest of the jagged rocky islets just offshore, topped by a navigational marker, is Mussel Rock. Black-coated, long-necked cormorants and a variety of other shorebirds inhabit these small offshore islands.

The San Andreas Fault enters the Pacific Ocean at Mussel Rock and reappears on the Point Reyes Peninsula. Look south from the vista point along the gentle curve of beaches and rocky shoreline beyond the Pacifica pier to see Point San Pedro jutting into

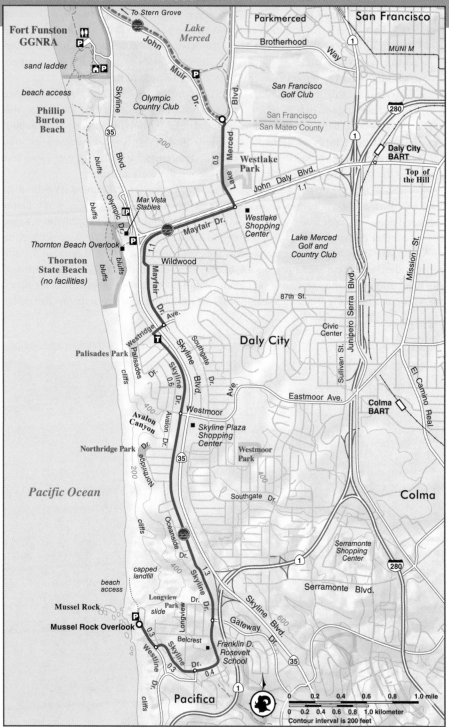

the sea. Just east of Pacifica lies the rounded flank of Sweeney Ridge, where another segment of the Bay Area Ridge Trail traverses the 3-mile-long ridgeline. Fort Funston lies to the north, and beyond, San Francisco's Ocean Beach stretches all the way to the Golden Gate. On a very clear day, the Marin Headlands and Point Reyes are visible farther north. Twenty-five miles offshore, the Farallon Islands appear from this perspective to stand guard over the narrow entrance to San Francisco Bay.

To start on this trail segment, head south on bumpy Westline Drive out of the Mussel Rock parking lot. In 0.25 mile turn left and start uphill on Skyline Drive. You will stay on Skyline for 2.6 miles through a residential neighborhood with sidewalks on both sides of the street. The neighborhood is a classic post-WWII Bay Area suburb, notable for its expanse of houses with boxy monostylistic architecture. The streets have few trees and the houses, all close to each other, are a patchwork of color.

About 0.4 mile up the hill, you pass Franklin D. Roosevelt Elementary School on your left. Turn around occasionally to see the expansive view south of the distant mountains and coast. At Oceanside Drive, the road heads downhill, only to go uphill once again before another downhill. If you are interested in a diversion, take a left on Carmel Avenue or Northridge Drive until you reach Northridge Park, or take a left on Westridge Avenue to Palisades Park. Both parks are on the bluff with views of the coast to the north and the hang gliders nearby, and have playgrounds and picnic tables. Even when it's foggy, the sound of the surf reminds the visitor of the ocean's incessant action below the cliffs.

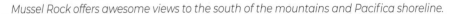

Mussel Rock offers awesome views to the south of the mountains and Pacifica shoreline.

Mussel Rock

While you're enjoying the view at the Mussel Rock vista point, read the interpretive panels to learn the site's history and natural history. From the late 1950s to 1978, the area to the north, now an open-space preserve and a paragliding site, was a landfill. To prevent ocean pollution, there is constant work on the site to keep the old landfill contained and the drainage working properly. It's a challenging effort with heavy winter storms and the eroding coastal bluffs. Just above the parking area is a refuse transfer station housed in the large concrete building.

Almost hidden, north of the canyon on a shelf midway between the cliffs and the ocean, lies more testimony to the relentless force of Pacific Ocean storms. The northern leg of the Ocean Shore Railroad ran along this coast from 1907 until its demise in 1920. Although planned to connect San Francisco and Santa Cruz, the tracks never bridged a gap south of Half Moon Bay. The railroad was abandoned in part because of landslides and high maintenance costs.

From Skyline Drive, take a right on Westridge Avenue and cross busy Skyline Boulevard (CA 35) with the signal. Turn left on Mayfair Drive, and follow this street through a residential neighborhood as it curves east, paralleling John Daly Boulevard. After 0.6 mile, when you reach Ashland Drive on your left, hikers can get on a tree-lined sidewalk between Mayfair and John Daly Boulevard. Bicyclists can continue to Crestwood Drive and merge left to get on John Daly Boulevard here.

At the corner of Lake Merced Boulevard and John Daly Boulevard (the west corner of Westlake Shopping Center), turn left and follow Lake Merced Boulevard on its east side. You begin to see the Olympic Club golf course on your left, and in 0.5 mile you reach John Muir Drive (and enter San Francisco), where you turn left to access the off-road path on the east side of the road.

This is the end of this Ridge Trail segment and the start of the next section.

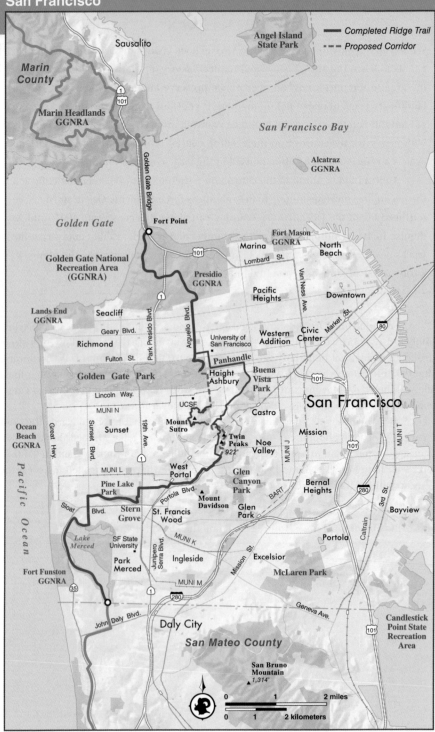

Completed Ridge Trail
Proposed Corridor

Marin County

Sausalito

Angel Island State Park

Marin Headlands GGNRA

San Francisco Bay

Golden Gate Bridge

Golden Gate

Fort Point

Alcatraz GGNRA

Golden Gate National Recreation Area (GGNRA)

Fort Mason GGNRA

Marina

North Beach

Lombard St.

Van Ness Ave.

Presidio GGNRA

Pacific Heights

Downtown

Lands End GGNRA

Seacliff

Park Presidio Blvd.

Arguello Blvd.

Geary Blvd.

Western Addition

Civic Center

Market St.

Richmond

University of San Francisco

Fulton St.

Panhandle

Golden Gate Park

Haight Ashbury

Buena Vista Park

San Francisco

Lincoln Way.

MUNI N

UCSF

Castro

Ocean Beach GGNRA

Great Hwy.

Sunset Blvd.

19th Ave.

Mount Sutro

Twin Peaks
922'

Noe Valley

Mission

MUNI J

MUNI T

Sunset

MUNI L

West Portal

Glen Canyon Park

Bernal Heights

Pacific Ocean

Pine Lake Park

Portola Blvd.

Mount Davidson

Glen Park

BART

280

3rd St.

Bayview

Sloat

Blvd.

Stern Grove

St. Francis Wood

Lake Merced

SF State University

Juniper Serra Blvd.

MUNI K

Portola

Caltrain

Park Merced

Ingleside

Mission St.

Excelsior

Fort Funston GGNRA

35

MUNI M

McLaren Park

John Daly Blvd.

1

280

Geneva Ave.

Candlestick Point State Recreation Area

Daly City

San Mateo County

San Bruno Mountain
1,314'

101

0   1   2 miles

0 1 2 kilometers

SAN FRANCISCO

Lake Merced to Stern Grove

From John Muir Drive to Sava Pool in San Francisco

LENGTH 4.1 miles one-way; car shuttle possible

ELEVATION GAIN/LOSS 295'/90' one-way

ACCESSIBILITY Hikers, bicyclists, and wheelchair users

AGENCY San Francisco Recreation and Parks

REGULATIONS Pine Lake Park and Stern Grove open 6 a.m.–10 p.m.; dogs must be leashed on park trails and city streets. Horses prohibited.

FACILITIES Restrooms at parking area on John Muir Boulevard; water and restrooms at Pine Grove Park and Stern Grove

THIS RIDGE TRAIL SEGMENT offers an opportunity to experience the natural side of San Francisco. On a mostly level route, you travel the length of Lake Merced, pass through residential neighborhoods, walk or ride by another freshwater lake in a sunny and protected glen, and visit iconic Stern Grove.

Getting Started

SOUTH TRAILHEAD Lake Merced Boulevard and John Muir Drive intersection, San Francisco. Parking lot on John Muir Drive, 0.3 mile north of intersection, or park along John Muir Drive. **(GPS: N37° 42.512', W122° 29.149')**

NORTH TRAILHEAD 20th Avenue and Wawona Street intersection, just west of 19th Avenue, San Francisco. Street parking. **(GPS: N37° 44.251', W122° 28.577')**

On the Trail

The Ridge Trail route starts at the northwest corner of John Muir Drive and Lake Merced Boulevard. This paved path is also the starting point for the Lake Merced Measured Mile, a 2.2-mile section of the Ridge Trail on the western shore of Lake Merced with mile and 0.5-mile markers. Look for the large MEASURED MILE signs along the way. Heading north 0.3 mile, you reach a parking lot, restrooms, a bridge over the lake, and paths down to the water.

Hikers and bicyclists share the path with runners and parents pushing strollers around Lake Merced. This scenic now-freshwater lake, an oasis in the paved city, occupies an ancient valley that was flooded at the end of the last Ice Age. As the seacoast rose, dunes built up, thus isolating this lake and Pine Lake in Stern Grove. Gradually, springs and groundwater changed the new lakes into a freshwater environment.

You reach the intersection with busy Skyline Boulevard at 1.1 miles. Stay on the path, unless you want to take a side trip to Fort Funston (see sidebar). A path across the street enters the former military site, but the official entrance is 0.4 mile south on Skyline Boulevard. A bit farther up the Ridge Trail, you can take a detour by turning right down Harding Road to enjoy picnic tables near the lake. On the Ridge Trail route, as you round the northwest corner of Lake Merced, you may hear the roar of a lion or the piercing scream of a peacock emanating from the forested west side of the street, which bounds one side of the San Francisco Zoo.

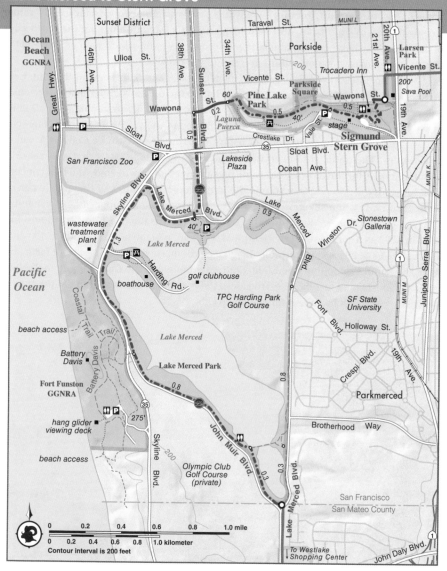

At 2.1 miles the Bay Area Ridge Trail route turns southeast on Lake Merced Boulevard, following the path along the lake. After passing parcourse stations set in a broad lakeside band, you cross Lake Merced Boulevard in 0.4 mile to the west side of Sunset Boulevard. This wide avenue, laid out in the tradition of the grand boulevards of Paris and Washington, DC, has landscaped borders and a parklike center strip and runs from Lake Merced to Golden Gate Park.

Stay on the Sunset Boulevard path for four blocks; then turn right on Wawona Street. Continue for three blocks through a residential neighborhood to Pine Lake Park at Crestlake Drive and 34th Avenue. You've come 3.1 miles.

Now you leave city streets to enter a steep-sided, tree-lined canyon. The paved path, often strewn with fragrant eucalyptus and cypress seedpods, descends rather steeply to marshy Pine Lake, and then levels off on a footpath hugging the north edge of the lake. Blackberry bushes and tall reeds crowd the path, which soon emerges at the first of four narrow meadows filling the rest of the canyon.

At the junction you find benches, picnic tables, and bathrooms at the Pine Lake Field House. Take the paved path that heads left up the meadow underneath large eucalyptus trees. This area is busy during camp season, with children partaking in all kinds of activities. Pass a dog play area, and enjoy this green valley, a refuge from the busy city.

You pass the main parking lot before entering Stern Grove's Concert Meadow at 3.8 miles. The paths are edged with handsome, low stone walls that also serve as additional seats for the crowds that come on summer Sundays to enjoy the free concerts held here. Mrs. Sigmund Stern started the long-standing tradition of fine public performances in 1931, when she gave the grove to San Francisco in honor of her husband.

Beyond Concert Meadow on the north hillside sits the charming Trocadero Inn, built in 1892 as a public hotel by George M. Greene, who owned the land for 40 years. The inn had a deer park, restaurant, dancing pavilion, rowing lake, and trout farm, and flourished until Prohibition, the Eighteenth Amendment to the Constitution, took effect in 1920. Refurbished in 1986, the Trocadero today appears much as it did at the turn of the century and can be rented for special events.

The Ridge Trail skirts Pine Lake, a quiet oasis in the city.

A Side Trip to Fort Funston

Across the street from the Ridge Trail, this former military site, as well as several others used in World Wars I and II for coastal defense, is now part of the vast Golden Gate National Recreation Area. Today Fort Funston's paved parking area covers the site of former Nike silos, and the elevated hang glider viewing deck and the adjacent hang glider launching site encompass an earlier military observation point.

You can walk out to the viewing deck for sweeping vistas of the Pacific Ocean— from Point San Pedro in the south to Point Reyes in the north. On a clear day, the view extends 25 miles offshore to the Farallon Islands. You may see an aerial display of hang gliders soaring on the ocean breezes.

Many trails traverse the site and there are two beach access points. When the fog hangs over the shore, there is a sense of solitude here, broken only by the shrieks of gulls. When coastal breezes sweep in and the surf crashes on the beach, the closeness to nature's power makes this almost a wilderness experience. And on clear, sunny days with the glint of sunshine on the breaking waves and flocks of shorebirds searching for clams, this is truly a glorious place to be.

You find picnic tables beside a small lily pond in a dense redwood grove near the Trocadero. Then the trail veers left and switchbacks up the steep hillside on a paved path through eucalyptus. At the top of the hill, veer left out to the street (the Wawona Clubhouse will be on your right). Cross Wawona Street and turn right. At the corner of 20th Avenue and Wawona, next to the Sava Pool building, you reach the end of this segment.

The next section of the Bay Area Ridge Trail begins here.

Stern Grove to the Presidio

From Wawona Street at 20th Avenue to Arguello Gate

LENGTH 6.6 miles one-way (plus 1.4 miles one-way on Mount Sutro Trail and 0.7 mile one-way on Phil Arnold Trail); car shuttle possible

ELEVATION GAIN/LOSS 920'/875' one-way

ACCESSIBILITY Hikers and bicyclists

AGENCY San Francisco Recreation and Parks

REGULATIONS Dogs must be leashed; horses prohibited

FACILITIES Water and restrooms in Larsen Park and Panhandle

SAN FRANCISCO'S SPECTACULAR BAY and ocean views reward you on gradual climbs along city streets and park paths. Visit a number of parks, playgrounds, and unique residential and commercial neighborhoods. The route takes you near Twin Peaks and Sutro

Tower, and through Buena Vista Park and the Panhandle. Be prepared for San Francisco's foggy and breezy weather.

Getting Started

SOUTH TRAILHEAD Stern Grove, 20th Avenue and Wawona Street intersection, just west of 19th Avenue. Street parking. (**GPS: N37° 44.251', W122° 28.577'**)

NORTH TRAILHEAD Presidio, Arguello Gate, Arguello Boulevard and West Pacific Avenue intersection, San Francisco. (**GPS: N37° 47.378', W122° 27.568'**) Besides street parking, limited parking is available on the west side of Arguello Boulevard (golf clubhouse), 100 yards inside the Presidio, or at Inspiration Point, less than 0.1 mile farther north on Arguello Boulevard.

On the Trail

Hikers and bicyclists start this trip at 20th Avenue and Wawona Street. Following the BAY AREA RIDGE TRAIL signs, go one block north on 20th Avenue and skirt the Larsen Park greensward. Before donating the land for a park in 1926, Carl Larsen had a chicken ranch here that supplied eggs for his downtown restaurant. Today, a swimming pool, baseball diamond, tennis and basketball courts, and playground serve neighborhood families.

From the corner of Vicente Street and 20th Avenue, proceed east, cross 19th Avenue, and continue uphill on Vicente Street. Saint Cecelia's, a Spanish Colonial building with a facade graced by handsome bronze doors, is the first of several churches you'll see on this trip.

Soon eucalyptus-covered Mount Davidson in Mount Davidson Park and its 103-foot concrete cross looms on your right; the soaring, spare, rusty-orange frame of 977-foot Sutro Tower rises on your left. Mount Davidson, the city's highest peak at 927 feet, commemorates surveyor George Davidson for exposing a false ownership claim to vast acreage in the southwest quarter of the city.

You leave Vicente Street's flowery front gardens and curve left onto West Portal Avenue. Here is a one-block opportunity to stop at a neighborhood restaurant or buy a deli lunch for a picnic later in Buena Vista Park. Turn right, uphill, on Ulloa Street, just before the streetcar line disappears into its tunnel. Continue through a residential neighborhood to the top of the hill, crowned by the colorful mosaic bell tower of St. Brendan's Church. At the intersection of Ulloa Street and Laguna Honda Boulevard, you have a sweeping view across the bay to the Marin Headlands and Mount Tamalpais.

Now descend gradually and curve right onto Sydney Way before turning left on Portola Drive, across which are more neighborhood shops and restaurants. In a few blocks you bear left onto Twin Peaks Boulevard. Pause at the Portola Drive/Twin Peaks Boulevard junction, and glance southeast across tree-filled Glen Canyon Park to see Mount Diablo rising above the East Bay Hills across the bay. The Creeks to Peaks Trail from Glen Canyon Park intersects here.

Onward and upward, make a quick left turn on Panorama Drive and in 50 yards make a sharp right to ascend Midcrest Way. (*See page 302 for a side trip leading off Midcrest.*) After turning left on Cityview Way, make a right turn on Skyview Way. The street names in this residential neighborhood attest to the remarkable vistas this Bay Area Ridge Trail route offers. In a quick succession of right turns on Aquavista and Marview Ways, you skirt the steep sides of Twin Peaks. On windy days you may see people flying kites from the top.

Bear northwest on Marview Way. After you pass Farview Court, look to the left for a detour up a trail past a reservoir and to the base of Sutro Tower, San Francisco's prominent radio-antenna landmark, and the second-tallest structure in the city (after the Salesforce Tower). At the intersection with Palo Alto Avenue, take a left. You pass houses with intricate brickwork, charming garden gates, and handsome redwood siding. Jog right on Glenbrook Avenue for a quick, steady descent. Bear right on Mountain Spring Avenue and then arc sharply left on Twin Peaks Boulevard. *(See page 302 for a side trip to Mount Sutro, just west of here.)*

Watch for RIDGE TRAIL signs and stay on Twin Peaks Boulevard as it turns right, passing Tank Hill, a former water tank site and now city-owned open space containing 60 native plant species. Beyond the Golden Gate you see the Point Bonita Lighthouse, and on a clear day, farther still to the tip of Point Reyes. Twin Peaks Boulevard becomes Clayton Street, where another reservoir sits encased in a solid steel tank.

Hikers and bicyclists diverge here and rejoin at Buena Vista Park. **Hikers** turn right on 17th Street, walk a few yards on its north side, and then mount a steep stairway to Upper Terrace. Head left on Upper Terrace at the top, continuing to Mount Olympus Park, a tiny, circular green space, once considered the geographical center of the city. The statue is missing from the pedestal, but benches offer a place to rest.

You then descend the stairway on the circle's northeast side to the lower leg of Upper Terrace and pass well-kept gardens and attractive homes, following a fairly level route to Buena Vista Park. If the day is sunny, you can see the ocean sparkling at

From Tank Hill Open Space on Twin Peaks Boulevard, you can look out over San Francisco neighborhoods, Golden Gate Park, the Presidio, the Golden Gate Bridge, Marin Headlands, and the bay.

the end of intersecting side streets, named for surveyors and developers of this area. At the entrance to Buena Vista Park, your view northwest points to the forested Presidio, where you are headed.

Bicyclists turn right as well on 17th Street and go left on Roosevelt Way, and left on Loma Vista. Turn right on Upper Terrace and rejoin **hikers.**

Along Buena Vista Avenue East, **hikers and bicyclists** pass several refurbished Victorian mansions and a former hospital converted to residences. **Hikers** have the option of walking the parallel trail in Buena Vista Park. Benches here offer more resting places. Or take a short side trip into the park, a 36-acre hilltop preserved in 1894 for its trees and views. It's said that the ornate marble gutters edging the path that circles the knoll are recycled tombstones from relocated cemeteries.

Continue downhill on this avenue to cross Haight Street. On the other side of Haight Street, Buena Vista Avenue East becomes Baker Street, which is lined with old Victorian houses; follow Baker Street for two blocks north to the Panhandle, a long, tree-canopied, grassy strip that leads to Golden Gate Park. Bear left on a park path in the Panhandle that parallels Fell Street. Rambling under some of the city's oldest trees, these paths replace a boulevard that once cut through the middle of the park, a space now filled with basketball courts, hopscotch games, and children's play equipment.

Just before Golden Gate Park, turn right onto Shrader Street and pass St. Mary's Hospital. Shrader Street ends at Fulton Street; the Ridge Trail route makes a slight jog right on Fulton Street and continues north on Parker Avenue. You go one block on Parker Avenue past twin-towered St. Ignatius Church on the University of San Francisco campus to McAllister Street, where you turn left. Admire the tight row of venerable, tiny, Stick-style homes, each trimmed in different colors.

Turn right onto Stanyan Street, jog north slightly, and cross Stanyan to pick up McAllister again. At the corner of Willard North and McAllister, note two small houses on the right, vestiges of pre-1906 San Francisco, tucked in among taller homes and apartments. Growing next to a white picket fence surrounding the corner house is a patriarch among buckeye trees with gnarled, twisted limbs.

Turn right onto Arguello Boulevard from McAllister Street. In a few blocks, you come to a playground donated by former mayor Angelo J. Rossi. Mount the concrete steps graced by circular flower-filled planters to see the playing fields, tennis courts, and swimming pool. In the last mile of your trip along this busy boulevard, look on its east side for Roosevelt Junior High School, an imposing, brick-faced public school, designed by distinguished architect Timothy L. Pflueger.

Two houses of worship stand on opposite corners of the intersection of Lake Street and Arguello Boulevard. The brown-shingled St. John's Presbyterian Church, dating from 1905, is listed in the National Register of Historic Places and considered one of the city's architecturally significant historic buildings. The monumental Neo-Byzantine–style Temple Emanu-El has a fine courtyard and stained-glass windows designed by Mark Adams.

After climbing a little in the last two blocks, you reach the Arguello Gate of the Presidio of San Francisco, the end of this Ridge Trail segment.

◆ ◆ ◆

The next segment of the Bay Area Ridge Trail begins here at the Arguello Gate.

From Twin Peaks you see down Market Street to the Financial District and the bay beyond.

Twin Peaks, Mount Sutro, and Golden Gate Park:
The Long-Term Ridge Trail Route

BECAUSE TWIN PEAKS AND MOUNT SUTRO, at 922 and 909 feet, respectively, are the second- and third-highest peaks in San Francisco (after Mount Davidson), it has been a long-term goal to route the Ridge Trail over these landmarks. In 2017 the Ridge Trail opened on Mount Sutro, but the rest of the route is not yet official. For another excursion on San Francisco's ridgetops, **hikers and bicyclists** can take side trips to experience the spectacular views from Twin Peaks and the quiet eucalyptus forests of Mount Sutro.

The Twin Peaks route diverges from the dedicated Ridge Trail at the intersection of Twin Peaks Boulevard and Midcrest Way (*see map opposite*). **Hikers** stay on the trail on the right side of the road as they climb Twin Peaks Boulevard. Eucalyptus and Monterey pine grow in this undeveloped area, and the traffic noise diminishes as you climb and look out across the city and bay. At 0.3 mile **hikers** follow the trail sign and cross the street (**bicyclists** stay on the road). The hiker path takes you up stairs to meet Twin Peaks Boulevard again, where you walk along the road and then cross the road to climb the steep trail through chaparral to the top of the hill. Hikers meet bicyclists here.

Take a right; bikers ride on the road and hikers walk on the trail on the side of the road that curves to the east (the road is currently closed to vehicular traffic). The views are phenomenal across San Francisco, the bay, and East Bay. At 0.8 mile you reach Christmas Tree Point Road. Turn left, where **hikers** can take a side trip and climb the steps to the summit of the north of the two Twin Peaks (the second peak is immediately south). At the top, you

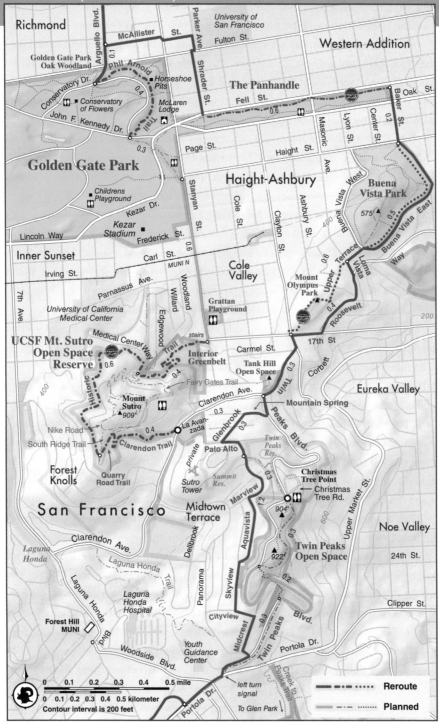

Richmond

Golden Gate Park
Oak Woodland

Conservatory Dr.

Arguello Blvd.

McAllister St.

Phil Arnold

Horseshoe Pits

Conservatory of Flowers

McLaren Lodge

John F. Kennedy Dr.

Parker Ave.

University of San Francisco

Fulton St.

Western Addition

The Panhandle

Fell St.

Shrader St.

Baker St.

Oak St.

Masonic Ave.

Lyon St.

Center St.

Page St.

Golden Gate Park

Childrens Playground

Kezar Dr.

Kezar Stadium

Frederick St.

Haight St.

Haight-Ashbury

Cole St.

Clayton St.

Ashbury St.

Buena Vista West

Buena Vista East

Buena Vista Park

575

Loma Vista

Way

Inner Sunset

Lincoln Way

Carl St.

MUNI N

Irving St.

7th Ave.

Parnassus Ave.

University of California Medical Center

Woodland

Willard

Edgewood

Medical Center Way

Historic

Trail

Cole Valley

Grattan Playground

stairs

Interior Greenbelt

Fairy Gates Trail

Mount Sutro
▲909'

La Avan-zada

Clarendon Ave.

Upper Terrace

Mount Olympus Park

Roosevelt

Carmel St.

17th St

Tank Hill Open Space

Corbett

Twin

Eureka Valley

Mountain Spring

Glenbrook

Palo Alto

UCSF Mt. Sutro Open Space Reserve
0.6

Nike Road

South Ridge Trail

Clarendon Trail

Quarry Road Trail

Forest Knolls

private

Sutro Tower

Summit Res.

Twin Peaks Res.

Peaks Blvd.

Christmas Tree Point
Christmas Tree Rd.

904'

San Francisco

Clarendon Ave.

Laguna Honda

Laguna Honda Blvd.

Midtown Terrace

Dellbrook

Laguna Honda Trail

Laguna Honda Hospital

Panorama

Marview

Aquavista

Skyview

922'

Twin Peaks Open Space

24th St.

Upper Market St.

Noe Valley

Forest Hill MUNI

Youth Guidance Center

Cityview

Midcrest

Twin Peaks

Portola Dr.

Clipper St.

Woodside Blvd.

0 0.1 0.2 0.3 0.4 0.5 mile

0 0.1 0.2 0.3 0.4 0.5 kilometer

Contour interval is 200 feet

left turn signal

Portola Dr.

To Glen Park

Creek to Peaks Trail

- - - · · · Reroute

- - - · · · Planned

have a 360-degree view from your vantage point at 904 feet above sea level: of the Pacific Ocean, the Golden Gate, and the Coast Range that encircles San Francisco Bay.

Other segments of the Bay Area Ridge Trail lie along the ridges of these mountains: Mount Tamalpais and Sonoma Mountain to the north; Vollmer, Mission, and Monument Peaks to the east; and Mount Umunhum and Kings Mountain to the south. Spread out before you is the beautiful city of San Francisco. With a good map you can identify its famous hills, historic buildings, skyscrapers, and many parks.

From Christmas Tree Road, you can also go right, past San Francisco's Central Radio Station, to the busy parking lot at Christmas Tree Point, where restrooms are available. Here you have amazing views east, north, and south of city neighborhoods, hilltop parks, and landmark public structures, such as the bronze-domed City Hall.

The Mount Sutro segment of the Ridge Trail, 1.5 miles long and dedicated in 2017, lies within the 61-acre Mount Sutro Open Space Preserve, owned by the University of California San Francisco (UCSF), and the city-owned Interior Greenbelt, managed by San Francisco Recreation and Parks. The route takes a clockwise circle below the summit of Mount Sutro, named for Adolph Sutro, who in the late 1800s owned 2,200 acres in San Francisco, including Mount Sutro, where he planted eucalyptus, cypress, and Monterey pines.

The singletrack Clarendon Trail heads into the eucalyptus trees below Aldea San Miguel Housing. You also pass through blackwood acacia, ivy, and blackberry bramble. At 0.25 mile take a left at the intersection for the Quarry Road Trail and Historic Trail. The Historic Trail is a route that was built in the early 1900s. You come to another junction in 0.1 mile; a side trip to the right will take you to the summit (a former Nike missile site), but head straight on the Historic Trail. To your left the views open a bit through the trees of the Sunset neighborhood. After passing another trail junction in 0.2 mile, you can see Golden Gate Park as well as the Marin Headlands and Mount Tamalpais in the distance. Red elderberry edges the trail, and soon the UCSF Parnassus Campus is below you and dramatic layers of red chert outcroppings appear along the trail.

The route crosses Medical Center Way at about 1 mile from Clarendon Avenue. A large board on the east side of the road has a trail map and reserve information. Go up the road and take a left down the Edgewood/Fairy Gates Trail, where the trail descends through cape ivy and nasturtium. Stay on the Historic Trail (to Stanyan Street) when you reach the intersection. As you head down the canyon, you are in a magical forest of towering ivy-covered eucalyptus. The trail eventually enters the Interior Greenbelt, a significant natural resource area, and you pass more chert outcroppings. One-half mile from Medical Center Way, the trail ends in a residential neighborhood on Stanyan Street.

The future Ridge Trail route will head down Stanyan Street and enter another dedicated Ridge Trail section in Golden Gate Park. Enter the park at Haight Street; then cross Kezar Drive and John F. Kennedy Drive. Head up Conservatory Drive, and find a trail immediately to your right. Take the Phil Arnold Trail into the oak, bay, and eucalyptus forest that winds through the woods. The trail is named for the chair of the Bay Area Ridge Trail Council, also a San Francisco housing commissioner. After passing a few junctions and the horseshoe pits, you come out onto a ridge with views of the Golden Gate Bridge and Marin Headlands. Passing through this cleared area, veer to the left and descend to Arguello; take a right and go a few blocks until you intersect the dedicated Ridge Trail segment at McAllister Street, which leads you to the Arguello Gate of the San Francisco Presidio.

◆ ◆ ◆

Twin Peaks hours are 5 a.m.–midnight. UCSF Mount Sutro Open Space Reserve hours are sunrise–sunset, and Interior Greenbelt hours are 5 a.m.–midnight. Dogs must be leashed.

San Francisco Presidio

From Arguello Gate to the Golden Gate Bridge in San Francisco

LENGTH 2.7 miles one-way; car shuttle possible

ELEVATION GAIN/LOSS 105/225' one-way

ACCESSIBILITY Hikers, bicyclists, and wheelchair users

AGENCY Presidio Trust and National Park Service

REGULATIONS Presidio trails open during daylight hours. Dogs must be leashed. Horses prohibited.

FACILITIES Water and restrooms at the golf clubhouse, Rob Hill Campground and Picnic Area, and Golden Gate Bridge Plaza

EXPLORE THE CHARM, SECLUSION, NATURAL WONDERS, and historic and cultural variety of the 1,491-acre Presidio. Stunning views await you on this trip through forests and along coastal bluffs that ends at the Golden Gate Bridge. Interpretive panels along the route provide information about the Presidio's unique natural and cultural history.

Getting Started

SOUTH TRAILHEAD Presidio Arguello Gate, Arguello Boulevard and West Pacific Avenue intersection, San Francisco. (**GPS: N37° 47.378', W122° 27.568'**) Besides street parking, limited parking is available on the west side of Arguello Boulevard (golf clubhouse), 100 yards inside the Presidio, or at Inspiration Point, less than 0.1 mile farther north on Arguello Boulevard, San Francisco.

NORTH TRAILHEAD Golden Gate Bridge Welcome Center, south of bridge, San Francisco. Parking lots (some with fee) are located next to the Welcome Center; farther east, on the north side of Lincoln Boulevard; and on west side of US 101/CA 1. (**GPS: N37° 48.454', W122° 28.500'**)

On the Trail

As you enter the Presidio through the Arguello Gate, take note of the gate's flanking stone columns. A prominent stars-and-stripes emblem proclaims the founding of the Presidio in 1776, and the insignia of the infantry, cavalry, and artillery decorate the columns. From

Marin Headlands GGNRA

Lime Point

Marin County

Golden Gate Bridge
west sidewalk
east sidewalk

Golden Gate

Fort Point

Enlarged Above (inset)

0 .1 .2 mile
0 .1 .2 kilometer

Fort Point National Historic Site

viewing area

Round House Café

Welcome Center

Toll Plaza

Presidio Promenade

Battery Cranston

Battery Marcus Miller

Battery Boutelle

Golden Gate Overlook

Langdon Ct.

Merchant Rd.

Lincoln

Coastal Trail

Blvd.

Battery East

Presidio

Fort Scott

Storey Ave.

1

101

Main map

Marine Dr.

Warming Hut bookstore & café

San Francisco Bay

Toll Plaza

Lincoln Blvd.

Coastal Trail

101

Storey

Golden Gate Overlook

Pacific Overlook

Ralston

Fort Scott

Golden Gate Promenade

Crissy Field
Mason St.

Presidio Visitor Center

transit center

Promenade

101

Girard Rd.

Enlarged Above

Coastal Trail

Batteries to Bluffs Trail

Washington

WWII Memorial Immigrant Point

Kobbe

Ave.

Central Magazine Rd.

Rob Hill Group Camp

Blvd.

McDowell

National Cemetery

Cemetery Overlook

Park

Blvd.

Main Post

Montgomery

Funston

Lincoln Blvd.

Officers Club

Lover's Lane

Presidio Blvd.

Baker Beach

Lincoln Blvd.

Nauman Rd.

Amatury Loop

Presidio (Presidio Trust/ GGNRA)

Presidio Hill 382'

Presidio Golf Course

golf clubhouse

Arguello Gate

Arguello Blvd.

Quarry Road

Ecology Trail

El Polin Spring

Inspiration Point

West Pacific Ave.

Julius Kahn Playground

Battery Caufield Rd.

Park Blvd.

Mountain Lake

Creek Trail

Lobos

Lobos Creek

Mountain Lake Park

Lake St.

Richmond District

California St.

Presidio Heights

Arguello Blvd.

25th Ave.

14th Ave.

12th Ave.

San Francisco

0   0.2   0.4   0.6   0.8   1.0 mile
0 0.2 0.4 0.6 0.8 1.0 kilometer
Contour interval is 200 feet

1776 to 1994, the Presidio was a military reservation, first under Spanish and then under Mexican control, and finally in 1847 it became a United States Army post; as of 1994 it has been a national park site. Since the founding of the Presidio, these gates have been closed only once—at the beginning of World War II.

Beyond the gate, turn right on the Ecology Trail and cross West Pacific Street; then bear left on the dirt trail. After 100 yards along Arguello Boulevard, take the crosswalk that leads to the Presidio Golf Course clubhouse. (You can take a detour here by staying straight for 0.1 mile to Inspiration Point, which overlooks San Francisco, and Alcatraz and Angel Islands in the bay.) Turn right on the sidewalk; then veer left to follow the trail into the woods.

In 0.1 mile on your right, look for the towering *Spire* sculpture, designed and built by artist Andy Goldsworthy in 2008. The 100-foot-high sculpture was created with 37 felled dying cypress trees from the site; a new forest has been planted around the spire. On your left and a bit farther down the trail, you thread through mature forests of cypress and then Monterey pine and eucalyptus. In 1883, Major W. A. Jones had trees planted on three ridgetops and around the parade ground. He intended to beautify the windswept sand dunes and the coastal scrub landscape, as well as to provide much-needed wind protection and to camouflage the military fort. Today's forest is composed of tall, spindly trees, so closely spaced that most of their branches are clustered at the top reaching for sunlight.

At 0.4 mile veer right at the intersection. You can see the golf course through the eucalyptus to your left and get glimpses of the bay through the trees on your right. Gradually descend to Washington Boulevard and after crossing the street, turn left and stay on the roadside trail for a short distance to Nauman Road, where **hikers** can take an alternate trail that skirts the back side of former Army officers' housing; from here, a trail leads to the San Francisco National Cemetery, built in the 1850s. From the cemetery overlook, you can see beyond the white gravestones, arranged in symmetrical rows on a gentle slope, to the opposite side of the Golden Gate.

The Ridge Trail hiking trail parallels Nauman Road in the woods and drops onto Amatury Loop. **Bicyclists** follow Nauman Road; both **hikers and bicyclists** turn left to descend the south side of Amatury Loop, following it past housing and a children's playground.

At busy Park Boulevard, look for the trail on the other side of the street and be careful when crossing. The dirt trail passes through a clearing, with recently planted cypress on your left and a more mature forest on your right. After 500 feet the Ridge Trail splits; **hikers** can go right and wind through the forest, and **bikers** veer left. The two trails eventually merge before reaching the paved Central Magazine Road that leads to Rob Hill Campground and some benches.

The road intersects Washington and Harrison Boulevards. Turn down Washington Boulevard, where the trail merges with the Juan Bautista de Anza National Historic Trail. The natural-surface path parallels the road for 0.2 mile, and you start getting scenic views of the Pacific and Marin Headlands. The West Coast Memorial to the Missing of WWII is on the other side of the street and worth a detour.

Cross Kobbe Avenue and, at Lincoln Boulevard, cross to the ocean side for a phenomenal view of the Golden Gate Bridge. You are now on the California Coastal Trail. Turn right and take in the view at the Pacific Overlook, which offers plenty of seating and interpretive panels to read. Keep heading north on the Coastal Trail, where you pass a parking lot, Langdon Street, and Fort Scott on your right. Fort Scott became the headquarters for San Francisco's coastal defenses in 1912. Its parade ground—an elongated, open greensward—is partially surrounded by former Army buildings.

Take a diversion to your left up to the Golden Gate Overlook, where you can see the bridge's towers framed between two enormous cypress trees, and get a fabulous view of Lands End, the Point Bonita Lighthouse, and the Marin Headlands. On a clear day, you can see west to the Farallons—small, rocky islands 25 miles offshore. To your west, you can also explore Battery Godfrey. The batteries along this stretch were built from 1892 to 1900 for soldiers to guard the Golden Gate against enemy attacks.

The Ridge Trail heads downhill after intersecting the trail to the overlook, passing Battery Boutelle and going over a pedestrian/bicyclist bridge. After Batteries Marcus Miller and Cranston, the wide trail then skirts the bluffs before approaching the bridge, offering spectacular views of the bridge and ocean. On weekends, bicyclists follow signs to access the path on the west side of the bridge. Otherwise, pedestrians and weekday cyclists follow the path under the bridge and up to the right onto the eastern bridge path. At the bridge overlook, tourists and locals alike flock on clear days to enjoy the world-class views of the Golden Gate, the bridge, San Francisco, and the bay and its enclosing hills.

The Coastal Trail approaches the Golden Gate Bridge and provides unobstructed views of the Marin Headlands.

Look out at the blue bay waters filled with sailboats heeling in the wind, windsurfers skimming across the waves, surfers at Fort Point, and great ships, mostly oceangoing freighters, cruising to or from distant ports. Sitting in a swirl of swift bay currents, Alcatraz Island was first a fortress and then a military and federal prison before becoming part of Golden Gate National Recreation Area.

To the east lie Coit Tower, the Transamerica Pyramid, other downtown sky-scrapers, and the Bay Bridge leading to the populous East Bay cities. The Campanile's tall shaft rises on the University of California, Berkeley, campus, and forested public parklands crown the surrounding hills.

Visit the welcome center for more information about the bridge and the Pre-sidio, or grab a bite at the Round House Café. If you have time, stop by the Presidio Visitor Center in the main parade ground, which has fascinating exhibits, maps, and videos about the Presidio. Consider taking the short, 0.4-mile trip from the toll plaza to Fort Point, a national historic site. Fort Point stands directly beneath the bridge; the impressive brick and mortar fortress was built from 1853 to 1861 as part of a defense system to protect San Francisco Bay.

◆ ◆ ◆

The next leg of the Bay Area Ridge Trail begins at the entry to the Golden Gate Bridge; see the first trip in this guidebook, which crosses the Golden Gate Bridge.

If you began your journey along the Bay Area Ridge Trail here and followed all the trips in this guidebook, described clockwise around San Francisco Bay, *congratulations!* You've traveled more than 375 miles, primarily along the ridges above the bay, experiencing outstanding views and learning about the natural environment and culture of the spectacular San Francisco Bay Area.

Appendix 1

Information Sources and Contacts for Bay Area Ridge Trail Parks and Watersheds

National Park Service

GOLDEN GATE NATIONAL RECREATION AREA
415-561-4700, nps.gov/goga

Marin Headlands
415-331-1540,
nps.gov/goga/marin-headlands.htm

Milagra Ridge
415-561-4323, nps.gov/goga/miri.htm

Muir Woods National Monument
415-561-2850, nps.gov/muwo

San Francisco Presidio
415-561-4323, nps.gov/prsf

Sweeney Ridge
415-561-4323, nps.gov/goga/sweeney.htm

JOHN MUIR NATIONAL HISTORIC SITE
925-228-8860, nps.gov/jomu

California State Parks

916-653-6995, parks.ca.gov
(Click "Visit a Park" at the website above to reach the sites for the parks below.)

BENICIA STATE RECREATION AREA
707-648-1911

BOTHE–NAPA VALLEY STATE PARK
707-942-4575

CASTLE ROCK STATE PARK
408-867-2952

JACK LONDON STATE HISTORIC PARK
707-938-5216

MOUNT TAMALPAIS STATE PARK
415-388-2070

ROBERT L. STEVENSON STATE PARK
707-942-4575

SAMUEL P. TAYLOR STATE PARK
415-488-9897

TRIONE-ANNADEL STATE PARK
707-539-3911

Regional, County, and City Agencies

CITY OF BENICIA PARKS & COMMUNITY SERVICES
707-746-4285, ci.benicia.ca.us

CITY OF DALY CITY
650-991-8001, dalycity.org

CITY OF FAIRFIELD
707-428-7614, fairfield.ca.gov

CITY OF NOVATO PARKS, RECREATION & COMMUNITY SERVICE
415-899-8900, novato.org

CITY OF PETALUMA PARKS AND RECREATION
707-778-4380,
cityofpetaluma.net/parksnrec

EAST BAY REGIONAL PARK DISTRICT
888-327-2757, ebparks.org

EAST BAY MUNICIPAL UTILITY DISTRICT
866-403-2683, ebmud.com

**GREATER VALLEJO
RECREATION DISTRICT**
707-648-4600, gvrd.org

**MARIN COUNTY
OPEN SPACE DISTRICT**
415-473-6387, marincountyparks.org

MARIN MUNICIPAL WATER DISTRICT
415-945-1455, marinwater.org

**MIDPENINSULA REGIONAL
OPEN SPACE DISTRICT**
650-691-1200, openspace.org

**NAPA COUNTY REGIONAL PARK AND
OPEN SPACE DISTRICT**
napaoutdoors.org

**SAN FRANCISCO
PUBLIC UTILITIES COMMISSION**
415-551-3000, sfwater.org

PRESIDIO TRUST
415-561-5300, presidio.gov

**SAN FRANCISCO RECREATION
AND PARKS**
415-831-2700, sfrecpark.org

**SAN JOSÉ DEPARTMENT OF
PARKS, RECREATION, AND
NEIGHBORHOOD SERVICES**
408-535-3570, sanjoseca.gov

SAN MATEO COUNTY PARKS
650-363-4020, sanmateocountyparks.org

**SANTA CLARA VALLEY
OPEN SPACE AUTHORITY**
408-224-7476, openspaceauthority.org

SANTA CLARA COUNTY PARKS
408-355-2200, sccgov.org/sites/parks

**SANTA CLARA VALLEY
WATER DISTRICT**
408-265-2600, valleywater.org

SOLANO COUNTY PARKS
707-784-6765, solanocounty.com

**SONOMA COUNTY REGIONAL
PARKS DEPARTMENT**
707-565-2041, parks.sonomacounty.ca.gov

**UNIVERSITY OF CALIFORNIA
SAN FRANCISCO**
415-476-1000, ucsf.edu

Nongovernmental Organizations

BAY AREA RIDGE TRAIL COUNCIL
415-561-2595, ridgetrail.org

JOHN MUIR LAND TRUST
925-228-5460, jmlt.org

SKYLAWN MEMORIAL PARK
650-227-3142,
skylawnmemorialpark.com

SKYLINE WILDERNESS PARK
707-252-0481, skylinepark.org

SOLANO LAND TRUST
707-432-0150, solanolandtrust.org

**VALLEY OF THE MOON
NATURAL HISTORY ASSOCIATION**
707-938-5216, jacklondonpark.com

Transportation Agencies

CALIFORNIA DEPARTMENT OF TRANSPORTATION
916-654-2852, caltrans.ca.gov

GOLDEN GATE BRIDGE HIGHWAY & TRANSPORTATION DISTRICT
415-921-5858, goldengate.org

Appendix 2

Transportation Agencies Serving the Bay Area Ridge Trail Route

For public-transit agencies and directions, dial 511 or visit 511.org. Also check transitandtrails.org for the locations of trails near public transportation.

AC TRANSIT (ALAMEDA, CONTRA COSTA, AND SAN FRANCISCO COUNTIES)
510-891-4777, actransit.org

BAY AREA RAPID TRANSIT (BART; San Francisco, Alameda, Contra Costa, San Mateo, and Santa Clara Counties)
510-464-6000, bart.gov

CALTRAIN (San Francisco, San Mateo, and Santa Clara Counties)
800-660-4287, caltrain.org

CAPITAL CORRIDOR (Solano, Contra Costa, Alameda, and Santa Clara Counties)
877-974-3322, capitolcorridor.org

COUNTY CONNECTION (Contra Costa County) 925-676-7500, countyconnection.com

FAIRFIELD AND SUISUN TRANSIT (FAST) 707-434-3800, fasttransit.org

GOLDEN GATE TRANSIT (Marin, Sonoma, and San Francisco Counties)
415-455-2000, goldengatetransit.org

MARIN TRANSIT 415-454-0902, marintransit.org

PETALUMA TRANSIT
707-778-4460, transit.cityofpetaluma.net

SAN FRANCISCO MUNICIPAL TRANSPORTATION AGENCY (SFMTA/Muni; San Francisco)
415-701-2311, sfmta.com/muni

SAMTRANS (San Mateo, Santa Clara, and San Francisco Counties)
800-660-4287, samtrans.com

SANTA ROSA TRANSIT 707-543-3333, srcity.org/1036/transit-and-citybus

SOLANO EXPRESS 800-535-6883, solanoexpress.com

SOLTRANS (Solano County) 707-648-4666, soltransride.com

SONOMA–MARIN AREA RAIL TRANSIT (SMART) 415-455-2000, sonomamarintrain.org

UNION CITY TRANSIT 510-675-5446, uctransit.org

VALLEY TRANSPORTATION AGENCY (Santa Clara County)
408-321-2300, 800-894-9908, vta.org

THE VINE (Napa County) 707-251-2800, ridethevine.com

WESTCAT (West Contra Costa County) 510-724-7993, westcat.org

Index

"Trail segment" below indicates segments of the Bay Area Ridge Trail.

About the Authors

A MILL VALLEY RESIDENT and native Northern Californian, **Elizabeth Byers** has lived in the San Francisco Bay Area for most of her life. As a child and teenager, she explored the beautiful mountains of Carmel Valley and Big Sur near her home. Her love of the outdoors led her to study environmental planning in college and graduate school at the University of California, Berkeley. She began working in the land conservation field in the mid-1980s, for 16 years as a project manager, program director, and writer at the Trust for Public Land (TPL) and then as a consultant for many nonprofits and agencies, including the Garden Conservancy, the Bay Area Ridge Trail Council, and TPL.

Photo: Robert K. Byers Jr.

In 1988, while at TPL, Elizabeth became one of the founding board members of the Bay Area Ridge Trail Council, and she stayed connected to the organization over the years. She coauthored the second edition of *The Conservation Easement Handbook,* copublished by TPL and the Land Trust Alliance in 2005, and was a photographer and project coordinator for the 2014 Golden Gate National Parks Conservancy publication *Alcatraz Gardens: Remembered, Reclaimed, Reimagined.* She is a mom to two children in their 20s who grew up on the lower slopes of Mount Tamalpais.

Elizabeth hiked, biked, and photographed the Ridge Trail to update this guidebook, often with family and friends, and this journey reconfirmed for her the magnificence of the Bay Area landscape.

Jean Rusmore, the author of this book's first three editions, grew up in what was once the small town of Anaheim, California, in the county that boasted orange and lemon groves as its namesake. She took her first backpacking trip at age 16, when she and a cousin ascended the slopes of Mount Wilson in the San Gabriel Mountains with some food and a jacket rolled up in a blanket. Her outdoor experience was enlarged through her husband, Ted, whom she met at the University of California, Berkeley. They skied and backpacked with their six children, and all looked forward to their annual Sierra backpacking trip.

When the Midpeninsula Regional Open Space District was established, Jean and her friend Frances Spangle decided to write a book about the new foothill preserves, *Peninsula Trails,* followed by *South Bay Trails,* both published by Wilderness Press. When the first segments of the Ridge Trail opened, they wrote pamphlets about each leg. These were later combined and published as the first edition of this book.